Cognitive Development and Working Memory

The intellectual development of human beings from birth to adulthood is a fascinating phenomenon. Understanding the constraints that limit children's intelligence, as well as discovering methods to improve it, has always been a challenging undertaking for developmental psychologists. This book presents a unique attempt to address these issues by establishing a dialogue between neo-Piagetian theorists and researchers specialized in typical and atypical working memory development.

The book integrates recent advances in studies of working memory development with theories proposed by the most prominent neo-Piagetian researchers who have emphasized the role of cognitive resources and working memory capacity in the development of thinking and reasoning. In the opening section, the main proponents of this tradition develop their theories of cognitive development in terms of available mental attention, processing efficiency and speed, inhibition and relational complexity. The second part of the book addresses the mechanisms that underpin the increase in working memory capacity and the respective roles of processing efficiency, storage capacity, and the use of reactivation processes of memory traces such as rehearsal. Finally, the central role played by working memory in atypical development and learning difficulties is examined.

This book provides psychologists, students and researchers who are interested in child development with an integrated and up-to-date series of chapters written by prominent specialists in the areas of working memory, attention, and cognitive development.

Pierre Barrouillet is Professor of Developmental Psychology at University of Geneva and Director of the Archives of Jean Piaget. His research investigates the development of numerical cognition, conditional reasoning, as well as the functioning and development of working memory.

Vinciane Gaillard is a Postdoctoral Research Fellow at Université Libre de Bruxelles (Belgium) Consciousness, Cognition, and Computation group, directed by Axel Cleeremans. Her main research interests concern implicit learning, consciousness, control, attention, working memory, development and aging.

Cognitive Development and Working Memory

A dialogue between neo-Piagetian and cognitive approaches

Edited by Pierre Barrouillet and Vinciane Gaillard

Psychology Press
Taylor & Francis Group
HOVE AND NEW YORK

Published in 2011
By Psychology Press
27 Church Road, Hove, East Sussex BN3 2FA

Simultaneously published in the USA and Canada
by Psychology Press
270 Madison Avenue, New York, NY 10016

Psychology Press is an imprint of the Taylor & Francis Group, an Informa business

© 2011 Psychology Press

Typeset in Times by RefineCatch Limited, Bungay, Suffolk
Printed and bound in Great Britain by TJ International Ltd, Padstow, Cornwall
Cover design by Sandra Heath

This publication has been produced with paper manufactured to strict environmental standards and with pulp derived from sustainable forests.

British Library Cataloguing in Publication Data
A catalogue record for this book is available from the British Library

Library of Congress Cataloging in Publication Data
Cognitive development and working memory : a dialogue between neo-Piagetian and cognitive approaches / edited by Pierre Barrouillet and Vinciane Gaillard.
    p. cm.
   Includes bibliographical references and index.
   ISBN 978–1–84872–036–7 (hb)
   1. Short-term memory. 2. Cognition. 3. Cognition in children.
   I. Barrouillet, Pierre. II. Gaillard, Vinciane.
   BF378.S54C64 2010
   155.4′1312—dc22   2010005189

ISBN: 978–1–84872–036–7 (hbk)

Contents

Figures and tables

Figures

Tables

Contributors

Tracy Packiam Alloway, Department of Psychology, University of Stirling, Stirling, UK. E-mail: t.p.alloway@stir.ac.uk

Glenda Andrews, School of Psychology, Griffith University, Gold Coast Campus, Australia. E-mail: g.andrews@griffith.edu.au

Lisa Archibald, School of Communication Sciences and Disorders, University of Western Ontario, London, ON, Canada. E-mail: larchiba@uwo.ca

Angela M. AuBuchon, Department of Psychological Sciences, University of Missouri, Columbia, MO. E-mail: amam87@mizzou.edu

Pierre Barrouillet, Faculty of Psychology and Educational Sciences, Université de Genève, Geneva, Switzerland. E-mail: Pierre.Barrouillet@unige.ch

Valérie Camos, LEAD CNRS, Université de Bourgogne and Institut Universitaire de France, Dijon, France. E-mail: valerie.camos@u-bourgogne.fr

Nelson Cowan, Department of Psychological Sciences, University of Missouri, Columbia, MO. E-mail: CowanN@missouri.edu

Andreas Demetriou, Department of Psychology, University of Cyprus, Nicosia, Cyprus. E-mail: ademetriou@ucy.ac.cy

Anik de Ribaupierre, Faculty of Psychology and Educational Sciences, Université de Genève, Geneva, Switzerland, E-mail: Anik.deRibaupierre@unige.ch

Delphine Fagot, Faculty of Psychology and Educational Sciences, Université de Genève, Geneva, Switzerland, E-mail: Delphine.Fagot@unige.ch

Vinciane Gaillard, Faculty of Psychological and Educational Sciences, Université Libre de Bruxelles, Brussels, Belgium, E-mail: vgaillar@ulb.ac.be

Amanda L. Gilchrist, Department of Psychological Sciences, University of Missouri, Columbia, MO. E-mail: algkb8@mail.mizzou.edu

Graeme S. Halford, School of Psychology, Griffith University, Mt Gravatt Campus, Australia. E-mail: halford@griffith.edu.au

Chris Jarrold, Department of Experimental Psychology, University of Bristol, Bristol, UK. E-mail: C.Jarrold@bristol.ac.uk

Janice Johnson, Department of Psychology, York University, Toronto, ON, Canada. E-mail: janicej@yorku.ca

Thierry Lecerf, Faculty of Psychology and Educational Sciences, Université de Genève, Geneva, Switzerland. E-mail: Thierry.Lecerf@unige.ch

Candice C. Morey, Experimental and Work Psychology, University of Groningen, Groningen, The Netherlands. E-mail: c.c.morey@rug.nl

Antigoni Mouyi, Pedagogical Institute of Cyprus, Nicosia, Cyprus. E-mail: mougi@ucy.ac.cy

Juan Pascual-Leone, Department of Psychology, York University, Toronto, ON, Canada. E-mail: juanpl@yorku.ca

J. Scott Saults, Department of Psychological Sciences, University of Missouri, Columbia, MO. E-mail: SaultsJ@missouri.edu

H. Lee Swanson, Graduate School of Education, University of California Riverside, Riverside, CA. E-mail: lee.swanson@ucr.edu

Helen Tam, Department of Experimental Psychology, University of Bristol, Bristol, UK. E-mail: Helen.Tam@bris.ac.uk

Christopher E. Zwilling, Department of Psychology, University of Illinois, Urbana-Champaign, IL. E-mail: cezresearch@gmail.com

1 Introduction

From neo-Piagetian theories to working memory development studies

Pierre Barrouillet and Vinciane Gaillard

The changes occurring in human intelligence from birth to the end of adolescence and the corollary increase in knowledge, skills, and abilities are probably among the most striking phenomena that can be studied in natural sciences. Though physical growth from the embryo to the mature organism is by itself astonishing, cognitive development is even more impressive as unique to our species and appears as the main fact of the extended developmental period that characterizes *Homo sapiens sapiens*. It does not come as a surprise that, from the very beginning of scientific psychology at the end of the nineteenth and the beginning of the twentieth centuries, the discovery of the mechanisms underlying cognitive development has been a fascinating challenge. There is no doubt that among these psychologists, Jean Piaget was the author who offered the most vivid picture of these developmental changes, contrasting the limitations of the young child's thinking with the capacity of the adolescent's and adult's formal thinking to grasp complexity and deal with abstract and hypothetical matters.

As noted by Nelson Cowan in this book, no scientific enterprise starts within an individual, and Piaget acknowledged the influence on his thinking, among others, of the ideas put forward by J. M. Baldwin (1894) about the role of the span of attention, which he conceived as the maximum number of mental elements that the child can simultaneously take into account, a limitation resulting from neurological constraints and a slow physical development. Of course, Piaget described cognitive development as a progression towards rationality through the construction of logical structures underlying behavior, but his account of the egocentric and intuitive thinking of young children as the incapacity to coordinate different points of view and dimensions echoes Baldwin's notion of a limited span of attention in children. Thus, right from the start, developmental psychologists surmised that most of the developmental differences between children and adults would come from the limited capacity of the former in embracing all the relevant aspects and dimensions of the situations they are faced with and try to understand. The cognitive revolution that occurred during the 50s and Miller's magical number provided the general theoretical framework to describe this limitation and how it is overcome with age. The mind was then understood as an information processing system whose capacity is limited by the amount of information that can be held active and ready for treatment and by the speed at which this information can be processed. The integration of this information processing approach within the Piagetian constructivism and structuralism led to theories of cognitive development known as neo-Piagetian (Case, 1985; Demetriou & Efklides, 1987; Demetriou & Raftopoulos, 1999; Halford, 1978, 1993; Pascual-Leone, 1970).

Among the main tenets of the neo-Piagetian theories is the idea that cognitive activities impose a load to the processing system (Morra, Gobbo, Marini, & Sheese, 2008), with the corollary idea, whose origin can be traced back as we have seen to J. M. Baldwin, that there is some processing or cognitive capacity, often considered as attentional, which is limited but increases with age and permits to cope with higher information load. Within the contemporary experimental cognitive psychology, this general processing capacity is described as the capacity of working memory. Devoted to maintain information temporarily active and ready for treatment in face of any distracting events, working memory is considered to be the "workbench of cognition" (Jarrold & Towse, 2006). From the seminal work of Baddeley and Hitch (1974), many theories have been proposed to account for the functioning and limited capacity of this system (Baddeley & Logie, 1999; Barrouillet, Bernardin, & Camos, 2004; Cowan, 2005; Engle & Kane, 2004; Ericsson & Kintsch, 1995), and for its development (Barrouillet, Gavens, Vergauwe, Gaillard, & Camos, 2009; Case, Kurland, & Goldberg, 1982; Towse & Hitch, 1995). From the commonality of concepts developed by neo-Piagetian and working memory theorists, a tradition of exchanges and mutual enrichment could have been expected between the two traditions of research. Surprisingly, and apart from some noticeable exceptions (Baddeley & Hitch, 2000; Cowan, Saults, & Elliott, 2002; Halford, Cowan, & Andrews, 2007; Kemps, De Rammelaere, & Desmet, 2000; Morra, 2000), the two realms have remained separated. The aim of the present book was to bridge this gap by offering an opportunity of dialog between both traditions. Issuing from a series of conferences held in Geneva in July 2008 for the 18th Advanced Course of the Archives Jean Piaget, it gathers preeminent neo-Piagetian theorists of cognitive development with specialists of the development of working memory.

A first part is devoted to neo-Piagetian theories and the role they assign to working memory in development. Though each of these theories develops its own account of what the cognitive resources are underlying cognitive development, these resources being described as mental attention, central executive resources, or capacity of a processing system, all of them agree that there is some limited capacity that increases with age and permits solution of more and more complex problems. With Juan Pascual-Leone's theory of constructive operators (TCO), Halford's Relational Complexity (RC) theory, and Demetriou's theory of experiential structuralism, three of the most important neo-Piagetian theories are represented and developed here. A second part addresses the arduous problem of the nature of the processes underlying working memory development. As Towse, Hitch, and Horton (2007) noted in their recent survey of the literature, although an extensive body of research has been devoted to working memory in children, it is not easy to discern a developmental model of working memory. Three contributions are presented here, issued from three different conceptions of working memory (the seminal multi-component model of Baddeley and Hitch, Cowan's embedded process model, and Barrouillet and Camos' time-based resource-sharing model). Of course, these contributions do not constitute a definitive answer to Towse, Hitch, and Horton's observation, but rather a body of proposals that could delineate the bases for a future integrative theory of working memory development. Finally, a third part illustrates the role of working memory in atypical development by investigating its impact on learning disabilities and the working memory profile of several atypical populations.

Neo-Piagetian theories and working memory

In Chapter 2, Juan Pascual-Leone and Janice Johnson present their theory of constructive operators (TCO), stressing the role of mental attention in cognitive development. They cogently note that working memory capacity has proven to be difficult to measure, and suggest that this is due to a failure to identify the functional units of processing, the "chunks," that can be activated, and to develop a theoretically grounded method for task analysis. They claim that TCO provides us with the organismic theory and the method of task analysis that permits the measurement of the hidden resources. According to this view, the functional units are the different schemes, and the hidden resource is mental attention. This construct can be measured by the size of the set of distinct schemes that can be endogenously activated and coordinated at a given developmental level. Mental attention increases with age, enabling the transition from one developmental stage to the next. From several original tasks including either verbal or visuo-spatial material, Pascual-Leone and Johnson observe that the maximum number of symbolic schemes that can be simultaneously activated, which is called M-power, evolves from 1 in the low preoperational stage to 7 in adolescents and adults, echoing Miller's magical number. Interestingly, they show that although the precise nature of the schemes involved changes from one task to another, M-power values remain remarkably constant across tasks and domains for a given developmental level. Finally, Pascual-Leone and Johnson evoke recent fMRI studies (functional magnetic resonance imaging) supporting their M-capacity construct.

Quantifying the complexity of cognitive tasks is also the main concern of Glenda Andrews and Graeme Halford in Chapter 3. According to their Relational Complexity (RC) theory, complexity is defined in terms of the complexity of the mental models that underlie thinking. Here, cognitive development is no longer characterized by the capacity to simultaneously activate an increasing number of schemes, but by the capacity to construct mental models involving more and more complex relations. A metric of complexity is provided, which is the number of independent variables that are related in a cognitive representation. Thus, whereas young children can only apprehend one dimension in unary relations, adolescents and adults can represent quaternary relations involving four slots, such as proportions, a developmental level corresponding to the stage of formal operations in Piaget's theory. Using traditional Piagetian tasks as transitive inferences and inclusion tasks, as well as a version of the Iowa Gambling Task adapted for children, Andrews and Halford show that children's performance depends on the relational complexity involved by the tasks, with evidence of consistency within individuals. All the tasks involving a same level of complexity are either failed or passed depending on the developmental level reached. As other neo-Piagetian theorists, Andrews and Halford assume that cognitive development is underpinned by a growth in processing resources, which are conceived as the capacity of the central executive component of Baddeley's model. The upper limit is not 7 as in Pascual-Leone's account, but 4, which corresponds to the working memory limitation of four chunks proposed by Cowan (2005). A large part of their chapter is devoted to brain imaging studies showing that activations in the prefrontal cortex are related to the relational complexity of the tasks.

In Chapter 4, Andreas Demetriou and Antigoni Mouyi present their theory that integrates the experimental, differential, and developmental traditions to propose a comprehensive model of the mental architecture of the mind. Their theory distinguishes three levels. A first level, named the *Specialized Domains of Thought*, is dedicated to the representation and processing of different aspects of our physical and social environment. This level reflects and processes the different fields of reality, namely the categorical, quantitative, spatial, causal, social, and verbal domains. These systems involve processes and abilities. A second level, named the *Hypercognitive System*, corresponds to a set of metacognitive representations and processes directed to the self. It involves processes such as self-monitoring, self-representation, and self-regulation. Consciousness is part of this system. Finally, a third system, named *Processing Potentials*, the most basic, involves general processes and functions such as processing, control of processing, and representational capacity or working memory. Interestingly, Demetriou and Mouyi integrate both Pascual-Leone's and Halford's views in suggesting that working memory capacity is defined as the maximum amount and complexity of the representations and mental acts that can be handled simultaneously. Another original proposal is that these components are involved in a cascade model in which age-related changes in speed of processing open the way for changes in control of processing, which in turn open the way for the enhancement of working memory that permits development in high-level cognitive processes such as reasoning. These hypothesized relations between processing speed, processing efficiency, working memory capacity, and reasoning performance echo Case's conceptions and are directly addressed in the following chapter by Anik de Ribaupierre and her colleagues.

In Chapter 5, Anik de Ribaupierre, Delphine Fagot, and Thierry Lecerf directly address the role of working memory in cognitive development. Do measures of working memory capacity predict children's performance in developmental tasks such as traditional Piagetian tasks? Using tasks designed by Pascual-Leone to measure mental attention capacity, they assess working memory capacity in large samples of children and observe that working memory measures account for almost all the age-related variance in Piagetian tasks. Interestingly, they extend their investigation to the entire life-span and to a large range of cognitive tasks including measures of fluid intelligence, processing speed, and inhibition. In several studies, they observe that there are global mechanisms underpinning cognitive development, but that a single factor is not sufficient to explain it. Moreover, the relative weight of the different factors seems to evolve along the life-span, with inhibitory processes playing a more important role in older adults. These studies nicely illustrate how cognitive development is complex and most probably multi-determined. The same is true for the development of working memory itself, as the following part of the book makes clear.

Underlying processes of working memory development

According to Hitch (2006), the most striking aspect of the development of working memory in childhood is the steady improvement in performance in all the complex span tasks. Complex span tasks are tasks combining storage and processing requirements, such as maintaining words while reading sentences (Daneman & Carpenter, 1980) or solving equations (Turner & Engle, 1989), or maintaining numbers while counting arrays of dots (Case, 1985). Many studies have demonstrated a clear age-related increase in complex spans (e.g., Gathercole, Pickering, Ambridge, & Wearing, 2004), but as we noted above, the question of the processes responsible for this development is still unsolved. The answer given by the late Robbie Case is well known: experience and maturation would lead to a dramatic age-related increase in processing efficiency; because more efficient processes are less resource-demanding, they free a larger part of capacities for storage, hence the developmental increase in complex spans. Case, Kurland, and Goldberg (1982) tested this "processing efficiency" hypothesis in an impressive series of experiments that have constituted the cornerstone of working memory studies in children for many years.

Nelson Cowan and colleagues open Chapter 6 with an erudite review of the debate among neo-Piagetians concerning working memory development. Detailing Case et al. (1982) and other studies focusing on the same "processing efficiency" hypothesis, they argue that if the emphasis on operational efficiency is understandable, at least for methodological reasons, it is far more difficult to estimate how much of working memory span task performance depends on information storage. Nonetheless, they review some of their recent studies on the development of storage capacity that provide us with provocative results.

Thus, contrary to a widespread belief in cognitive science, ingenious experimental designs reveal that older children and adults differ more from younger children in their basic storage capacity than in their capacity to focus on relevant information and filter out irrelevant information. Even more surprisingly, it appears that storage capacity increases with age but that the size of the chunks maintained in working memory remains stable across age. This does not dismiss the role of the age-related increase in processing efficiency, and based on novel results, Cowan and colleagues propose the balanced conclusion that both storage and processing efficiency play an important role.

Valérie Camos and Pierre Barrouillet also assume that processing efficiency and storage capacity play a role in working memory development, but they suggest that both factors depend on attentional capacity. In Chapter 7, they present their time-based resource-sharing model according to which attention is incessantly and rapidly switched back and forth from processing to maintenance activities. When attention is occupied by the processing component of working memory span tasks, memory traces suffer from a time-related decay that can be counteracted by refreshing these traces through attentional focusing before resuming processing activities. Camos and Barrouillet review recent studies that investigated the development of this switching process, and found that it is effective at least from the age 8 onwards, its efficiency increasing with age. However, it seems that 5-year-old children do not switch their attention from processing to storage during the processing component of the task. The critical change occurring between 5 and 7 in the use of strategies to reactivate decaying memory traces would introduce a qualitative change in working memory development.

In Chapter 8, Chris Jarrold and Helen Tam question this hypothesis of a qualitative change by investigating the development of the process of rehearsal. It is commonly acknowledged that children do not actively rehearse verbal material for maintenance purposes before 7 years of age. Using both simple and complex span tasks, Jarrold and Tam propose a more balanced conclusion. Focusing on traditional markers of rehearsal such as word length effect under probed recall, speech rate-span correlations, and phonological similarity effect for visually presented materials, they observe that rehearsal-related phenomena do not appear before 7 years of age. However, in the context of working memory span tasks administered to large samples of children, they find some evidence for rehearsal in young children. These seemingly contradictory findings generate a thoughtful discussion about qualitative and quantitative changes in development that has both theoretical and methodological implications.

One of the strengths of Jarrold and Tam's investigations is to involve evidence from atypical development, demonstrating that the analysis of performance in atypical populations sheds light on working memory development phenomena. In the other way around, and as the last part of this book illustrates, analyzing working memory functioning in typical and atypical populations allows a better understanding of developmental disorders.

Working memory in typical and atypical development

Baddeley's multi-component approach of working memory and the clear distinctions it introduces between several cognitive domains has always proved particularly useful to analyze task demands as well as individuals' specific impairments. The two chapters of this third part perfectly illustrate the usefulness of the concept of working memory in understanding cognitive development in typical and atypical populations. In Chapter 9, Lee Swanson analyzes the role of working memory deficits in reading and math disabilities. Particularly interesting is the longitudinal approach adopted in his studies. Going beyond the frequent observation that academic achievement is closely related to working memory capacity (e.g., Lépine, Barrouillet, & Camos, 2005), Swanson demonstrates that *growth* in working memory is an important predictor of math and reading achievement. Of interest is also the fine-grained analysis of the contribution of the different components of working memory to learning disabilities. For example, it appears that reading disabilities do not exclusively result from deficient growth in the phonological loop but also, as observed for math disabilities, in the executive component of working memory. Pursuing further his analysis, Swanson is able to identify those executive functions that are deficient and those that are intact in children with reading disabilities. These studies are of course particularly important to understand learning disabilities, and thus have a high educational and societal relevance, but they also inform us about the relevance of the construct of working memory for psychology, by demonstrating in several experiments that working memory growth contributes unique variance in academic achievement beyond short-term memory, intelligence, inhibition, or processing speed.

Finally, Tracy Packiam Alloway and Lisa Archibald characterize the short-term and working memory impairments associated with several developmental disorders that have a strong impact on learning such as Specific Language Impairment, Developmental Coordination Disorder, Attention Deficit and Hyperactive Disorder, and Autistic Spectrum Disorder. Each of these disorders is associated with a selective profile of strengths and weaknesses across the different functions of working memory as described in Baddeley's multi-component model and as measured by the Automated Working Memory Assessment (AWMA, Alloway, 2007), a cognitive test that permits to determine the profile of a student's verbal and visuo-spatial working memory skills. Alloway and Archibald recall that about 10% of children in a typical classroom have working memory difficulties that can impact their learning. The capacity of the AWMA scale to discriminate between different developmental disorders strongly suggests that, beyond the difficulties encountered by researchers in defining the functional units of processing and measuring working memory capacity, our knowledge of working memory functioning is sufficiently advanced to yield measures with discriminative and predictive power.

Overall, the contributions gathered in this book provide an up-to-date overview of the current research on the relations between working memory and cognitive development. The diversity of responses given to key questions such as the nature of the units of processing, the maximum number of units that can be maintained active, the nature of the resources involved, or the factors underlying working memory development clearly indicates that we are still far from a comprehensive and unified theory of working memory and cognitive development. Nonetheless, beyond their diversity, the different chapters testify for an increasing mutual acknowledgement of the advances in the other domains, bridging the gap between the general theories of cognitive development and the models of working memory development.

References

Alloway, T. P. (2007). *Automated Working Memory Assessment (AWMA)*. London: Pearson Assessment.

Baddeley, A. D., & Hitch, G. (1974). Working memory. In G.A. Bower (Ed.), *Recent advances in learning and motivation* (Vol. 8, pp. 647–667). New York: Academic Press.

Baddeley, A. D., & Hitch, G. (2000). Development of working memory: Should the Pascual-Leone and Baddeley and Hitch models be merged? *Journal of Experimental Child Psychology, 77*, 128–137.

Baddeley, A. D., & Logie, R. H. (1999). Working memory: The multiple-component model. In A. Miyake & P. Shah (Eds.), *Models of working memory: Mechanisms of active maintenance and executive control* (pp. 28–61). Cambridge: Cambridge University Press.

Baldwin, J. M. (1894). *Mental development in the child and the race*. New York: Macmillan.

Barrouillet, P., Bernardin, S., & Camos, V. (2004). Time constraints and resource-sharing in adults' working memory spans. *Journal of Experimental Psychology: General, 133*, 83–100.

Barrouillet, P., Gavens, N., Vergauwe, E., Gaillard, V., & Camos, V. (2009). Working memory span development: A Time-Based Resource Sharing Model account. *Developmental Psychology, 45*, 477–490.

Case, R. (1985). *Intellectual development: Birth to adulthood*. New York: Academic Press.

Case, R., Kurland, M., & Goldberg, J. (1982). Operational efficiency and the growth of short-term memory. *Journal of Experimental Child Psychology, 33*, 386–404.

Cowan, N. (2005). *Working memory capacity*. Hove, UK: Psychology Press.

Cowan, N., Saults, J. S., & Elliott, E. M. (2002). The search for what is fundamental in the development of working memory. In R. Kail & H. Reese (Eds.), *Advances in Child Development and Behavior, 29*, 1–49.

Daneman, M., & Carpenter, P. A. (1980). Individual differences in working memory and reading. *Journal of Verbal Learning and Verbal Behavior, 19*, 450–466.

Demetriou, A., & Efklides, A. (1987). Experiential structuralism and neo-Piagetian theories: Toward an integrated model. *International Journal of Psychology, 22*, 679–728.

Demetriou, A., & Raftopoulos, A. (1999). Modeling the developing mind: From structure to change. *Developmental Review, 19*, 319–368.

Engle, R. W., & Kane, M. J. (2004). Executive attention, working memory capacity, and a two-factor theory of cognitive control. In B. Ross (Ed.), *The psychology of learning and motivation* (Vol. 44, pp. 145–199). New York: Elsevier.

Ericsson, K. A., & Kintsch, W. (1995). Long-term working memory. *Psychological Review, 102*, 211–245.

Gathercole, S. E., Pickering, S. J., Ambridge, B., & Wearing, H. (2004). The structure of working memory from 4 to 15 years of age. *Developmental Psychology, 40*, 177–190.

Halford, G. S. (1978). Toward a working model of Piaget's stages. In J. A. Keats, K. F. Collis, & G. S. Halford (Eds.), *Cognitive development: Research based on neo-Piagetian approach* (pp. 169–220). London: Wiley.

Halford, G. S. (1993). *Children's understanding*. Hillsdale, NJ: Lawrence Erlbaum.

Halford, G. S., Cowan, N., & Andrews, G. (2007). Separating cognitive capacity from knowledge: A new hypothesis. *Trends in Cognitive Sciences, 11*, 237–242.

Hitch, G. (2006). Working memory in children: A cognitive approach. In E. Bialystok & F. I. Craik (Eds.), *Lifespan cognition: Mechanisms of change* (pp. 112–127). New York: Oxford University Press.

Jarrold, C., & Towse, J. N. (2006). Individual differences in working memory. *Neuroscience, 139*, 39–50.

Kemps, E., De Rammelaere, S., & Desmet, T. (2000). The development of working memory: Exploring the complementarity of two models. *Journal of Experimental Child Psychology, 77*, 89–109.

Lépine, R., Barrouillet, P., & Camos, V. (2005). What makes working memory spans so predictive of high-level cognition? *Psychonomic Bulletin and Review, 12*, 165–170.

Morra, S. (2000). A new model of verbal short-tem memory. *Journal of Experimental Child Psychology, 75*, 191–227.

Morra, S., Gobbo, C., Marini, Z., & Sheese, R. (2008). *Cognitive development: Neo-Piagetian perspectives*. New York: Lawrence Erlbaum.

Pascual-Leone, J. A. (1970). A mathematical model for the transition rule in Piaget's developmental stage. *Acta Psychologica, 32*, 301–345.

Towse, J. N., & Hitch, G. J. (1995). Is there a relationship between task demand and storage space in tests of working memory capacity? *The Quarterly Journal of Experimental Psychology, 48A*, 108–124.

Towse, J. N., Hitch, G., & Horton, N. (2007). Working memory as the interface between processing and retention: A developmental perspective. *Advances in Child Development and Behavior, 35*, 219–251.

Turner, M. L., & Engle, R. W. (1989). Is working memory task dependent? *Journal of Memory and Language, 28*, 127–154.

Part I

Neo-Piagetian theories and working memory

2 A developmental theory of mental attention

Its application to measurement and task analysis

J. Pascual-Leone and Janice Johnson

> In general *attention* is a *tending of the ego towards an intentional object*, towards a unity which "appears" continually in the change of the modes of its givenness [. . .]; it is a tending-toward in realization.
>
> (Husserl, 1948/1973, p. 80)

> One might further argue that the discovery of the structural assumptions underlying the phenomena is the basic goal of science and that measurement is "only" a consequence of these assumptions. In this sense measurement is a by-product of theory. Only when the assumptions of the theory are satisfied by the data can measurement be obtained.
>
> (Coombs, Dawes, & Tversky, 1970, p. 30)

> The four-chunk storage limit that I have documented is meant as a starting point under the simplest of circumstances, on the road to the eventual goal of quantifying working memory storage limits in more complex situations. It was not meant as an end point.
>
> (Cowan, 2005, p. 149)

Working memory is an organismic construct that captures the notion of a limited capacity to "keep in mind" information. Measuring the capacity of working memory has proven to be difficult, and there is no consensus in the literature about its limit – as the last epigraph suggests. This difficulty may stem from failure to apply, or explicitly create, sensible principles for valid and direct (fundamental) measurement. Instead, research psychologists tend to use somewhat arbitrary ways of scoring without giving much attention to organismic processes that the numeric scoring represents. In this chapter we advance towards a solution of this problem by formulating an explicit organismic model of mental (i.e., voluntary, executive) attention – a construct often regarded as the maturational component of working memory. We discuss explicitly principles of fundamental measurement relevant for this measurement, and clarify the concept of functional units of processing (often called chunks) by discussing in detail the construct of organismic schemes, to show how "chunks" are explicated within a constructivist evolutionary epistemology. Then, after discussing our model of mental attention, we present data supporting the fruitfulness of our approach. We begin with fundamental measurement, because this concept must be clear to see how our psychological approach can help to solve the working-memory measurement problem.

Fundamental measurement (Suppes & Zinnes, 1963) uses a formal (often numerical) relational system to *represent* an empirical relational system. Such a representation is made possible by "the assignment of numbers to objects in such a way that the observed relations among objects are reflected by the corresponding relations among the numbers assigned to them" (Coombs et al., 1970, p. 29). Thus objects from an empirical relational system, and stable functional relations amongst them, are mapped onto objects – often numbers – and relations of a formal relational system. When the direction of mapping can be reversed, that is, formal and empirical structures can represent/map each other, the mapping generated is an *isomorphism*. Notice that in fundamental measurement both the formal and empirical systems result from theory-guided rational choices or modeling: The characterization of the field of study as an empirical relational system results from a constructive abstraction process in which "raw data of our experience are classified and structured as objects and relations" (Coombs et al., 1970, p. 11). When both the empirical mapped structure and the formal-mapping structure are suitably configured by the researcher, one can define fundamental measurement as an isomorphic mapping (Narens, 1985).

Classic physical measurement generally is fundamental and *extensive*, in the sense that it is based on semantic-pragmatic procedures analogous to the arithmetical operation of addition: an empirical *concatenation operation*, that is, counting the reiteration of suitable displacements of a unit (such as a centimeter) over the length to be estimated, or the juxtaposition of objects in a balance, or the displacement of mercury over the thermometer's metric scale. When such a concatenation operation is impossible, specialists talk instead of *intensive* measurement. Examples of *intensive properties* are heat, or degree of attention, or most other psychological qualitative variables. It is now well recognized that one does not need to have extensive measurement to produce *interval scales* (i.e., scales of measurement in which not only the values, but the intervals between values can be meaningfully compared and treated as invariant). The Coombs et al. (1970) quote in the epigraph emphasizes that theory is important for fundamental measurement. Furthermore, measurement of psychological organismic variables is particularly in need of theory, because organismic processes, being hidden, must be "invented" before they can be "discovered" and described via empirical experimentation and measurement (Pascual-Leone & Sparkman, 1980). In this sense we should talk of three facets of measurement, and not just two: The *formal model* and the *empirical model*, which respectively produce the measurement's formal relational system and empirical relational system, and also the *organismic or general theory*, which informs and justifies the procedure for measurement and the formal and empirical models. Also necessary is an explicit method of *task analysis* (based on the general theory) that can coordinate formal and empirical models with the actual procedures of successful measurement. Crucial to fundamental measurement is the aptitude of the chosen formal relational system to *epistemologically reflect* (or mirror in its functional structure) the functional structure in the empirical domain. Such epistemological reflection emerges as *functional invariant* in the context of praxis (Gibson, 1979; Reuchlin, 1962; Ullmo, 1967) – and, when well defined, is an *isomorphism*.

Consider an example in a simple perceptual domain: Imagine different human or animal faces and faces made with geometric shapes that replace eyes, nose, mouth, head. The term "face" is applied to all of them, because a similar relational pattern emerges under exploration, which the visual scan-paths basically preserve in each, as the gaze goes from one "face" feature to the other: This is the (functionally) *invariant* relational pattern of "a face." We commonly express this idea by saying that each drawing *reflects* the structure of a face. This purely perceptual functional invariant relates to the similar semantic-pragmatic interpretations (or perceptual cognition) that each drawing elicits, which justifies the claim that symbols of a face embody an *isomorphism* between two systems, one more perceptual and the other more cognitive.

The first epistemological thesis of this chapter is that, if a suitable organismic theory and method of task analysis are available, it is possible to do fundamental measurement of a "hidden" organismic resource, which often is called endogenous effortful attention, that is responsible for developmental differences in problem-solving ability. This sort of attention has been called alternatively voluntary attention, focus of attention, executive attention, and (biogenetic component of) working memory. We call it *mental attention*, and we contrast it with *spontaneous attention* (an effortless, often exogenous, perceptual or imaginal sort of attention that also occurs in mind wandering; Berger, Henik, & Rafal, 2005; Christoff, Gordon, Smallwood, Smith, & Schooler, 2009; Hopfinger & West, 2006; Posner & Peterson, 1990). Mental attention grows with and regulates cognitive development. As a construct it may underpin what Binet (1910; Binet & Simon, 1905/2004) considered the root of developmental intelligence and judgement (Pascual-Leone & Johnson, 2005); what Spearman (1927) regarded as the organismic foundation of his *g* factor (Pascual-Leone & Goodman, 1979; Pascual-Leone & Johnson, 2005); what Piaget called *operativity* (e.g., centration and decentration of reflective attention – his mental "field of equilibrium"); and what James (1892/1961) called voluntary attention that monitors the stream of thought.

Attention is an intensive, purely qualitative resource of humans and other mammals. We have long had the intuition (Pascual-Leone, 1970) that *mental* attention could be measured by *the size of a set:* the set of distinct *schemes* (semantic-pragmatic processes) that a person can *endogenously activate* and coordinate together to synthesize a distinct mental state (or a percept) as integrated totality. Indeed, mental attention (like William James' [1892/1961] voluntary attention; or Husserl's [1948/1973] intentional syntheses of consciousness) appears to subjective experience as if it were a limited resource, which can only encompass, and simultaneously boost with activation, a small set of separate representational and operative schemes (relevant separate pieces of information). Restle (1959) proposed a metric for set-theoretical measures. In our case, however, because we propose a set-theoretical measure for *mental* attention, and units of information (i.e., *schemes*) are in the mind of the beholder, we must first make available a method of *metasubjective* – mental if you will – *task analysis*, to demarcate task-relevant schemes needed for the acts of mental attention.

In what follows we present a brief summary of the organismic general model informing our task analysis method. Then, to clarify the important concept of misleading situations, we give several examples of tasks measuring mental attention (*M-tasks*), outlining their task analyses and illustrating with some data. We discuss measurement of mental attention as a new form of additive conjoint measurement (Coombs et al., 1970) and illustrate the invariance of our *M*-measurement results across types of tasks as well as across age-group samples.

Theory of constructive operators: Schemes and other organismic operators

The causal texture of the environment and organismic schemes

Proper measurement of mental attention needs clear ways to identify organismic units of information, the schemes, and a clear formulation of mental attention. This is what the theory of constructive operators can provide. Kant (1781/1965; Pascual-Leone, 1998) saw the schema as the organism's way of bridging the gap between organism and its situational context, capturing actual constraints/resistances of the current situation. However, schemas or schemes of Kant or Piaget are neither *organismic* (i.e., embodied in the brain and behavioral processes) nor *situated* (i.e., contextualized to a situation). They also fail to show the link of schemes/schemas with constructivist processes in evolutionary epistemology (Pascual-Leone, 2006b).

Human *activity* (understood as goal-directed interaction with situations in order to control or understand objects/persons – Leontiev, 1981) can be expressed in praxis or practice. By *praxis* we mean cognitive/motor goal-directed actions addressed to the environment, to satisfy *central* and *intrinsic* personal needs (i.e., affective goals). *Practice* is similar to a conscious or unconscious praxis that often uses automatized operations, enacted to satisfy *marginal* and predominantly *extrinsic* needs or affective goals. Actual goals always involve an affective/emotive component that is explicit or implicit within the organism's internal constraints (Pascual-Leone & Johnson, 2004).

We think of reality-out-there as a universe of species-specific *resistances* to our goals (externally determined constraints or relational/perceptual patterning in experiential outcomes) *that emerge during the individual's activity*, both praxis and practice, within a given context/situation. For instance, when I hit the table with my knuckle, I hear the sound and simultaneously feel the blow on my finger – these are resistances expressing two different "objects" clashing. As in this example, resistances often are found to have dependency relations with one another. Reality is populated with *packages of interdependent resistances* that are relative to each species (any physical object is one such sort of package). An example from Kagan (2002, p. 72) can serve as illustration: ". . . a person who has just cut his finger on a knife and watches the blood ooze over his palm has no uncertainty about the existence of objects that can cause blood to flow, and is certain that he feels different than he did moments earlier." The finger and the knife are *real* packages of resistances (they are *distal objects*, construed by each of us to coordinate the respective interdependent external resistances); and the cutting action (a key resistance of the knife) here serves to expose a conditional key resistance of the finger (i.e., when cut it will bleed).

These packages can be interpreted, without falling into empiricist excess, as indexing *real* functional *invariants* (cf. Gibson, 1979; Nakayama, 1994; Nozick, 2001; Ullmo, 1967), that is, recurrent relational aspects of reality that animals can cognize and in a constructivist manner learn to re-present to themselves. Motivation (which functionally intertwines affect/emotion, cognition, and reality) leads higher animals to *internalize* (constructively learn) these packages and their interdependencies, to learn the *causal texture of the environment* (Tolman & Brunswik, 1966).

From this constructivist-epistemology perspective, it is appropriate to recognize that *internalization* (neural reflective abstraction) of reality packages results from our activity and occurs in three distinct *modes or categories* of invariants – differently *packaged resistances*. (1) First are packaged resistances that stand for the *targets* of the person's praxis or practice and that underpin semantic-pragmatic "objects of experience" – whether external or internal/mental experience; we call these packages *obs*. (2) Packages that stand for *patterns of action* or *mental operation* (praxis or practice) can change *obs*, or the relations among *obs*, in expectable ways. We call these packages *pros*, because they are constructivist substrata for procedures and operative processes. (3) Finally, there are packages of resistances, simple or complex, that give *adjunct information* about *obs*, *pros*, and situations in which they usefully can be applied. These packages, which we call *ads*, describe properties or relations pertaining to *obs* (or situations) and can also describe conditions or parameters that *pros* need to satisfy to be applicable to particular *obs* and situations. *Ad*jectives, *ad*verbs, the meaning of relative clauses, and *ad*vertisements, all have this category of *adjunct-information* as their reality foundation.

In the quote of Kagan above, the finger, the knife, the blood, and the palm are each represented in the person's brain as *ob*-indexing processes. The category description "objects that can cause blood to flow" is an *ad*-indexing process that causally relates *obs* such as knives to parts of the body (e.g., fingers) and to blood. The brain representation of the knife's action, which actually caused the blood to flow, stands for a *pro*. By reflectively abstracting from experience *obs*, *pros*, and *ads* related to praxis and practice, intelligent animals can internalize descriptive representations and causal relations relevant for life in their environment.

When constructively *internalized* (i.e., learned via epistemological reflection of *real* resistances), *pros* appear as blueprints of people's actions or transformations, which Piaget and neo-Piagetians would call *operative schemes* or *operatives* (essentially procedural knowledge). In contrast, both *obs* and *ads* are internalized as coded descriptions of states, which Piaget and neo-Piagetians often call *figurative schemes* or *figuratives* (related to declarative/representational knowledge, although they can be either explicit or implicit). A main difference between *obs* and *ads* seems to be motivational: *obs*, but not *ads*, serve as possible targets for the person's praxis. Notice further that abstraction and *internalization* of *obs*, *ads*, and *pros* cannot be made in a piecemeal manner. These three functional categories constitute a dialectical trio: They emerge together in the context of activity within situations, as partial constituents of the activity being internalized; that is, *they are abstracted together in coordinated packages that produce the organismic schemes.*

Information is carried in the brain by distinct unitized collections of neurons, often distributed over the brain, that are co-functional (vis-à-vis certain activities) and co-activated in some tasks. These functional collections are the *organismic schemes*. Schemes in the organism are *situated* (i.e., situation specific) and self-propelling causal factors that *overdetermine* (i.e., conjointly determine beyond the need) manifest performance; their identification facilitates process and task analysis (Pascual-Leone, 1970, 1995; Pascual-Leone & Goodman, 1979; Pascual-Leone & Johnson, 1991, 2005; Pascual-Leone, Johnson, Baskind, Dworsky, & Severtson, 2000).

As dynamic systems, schemes are abstracted across situations for a given sort of praxis, internalizing models of *obs*, *ads*, and *pros* in their interaction. From a structural perspective, a scheme can be understood as expressing the well-learned coordination of three components: (1) a *functional system* that embodies the gist of the scheme's semantic-pragmatic organization (the configuration of related *pros* or *obs*, and the scheme goals); (2) a set of *conditions* (related to *ads*, *obs*, or *pros*) that release the scheme; and (3) a set of *effects* (related to *pros*, *obs*, or *ads*) that follow from the scheme's application to experienced reality. Schemes must be internally consistent to be formed, and they are recursive. They can be defined at different epistemological levels, so that many schemes appear to be functionally nested in the sense that conditions and/or effects of schemes can in turn be constituted by (copies of) other lower-level schemes, even though these distinct schemes remain functionally autonomous albeit related.

A clear example of this functional nesting occurs with the contrast between *executive* schemes and ordinary *action* schemes. *Executive schemes* (i.e., *executives*) are higher-level units that embody plans/blueprints for action and strategy. They define tasks within situations, and (induced by affective schemes) they can regulate application of organismic resources (hidden operators, see below) to the action schemes. Via these organismic resources, executives also can monitor and control application of suitable action schemes to the task at hand – whether *figurative* (i.e., representational, including "objects" and "parameters") or *operative* (procedural) *action schemes* – to generate perceptual experience or performance. Initially, executives are separate from the action schemes to which they apply, so that mental attention must be used separately to activate all these nested schemes. However, with practice, a chunking or associative-learning process that we call *logical*-structural *content* (or *LC*) *learning* develops, which transforms the hierarchical package into a single *chunk* (called in our theory *LC-structure* – an automatized circuit) that can be boosted with mental energy as a single unit. These complex schemes, often called *structures* or schemas, could be interpreted as neuronal circuits or semantic networks (Fuster, 1995; Kagan, 2002).

Schemes overdetermine performance because they are *self-propelling* (Piaget's *assimilation* function) and tend to *apply* to the situation (i.e., fire as collections of neurons) under minimal conditions of activation. Every scheme has a dual reality: As a *package of qualitative functional characteristics* that can inform (i.e., inject form into) experience when it applies, and as a variable *quantitative parameter* (i.e., *activation weight* for its neural network area) – which conditions the probability that the scheme will become hyperactivated and apply (perhaps via neuronal synchronization) to cause performance. Schemes are like recursive procedures and can be learned: It is common to have scheme hierarchies (i.e., schemes of schemes of schemes, etc.), which we call *structures* or *schemas* (e.g., the coordinated "program" or "script" that governs our behavior in restaurants or within familiar sorts of problem solving). Long-term memory can be best explicated as a manifold repertoire of schemes or structures sorted in kinds: *executive* schemes (prefrontal), *operative* schemes (frontal), *figurative* schemes (i.e., perceptual or representational or linguistic – occipital, parietal, or temporal), coordinated packages of automatized *operative/motor* schemes (frontal right hemisphere, basal ganglia, and cerebellum), *affective/emotion* schemes (broadly defined limbic system), *analytical* schemes *produced with mental effort* (initially in the left hemisphere), *global or holistic automatized* schemes (right hemisphere), etc. Experiences are possible only because schemes produce, assimilate, or structure them via dynamic syntheses.

Hidden operators and the process of mental attention

With the theory of schemes alone one cannot explain *general* organismic constraints (i.e., those applying across kinds of schemes and across content domains) such as "central" working-memory capacity limits, "central" inhibitory mechanisms, structural versus content learning, "central" resolution of schemes' *competition* within the network, or the emergence of truly-novel performances via unplanned dynamic syntheses. It is often thought that prefrontal lobes and other areas carry out these general regulation functions by controlling activity of specific processes elsewhere in the cortex (such as posterior areas) – even though such controlling power is limited.

To explain these regulation functions we postulate that the brain, in addition to a repertoire of *schemes* (i.e., cofunctional collections of neurons), has a small set of general purpose functional resources that we call *hidden* or silent *operators* (Pascual-Leone, 1987, 1995, 2000a, 2000b; Pascual-Leone & Johnson, 1991, 2005; Pascual-Leone et al., 2000). They are functional mode-general mechanisms of brain "hardware," defined as molar procedures whose computational details are unspecified (therefore the name *operators*), which constrain schemes to change their activation level, produce new schemes, synthesize truly-novel performances, etc. These operators are *hidden* because they lack substantive content referents, which schemes have (i.e., perceptual, motor, representational, etc.). Instead, hidden operators express/explain purely-relational multivariate constraints – surprising patterns or "anomalies" (exhibited under specific empirical circumstances) that a pure theory of schemes cannot explain. They are our attempt to formulate, as categories of constructs within a psychological theory, some *purely-organismic constraints* that the brain's cortical architecture imposes on psychological processes and behavior. The hidden operators currently entertained in our theory are summarized by Pascual-Leone and Johnson (2005) and Pascual-Leone (1995). Here we discuss briefly only operators that intervene in *spontaneous, perceptual* attention versus those that intervene to produce the phenomena of *mental* attention. Notice that organismic resources causing mental attention function as activation boosters of information-carrying neuronal processes, which ensures that coactivated and cofunctional schemes (aspects of the experience, such as objects or actions) are dynamically synthesized into complex manifolds of unitized experience, as suggested by Husserl in our first epigraph on *intentional* objects (the meaningful target of our praxis).

Spontaneous attention, that is, William James' (1892/1961) immediate attention, occurs under various circumstances: effortless attention driven by salient or novel *perceptual experiences*; automatized habits that effortlessly call and monitor the direction of attention; affects or emotions that drive the attending process; wanderings of the mind effortlessly driven by prominent experiential or personal processes within the inner stream of thought – either during dreams in sleep or during inattention to many tasks of our daily work. Spontaneous attention is the normal sort of attention in mammals, as pets and children easily demonstrate. Situations that elicit spontaneous attention are intrinsically self-motivating: They elicit immediate attention and typically are *facilitating* (Pascual-Leone & Johnson, 2005). A *situation is facilitating* when by itself it activates only schemes that are relevant for the task at hand – the activity towards which the person is motivationally oriented. Recent neuroscience research has established that spontaneous-attention activity is expressed in the cortex as activation of the medial frontal gyrus and other related areas. These interrelated areas have been named the default network

(Buckner, Andrews-Hanna, & Schacter, 2008; Christoff et al., 2009; Raichle, MacLeod, Snyder, Powers, Gusnard, & Schulman, 2001), because they are activated in situations in which active, voluntary, executive-driven attending is not required. In our theory, spontaneous attention is essentially the product of affects (which include arousal processes), content learning (*C-* and *LC*-learning), and sensorial or Gestaltist salience in the perceptual field (*F*-operator, see below).

Mental attention, also known as endogenous, active, effortful, voluntary, and executive attention, or as working memory, is our name for the executive-driven attentional "brain energy" that William James (1892/1961), Spearman (1927), and Luria (1973), among others, saw as activating *task-relevant* processes in the cortex when they are not strong enough to co-determine the intended performance. We call this form of attention *mental* instead of executive attention – a currently popular denotation – for three main reasons: (1) It is used to boost activation of all sorts of schemes, not just executives; (2) it is driven not just by executives but also by affective and emotional schemes (Pascual-Leone, 1991; Pascual-Leone & Johnson, 2004; Pessoa, 2009); (3) mental attention can be recognized to exist already in children after 2 months of life (its growth indexes Piaget's sensorimotor stages), whereas executive schemes cannot be found until after 12 months of age (Alp, 1994; Benson, 1989; Diamond, 2006; Pascual-Leone & Johnson, 1999a). Our constructive-operators model for mental attention is discussed below.

Within facilitating situations, mental attention can join forces with spontaneous attention. In misleading situations, however, mental attention is in competitive opposition to the misleading/distracting effects of spontaneous attention. In a *misleading situation* strong, prepotent responses (schemes) are elicited that contradict what the person wants (or should like) to do. Salient cues exist in such situations that lead performers to error, and these error factors cannot be ignored because they are intertwined or embedded with task-relevant cues or processes. We encounter misleading contexts when shopping in supermarkets or pharmacies. Products often are placed inside excessively large packaging, giving the illusion that packages contain more product than they in fact do – creating a misleading situation when one wishes to appraise the cost. Many everyday or laboratory *problem-solving tasks* involve misleading situations, and control of these error factors is key to success. This control involves becoming aware, keeping these factors in mind, inhibiting misguided impulsive responses, and applying necessary corrections – usually with the help of mental attention. The need to inhibit misleading schemes (i.e., competing but unwanted activated brain circuits) forces use of mental attention to activate alternative task-relevant processes. The number of relevant processes (i.e., schemes) simultaneously activated by mental attention can be used to measure its capacity: We call this measure *mental (M-) power*. *M*-power increases with age up to adolescence. In our view, growth of *M*-power is the key causal mechanism for developmental stage transitions (Pascual-Leone, 1970).

Everyday problem solving often illustrates the learned origin of misleading error factors (error-learning habits). An experience of Pascual-Leone (JPL), when he was a 20-year-old medical student living in his parents' home, can serve as illustration. His mother always wanted the family to turn off the light when leaving a room at night and, as an obedient fellow, JPL tried hard to do so. One day he noticed that he often involuntarily turned *on* the light when leaving rooms in the middle of the day. He had evolved a habit (scheme) such as: **if** *I leave a room* **and** *the room is illuminated*, **then** *I move hand to the switch* to *turn off the light*. This was a good scheme at night to satisfy his mother's injunction; however, by day it caused a misleading situation. To correct this error factor he had to become aware of it, to inhibit the response, if needed, when room lights were not on and light was entering through a window. That is, he had to incorporate another condition into his scheme: **if** *I leave a room,* **and** *the room is illuminated,* **and** *lights in the room are on* (or light does not enter from outside), **then** . . ."

This example makes an important point: Boosting additional relevant schemes with mental attention can serve to control misleading situations (perhaps without having to use inhibition). This is why growth of mental attention during developmental stages is best assessed in misleading situations. The measure of mental attention often used to recognize this growth is set-theoretical: the size of the set of task-relevant schemes simultaneously to be attended to, to pass a task item. In our studies such set measure increases across classes/levels of items from 2 to 8.

As a form of fundamental measurement we contrast mental demand (Md) of items with the person's measure of mental capacity (his/her M-power or Mp). In this way we assess whether $Mp = Md$, in which case the participant should solve the task, or $Mp < Md$, which should cause the participant to fail. This difference between Mp and Md can be interpreted as expressing the actual processing difficulty within the organism (i.e., *organismic* difficulty) of the task (Pascual-Leone, 1970). In addition, this difference between a hidden organismic measure such as Mp and the task difficulty Md (tacitly computed by the organism) can be construed over age-group samples as a case of additive conjoint measurement (Coombs et al., 1970; Krantz, Luce, Suppes & Tversky, 1971), which we illustrate later. A quote from Coombs et al. (1970, p. 28) applies well to what happens with this organismic Mp versus Md difference in M-measurement: "It is interesting to note that one obtains an additive measurement scale in the absence of any physical concatenation operation. The numerical addition [difference in our case – JPL] represents the combination of two treatments, which are, so to speak, added inside the organism."

A model of endogenous mental attention

We symbolize mental attention as a searchlight model constituted by a system of four organismic operators: $< E, M, I, F >$. E is a set of attentional executive schemes. These executive processes can mobilize and allocate the two main attentional resources, that is, attentional activation (called *M-operator*), and the attentional inhibition or interruption (called *I-operator*). *F* is the Gestaltist *field factor*, that is, lateral inhibition in layer 4 of the cortex (e.g., Edelman, 1987), which helps to produce the closure of performance and generates the beam of attention by inhibiting schemes outside this beam.

The beam of attention is symbolized in Figure 2.1. Operators *E, M*, and *I* are expressed in the prefrontal lobe, and their coordinated application to action schemes produces *focal centration* (or *M*-centration). This is the inner ellipse. Notice that in Figure 2.1 we call H the repertoire of *habitual* schemes (this is long-term memory) in *M*-centration, and call H' the part of long-term memory that is outside. The outer ellipse symbolizes the field of activated schemes (*field of activation*), and the middle ellipse symbolizes the field of *all* hyperactivated schemes, which is often called *focus of attention* or *working memory*. Therefore, there are schemes in the focus of attention that are not hyperactivated by means of *M*-capacity. Rather, their high activation is caused by some other organismic factors such as associative content learning (*C*), logical-content learning (*LC*), effortful logical-structural learning (*LM*, i.e., learning made possible by boosting with *M*-capacity the chosen schemes), or affect (*A*), etc. These hyperactivated schemes located outside the *M*-centration tend to be automatically (or effortfully) interrupted/inhibited to some degree with each new act of mental (*M*-) centration (Morra, 2000; Pascual-Leone, Romero Escobar, Johnson, & Morra, 2006; Romero Escobar, 2006).

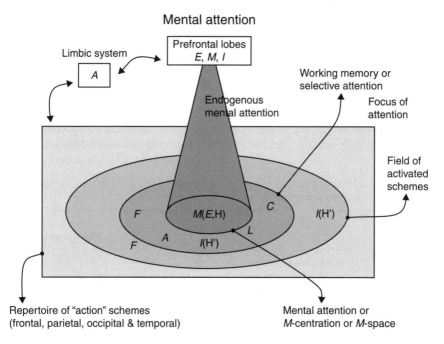

Figure 2.1 Model of endogenous mental attention.

Figure 2.1 in fact illustrates the case of a facilitating situation, in which one can distinguish within the field of hyperactivated schemes (focus of attention, middle ellipse) those that are being boosted by *M*-capacity (this is the inner ellipse), and those that are instead boosted by other organismic factors such as associative learning, affect, or Gestalt saliency (hidden operators *C, LC, A, F*). In the case of misleading situations, however, highly-activated misleading schemes are already in the focus of attention and consequently the person's executive processes (*E* operator) seek to inhibit (*I* operator) these misleading schemes to cope with the task. As a result they inhibit at the same time most hyperactivated schemes outside *M*-centration, which eliminates the middle ellipse reducing the focus of attention to the inner ellipse. This is another reason why misleading situations make better tasks for estimating *M*-demand via task analysis. *M*-demand is the minimal amount of *M*-capacity needed to solve a given task.

Maturational growth of *M*-capacity and *M*-measurement

Mental attention, and with it the power (set-theoretical measure) of *M*-capacity, increases during normal child development from early months of life to adolescence; this measure, called *M*-power (*Mp*), gives a numerical characteristic to developmental stages (Pascual-Leone, 1970). Indeed, each maturationally achieved *Mp* level enables the transition from one cognitive-developmental stage to the next – provided that suitable learning has taken place (Johnson, Fabian, & Pascual-Leone, 1989; Pascual-Leone, 1970, 1987, 2000a; Pascual-Leone & Baillargeon, 1994; Pascual-Leone & Ijaz, 1989; Pascual-Leone & Johnson, 1999a, 2005; Pascual-Leone et al., 2000).

Table 2.1 gives Piaget's substages of cognitive development from 3 years of age onward, with corresponding expected *M*-capacity values. In this table *M*-capacity is given with two scales *e* plus *k*. The scale *e* corresponds to *M*-capacity found during the sensorimotor period, and its upper bound estimates the number of sensorimotor schemes that 3-year-olds can simultaneously boost with mental attention. During the symbolic-processing years (up

Table 2.1 Predicted *M*-capacity values as a function of age, and their correspondence to the Piagetian substage sequence

M-capacity (e + k)	*Piagetian substage*	*Normative chronological age*
$e + 1$	Low preoperations	3, 4 yrs
$e + 2$	High preoperations	5, 6 yrs
$e + 3$	Low concrete operations	7, 8 yrs
$e + 4$	High concrete operations	9, 10 yrs
$e + 5$	Substage introductory to formal operations	11, 12 yrs
$e + 6$	Low formal operations	13, 14 yrs
$e + 7$	High formal operations	15 – adult

to and beyond adolescence) this amount *e* of mental attention is used to activate task-relevant *executive* schemes. *In this paper the **e** scale is not discussed, but treated as a constant.* We discuss the **k** scale, whose growth with age is presented in Table 2.1. The value *k* indicates the number of symbolic schemes that can be simultaneously hyperactivated with *M*-capacity at each substage during the school years. At the end of this pattern of *M*-growth, in late adolescence, the value of *k* can be as much as 7 – no doubt the "magical number seven" of George Miller (1956); this is what our task analyses and much data show. We have determined, however, that participants often do not mobilize all *M*-capacity they have available (Pascual-Leone, 1970): There is a lower bound or *functional M*-capacity often used by participants, which is equal to 4 or 5 *k*-units in adults; and there is an upper bound or *M-reserve* (*structural M*-capacity, Pascual-Leone, 1970). The *M*-reserve is equal to 7 in adolescents (15–16 year) and adults (Arsalidou, 2008; Arsalidou, Pascual-Leone, & Johnson, 2010; Pascual-Leone, 1970, 2006a). Our estimates come from many tasks and much data, some of which we briefly summarize below. The measure of *M* is probabilistic, changing with causal variables such as alertness, fatigue, appraised difficulty of the task, state of health, etc. (Pascual-Leone, 1970).

M-capacity is a hidden organismic construct in the sense that we must co-vary conjointly participants' capacity and tasks' processing demand to obtain estimates of participants' *M*-power as an empirical invariant in the data. This need to conjointly vary the two organismic variables suggests that *M*, as an empirical construct, results from what Bohm (1980) has called an "implicate order"; in our case, a complex, purely-relational, organismic-and-situational system of *constraints*. *M* is a special sort of latent variable that Bohm and others call a *hidden variable*. The key characteristic of *M* as hidden variable is that the effect on manifest performance of participants' mental-capacity power (*Mp*) is *relative to* the mental demand (*Md*) of task items (e.g., items will be passed only if *Mp* is equal to or larger than the task's *Md*). We have tested empirically the reality of such *Mp/Md trade-off* and its relationship to participants' cognitive style of processing (e.g., Baillargeon, Pascual-Leone, & Roncadin, 1998; Pascual-Leone & Baillargeon, 1994). Because *M*-capacity is a hidden organismic variable, theory-guided task analysis must inform the *a priori* construction of measuring tasks, as well as construction of appropriate *M-scores*, so that they epistemologically reflect the intended trade-off.

We give four characteristics that good measures of *M*-capacity should have (for more detail on *M-measurement* see Pascual-Leone & Baillargeon, 1994; Pascual-Leone et al., 2000).

1   All items must have a reduced need for executive control (a minimal *E*-demand), which is achieved in at least three ways: (a) doing executive pretraining; (b) maintaining the same executives in all task items while increasing *M*-demand from one class of item to the next, thus facilitating

intra-task executive learning; (c) creating valid alternative forms of the same *M*-task, then administering both forms in succession (the first one will induce executive learning transferable to the second).

2   An *M*-task is constituted by relevant *classes* of items (homogeneous scales) such that each class indexes one given *M*-demand value, all relevant values being represented in items of the task. These scales differ only in *M*-demand, with other aspects kept constant.

3   Although executive and action schemes required by items are available to participants (perhaps due to pretraining), the problem to be solved (i.e., the task as such) is not trained: It is novel.

4   *M*-measurement tasks can be constructed in facilitating or misleading situations. Misleading situations require, in addition to *M*-capacity, *moderate* use of effortful attentional inhibition. Misleading situations are more culture-fair for theoretical and empirical reasons (Pascual-Leone et al., 2000), making them better for *M*-measurement.

M-tasks and metasubjective task analysis

The *M*-demand of a task is the minimal amount of *M*-capacity needed to solve it. *M*-demand is measured by the maximal number of separate symbolic schemes that must be *simultaneously* boosted with *M*-capacity during the task solution. This number is estimated by means of metasubjective task analysis. The schemes (operative and figurative) identified in the analysis should meet three conditions: (1) reflect the affordances provided by the task and/or the actions demanded by it; (2) require activation with *M*-capacity (e.g., not be automated or *LC* driven); and (3) if coordinated via dynamic synthesis, be able (along with other highly activated schemes) to produce the intended performance (Pascual-Leone & Johnson, 1991, 2005).

Predictions from task analyses are tested against developmental performance patterns; and when needed, adjustments could be done to task analyses, if theoretically justified. We describe four *M*-tasks and their task analyses. We subsequently present representative data on these tasks.

The *Figural Intersections Task* (*FIT*) is an individual or group-administered paper-and-pen test. In this task between 2 and 8 shapes are presented on the right-hand side of the page, and are shown overlapping on the left-hand side (see Figure 2.2). Participants first place a mark inside each discrete shape on the right. Next, they must place a single mark that is inside all relevant overlapping shapes on the left at the same time – *the common intersection*. Relevant shapes are those also found on the right side. However, right and left side shapes are not perceptually identical: They often differ in size and are rotated, although the shape is preserved.

Guided training gives participants knowledge of needed executive and action schemes. Task difficulty varies with the number of relevant shapes to be intersected. Key misleading factors in this task are the number of *partial* intersections (i.e., intersections among relevant shapes that are not the

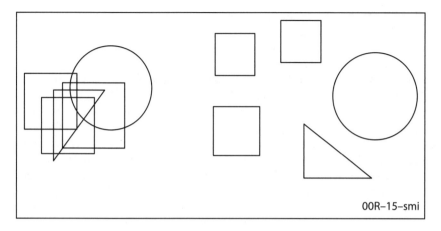

00R–15–smi

Figure 2.2 Sample class 5 item from Figural Intersections Task (FIT).

common intersection – activated by content, i.e., *C*- and *LC*-operators), which increases rapidly with the number of figures; and also the Gestalt field-factor effects (*F* operator) that produce an automatic overall perceptual pattern that makes it hard to analytically (*M*- and *LM*-processing) segregate shapes to extract the site of common intersection (Pascual-Leone & Baillargeon, 1994). This analytical process of extraction needs mental attention. Pascual-Leone and Baillargeon (1994) give a detailed task analysis of the FIT and also use Latent Class Analysis (Clogg & Sawyer, 1981) to test assumptions of our "mental power versus mental demand (*Mp/Md*)" trade-off model for the task. They demonstrate that Lazarsfeld's latent-distance scaling model (which generates ordered latent *Mp* classes of participants) fits very well our FIT theoretical model and data.

To begin task analysis of FIT, look again at Figure 2.2. The subtask at the right side of the page is facilitating – past perceptual learning (*C* and *LC* operators) and perceptual saliency (*F* operator) help in task completion. The subtask of the left side, however – that is, to place a mark in the common area of intersection – is misleading, particularly with many shapes. Gestaltist perceptual-field factor (*F*-operator) hinders perception of the common intersection, which is embedded in the pattern of overlapping shapes.

A brief summary of the FIT left-hand subtask analysis appears in Formula 1, which assumes participants use an *analytical total-intersection strategy*. Notice that a metasubjective task analysis has to model a single strategy, and we adopt the one participants commonly use (Pascual-Leone & Baillargeon, 1994). Every distinct strategy demands a different task analysis.

$$M\,[OP_i\,(\{\,f1\,\}_{LC,\,F}\,,\,f2,\,f3,\,f4,\,f5)] \to i12345 \qquad (1)$$

In this formula, the boosting of all relevant schemes with mental attention ($M[...]$) provokes the dynamic synthesis ($\rightarrow$) of a truly-novel representation: the total intersection **i12345**. This dynamic synthesis is generated by schemes' tendency to apply together and *overdetermine* the (in this task perceptual) outcome. Such overdetermination is symbolized by the arrow ($\rightarrow$).

The main purpose of task analysis is to model steps (microanalysis) of a task solution, and to estimate its mental demand when solved without external aid. Using symbolic (operator logic) notation informally, we represent the most *M*-demanding step of the chosen strategy: To use mental attention to focus on the operative scheme (OP_i) that searches and finds the common intersection by the strategy of attending to relevant shapes, one by one, segregating them in perception. The symbols **f1, f2, ... f5** stand for these shapes to be intersected. These schemes are inside the brackets of *M*-capacity (symbolized by $M[...]$) to express that they are being boosted by *M*. However, shape **f1** is inside braces {...} to indicate that it is not boosted by *M*. This is because participants take **f1** as *background shape* for visual exploring, and thus **f1** becomes overlearned (*LC*) and salient – facilitated by the perceptual field (*F*), and not needing additional boosting. A likely strategy for the item in Figure 2.2 would be to take the salient circle as background figure. The schemes for the operative process (OP_i) and the shapes **f2, f3, f4**, and **f5** will each need to be boosted with *M*-capacity, because on the left side each shape has to be actively extracted from the perceptually salient overall pattern of figures. If we count the number of distinct schemes to be boosted, that is, the task's mental demand, it is equal to the number *n* of figures to be intersected: $Md = n$.

The FIT is constituted by randomly ordered items, each belonging to one item class defined by its *M*-demand (*Md*). Classes of items vary from $Md = 2$ (i.e., two relevant figures to be intersected) to $Md = 8$. FIT *M*-score is the highest item class a participant passes reliably (i.e., at least 66% correct – exact percentage changes with number of items in the task version) given similarly reliable performance on lower item classes (allowing for one lower item class to be below 66% correct).

We and others have studied FIT extensively (e.g., Laudy, Zoccolillo, Baillargeon, Boom, Tremblay, & Hoijtink, 2005; Morra, 1994; Pascual-Leone & Baillargeon, 1994; Pennings & Hessels, 1996). Pascual-Leone and Baillargeon (1994) and many others have demonstrated that participants succeed items when their $Mp = Md$; otherwise they fail.

The *Color Matching Tasks* (*CMT*) were developed in our laboratory with Arsalidou (2008; Arsalidou et al., 2010). They are comprised of two modified 1-back tasks, in which the stimuli are patterned figures (either a clown or a set of balloons) with different colors. The colors of successive figures must be compared to determine whether the set of current-figure colors (*target colors*) is the same or different from that of the previous figure (*criterion colors*). Irrelevant features to be ignored are the colors blue and green, location of colors in the figure, repetition of colors in the same figure, and colors in the clown's face. The two tasks differ in the form of the stimulus figure:

CMT-Balloon has as figure a bundle of balloons of various colors; CMT-Clown has a clown with a varicolored costume. The Balloon task presents a *facilitating situation*: The colors are the balloons' most salient feature, because in everyday life basic balloons are distinguishable only by their colors. In contrast, the Clown task is more difficult, because it presents a *misleading situation*: The salient aspect of the stimulus is the charming clown itself with its expressive face (which must be ignored). As a result, relevant colors in the clown figure are less easy to see, hindered by the salience of the clown's body and costume – where relevant colors are embedded. CMT-Clown was designed as an *M*-measure, and has classes of items differing only in the items' *M*-demand. To ensure that they had executive and action schemes needed for the task, children were tested first with the alternative version CMT-Balloon and then with CMT-Clown.

The two CMT versions (Balloon and Clown) are computerized tasks (Arsalidou, 2008; Arsalidou et al., 2010). They have a brief pretraining in which the relevant strategy and the needed executive and action schemes are suggested and practiced. Figures are presented in sequence, and for each the participant must indicate whether the current set of relevant target colors is the same as those in the previous (criterion) figure. There also are *baseline items* (containing only the irrelevant colors, blue and green), which do not require a response. Items are presented in pseudorandom blocks of classes. *M*-score in the CMT is the *M*-demand of the highest item class passed reliably (i.e., at least 70% of items correct) – given a similarly reliable performance on lower classes, and allowing performance on only one lower class to fall below 70% correct.

We used metasubjective task analysis to estimate the *M*-demand of CMT-Clown items. The task analysis is summarized in Formula 2, and it will help readers to consult the formula as they read the explanation below.

(1) $M[\text{SCAN\&IDEN}^{L1}$ ($\{\#\text{IGN: f, irrC, locC, repC}\}_{L1} <$
$\underline{cc1}, \underline{cc2}, \ldots \underline{ccn} > \underline{tci})]$

(2) $M[\text{MATCH\&PRESS}$ ($< \underline{cc1}, \underline{cc2}, \ldots \underline{ccn} > \underline{tci})]$

(3) $M[\text{RESET}^{L3}/\text{RECUR}^{L2}$ ($\{\#\text{set.c'} \leftarrow \}_{L3} \underline{\text{set.t}}/\#\text{set.t}:\{\text{tci'} \leftarrow \text{tci}\}_{L2})]$ (2)

The task has an overall executive procedure that consists of three successive steps. In this task analysis the executive process is not represented, because it is assumed not to be boosted with *M*-capacity for symbolic processing (i.e., *k* scale of *M*-power), but instead boosted with *M*-capacity for sensorimotor processes (i.e., *e* scale of *M*-power; Pascual-Leone & Johnson, 2005). We symbolize *operative schemes* with capital letters, and *figurative schemes* with lower case. *Parameters*, which prescribe conditions to the application of operatives, are identified by #. In the first step (1) a participant must *scan*, one by one, and *identify* (**SCAN&IDEN**) the relevant target colors found in the current Clown item. As the participant scans and identifies he/she has to *ignore* (**#IGN**) the face colors (**f**), irrelevant colors (**irrC**), location of colors (**locC**), and repeated colors (**repC**). These, and the embedding context which is the Clown itself, are features making the task misleading. We assume that this injunction to ignore is already chunked with the operative **SCAN&IDEN**. We symbolize such chunking by placing these **#IGN** schemes inside braces (curly brackets) subscripting the letter *L1* to the second brace, and simultaneously placing a superscripted *L1* on **SCAN&IDEN**. This signifies that the latter is the operative-scheme portion of a chunk that controls the former. The *L-boosting process*, symbolized by *L1, L2,* and *L3* in Formula 2, corresponds to multiple schemes that are so highly associated (structured together) that the chunk requires only one unit of *M*-energy to be hyperactivated.

Step (1) in the model shows a moment when the participant, who moments before scanned the current set of target colors (**set.t**), is now keeping in mind one of them (**tc$i$**) along with the total set of criterion colors (**set.c**) from the previous item. Step 1 shows the schemes kept in mind. Participants must keep in mind (boosted with *M*-capacity) *each* of the criterion colors separately, because they are no longer present, and next he/she will have to match them, one by one, with each of the target colors (**tc$i$**). This total set of criterion colors is symbolized in step (1) as **<cc1, cc2, . . ., cc$n$>**.

In step (2) participants, pursuing the analysis begun in step 1, have to match each and every target color **tc$i$** with the total set of criterion colors (to check whether the color in question is among the criterion colors). This is done by keeping in mind (boosted with *M*-capacity) the operative scheme (**MATCH&PRESS**) of step 2, *and* the *n* criterion-color schemes of step 1. Finally, step (3) plays a dual function, indicated by the incompatibility sign (/) that separates operatives **RESET** and **RECUR**; this logical connective symbolizes that one or the other operative, *but not both*, will be applied at suitable moments of the task process. **RESET** applies whenever a new item is introduced, to ensure that the set of target colors (**set.t**) of the just finished item is retained with its function changed (←), now becoming the new set (**set.c'**) of criterion colors (**#set.c'←et.t**) – a change that is chunked (subscripted *L3*) with **RESET**. In contrast, **RECUR** applies within the processing of each item. The **RECUR** operative changes *M*-centration within the set of target colors from one target color matched to another target color (**tc$i$'**) not yet matched (**#set.t: tc$i$'←tc$i$**). This change process is chunked (subscripted *L2*) with **RECUR**.

Formula 2 has *underlined* schemes that in each step must have their activation boosted using *M*-capacity, because they are not salient and are not subordinate parts of an activated chunk. Counting these underlined schemes for each step we find that in steps (1) and (2) the number of schemes to be boosted by *M* is equal to $2 + n$, where *n* is the number of criterion colors in the trial item. For example, in step (1) participants must use *M*-capacity to boost the operative **SCAN&IDEN**, each of the colors **cc1** to **cc$n$** of the criterion set, and the target-set color (**tc$i$**) that they try to match against the criterion set. In step (3) this number is equal to 2: One of the two mutually incompatible (/)

operatives, and the scheme of their respective parameter (#) that is not chunked (is outside braces of *L2* or of *L3*). Thus participants should be able to solve a given CMT-Clown item, assuming they have the necessary schemes, when their *M*-power (*Mp*, i.e., the measure of *M*-capacity) is equal to $2 + n$. Because classes of items differ in the number of relevant colors presented, the value of *n* varies with the item class from 1 to 6, so that corresponding *M*-demand varies from 3 (i.e., $2 + 1$) to 8 (i.e., $2 + 6$).

The *Mental Attention Memory task* (*MAM*) is a modified verbal span measure. Participants free-recall consonants under three conditions of misleadingness. The consonants are presented on a card, arranged in a circular pattern. Number of consonants presented is equal to 4 plus the predicted *M*-power for the age group (e.g., 9–10-year-olds, with a predicted *M*-power of 4, receive 8 consonants). This keeps the supraspan list of similar difficulty for all age groups. As an illustration we describe the subtask called Telephone MAM. After reading aloud all consonants on a stimulus card (one consonant per second), participants must recall each consonant aloud and dial it on an old-fashion rotary telephone (i.e., on a dial that identifies positions with both numbers and letters). Since participants (children and young adults) do not know the location of consonants on the dial, they must search for them, thus suffering interference with recall of consonants from the card. This interference creates a *misleading situation*, and as a result they can only recall consonants they can keep active with *M-capacity*.

Romero Escobar (2006; Pascual-Leone et al., 2006) did mathematical modeling of the MAM, based on task analyses presented by Pascual-Leone and Johnson (1999b), and found excellent fit of developmental data to the model. For our present purpose, however, it may suffice to refer to the task analysis of FIT (see Formula 1) with an alternative interpretation. In this new interpretation, the various symbols for FIT shapes (**f1, f2, f3, f4, . . .**) stand for consonants that have been read and must be recalled/dialled; the operative scheme OP_i now stands for the process of recalling and/or dialling, and the symbol within braces, which we modify from Formula 1 as $\{f1\}_{LI}$, represents a consonant that already is chunked with OP_i^{LI}, because this search-of-consonants process is well-practiced enough to have a built-in place for the currently searched consonant. *M*-score is mean number of recalled consonants.

The *Direction Following Task* (*DFT*) was developed in our laboratory with Cunning (2003; Cunning, Johnson, & Pascual-Leone, 2004); it is an *M*-capacity measure in the language domain. It requires children to follow directions of increasing complexity (e.g., "Place a small blue square on a yellow space"). The task employs 20 foam shapes and a display board. The shapes consist of large and small squares and circles in the colors blue, green, red, yellow, and white. Shapes are arranged at random on a white board with two sides: a bare side for displaying shapes and a folding top that opens to reveal 10 large and small spaces in blue, green, red, yellow, and white where shapes can be placed according to the direction given.

DFT items are instructions consisting of a simple repetitive command ("place X on Y"). Complexity is manipulated by increasing the number of shapes, locations, and characteristics specified in a command to be enacted. Items are sorted into nine levels or classes of increasing complexity, with five items per level. The task also includes five practice items. Each item is scored as passed/failed, where passing requires that all elements be correct and enacted in the order of mention in the command. DFT M-score corresponds to the M-demand of the highest level at which 60% (3/5) of items are passed, assuming similarly reliable passing of lower levels, and allowing one lower level of items to be passed at rate 40% (2/5).

A metasubjective task analysis was conducted for each level of items in the DFT. As an example, we analyze in Table 2.2 the M-demand estimates for items from three of the nine levels of difficulty available in this task. Here, as in other task analyses, operative schemes are indicated by capital letters, and figurative schemes are represented by lower case letters.

Subscripted $L1$ indicates structures that are chunked with, and boosted by, a scheme superscripted by $L1$. This code indicates that schemes placed inside braces do not require M-capacity, because they are boosted into activation by the $L1$ scheme. One object (e.g., circle or square) is assumed to be boosted by the operative scheme **PLACE**, due to linguistic practice, contextual features, and automatization. The operative **PLACE** involves the location, apprehension, and relocation of an object. We also assume that the object in question is chunked with *one* of its characteristics (in real life size and color usually are tied to shape as object descriptors). This chunking occurs only for the first object-scheme (figurative) per instruction, whether or not it is a compound instruction, because memory load and time cost should prevent more chunking.

Table 2.2 Task analysis of sample Direction Following Task (DFT) items

DFT items	*Enumeration of schemes*	*M-demand*
Level 1: Place a blue square on a white space.	M[PLACE^{L1} ({blue-square}$_{L1}$: white)]	$e + 2$
Level 5: Place a red square and a white circle on a small yellow space.	M[PLACE^{L1} ({red-square}$_{L1}$ ∧ (white, circle : small, yellow)]	$e + 5$
Level 7: Place a green circle on a yellow space and a blue square on a red space.	M[PLACE^{L1}(#AND ({green-circle}$_{L1}$: yellow) (blue, square : red))]	$e + 6$

Items at Level 1 (e.g., "Place a blue square on a white space") are predicted to have M-demand of $e + 2$. One M-unit is required to boost the operative **PLACE**, which is chunked with and thus automatically activates the figurative **blue-square**. The figurative **white**, representing the destination of the object, requires a second unit of M-capacity. An item at Level 5 (e.g., "Place a red square and a white circle on a small yellow space") is predicted to have M-demand of $e + 5$. Again **PLACE** boosts **red-square**, requiring one unit of M. The next object to be placed requires two units of M-capacity – one for each of the figuratives **white** and **circle**. Two additional units are needed for location characteristics represented by the figuratives **small** and **yellow**. Starting at Level 7, items have an additional characteristic – placing objects on two different spaces – and this is represented by the parameter **#AND**. Here, **#AND** represents the temporal sequence of *two* objects to be placed at *two separate* locations (i.e., "first this here – then that there"). This is a parameter (or condition) on **PLACE** and requires an additional unit of M-capacity. Below we present representative data on the M-tasks we have described.

Developmental adequacy of CMT and FIT (a conjoint measurement test)

In her doctoral work, Arsalidou (2008; Arsalidou et al., 2010) studied the Color Matching Tasks, comparing performance with FIT in both children and adults. We briefly summarize developmental results (fully presented elsewhere) focussing on performance on CMT-Clown relative to FIT, and the relationship between participants' predicted M-power (Mp) versus items' M-demand (Md) – what we called above the Mp/Md trade-off (Pascual-Leone & Baillargeon, 1994). Participants were 112 children (ages 7–8, 9–10, 11–12, and 13–14 years) and 37 young adults (mean age 19 years). Children came from grades 2, 4, 6, and 8 of a single urban public school; adults were university students, from an introductory course. Figure 2.3 shows the mean M-score on CMT-Clown and FIT, as a function of age group. The black bars indicate the theoretically predicted M-score for each age group.

Scores on FIT and CMT-Clown are very close at all ages, and both are very close to theoretical predictions. Using repeated measures analysis of variance, Arsalidou (2008) found that CMT-Clown scores did not differ from FIT at any age. Furthermore, using paired t-tests *for equivalence* (Wellek, 2003) she demonstrated that (within an individual equivalence interval of +/– 1) M-scores on CMT-Clown and FIT largely are statistically equivalent; and both are also equivalent to theoretically predicted M-scores (some exceptions to this pattern occur in children 11 years and older).

Table 2.3 shows the proportion of participants passing 70% of CMT-Clown items, as a function of both age group (which indexes participants' M-power, i.e., Mp) and items' M-demand (Md). Our theory predicts a trade-off between Mp/Md such that, in misleading tasks, participants should pass a class of items only if their Mp is equal to or greater than the items' Md.

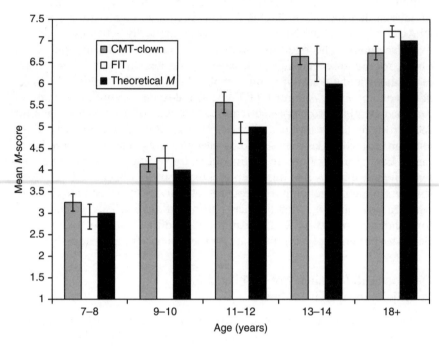

Figure 2.3 Mean *M*-scores on Clown Color-Matching Task (CMT) and Figural
Intersections Task (FIT); bars show standard errors.

Table 2.3 Proportion of participants passing CMT-Clown items, as a function of age
group (theoretical *M*-capacity) and predicted item *M*-demand

		Predicted M-demand of item class					
Age	*Theoretical M-capacity of age group*	*3*	*4*	*5*	*6*	*7*	*8*
7–8	$e + 3$	**0.69**	0.46	0.08	0.04	0.04	0.00
9–10	$e + 4$	0.97	**0.79**	0.31	0.10	0.03	0.07
11–12	$e + 5$	1.00	0.93	**0.68**	0.43	0.07	0.11
13–14	$e + 6$	0.93	0.93	0.89	**0.74**	0.52	0.11
18+	$e + 7$	0.97	0.97	0.89	**0.86**	0.43	0.22

Note. Within age group, proportions indicate participants who passed at least 70% of items in a
given item class. Bolded proportions highlight the highest *M*-demand class passed by at least
60% of participants. The highlighted staircase represents the theoretically predicted cut off for
each age group (i.e., the point at which predicted *Md* becomes greater than theoretical *Mp*).

Pascual-Leone and Baillargeon (1994) have demonstrated this trade-off in
performance on FIT. In each row of Table 2.3 performance is high under the
"staircase" diagonal line and is low above this line. Each step of the "staircase" line corresponds to data sets where participants' *Mp* theoretically

matches the items' *Md*; and consequently the *Mp/Md* trade-off prediction of Pascual-Leone and Baillargeon (1994) is supported also with CMT-Clown.

Furthermore, if as suggested above, *M*-measurement in misleading situations corresponds to an additive conjoint measurement structure, then data in Table 2.3 should satisfy the cancellation axiom that is characteristic of additive conjoint measurement (e.g., Krantz et al., 1971, ch. 6). The *cancellation axiom* says for all *a, b, c* in one measurement dimension (e.g., in our case *Mp* – rows in Table 2.3) and *p, q, r* in the other conjoint dimension (*Md* – columns in Table 2.3), the following implication is true. Calling $m(a,q)$ the measure of data satisfying values *a and q*, if $m(a,q) \leq m(b,p)$, and $m(b, r) \leq m(c,q)$, then $m(a,r) \leq m(c,p)$. Let us, for example, assign the letters *p, q, r* to the first three data columns in Table 2.3 and the letters *a, b, c* to the first three rows. Substituting the corresponding data values in the cancellation axiom formula we obtain: **If** .46 ≤ .97 **and** .31 ≤ .93 **then** .08 ≤ 1.0. Thus, in this case the cancellation axiom holds. We have verified that this cancellation axiom holds for all possible sequence assignments of *p, q, r* and of *a, b, c* to data in Table 2.3. Pascual-Leone and Baillargeon (1994, Table 5) reported a different table with similar "staircase" diagonals for FIT data. Although the authors fail to mention it, the cancellation axiom applies very well to the data they report. Thus CMT-Clown and FIT exhibit an additive conjoint measurement structure.

We can have some insight into the significance of this cancellation axiom by observing that it is based on an additive representation (Coombs et al., 1970). Consequently we have: $m(a, q) \leq m(b, p)$ **if and only if** $f(a) + g(q) \leq f(b) + g(p)$, which is equivalent to the difference $f(a) - g(p) \leq f(b) - g(q)$. Therefore, doing a similar transformation in other terms of the cancellation axiom: **If** $f(a) - g(p) \leq f(b) - g(q)$, **and** $f(b) - g(q) \leq f(c) - g(r)$ **then** $f(a) - g(p) \leq f(c) - g(r)$. This shows that the cancellation axiom reduces to a transitivity relation applied to the ordering of intervals between the two dimensions of variation, in our case *Mp* and *Md*. Note that in our case the two functions *f* and *g* stand, respectively, for the choice of chronological age in normal child participants and for the number of schemes simultaneously kept in mind to solve the item in question. This axiom suggests that the conjoint dimensions of variation are mutually independent, and their values grow monotonically, and in congruence, throughout the item levels; and, last but not least, *Md* is more potent than (dominant over) *Mp* – possibly because, unlike *Mp*, by-design *Md* does not have individual variation of values (all items within a class have, when well designed, the same *Md* value).

Invariance of mean *M*-scores across content domains and populations

Our system of *M*-measurement exhibits the very uncommon characteristic, for a psychological measure, of having values that are reasonably invariant across content domains. They also are invariant across populations of many sorts. We illustrate these important characteristics of *M*-measures using data from different studies in our laboratory.

Figure 2.4 shows the mean *M*-scores of 26 mainstream and 26 cognitively gifted 9- to 11-year-old children (gifted children identified by their school board) on our measures FIT, MAM, and DFT (Johnson, Pascual-Leone, Im-Bolter, & Verrilli, 2004). Black bars indicate theoretically predicted *M*-scores based on chronological age.

As can be seen, there is considerable group-mean invariance of *M*-scores across the content domains of the three *M*-tasks (visuospatial, verbal, and linguistic). In the gifted sample, nonetheless, DFT and FIT (which have greater executive demand than MAM) exhibit somewhat higher scores, which may be characteristic of giftedness. In other research, we have demonstrated that FIT scores can be used to predict giftedness in children (Johnson, Im-Bolter, & Pascual-Leone, 2003; Pascual-Leone, Johnson, Calvo, & Verrilli, 2005).

Figure 2.5 shows for the same samples mean proportion pass on FIT and DFT items, grouped by their predicted *M*-demands (Johnson et al., 2004). Consistent with data in Figure 2.4, gifted perform better than mainstream children. However, within each sample, and for each *M*-class of items, performance levels on FIT and DFT are almost identical.

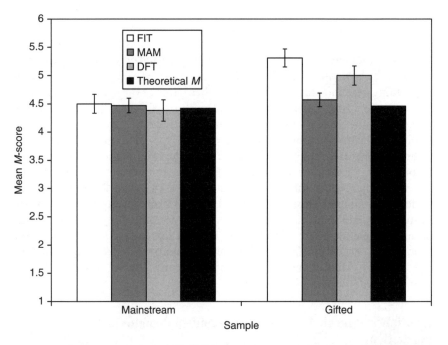

Figure 2.4 Mean *M*-scores on Figural Intersections Task (FIT), Mental Attention Memory (MAM) task, and Direction Following Task (DFT) for age-matched gifted and mainstream children bars show standard errors.

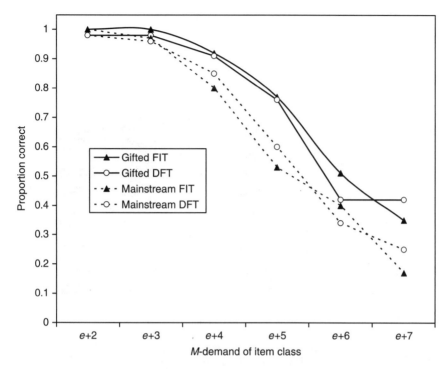

Figure 2.5 Mean proportion of items passed on Figural Intersections Task (FIT) and Direction Following Task (DFT), as a function of items' *M*-demand. Samples are age-matched gifted and mainstream children (Johnson et al., 2004).

Figure 2.6 shows the mean *M*-scores on FIT, DFT, and MAM of 7- to 12-year-old children with specific language impairment and a normal-language control sample, matched on age and performance IQ (*N* = 45 in each sample; Im-Bolter, Johnson, & Pascual-Leone, 2006). Children with language impairment underperformed significantly on *M*-measures relative to both theoretically-expected *M*-scores and controls. Nonetheless the three *M*-measures exhibit invariance of mean scores over the three content domains in each sample.

The upper bound of *M*-capacity in adults

It generally is claimed that the upper bound of working memory in adults is about 4 (Cowan, 2005), even though Barrouillet, Gavens, Vergauwe, Gaillard, and Camos (2009) have argued that such working memory capacity may be artificially inflated by participants' ability to rapidly shift attention from one to another object (scheme) kept in mind, to refresh the schemes' activation level and remember them better. This upper bound level of working

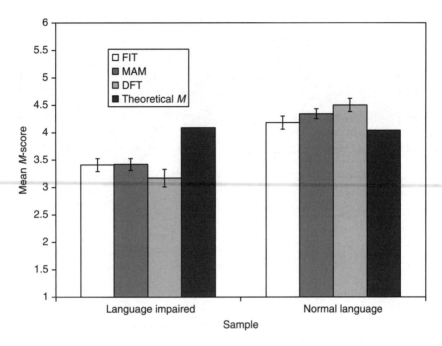

Figure 2.6 Mean *M*-scores on Figural Intersections Task (FIT), Mental Attention
Memory (MAM) task, and Direction Following Task (DFT) for children
with language impairment and normal language; bars show standard errors.

memory capacity is important because we claim, as have others (e.g., Case,
1998; Cowan, 2005), that endogenous attention is a maturational component
of working memory. As already indicated, we claim that *M*-capacity has an
upper bound of 7 (adults' structural *reserve* of *M*-capacity).

Cowan (2001, 2005) has found a limit of about 4 chunks to be the capacity
of the focus of attention in adults. His counting comes from the number of
figurative chunks (schemes) recalled in the final performance, when adults are
tested under appropriate conditions. In contrast with the sort of metasubjective task analysis we have illustrated above, Cowan's counting does not
include operative schemes needed to produce the performance, nor other
figuratives that may be needed in the course of the task. Elsewhere, Pascual-
Leone (2001) has presented task analyses of some of Cowan's tasks and estimated an *M*-demand above 4 units (see also Morra, 2001). Nonetheless,
adults do not always employ their full *M*-capacity in performance, and this
may result in a lower bound of 4 or 5 (this is adults' frequent functionally-
used level of *M*-capacity). Thus we can expect a probabilistic oscillation of
adults' measured *M*-capacity, often between the values 4 and 7 (Arsalidou,
2008; Arsalidou, Pascual-Leone, Johnson, & Taylor, 2008; Pascual-Leone
1970, 2006a).

Figure 2.7 shows the mean *M*-scores obtained by young adult samples in five studies using FIT, DFT, and MAM (Cunning, 2003; Hitzig, 2008; Johnson & Pascual-Leone, 2003; Leyson-Aro, 2002; Mongroo, 2003). As predicted, the average *M*-score across tasks and samples is 6 (see also adult sample in Figure 2.3).

Figure 2.8 shows data from three studies using the DFT with adults in Canada and Italy (Cunning, 2003; Johnson & Pascual-Leone, 2003; Morra, 2007). Sample Canada 3 received DFT items in random order; other samples received them in order of increasing complexity. The Italian data were collected in Sergio Morra's laboratory in Genova.

All Canadian samples yield very similar performance patterns, with passing rate of 60% in adults for items with *M*-demand equal to 7 (although performance dips a bit for items of *M*-demand 6). All three Canadian samples obtain a mean *M*-score of 6. Performance of adults tested in Italian parallels that of the Canadian samples tested in English, with the exception of the Italians' maintaining high performance on items with demand of 6; their mean *M*-score is 7. Motivational and linguistic factors may underlie the somewhat higher performance of Italian participants. In all, results support our prediction of an upper bound equal to 7 symbolic schemes in adults.

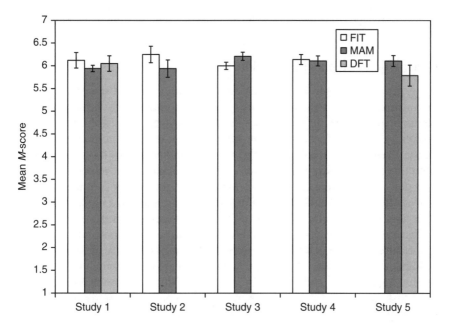

Figure 2.7 Mean *M*-scores on Figural Intersections Task (FIT), Mental Attention Memory (MAM) task, and Direction Following Task (DFT) from five studies with university-student samples; bars show standard errors.

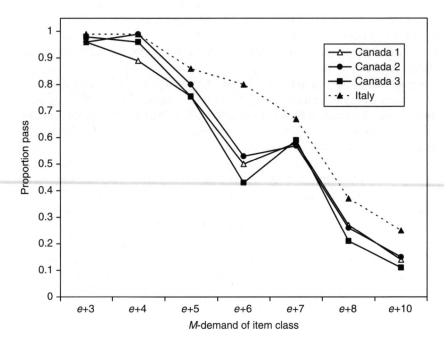

Figure 2.8 Mean proportion of items passed on Direction Following Task (DFT), as a function of items' *M*-demand for four adult samples from Canada and Italy.

General discussion and conclusion

We began this chapter with fundamental measurement and the possibility of organismic set-theoretical measures of mental attention (a maturational component of working memory). These *M*-measures (which quantify naïve notions of a capacity to "keep in mind" ideas under unfavorable circumstances) reflect epistemologically, or mirror, the organism's limit in effortful simultaneous processing of schemes – organismic chunks of information. We then described our theory of organismic schemes, intimating their constructivist evolutionary-epistemology foundation; and summarized a model of mental attention, suggesting its relation to some current working memory theories.

Because metasubjective task analysis is central to our organismic approach to measurement, we described four very different *M*-capacity tasks: FIT (visuospatial, intersection of figures), CMT (visual, color matching), MAM (verbal, free recall), and DFT (linguistic, direction following). We summarized task analyses of each *M*-task, using logical symbolic models that make explicit processes involved and the schemes that need boosting with mental attention. These analyses make clear that although the schemes change with each task, the *number* of symbolic schemes that each age group can simultaneously activate with *M*-capacity appears to be constant across tasks and across content domains. This number (*M*-power) increases across ages as predicted, so that intervals between these age-characteristic *Mp* values remain invariant across content domains. Such finding is consistent with Pascual-Leone and Baillargeon (1994), who working with FIT, concluded that *M*-measurement has the power of an *interval scale*. This interval-scale conclusion is reinforced by present findings using CMT-Clown, suggesting that *M*-measurement is an organismic variant of additive conjoint measurement. In our method, the dimensions of variation being conjoint are the *M*-power of participants' mental attention versus (minus) the *M*-demand of task items. The difference between these two values expresses the *organismic difficulty* of the task in question (Pascual-Leone, 1970), as our present data suggest. Our method is a variation of additive conjoint measurement, because the so-called cancellation axiom of conjoint measurement, a key axiom, is satisfied by developmental data with CMT-Clown. FIT data published by Pascual-Leone and Baillargeon (1994) appear also to satisfy the cancellation axiom, an axiom that could be interpreted as establishing the independence of the two conjoint dimensions of variation (*Mp* and *Md*); and establishing existence of a transitivity rule between value intervals defined by this measure – another piece of evidence that supports a claim of interval scale for *M*-measurement.

We also have supported our claim that mental attention (*M*-capacity) in adults, and therefore working memory, has an upper bound or *reserve* of *M*-capacity, estimated to be equal to 7. It may also have a lower bound or *usual functional level* that we estimate to be equal to 4 or 5. Failure of adult subjects to always employ their full capacity, as well as failure of researchers to count task-relevant schemes other than "objects" or attributes appearing in the final performance, may account for current differences among working memory researchers (e.g., Cowan, 2001, 2005; Halford, Cowan, & Andrews, 2007; Pascual-Leone, 2000a, 2001).

Finally, we should report that in a doctoral dissertation from our laboratory, Arsalidou (2008; Arsalidou et al., 2008) used fMRI to study young adults completing CMT-Clown. She found that the different *M*-capacity levels, which in normal children grow till adolescence to the upper bound of 7, re-appear in adults as distinct graded levels of activation in the appropriate areas of the prefrontal lobe. These cortical levels are highly correlated with behavioral performance on corresponding levels of CMT-Clown as well as FIT, a different *M*-measure. Arsalidou's confirmation of predictions using fMRI with adults suggests again that our method of measurement yields an interval scale, because only an interval scale could be transferred in similarly graded levels to neuronal cortical activity; levels of cortical activity that, for added validity, correlate highly with a very different *M*-measure.

Author note

Preparation of this chapter was facilitated by an operating grant (#410-2006-2325) from the Social Sciences and Humanities Research Council of Canada

(SSHRC). Research reported here was supported by this and by an earlier SSHRC grant (#410-2001-1077). We thank the following lab members or colleagues who contributed data to this chapter: M. Arsalidou, F. Bracco, G. Calvini, S. Cunning, S. Hitzig, N. Im-Bolter, C. Leyson-Aro, T. Mongroo, S. Morra, E. Polak, and E. Verrilli. We are grateful to M. Arsalidou, C. Balioussis, C. Lee, S. Morra, M. Romero Escobar, and E. Verrilli for comments on an earlier version of the chapter.

References

Alp, I. E. (1994). Measuring the size of working memory in very young children: The Imitation Sorting Task. *International Journal of Behavioral Development, 17,* 125–141.

Arsalidou, M. (2008). *Context, complexity, and the developmental assessment of attentional capacity.* Unpublished doctoral dissertation, York University, Toronto, ON, Canada.

Arsalidou, M., Pascual-Leone, J., & Johnson, J (2010, October). Misleading cues improve developmental assessment of working memory capacity: The colour matching tasks. *Cognitive Development, 25,* 262–277.

Arsalidou, M., Pascual-Leone, J., Johnson, J., & Taylor, M. J. (2008, June). *Neural responses to a visuospatial task with six levels of mental demand* [Abstract]. *Canadian Journal of Experimental Psychology, 62,* 262.

Baillargeon, R., Pascual-Leone, J., & Roncadin, C. (1998). Mental-attentional capacity: Does cognitive style make a difference? *Journal of Experimental Child Psychology, 70,* 143–166.

Barrouillet, P., Gavens, N., Vergauwe, E., Gaillard, V., & Camos, V. (2009). Working memory span development: A time-based resource-sharing model account. *Developmental Psychology, 45,* 477–490.

Benson, N. (1989). *Mental capacity constraints on early symbolic processing: The origin of language from a cognitive perspective.* Unpublished doctoral dissertation, York University, Toronto, ON, Canada.

Berger, A., Henik, A., & Rafal, R. (2005). Competition between endogenous and exogenous orienting of visual attention. *Journal of Experimental Psychology: General, 123,* 207–221.

Binet, A. (1910). Que-ce qu'une émotion? Que-ce qu'un acte intellectuel? [What is an emotion? What is an intellectual act?] *L'Année Psychologique, 17,* 1–47.

Binet, A., & Simon, T. (2004). *L'élaboration du premier test d'intelligence: Oeuvres choisies II* [Elaboration of the first test of intelligence: Selected works] (S. Nicolas, Ed.). Paris: L'Harmattan. (Original work published in 1905.)

Bohm, D. (1980). *Wholeness and the implicate order.* Boston: Routledge & Kegan Paul.

Buckner, R. L., Andrews-Hanna, J. R., & Schacter, D. L. (2008). The brain's default network. *Annals of the New York Academy of Sciences, 1124,* 1–38.

Case, R. (1998). The development of conceptual structures. In W. Damon (Series Ed.) & D. Kuhn & R. S. Siegler (Vol. Eds.), *Handbook of child psychology: Vol. 2. Cognition, perception, and language* (5th ed., pp. 745–800). New York: Wiley.

Christoff, K., Gordon, A. M., Smallwood, J., Smith, R., & Schooler, J. W. (2009). Experience sampling during fMRI reveals default network and executive system contributions. *Proceedings of the National Academy of Sciences of the United States of America, 106*, 8719–8724.

Clogg, C. C., & Sawyer, D. O. (1981). A comparison of alternative models for analyzing the scalability of response patterns. In S. Leinhardt (Ed.), *Sociological methodology* (pp. 240–280). San Francisco: Jossey-Bass.

Coombs, C. H., Dawes, R. M., & Tversky, A. (1970). *Mathematical psychology: An elementary introduction*. Englewood Cliffs, NJ: Prentice-Hall.

Cowan, N. (2001). The magical number 4 in short term memory: A reconsideration of mental storage capacity. *Behavioral and Brain Sciences, 24*, 87–185.

Cowan, N. (2005). *Working memory capacity*. New York: Psychology Press.

Cunning, S. (2003). *The Direction Following Task: Assessing mental capacity in the linguistic domain*. Unpublished doctoral dissertation, York University, Toronto, ON, Canada.

Cunning, S., Johnson, J., & Pascual-Leone, J. (2004, July). Following directions: Another route to processing limits in language. In S. Morra & J. Johnson (Conveners), *Verbal working memory and cognitive development*. Symposium conducted at the meeting of the International Society for the Study of Behavioral Development, Ghent, Belgium.

Diamond, A. (2006). The early development of executive functions. In E. Bialystok & F. Craik (Eds.), *Lifespan cognition: Mechanisms of change* (pp. 70–95). New York: Oxford University Press.

Edelman, G. M. (1987). *Neural Darwinism*. New York: Basic Books.

Fuster, J. M. (1995). *Memory in the cerebral cortex*. Cambridge, MA: MIT Press.

Gibson, J. J. (1979). *The ecological approach to visual perception*. Boston: Houghton Mifflin.

Halford, G., Cowan, N., & Andrews, G. (2007). Separating cognitive capacity from knowledge: A new hypothesis. *Trends in Cognitive Sciences, 11*, 236–242.

Hitzig, S. (2008). *The role of age and circadian arousal in complex task solution*. Unpublished doctoral dissertation, York University, Toronto, ON, Canada.

Hopfinger, J. B., & West, V. M. (2006). Interactions between endogenous and exogenous attention on cortical visual processing. *NeuroImage, 31*, 776–789.

Husserl, E. (1973). *Experience and judgment: Investigations in a genealogy of logic* (L. Landgrebe, Ed.; J. S. Churchill & K. Ameriks, Trans.). Evanston, IL: Northwestern University Press. (Original work published in 1948.)

Im-Bolter, N., Johnson, J., & Pascual-Leone, J. (2006). Processing limitation in children with specific language impairment: The role of executive function. *Child Development, 77*, 1822–1841.

James, W. (1961). *Psychology: The briefer course* (G. Allport, Ed.). New York: Harper Torchbook. (Original work published in 1892.)

Johnson, J., Fabian, V., & Pascual-Leone, J. (1989). Quantitative hardware-stages that constrain language development. *Human Development, 32*, 245–271.

Johnson, J., Im-Bolter, N., & Pascual-Leone, J. (2003). Development of mental attention in gifted and mainstream children: The role of mental capacity, inhibition, and speed of processing. *Child Development, 74*, 1594–1614.

Johnson, J., & Pascual-Leone, J. (2003). *Effect of item order on adult performance in the Direction Following Task*. Unpublished research report, York University, Toronto, ON, Canada.

Johnson, J., Pascual-Leone, J., Im-Bolter, N., & Verrilli, E. (2004, July). *Executive functions and mental attention in cognitively gifted children*. Poster session presented at the meeting of the International Society for the Study of Behavioral Development, Ghent, Belgium.

Kagan, J. (2002). *Surprise, uncertainty, and mental structures.* Cambridge, MA: Harvard University Press.

Kant, I. (1965). *Critique of pure reason* (N. K. Smith, Trans.). New York: St. Martin's Press. (Original work published in 1781.)

Krantz, D. H., Luce, R. D., Suppes, P., & Tversky, A. (1971). *Foundations of measurement: Vol. 1. Additive and polynomial representations.* New York: Academic Press.

Laudy, O., Zoccolillo, M., Baillargeon, R. H., Boom, J., Tremblay, R. E., & Hoijtink, H. (2005). Applications of confirmatory latent class analysis in developmental psychology. *European Journal of Developmental Psychology, 2,* 1–15.

Leontiev, A. N. (1981). The problem of activity in psychology. In J. V. Wertsch (Ed.), *The concept of activity in Soviet psychology.* Armonk, NY: Sharpe.

Leyson-Aro, C. (2002). *Does cognitive arousal enhance problem solving capabilities?* Unpublished Honours BA thesis, York University, Toronto, ON, Canada.

Luria, A. R. (1973). *The working brain* (B. Haigh, Trans.). Middlesex, UK: Penguin Books.

Miller, G. A. (1956). The magical number seven, plus or minus two: Some limits on our capacity for processing information. *Psychological Review, 63,* 81–97.

Mongroo, T. (2003). *Can sound-shadowing increase mental alertness?* Unpublished Honours BA thesis, York University, Toronto, ON, Canada.

Morra, S. (1994). Issues in working memory measurement: Testing for M capacity. *International Journal of Behavioral Development, 17,* 143–159.

Morra, S. (2000). A new model of verbal short-term memory. *Journal of Experimental Child Psychology, 75,* 191–227.

Morra, S. (2001). Nothing left in store . . . but how do we measure attentional capacity? *Behavioral and Brain Sciences, 24,* 132–133.

Morra, S. (2007). *Italian data on the CSVI and the DFT.* Unpublished research report, University of Genova, Italy.

Nakayama, K. (1994). James J. Gibson: An appreciation. *Psychological Review, 10,* 329–335.

Narens. L. (1985). *Abstract measurement theory.* Cambridge, MA: MIT Press.

Nozick, R. (2001). *Invariances: The structure of the objective world.* Cambridge, MA: Belknap.

Pascual-Leone, J. (1970). A mathematical model for the transition rule in Piaget's developmental stages. *Acta Psychologica, 32,* 301–345.

Pascual-Leone, J. (1987). Organismic processes for neo-Piagetian theories: A dialectical causal account of cognitive development. *International Journal of Psychology, 22,* 531–570.

Pascual-Leone, J. (1991). Emotions, development and psychotherapy: A dialectical constructivist perspective. In J. Safran & L. Greenberg (Eds.), *Emotion, psychotherapy and change* (pp. 302–335). New York: Guilford.

Pascual-Leone, J. (1995). Learning and development as dialectical factors in cognitive growth. *Human Development, 38,* 338–348.

Pascual-Leone, J. (1998). SSSs or functionalist modes of processing? A commentary on Kargopoulos and Demetriou's paper. *New Ideas in Psychology, 16,* 89–95.

Pascual-Leone, J. (2000a). Is the French connection neo-Piagetian? Not nearly enough! *Child Development, 71,* 843–845.

Pascual-Leone, J. (2000b). Reflections on working memory: Are the two models complementary? *Journal of Experimental Child Psychology, 77*, 138–154.

Pascual-Leone, J. (2001). If the magical number is 4, how does one account for operations within working memory? *Behavioral and Brain Sciences, 24*, 136–138.

Pascual-Leone, J. (2006a, June). *Is working memory a product of mental/executive attention?* Invited address presented at the 3rd European Working Memory Symposium (EWOMS-3), Genova, Italy.

Pascual-Leone, J. (2006b). Mental attention, not language, may explain evolutionary growth of human intelligence and brain size. *Behavioral and Brain Sciences, 29*, 19.

Pascual-Leone, J., & Baillargeon, R. (1994). Developmental measurement of mental attention. *International Journal of Behavioral Development, 17*, 161–200.

Pascual-Leone, J., & Goodman, D. (1979). Intelligence and experience: A neo-Piagetian approach. *Instructional Science, 8*, 301–367.

Pascual-Leone, J., & Ijaz, H. (1989). Mental capacity testing as a form of intellectual-developmental assessment. In R. Samuda, S. Kong, J. Cummins, J. Pascual-Leone, & J. Lewis. *Assessment and placement of minority students* (pp. 143–171). Toronto: Hogrefe International.

Pascual-Leone, J., & Johnson, J. (1991). The psychological unit and its role in task analysis: A reinterpretation of object permanence. In M. Chandler & M. Chapman (Eds.), *Criteria for competence* (pp. 155–187). Hillsdale, NJ: Erlbaum.

Pascual-Leone, J., & Johnson, J. (1999a). A dialectical constructivist view of representation: Role of mental attention, executives, and symbols. In I. E. Sigel (Ed.), *Development of mental representation: Theories and applications* (pp. 169–200). Mahwah, NJ: Erlbaum.

Pascual-Leone, J., & Johnson, J. (1999b, June). Process-organismic factors in developmental task analysis: A demonstration by contrasted experimental models. In J. Johnson (Chair), *Developmental task analysis: New methods and results.* Invited symposium conducted at the meeting of the Jean Piaget Society, Mexico City, Mexico.

Pascual-Leone, J., & Johnson, J. (2004). Affect, self-motivation, and cognitive development: A dialectical constructivist view. In D. Y. Dai & R. S. Sternberg (Eds.), *Motivation, emotion, and cognition: Integrative perspectives on intellectual functioning and development* (pp. 197–235). Mahwah, NJ: Erlbaum.

Pascual-Leone, J., & Johnson, J. (2005). A dialectical constructivist view of developmental intelligence. In O. Wilhelm & R. Engle (Eds.), *Handbook of understanding and measuring intelligence* (pp. 177–201). Thousand Oaks, CA: Sage.

Pascual-Leone, J., Johnson, J., Baskind, S., Dworsky, S., & Severtson, E. (2000). Culture-fair assessment and the processes of mental attention. In A. Kozulin & Y. Rand (Eds.), *Experience of mediated learning: An impact of Feuerstein's theory in education and psychology* (pp.191–214). New York: Pergamon.

Pascual-Leone, J., Johnson, J., Calvo, A., & Verrilli, E. (2005, August). *Can latent giftedness be indexed by mental-attentional capacity?* Poster session at the 16th Biennial World Conference of the World Council for Gifted and Talented Children, New Orleans, LA.

Pascual-Leone, J., Romero Escobar, E. M., Johnson, J., & Morra, S. (2006, June). *Mathematical modeling of free recall in the mental attention memory task.* Poster session at the meetings of the Psychometric Society, Montreal, QC, Canada.

Pascual-Leone, J., & Sparkman, E. (1980). The dialectics of empiricism and rationalism: A last methodological reply to Trabasso. *Journal of Experimental Child Psychology, 29*, 88–101.

Pennings, A. H., & Hessels, M. G. P. (1996). The measurement of mental attentional capacity: A neo-Piagetian developmental study. *Intelligence, 23*, 59–78.

Pessoa, L. (2009). How do emotion and motivation direct executive control? *Trends in Cognitive Sciences, 13*, 160–166.

Posner, M. I., & Peterson, S. E. (1990). The attention system of the human brain. *Annual Review of Neuroscience, 13*, 25–42.

Raichle, M. E., MacLeod, A. M., Snyder, A. Z., Powers, W. J., Gusnard, D. A., & Schulman, G. L. (2001). A default mode of brain function. *Proceedings of the National Academy of Sciences of the United States of America, 98*, 676–682.

Restle, F. (1959). A metric and ordering of sets. *Psychometrica, 24*, 207–220.

Reuchlin, M. (1962). *Les méthodes quantitatives en psychologie.* Paris: Presses Universitaires de France.

Romero Escobar, E. M. (2006). *A model of free recall using the Mental Attention Memory task.* Unpublished master's thesis, York University, Toronto, ON, Canada.

Spearman, C. E. (1927). *The abilities of man, their nature and measurement.* New York: MacMillan.

Suppes, P., & Zinnes, J. L (1963). Basic measurement theory. In R. D. Luce, R. R. Bush, & E. Galanter (Eds.), *Handbook of mathematical psychology* (Vol. 1, pp. 2–76). New York: Wiley.

Tolman, E. C., & Brunswik, E. (1966). The organism and the causal texture of the environment. In K. R. Hammond (Ed.), *The psychology of Egon Brunswik* (pp. 457–486). New York: Rinehart and Winston.

Ullmo, J. (1967). Les concepts physiques. In J. Piaget (Ed.), *Logique et connaissance scientifique* (pp. 623–705). Paris: Gallimard.

Wellek, S. (2003). *Testing statistical hypotheses of equivalence.* Boca Raton, FL: Chapman and Hall/CRC.

3 Recent advances in Relational Complexity theory and its application to cognitive development

Glenda Andrews and Graeme S. Halford

In Piagetian theory, cognitive development was characterized as a progression through a series of stages that culminated in formal operational logic. For Piaget (1947/1950), logic reflected properties that are inherent in thought. However, the assumption that human thought is logical has been questioned and alternative models that do not incorporate this assumption have been proposed. These include information processing theories (Anderson, 1983; Newell & Simon, 1972), as well as approaches based on heuristics (Kahneman, Slovic, & Tversky, 1982), rational analysis (Anderson, 1990, 1991) and mental models (Johnson-Laird & Byrne, 1991; Markovits & Barrouillet, 2002). One implication of these developments is that if human reasoning is not logical then criteria based on normative logic will be inappropriate for evaluating thinking. Different criteria for evaluating reasoning in children and adults are required.

In the current and earlier versions of Halford's theory (Halford, 1982, 1987, 1993; Halford & Wilson, 1980; Halford, Wilson, & Phillips, 1998) there is an emphasis on providing an objective basis for quantifying the complexity of cognitive tasks and the resulting demand on cognitive resources. Halford and Wilson (1980) expressed complexity in terms of levels of representational structure as derived from Category Theory. In the most recent refinement, Relational Complexity theory (Halford et al., 1998), complexity is defined in terms of the complexity of the mental models that underlie thinking. Cognitive development is characterized as the ability to construct mental models that involve more complex relations. Thus relational complexity replaces Piaget's psycho-logic as the index of cognitive development.

If relational complexity is to serve an alternative criterion to logic and provide a viable account of cognitive development, then there are a number of requirements that should be met. First, the theory should provide a principled way to analyse cognitive tasks and to quantify their complexity. Second, the theory should be applicable in different content domains. Third, the theory should be capable of making predictions in advance of data. Fourth, predictions derived from the theory should be supported by empirical evidence. Relational Complexity theory makes many predictions. Of most relevance here are the effects of task complexity on performance, the relative sensitivity of tasks with different complexity levels to age-related change, the extent to which tasks at a given complexity level form an equivalence class, and within-person consistency in performance.

In this chapter, we illustrate application of the relational complexity approach to a selection of tasks used in cognitive developmental research. Our purpose is to evaluate the extent to which Relational Complexity theory meets the requirements outlined above. In Relational Complexity theory, as in other neo-Piagetian theories, including those of Case (1992), Pascual-Leone (1970) and Demetriou, Efklides, and Platsidou (1993), cognitive development is underpinned by growth in information processing resources. We will outline our views regarding the nature of this resource, and its links with reasoning. Finally we will demonstrate that our approach is consistent with research about brain function and maturation of the prefrontal cortex. We start by describing the theory.

Relational Complexity theory

Relational Complexity theory (Halford, 1993; Halford, Wilson, & Phillips, 1998) proposes that explicit symbolic processing, which includes many of the phenomena studied by Piaget, involves processing of relations. Relational processing imposes demands on central processing resources. It can be differentiated from processes that are more automatic, modular, or implicit, which impose low processing demands. Two important components of the theory are the Relational Complexity metric and the Method for Analysis of Relational Complexity, which is a set of principles for applying the metric.

Relational Complexity metric

Complexity corresponds to the number of variables that are related in a cognitive representation, or the number of slots that must be filled. A metric of relational complexity is defined such that the simplest (unary) relations have a single slot. An example is class membership. The fact that Fido is a dog can be expressed as *dog*(Fido). Binary relations have two slots. An example is *larger-than*(elephant, mouse). Ternary relations have three slots as in *arithmetic addition*(2, 3, 5). Quaternary relations have four slots, as in *proportion*(2, 3, 6, 9).

Because each slot in a relation can be filled in different ways, the slots function as variables that can take on different values, as shown next for the binary relation *larger-than*.

> *larger-than*(_____, _____)
> *larger-than*(elephant, mouse)

larger-than(mountain, molehill)
larger-than(ocean-liner, rowing-boat)

More complex relations are predicted to impose higher processing loads than less complex relations. Thus, ternary relations impose higher loads than binary relations, and quaternary relations impose a higher load than ternary relations. The predicted median ages of attainment are 1 year for unary relations, 2 years for binary relations, 5 years for ternary relations and 11 years for quaternary relations (Halford, 1993). There is an approximate correspondence between these complexity levels and the major Piagetian stages: Unary to quaternary relations correspond to preconceptual, intuitive, concrete operational and formal operational stages respectively. On average, adult humans are limited to processing quaternary relations, or four interacting variables in the same decision (Halford, Baker, McCredden, & Bain, 2005).

The theory incorporates two strategies that can sometimes be used to reduce complexity and processing load. One such strategy involves decomposing or segmenting complex tasks into less complex components that do not overload capacity. To illustrate, consider the English object-relative sentence (i) and the subject-relative sentence (ii). Object-relatives are difficult to segment, whereas subject-relatives are easily segmented by native English speakers. Consequently, subject-relatives are easier to comprehend than object-relatives (Andrews, Birney, & Halford, 2006).

The clown that the teacher that the actor liked watched laughed (i)
The actor liked the teacher that watched the clown that laughed (ii)

Another strategy for reducing complexity is conceptual chunking, whereby concepts are recoded into fewer variables. For example, the ternary-relational concept velocity, defined as *velocity = distance/time*, can be recoded into a unary-relational concept as when speed is indicated by the position of a pointer on a dial. However, the reduction in processing load occasioned by conceptual chunking comes at the cost of temporary loss of access to the relationships that make up the concept. For example, a unary-relational representation of velocity would not be sufficient for determining how velocity changes as a function of time or of distance.

Method for the Analysis of Relational Complexity

One principle is that complexity analyses should be based on the cognitive processes actually employed in the task. Detailed task analyses are necessary to identify the processes involved and the strategies most likely to be employed. Consider the case of transitive inference. In transitive reasoning problems, participants are given premise information (A > B and B > C) and then they are asked to infer the relation between nonadjacent elements, A and C (A > C). A more concrete example is:

Tony is taller than Chris,
Chris is taller than David,
Therefore, Tony is taller than David

There is evidence that most people make transitive inferences by mentally arranging the elements into an ordered array, either from left to right or top to bottom. Once they have constructed the order, A > B > C, they can easily conclude, by inspecting the array, that A > C. Evidence from a study that used a dual-task paradigm with probe reaction time as the secondary task showed that constructing the ordered array (integrating premises) is the most demanding part of the task (Maybery, Bain, & Halford, 1986). Therefore, the complexity analysis of transitive inference should focus on premise integration.

Another principle relates to chunking and segmentation. Complexity is reduced when tasks are decomposed or when variables are chunked, therefore it is essential that complexity analyses take account of opportunities to engage in these strategies. The principle is that variables can be chunked or segmented only if the relations between them do not need to be processed. For example, in simple oddity tasks, arrays of three or more objects are presented and children are asked to choose the odd object in the array. In a four-element array of three blue circles and one red circle, the relevant relation is the different-colour relation between the red circle and blue circles. The task is binary-relational because the class, red circles can be compared to a chunked representation of the class, blue circles (Chalmers & Halford, 2003). Chunking can also occur in other tasks that depend on distinguishing (say) a red object from blue, green and yellow objects. In this case, blue, green, and yellow are chunked into a single class (non-red) which can then be compared to red. This reduces task complexity to the binary-relational level. However, such chunking is feasible only when the relations between the chunked elements (blue, green, yellow) are not important to success on the task. In general, where A is compared with B and C (e.g., red is different from blue and green), B and C can be chunked if the relation between them need not be processed.

Tasks that impose high processing loads are those in which chunking and segmentation are constrained. This can be illustrated using the Dimensional Change Card Sorting task (DCCS, Zelazo, 2006), which is used to assess executive function in preschool aged children. The task involves sorting objects according to their colour on some trials and according to their shape on other trials. For example, a red boat would be sorted with red flower in the colour game, but when the context changes to the shape game, the red boat is sorted with the blue boat. Children under 5 years sort correctly by the first dimension, but they experience difficulty switching between dimensions (i.e., from colour to shape or vice versa). According to both Relational Complexity theory and Cognitive Complexity and Control theory (Zelazo, Müller, Frye, & Marcovitch, 2003), the difficulty stems from the complexity of the task. In

Cognitive Complexity and Control theory, the task requires children to integrate two incompatible pairs of bivalent rules into a single rule system via a higher-order rule (Zelazo, Jacques, Burack, & Frye, 2002). In Relational Complexity theory, the task is ternary-relational. Complexity cannot be reduced because the DCCS is difficult to decompose into two subtasks. However, when the task is modified in a way that facilitates decomposition, as was done by Halford, Bunch, and McCredden (2007a), the majority of 3-, 4-, 5- and 6-year-olds succeed.

Another principle is that the complexity analysis applies to information that is being processed in the current step of the task, rather than to information that is being stored for future processing. When tasks have multiple steps, task complexity corresponds to the most complex step. The processing load imposed will depend on the number of interacting variables that must be represented in parallel to perform the most complex process of the task, using the least demanding strategy available. Thus, demand corresponds to the peak load imposed during performance of the task, rather than to the total amount of processing involved. Complexity and number of steps can be manipulated independently as shown by Birney, Halford, and Andrews (2006).

When applying Relational Complexity theory, there are some additional methodological issues that should be considered. The tasks used must be appropriate for the sample of participants, young children in cognitive developmental research. Task instructions and requirements should be communicated clearly. Verbal instructions can often be accompanied by nonverbal demonstrations, thereby reducing reliance on language comprehension skills. Embedding tasks within an appropriate story or game context can make the task goals more meaningful to young children. The task content should be such that children have the requisite declarative and procedural knowledge. Training and practice items can be used to ensure familiarity with materials, task procedures, and goals. A common practice in research on Relational Complexity theory is to include test items at two or more levels of complexity. Items at all complexity levels use similar or identical instructions, materials, procedures, and have similar knowledge requirements. This ensures that complexity is not confounded with other aspects of the task and helps to eliminate interpretations of task performance that implicate such factors.

Applying and evaluating Relational Complexity theory

In this section we demonstrate application of the Relational Complexity approach to three tasks used in cognitive developmental research. Our focus will be on tasks at the binary-relational and ternary-relational levels of complexity, which we have used with children aged 3 to 8 years. In other work we have examined ternary-, quaternary-, and quinary-relational levels of complexity in older children and adults (Andrews et al., 2006; Birney et al., 2006). The Relational Complexity approach is also being used to investigate cognitive ageing (Andrews & Todd, 2008; Zielinski, 2006). The three tasks discussed in this section are transitive inference, class inclusion, and the children's gambling task. Transitive inference and class inclusion tasks have their roots in the Piagetian tradition. The children's gambling task is an adaptation of the Iowa gambling task used to investigate decision making in adults. For each task, we summarize the complexity analysis, each of which is reported in more detail elsewhere. We then report empirical findings that are relevant to predictions derived from Relational Complexity theory. Three hypotheses will be addressed in this section. The complexity hypothesis states that task items that are analysed as ternary-relational will be more difficult than comparable tasks at the binary-relational level of complexity. The second hypothesis is that ternary-relational items will be more sensitive than binary-relational items to age-related change during this period of childhood. The third hypothesis is that the median age of attainment for ternary-relational tasks is approximately 5 years. In later sections we address whether tasks at the same level of complexity constitute equivalence classes, the extent to which individuals perform consistently in different content domains, and the domain generality of the Relational Complexity approach to cognitive development.

Transitive inference

As noted above, transitive reasoning is demonstrated when an inference A R C is deduced from premises A R B and B R C, where R is a transitive relation, and A, B, and C are the elements related. Determining the relation between A and C requires that premises A R B and B R C be integrated to form an ordered triple, A R B R C. Premise integration relates three elements, therefore it is ternary-relational (Halford, 1993). There is a constraint on segmentation because both premises must be considered in the same decision. Transitive inference imposes a processing load because the premises have to be integrated in working memory.

Andrews and Halford (1998, 2002) assessed transitive inferences about vertical spatial position using a modification of Pears and Bryant's (1990) procedure in which children build towers using coloured squares. Each premise display consisted of four pairs of coloured squares in which one colour was higher than another as shown in Figure 3.1. The premises together define a unique vertical ordering of five coloured squares. In the example in Figure 3.1, the correct top-down order is yellow, green, red, blue, purple. More generally, A > B > C > D > E, where A is the top position and E is the bottom position.

Five-term tasks such as this are preferable to three-term tasks because the former preclude use of a non-transitive labelling strategy. In tasks with three terms, A, B, and C, element A can be labelled as large because it occurs only once in the premises as the larger element. Element C can be labelled as small, because it occurs only once in the premises as the smaller element. Responses can be then based on one or both of these labels, without integrating the premises. In 5-term tasks there are four premises, A > B, B > C, C > D, and D > E, and children infer the relation between elements B and D. Notice that elements B and D each occur in two premises. The labelling strategy is no

Premises

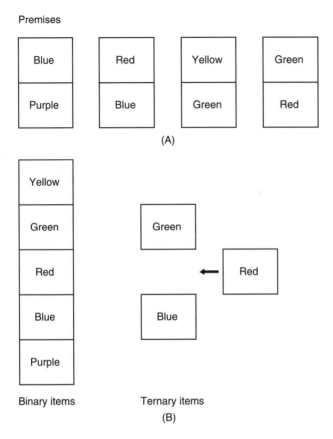

Figure 3.1 (A) An example premise display for the transitive inference task. (B) Binary-relational items required construction of a five-square tower, placing adjacent squares in succession. Ternary-relational items required placement of nonadjacent squares (green, blue) followed by the intermediate square (red). (Based on Andrews & Halford (2002) *Cognitive Psychology*, *45*, 153–219.)

longer effective because elements B and D would be labelled as larger in one premise and smaller in another premise (Andrews & Halford, 1998).

In our procedure children used coloured squares identical to those in the premise displays to construct their towers. Binary- and ternary-relational items were presented using similar procedures and instructions. All items required children to use premise information to construct their towers. The important difference was that two premises had to be integrated in a single decision in the ternary-relational items, whereas in binary-relational items each decision could be made by considering a single premise. In the binary-relational items, children constructed 5-square towers, beginning with an internal pair, either BC or

CD. In Figure 3.1, BC is represented by green-red. To place green and red correctly children would have to refer to the premise pair, green *above* red. Adding each subsequent square required consideration of a single premise. To place blue, children would need to refer to the premise, red *above* blue, then place blue below red yielding the order green, red, blue. This is a concatenation strategy. It entails processing one binary relation at a time.

In the ternary-relational items, two squares corresponding to positions B and D were handed to the child who attempted to place the squares in the correct order (i.e., B above D). In Figure 3.1, B and D are represented by green and blue. Two premises, green *above* red and red *above* blue, had to be integrated to form the ordered set, green *above* red *above* blue, from which green *above* blue could be deduced. Notice that no single square can be assigned to its position without considering both premises. As a check on guessing, square C (red) was placed after squares B and D (green and blue). If the child integrated BC and CD to conclude that B is *above* D, then the correct position of C, between B and D, should be obvious. Credit was given for items where B, D, and C were placed correctly.

Figure 3.2 shows results for 136, 4- to 8-year-old children (Andrews & Halford, 2002, Experiment 1). As predicted, the binary-relational items were easier than the ternary-relational items. Performance improved with age; however, the age effect was stronger for the ternary-relational items than for the comparable binary-relational items, as evidenced by the significant Age × Complexity interaction. A similar pattern emerged when we examined the percentages of children who performed significantly above chance level, based on binomial tests. The majority of children (83.3% to 100%) in each age

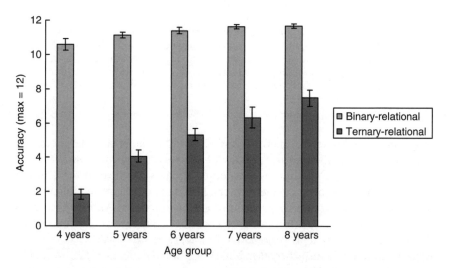

Figure 3.2 Mean correct responses on the binary-relational and ternary-relational transitive inference items by age group. Error bars represent standard errors.

group succeeded on the binary-relational items. The corresponding percentages for the ternary-relational items were 6.4% (4-year-olds), 46.7% (5-year-olds), 66.7% (6-year-olds), 71.4% (7-year-olds), and 86.7% (8-year-olds). Thus the ternary-relational items were more sensitive to age during this period of childhood.

Class inclusion

Class inclusion tasks involve reasoning about hierarchically related classes. The simplest hierarchy consists of a superordinate class and two (nonempty) subclasses. For example, in a hierarchy containing three yellow squares and two blue squares, the superordinate class is squares, the major subclass is yellow things, and the minor subclass is blue things. A key insight when making inferences based on classification hierarchies is to recognize the asymmetric nature of the relations between a superordinate class and its subclasses (Markman & Callanan, 1984); namely that all members of a subclass are included in the superordinate class, but the reverse is not necessarily true, that is, not all members of the superordinate class are included in a particular subclass. To understand asymmetry, the relations among a minimum of three classes (superordinate, subclass 1, subclass 2) must be considered, therefore complexity is ternary-relational.

Class inclusion can be assessed using displays that consist of coloured geometric shapes that comprise an inclusion hierarchy, as described above. For each display there were three critical questions. Subclass comparison questions, *Are there more yellow things or more blue things?*, are binary-relational because two entities are compared. Superordinate-major subclass comparison questions, *Are there more squares or more yellow things?*, are ternary-relational because recognition that the superordinate class necessarily includes more elements than the major subclass requires all three classes to be considered. This is the traditional Piagetian class inclusion test. Superordinate-minor subclass comparison questions, *Are there more squares or more blue things?*, are included because errors on these questions provide an estimate of guessing rates (see Hodkin, 1987, for further explanation). Ternary-relational scores were calculated by subtracting errors on the superordinate-minor subclass comparison questions from correct responses to the superordinate-major subclass question. Binary-relational scores were based on correct responses to subclass comparison questions.

In Figure 3.3 we present data for 442 children, who each participated in one of six experiments conducted in our labs. The sample includes 82 3-year-olds, 121 4-year-olds, 130 5-year-olds, 58 6-year-olds, and 51 7- and 8-year-olds. The pattern is consistent with our relational complexity analysis and with the complexity hypothesis in that binary-relational items were easier than the ternary-relational items.

There is an Age × Complexity interaction showing that the age effect was stronger on the ternary-relational item. All age groups performed above

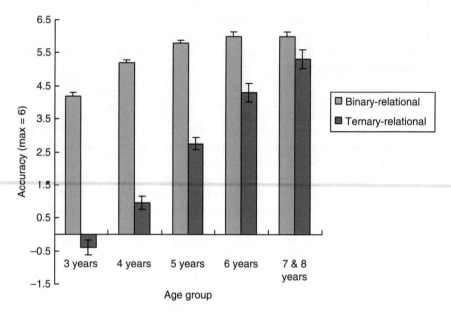

Figure 3.3 Mean correct responses on the binary-relational and ternary-relational
class inclusion items by age group. Error bars represent standard errors.

chance level on the less complex binary–relational items, but only the older
groups did so on the ternary-relational items. The pattern of findings is very
similar to transitive inference results, reported above. The ternary-relational
items were more sensitive to age and the median age of attainment for the
ternary-relational items was approximately 5 years.

Children's gambling task

In the Iowa Gambling Task (Bechara, Damasio, Damasio, & Anderson,
1994) participants are given an initial stake of play money and instructed to
win as much money as possible by choosing cards from four decks, which
have different gain-loss profiles. The two disadvantageous decks offer high
gains but higher losses, and a net loss over trials. The two advantageous decks
offer smaller gains but minimal losses, and a net gain over trials. Unimpaired
adults quickly learn to identify the advantageous decks and select from them,
while avoiding the disadvantageous decks. Their performance improves
across trial blocks. Patients with frontal brain lesions continue to select from
the disadvantageous decks. They show no improvement across trial blocks.

The task has been modified for use with children. In Kerr and Zelazo's
(2004) 2-deck version, the rewards are M&M sweets rather than money. The
cards display happy and sad faces, indicating the numbers of M&Ms won and
lost. For example, a card with two happy faces and four sad faces implies a gain

of two M&Ms and a loss of four M&Ms (a net loss of two). Kerr and Zelazo presented five 10-trial blocks. The 3-year-olds' pattern of choices resembled those of the frontal lobe patients in that selections from the advantageous deck decreased over successive trial blocks. For 4-year-olds, selections from the advantageous deck increased across blocks. Kerr and Zelazo interpreted their findings in terms of Cognitive Complexity and Control theory (Zelazo et al., 2003). Older children appreciate net gains because they formulated a higher-order rule. However, they did not test this complexity explanation.

Bunch, Andrews, and Halford (2007) provided a direct test of the complexity hypothesis. According to our relational complexity analysis the task requires integration of the differences between the two decks in gains and losses. Each difference involves a binary relation. Thus two binary relations must be integrated into a ternary relation involving three variables (deck, magnitude of gain, magnitude of loss). We predicted that children would be able to process the ternary relations required for success by 5 years. Younger 3- and 4-year-old children should be able to process the component binary relations, but they should experience difficulty integrating these binary relations into a ternary relation.

To test these predictions, Bunch et al. (2007) designed two less complex binary-relational versions of the children's gambling task (CGT). In the binary-gain version, the advantageous and disadvantageous decks differed in terms of the gain values, while the loss values were held constant across decks. The advantageous deck could be identified by focusing on gains alone. This involves the binary relation between two variables (deck, magnitude of gain). In the binary-loss version, the decks differed in terms of the loss values, while the gain values were held constant across decks. The advantageous deck could be identified by focusing on losses alone. This involves the binary relation between two variables (deck, magnitude of loss). The 3-, 4-, and 5-year-old children completed the two binary-relational versions and the ternary-CGT. The procedures for the three versions were closely matched. The findings are presented in Figure 3.4.

Children performed comparably on the binary-loss and binary-gain versions, so these two versions were combined. On the binary-relational versions, choices from the advantageous deck increased across blocks in all three age groups. On the ternary-relational version, choices from the advantageous deck increased across trial blocks for 5-year-olds, but not for 3- or 4-year-olds. The 3-year-olds' means for trial blocks 2, 3, and 4 were significantly below chance. The 4-year-olds' means for blocks 2 to 5 did not differ significantly from chance. The 5-year-olds' means for blocks 1 to 5 were significantly above chance. Younger children dealt with each component of the task in isolation, but they did not integrate information about gains and losses to identify the advantageous deck. Thus, the ternary-relational version was more sensitive than the less complex binary-relational version to age. Inspection of individual responses showed that the median ages of mastery on the binary-relational and ternary-relational versions were 3 years (or earlier) and 5 years respectively.

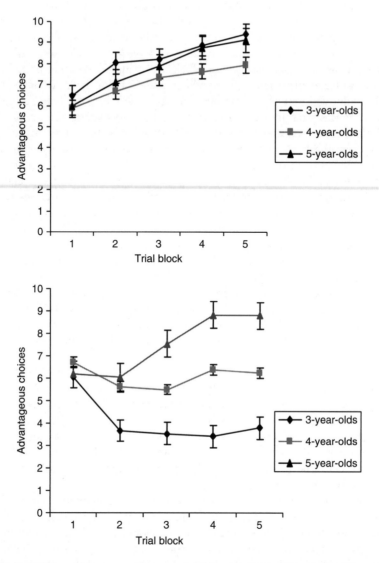

Figure 3.4 Mean correct responses on the binary-relational (upper) and ternary-relational (lower) versions of the children's gambling task by age group. Error bars represent standard errors.

These empirical findings support the predictions of Relational Complexity theory in that (i) ternary-relational items are more difficult than comparable binary-relational items within the same task, (ii) the ternary-relational items are more sensitive than the binary-relational items to age differences in 3- to 8-year-old children and (iii) children succeed on ternary-relational tasks from median age of 5 years whereas younger children succeed on comparable binary-relational versions.

Domain generality

The patterns of performance described above for transitive inference, class inclusion, and the children's gambling task have also been observed in other cognitive developmental tasks. These include estimation of tilt from weight and distance information (Andrews, Halford, Murphy, & Knox, 2009), property inferences based on classification hierarchies (Halford, Andrews, & Jensen, 2002), balance-scale reasoning (Halford, Andrews, Dalton, Boag, & Zielinski, 2002), theory of mind (Andrews, Halford, Bunch, Bowden, & Jones, 2003), hypothesis testing, counting and cardinality, and sentence comprehension (Andrews & Halford, 2002). In many cases (e,g., theory of mind, balance scale, gambling task) these predictions were made in advance of data, so they are genuine predictions rather than post hoc interpretations.

Relational Complexity theory is now being applied not only to cognitive developmental tasks from the traditional cool, cognitive domains (e.g., transitive inference, class inclusion) but also to tasks (e.g., gambling task, delay of gratification) from so-called hot domains that also include a motivational component (Andrews, Bunch, & Halford, 2007; Bunch, 2006). This research extends the scope of Relational Complexity theory and further demonstrates that the Relational Complexity approach is applicable to a broad range of content domains.

Equivalence classes

One of the requirements we noted at the outset was that tasks at the same level of complexity should form equivalence classes. This means that they should be of approximately equal difficulty irrespective of their content. This does not necessarily imply simultaneous acquisition of concepts, partly because acquisition will also be affected by knowledge. However, when relevant declarative and procedural knowledge is available, there should be some evidence of equivalence across content domains.

The most direct test of this hypothesis was provided by Andrews and Halford (2002). Our analysis was based on the performance of 241 children on ternary-relational items from five content domains (transitive inference; class inclusion; hierarchical classification; hypothesis testing; counting and cardinality) and binary-relational items from four of these content domains. The data analysed were the pass-fail scores for these tasks. The Rasch procedure assumes that a common source of difficulty underlies the task and the analysis yields locations that indicate calibration of items on a linear continuum. As shown in Figure 3.5, the binary-relational items of the four tasks were located at similar locations on this continuum. The ternary-relational items were also clustered together but at a higher location on the continuum.

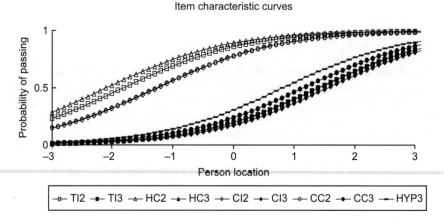

Figure 3.5 Item characteristic curves for binary- and ternary-relational items. Experiments 1 and 2 are combined. TI2 means binary-relational transitive inference; TI3 ternary-relational transitive inference; HC2 means binary-relational hierarchical classification; HC3 means ternary-relational hierarchical classification; CI2 means binary-relational class inclusion; CI3 means ternary-relational class inclusion; CC2 means binary-relational counting-cardinality; CC3 means ternary-relational counting-cardinality; HYP3 means ternary-relational hypothesis testing. Reprinted from Andrews, G. & Halford, G. S. (2002). A cognitive complexity metric applied to cognitive development. *Cognitive Psychology*, *45*, 153–219, with permission from Elsevier.

This indicated that the binary-relational items were mastered at lower levels of ability than the ternary-relational items. The 98% confidence intervals for all binary-relational tasks overlapped, as did the confidence intervals for all ternary-relational tasks. Importantly, there was no overlap between the two clusters of curves. These results suggest that the four binary tasks constitute an equivalence class, and the five ternary tasks constitute an equivalence class of conceptual complexity and that the binary- and ternary-relational tasks tap different levels of difficulty on a common underlying dimension.

Within-person consistency

This research also provided evidence of consistency within individuals. Performance on the tasks was strongly inter-correlated and all tasks loaded on a single factor which accounted for 43% and 55% of the variance in Experiments 1 and 2, respectively (Andrews & Halford, 2002). We have used these tasks (or subsets thereof) as predictors of children's performance on marker tests of cognitive development including fluid intelligence (Andrews & Halford, 2002), executive function assessed using the NEPSY battery (Bunch & Andrews, under review; Korkman, Kirk, & Kemp, 1998), balance scale reasoning (Halford et al., 2002), theory of mind (Andrews et al., 2003), property inference based on classification hierarchies (Halford, Andrews, & Jensen, 2002), and estimating tilt from weight and distance information (Andrews et al., 2009). The general finding is that measures of relational processing account for large proportions of the age-related variance in these criterion tasks as well as for significant variance independent of age. We interpret these findings as showing that the tasks tap a common underlying relational processing ability that undergoes considerable development between 3 years and 8 years of age. Comparable findings with tasks at higher levels of complexity have also been reported in young adults (Andrews et al., 2006) and in ageing samples (Andrews & Todd, 2008).

Nature of the resources construct

Thus far we have focused on relational complexity as a source of cognitive load. We turn now to the information processing resource whose capacity increases during childhood and allows children to process more complex relations. As noted already, in the Relational Complexity approach there is an emphasis on active processing as information about different variables is integrated to construct mental models that enable thinking. Information that is being stored for future processing contributes to overall task difficulty but not to relational complexity per se. It is also the case that tasks used to assess reasoning in children and adults involve a wide range of contents and are presented in many different formats. This imposes some constraints in that the underlying information processing resource needs to be suitable for active processing, rather than maintenance only, and to be central or multi-modal rather than being restricted to any specific type of information or modality. One potential candidate that meets these constraints is the central executive component of Baddeley and Hitch's influential model of working memory (Baddeley, 1990). Elsewhere (Halford et al., 2007c) we have suggested that central executive resources might be specialized for processing relational information. The empirical findings of Halford et al. (2005) suggest that adults' central executive capacity is sufficient to handle quaternary relations in cognitive tasks. The limits of four interacting variables in the same decision for adults and a smaller number for children are comparable to the working memory limitation of approximately four chunks proposed by Cowan (2001), who specified the conditions under which the limitation will and will not be observed.

We have proposed an explanation for the frequently observed associations between reasoning and working memory in adults (Halford, Cowan, & Andrews, 2007b). The essential link is that both involve elements that are bound to a coordinate system. Serial recall tasks, for example, require participants to maintain the items and also their ordinal positions. In this case the coordinate system is ordinal position. Transitive inference tasks require the elements to be bound to slots in a spatial array or mental model in a way that is consistent with the premises. The coordinate system is the horizontal or vertical spatial array that reasoners construct. Maintaining bindings between elements and slots is common to both working memory and reasoning. However, in the former case, the coordinate system is provided when the items are presented, whereas in the latter case it must be constructed by the reasoner. In general, coordinate systems in reasoning require explicit relational representations, whereas the coordinate systems that underpin working memory can be less explicit. Binding elements to the slots in a coordinate system, maintaining and updating these bindings all demand attentional capacity. The observed links between reasoning performance and composite measures of working memory capacity in adults (e.g., Kane, Hambrick, Tuholski, Wilhelm, Payne, & Engle, 2004; Wilhelm & Oberauer, 2006) are likely due to their common demands on this limited attentional resource (Halford et al., 2007b). Working memory tasks that require dynamic updating of these bindings would more closely approximate those of the reasoning tasks in this respect and as a result they might be stronger predictors of reasoning. There is scope for further research to investigate this prediction in both adults and children.

Brain regions involved in relational processing

Circuits involving the prefrontal cortex (PFC) are activated during working memory tasks (Postle et al., 2006). This area is also well suited to representing relations (Robin & Holyoak, 1995). This is especially the case for the lateral PFC regions (Brodmann Areas BA9; BA10; BA46). Relations are central to analogy and fMRI studies of analogy have indicated activation of the left frontopolar cortex (Bunge, Wendelken, Badre, & Wagner, 2005), the left frontal pole, BA9, BA10 (Green, Fugelsang, Kraemer, Shamosh, & Dunbar, 2006), the right BA11/47 and left BA45 (Luo et al., 2003). Smith, Keramatian, and Christoff (2007) demonstrated that a relational match-to-sample task reliably activates rostrolateral PFC.

PFC activation has been shown to be sensitive to relational complexity manipulations in several studies. Kroger, Sabb, Fales, Bookheimer, Cohen, & Holyoak (2002) parametrically varied relational complexity of modified Ravens matrix problems and found selective activation of the left anterior PFC. Waltz et al. (2004) found that PFC dysfunction was associated with impaired relational integration in Alzheimer's patients. Christoff and Owen (2006) concluded that the functions of the rostrolateral prefrontal cortex (BA10) are related to cognitive complexity, rather than to cognitive domain. A recent study in our lab showed that relational processing in four different tasks was impaired in patients who had suffered a stroke. Performance decrements were apparent relative to control participants at binary-, ternary-, and quaternary-relational levels of complexity. Within the stroke group, damage to frontal lobes was associated with greater impairment and this was most apparent at higher complexity levels (Andrews, Shum, Halford, Chappell, & Birney, 2008).

A number of studies have investigated the brain regions involved in transitive inference. A lesion study by Waltz et al. (1999) found that prefrontal patients were seriously impaired in ability to integrate relations, but were unimpaired in episodic memory and semantic knowledge. Patients with temporal lobe damage showed the opposite pattern. Goel (2007) reviewed five recent PET and fMRI studies of explicit transitive inference. Activation patterns varied widely as a function of task variables; however, all studies reported increased activation relative to baseline in left dorsolateral PFC, either BA9, BA46 or both regions. One of the five studies (Fangmeier, Knauff, Ruff, & Sloutsky, 2006) used event-related fMRI study which allowed them to distinguish between activation associated with premise encoding and activation associated with premise integration. Premise integration produced additional activation in BA10 and cingulate (BA32).

Processing of complex relations might depend on the functional maturity of these brain regions. There is abundant evidence that the prefrontal regions are the last to reach maturation (e.g., Huttenlocher & Dabholkar, 1997; Paterson et al., 2006). Myelination continues in the dorsal, medial, and lateral regions of the frontal cortex well into adolescence (Nelson, Thomas, & de Haan, 2006). Within the prefrontal regions, grey matter maturation occurs earliest in orbitofrontal cortex (BA11), later in ventrolateral (BA44, BA45, BA47), and later still in dorsolateral PFC (BA9; BA46) coinciding with its later myelination (Gogtay et al., 2004). The DL-PFC and RL-PFC are similar in terms of cortical thickness during childhood and cortical thinning in the two regions occurs at comparable rates, at least from 8 years of age (O'Donnell, Noseworthy, Levine, & Dennis, 2005). The correspondence between regions that recruit complex relational processing and those that are slowest to reach maturity is consistent with the Relational Complexity approach to cognitive development.

Brain imaging studies of the developing brain are still quite rare. However, performance on the Piagetian *A*-not-*B* task appears to be associated with maturity of brain systems involving the prefrontal cortex. In this task, infants watch while the experimenter hides an attractive toy at one location (A). They then search for and retrieve the toy from that location. After several such repetitions, the experimenter hides the toy at location B. Infants under about 8 months of age commit the A-not-B error. That is, they continue to search at location A, despite having seen the toy hidden at location B. Avoidance of the A-not-B error would appear to involve forming, maintaining, and dynamically updating the binding between an object and its location, so success on this task would indicate that infants are processing unary relations.

Bell and Fox (1992) found that 12-month-olds who could tolerate longer delays between hiding and searching had more mature patterns of EEG brain activity than those who could tolerate shorter delays only. In a separate study, Bell (2001) recorded EEG activity while 8-month-olds performed a looking version of the *A*-not-*B* task. High performing infants showed task-related increases in EEG power in four scalp regions (frontal pole, medial frontal, parietal, occipital), suggesting the involvement of both frontal and non-frontal brain regions. They also showed increased EEG coherence between medial frontal and parietal sites, suggesting that these regions were working together in the task, and lower coherence between two frontal pairs of electrodes in the right than left hemisphere, consistent with more advanced differentiation. Low performing infants showed more hemispheric symmetry.

Imaging studies involving children aged from 8 to 12 years (e.g., Crone, Wendelken, van Leijenhorst, Honomichl, Christoff & Bunge, 2009) are consistent with the complexity account of PFC function. Extending brain imaging research to examine relational processing in younger 3- to 8-year-old children is an important area for future research, although the difficulties associated with using these techniques with young children are not trivial.

Conclusion

We described Relational Complexity theory with an emphasis on two components that together provide a principled way to analyse cognitive tasks and to estimate their complexity. The theory has been shown to be capable of making predictions in advance of data. The empirical research reviewed supports the domain generality of the Relational Complexity approach, its predictions regarding the effects of task complexity on performance, the relative sensitivity of tasks with different complexity levels to age-related change, and the median ages of attainment during childhood. There is evidence of within-person consistency in performance, and for the interpretation that tasks with the same complexity level form equivalence classes. Although much work remains, we tentatively conclude that complexity as defined in Relational Complexity theory provides a viable alternative to normative logic as a criterion for cognitive development. We propose that both working memory and reasoning involve dynamic binding of elements into a coordinate system and that both require central attentional resources. Recent cognitive neuroscience research suggests that complex relational processing in adulthood depends on the integrity of the prefrontal regions of the brain. Therefore developmental advances in the ability to process complex relations might depend on the functional maturity of these brain regions.

References

Anderson, J. R. (1983). *The architecture of cognition.* Cambridge, MA: Harvard University Press.

Anderson, J. R. (1990). *The adaptive character of thought (Vol. 1).* Hillsdale, NJ: Erlbaum.

Anderson, J. R. (1991). Is human cognition adaptive? *Behavioral and Brain Sciences, 14,* 471–517.

Andrews, G., Birney, D. P., & Halford, G. S. (2006). Relational processing and working memory capacity in comprehension of relative clause sentences. *Memory and Cognition, 34*, 1325–1340.

Andrews, G., Bunch, K. M., & Halford, G. S. (2007, March–April). *The roles of the hot and cool systems and task complexity in young children's performance on a delay of gratification task.* Poster presented at the 2007 Biennial Meeting of the Society for Research in Child Development, Boston, Massachusetts.

Andrews, G., & Halford, G. S. (1998). Children's ability to make transitive inferences: The importance of premise integration and structural complexity. *Cognitive Development, 13(4)*, 479–513.

Andrews, G., & Halford, G. S. (2002). A cognitive complexity metric applied to cognitive development. *Cognitive Psychology, 45*, 153–219.

Andrews, G., Halford, G. S., Bunch, K. M., Bowden, D., & Jones, T. J. (2003). Theory of mind and relational complexity. *Child Development, 74*, 1435–1458.

Andrews, G., Halford, G. S., Murphy, K., & Knox, K. (2009). Integration of weight and distance information in young children: The role of relational complexity. *Cognitive Development, 24*, 49–60.

Andrews, G., Shum, D., Halford, G. S., Chappell, M., & Birney, D. P. (2008, December). *Relational processing following stroke.* Gold Coast conference of the Griffith Institute of Health & Medical Research, Surfers Paradise.

Andrews, G., & Todd, J. M. (2008). Two sources of age-related decline in comprehension of complex relative clause sentences. In N. B. Johansen (Ed.), *New research on short-term memory research* (pp. 93–123). New York: NovaScience Publishers.

Baddeley, A. D. (1990). *Human memory: Theory and practice.* Needham Heights, MA: Allyn & Bacon.

Bechara, A., Damasio, A. R., Damasio, H., & Anderson, S. W. (1994). Insensitivity to future consequences following damage to human prefrontal cortex. *Cognition, 50*, 7–15.

Bell, M. A. (2001). Brain electrical activity associated with cognitive processing during a looking version of the A-Not-B task. *Infancy, 2*, 311–330.

Bell, M. A., & Fox, N. A. (1992). The relations between frontal brain electrical activity and cognitive development during infancy. *Child Development, 63*, 1142–1163.

Birney, D. P., Halford, G. S. & Andrews, G. (2006). Measuring the influence of complexity on relational reasoning: The development of the Latin Square Task. *Educational and Psychological Measurement, 66*, 146–171.

Bunch, K. M., (2006). *A relational complexity approach to the development of hot/cool executive functions.* Unpublished doctoral dissertation. Griffith University, Australia.

Bunch, K. M., & Andrews, G. (under review). Development of relational processing in hot and cool tasks.

Bunch, K. M., Andrews, G., & Halford, G. S. (2007). Complexity effects on the children's gambling task. *Cognitive Development, 22*, 376–383.

Bunge, S. A., Wendelken, C., Badre, D., & Wagner, A. D. (2005). Analogical reasoning and prefrontal cortex: Evidence for separable retrieval and integration mechanisms. *Cerebral Cortex, 15*, 239–249.

Case, R. (1992). *The mind's staircase: Exploring the conceptual underpinnings of children's thought and knowledge.* Hillsdale, NJ: Erlbaum.

Chalmers, K. A., & Halford, G. S. (2003). Young children's understanding of oddity: Reducing complexity by simple oddity and "most different" strategies. *Cognitive Development, 18*, 1–23.

Christoff, K., & Owen, A. M. (2006). Improving reverse neuroimaging inference: Cognitive domain versus cognitive complexity. *Trends in Cognitive Sciences, 10*, 352–353.

Cowan, N. (2001). The magical number 4 in short-term memory: A reconsideration of mental storage capacity. *Behavioral and Brain Sciences, 24*, 87–185.

Crone, E. A., Wendelken, C., van Leijenhorst, L., Honomichl, R. D., Christoff, K., & Bunge, S. A. (2009). Neurocognitive development of relational reasoning. *Developmental Science, 12*, 55–66.

Demetriou, A., Efklides, A., & Platsidou, M. (1993). The architecture and dynamics of developing mind: Experiential structuralism as a frame for unifying cognitive developmental theories. *Monographs of the Society for Research in Child Development, 58* (5, Serial No. 234).

Fangmeier, T., Knauff, M., Ruff, C. C., & Sloutsky, V. (2006). fMRI evidence for a three-stage model of deductive reasoning. *Journal of Cognitive Neuroscience, 18(3)*, 320–334.

Goel, V. (2007). Anatomy of deductive reasoning. *Trends in Cognitive Sciences, 11*, 435–441.

Gogtay, N., Giedd, J. N., Lusk, L., Hayashi, K. M., Greenstein, P., Vaituzis, A. C., et al. (2004). Dynamic mapping of human cortical development through early adulthood. *Proceedings of the National Academy of Sciences of the United States of America, 101*, 8174–8179.

Green, A. E., Fugelsang, J. A., Kraemer, D. J. M., Shamosh, N. A., & Dunbar, K. N. (2006). Frontopolar cortex mediates abstract integration in analogy. *Brain Research, 1096(1)*, 125–137.

Halford, G. S. (1982). *The development of thought*. Hillsdale, NJ: Lawrence Erlbaum Associates.

Halford, G. S. (1987). A structure-mapping approach to cognitive development. *International Journal of Psychology, 22*, 609–642.

Halford, G. S. (1993). *Children's understanding: The development of mental models*. Hillsdale, NJ: Lawrence Erlbaum Associates.

Halford, G. S., Andrews, G., Dalton, C., Boag, C., & Zielinski, T. (2002). Young children's performance on the balance scale: The influence of relational complexity. *Journal of Experimental Child Psychology, 81*, 417–445.

Halford, G. S., Andrews, G., & Jensen, I. J. (2002). Integration of category induction and hierarchical classification: One paradigm at two levels of complexity. *Journal of Cognition and Development, 3(2)*, 143–177.

Halford, G. S., Baker, R., McCredden, J. E., & Bain, J. D. (2005). How many variables can humans process? *Psychological Science, 16*, 70–76.

Halford, G. S., Bunch, K., & McCredden, J. E. (2007a). Problem decomposability as a factor in complexity of the Dimensional Change Card Sort Task. *Cognitive Development, 22*, 384–391.

Halford, G. S., Cowan, N., & Andrews, G. (2007b). Separating cognitive capacity from knowledge: A new hypothesis. *Trends in Cognitive Sciences, 11*, 237–242.

Halford, G. S., Phillips, S., Wilson, W. H., McCredden, J. E., Andrews, G., Birney, D. P., et al. (2007c). Relational processing is fundamental to the central executive and it is limited to four variables. In N. Osaka, R. Logie, & M. D'Esposito (Eds.), *The cognitive neuroscience of working memory* (pp. 261–280). Oxford: Oxford University Press.

Halford, G. S., & Wilson, W. H. (1980). A category theory approach to cognitive development. *Cognitive Psychology, 12*, 356–411.

Halford, G. S., Wilson, W. H., & Phillips, S. (1998). Processing capacity defined by relational complexity: Implications for comparative, developmental, and cognitive psychology. *Behavioural and Brain Sciences, 21*, 803–831.

Hodkin, B. (1987). Performance model analysis in class inclusion: An illustration with two language conditions. *Developmental Psychology, 23*, 683–689.

Huttenlocher, P. R., & Dabholkar, A. S. (1997). Regional differences in synaptogenesis in human cerebral cortex. *The Journal of Comparative Neurology, 387*, 167–178.

Johnson-Laird, P. N., & Byrne, R. M. J. (1991). *Deduction.* Hillsdale, NJ: Lawrence Erlbaum Associates.

Kahneman, D., Slovic, P., & Tversky, A. E. (1982). *Judgment under uncertainity: Heuristics and biases.* London: C. U. P.

Kane, M. J., Hambrick, D. Z., Tuholski, S. W., Wilhelm, O., Payne, T. W., & Engle, R. W. (2004). The generality of working memory capacity: A latent variable approach to verbal and visuospatial memory span and reasoning. *Journal of Experimental Psychology: General, 133*, 189–217.

Kerr, A., & Zelazo, P. D. (2004). Development of "hot" executive function: The children's gambling task. *Brain and Cognition, 55*, 148–157.

Korkman, M., Kirk, U., & Kemp, S. L. (1998). *NEPSY. A developmental neuropsychological assessment.* San Antonio, TX: Harcourt Brace.

Kroger, J. K., Sabb, F. W., Fales, C. L., Bookheimer, S. Y., Cohen, M. S., & Holyoak, K. J. (2002). Recruitment of anterior dorsolateral prefrontal cortex in human reasoning a parametric study of relational complexity. *Cerebral Cortex, 12*, 477–485.

Luo, Q., Perry, C., Peng, D., Jin, Z., Xu, D., Ding, G., et al. (2003). The neural substrate of analogical reasoning: An fMRI study. *Cognitive Brain Research, 17(3)*, 527–534.

Markman, E. M., & Callanan, M. A. (1984). An analysis of hierarchical classification. In R. S. Sternberg (Ed.), *Advances in the psychology of human intelligence* (Vol. 2, pp. 325–365). Hillsdale, NJ: Erlbaum.

Markovits, H., & Barrouillet, P. (2002). The development of conditional reasoning: A mental models account. *Developmental Review, 22*, 5–36.

Maybery, M. T., Bain, J. D., & Halford, G. S. (1986). Information-processing demands of transitive inference. *Journal of Experimental Psychology: Learning, Memory & Cognition, 12*, 600–613.

Nelson, C. A., III, Thomas, K. M., & de Haan, M. (2006). Neural bases of cognitive development. In D. Kuhn & R. Siegler (Eds.), *Handbook of child psychology: Cognition, perception, and language* (6th ed., Vol. 2, pp. 3–57). Hoboken, NJ: John Wiley & Sons Inc.

Newell, A., & Simon, H. A. (1972). *Human problem solving.* New York: Prentice-Hall.

O'Donnell, S., Noseworthy, M. D., Levine, B., & Dennis, M. (2005). Cortical thickness of the frontopolar area in typically developing children and adolescents. *Neuroimage, 24*, 948–954.

Pascual-Leone, J. A. (1970). A mathematical model for the transition rule in Piaget's developmental stages. *Acta Psychologica, 32*, 301–345.

Paterson, S. J., Heim, S., Friedman, J. T., Choudhury, N., & Benasich, A. A. (2006). Development of structure and function in the infant brain: Implications for cognition, language and social behaviour. *Neuroscience & Biobehavioral Reviews, 30*, 1087–1105.

Pears, R., & Bryant, P. (1990). Transitive inferences by young children about spatial position. *British Journal of Psychology*, *81*, 497–510.

Piaget, J. (1950). *The psychology of intelligence* (M. Piercy & D. E. Berlyne, Trans.). London: Routledge & Kegan Paul. (Original work published 1947.)

Postle, B. R., Ferrarelli, F., Hamidi, M., Feredoes, E., Massimini, M., Peterson, M., et al. (2006) Repetitive transcranial magnetic stimulation dissociates working memory manipulation from retention functions in the prefrontal, but not posterior parietal cortex. *Journal of Cognitive Neuroscience*, *18*, 1712–1722.

Robin, N., & Holyoak, K. J. (1995). Relational complexity and the functions of the prefrontal cortex. In M. S. Gazzaniga (Ed.), *The cognitive neurosciences*. Cambridge, MA: MIT Press.

Smith, R., Keramatian, K., & Christoff, K. (2007). Localising the rostrolateral prefrontal cortex at the individual level. *NeuroImage*, *36*, 1387–1396.

Waltz, J. A., Knowlton, B. J., Holyoak, K. J., Boone, K. B., Mishkin, F. S., de Menezes Santos, M., et al. (1999). A system for relational reasoning in human prefrontal cortex. *Psychological Science*, *10*, 119–125.

Waltz, J. A., Knowlton, B. J., Holyoak, K. J., Boone, K. B., Back-Madruga, C., McPherson, S., et al. (2004). Relational integration and executive function in Alzheimer's disease. *Neuropsychology*, *18(2)*, 296–305.

Wilhelm, O., & Oberauer, K. (2006). Why are reasoning ability and working memory capacity related to mental speed? An investigation of stimulus-response compatibility in choice reaction time tasks. *European Journal of Cognitive Psychology*, *18*, 18–50.

Zelazo, P. D. (2006). The Dimensional Change Card Sort (DCCS): a method of assessing executive function in children. *Nature Protocols*, *1*, 297–301.

Zelazo, P. D., Jacques, S., Burack, J. A., & Frye, D. (2002). The relation between theory of mind and rule use: Evidence from persons with autism-spectrum disorders. *Infant and Child Development*, *11*, 171–195.

Zelazo, P. D., Müller, U., Frye, D., & Marcovitch, S. (2003). The development of executive function. *Monographs of the Society for Research in Child Development*, *68(3)*, 1–155.

Zielinski, T. A. (2006). *Performance of aging subjects on tasks varying in relational complexity*. Unpublished doctoral dissertation, University of Queensland.

4 Processing efficiency, representational capacity, and reasoning

Modeling their dynamic interactions

Andreas Demetriou and Antigoni Mouyi

Introduction

This chapter reviews the neo-Piagetian theory of Demetriou and his colleagues and his research on the development of mental processing. Mental processing can be defined in terms of three dimensions: content, processes and mechanisms, and potentials or capacity. Content refers to mental representations that carry information about the world. Processes and mechanisms refer to conscious and subconscious mental actions that when applied on representations they transform, connect, combine, or integrate them for the sake of understanding and problem solving. Finally, potentials or capacity refer to the amount and the complexity of the representations that can be handled simultaneously (or within a very narrow window of time).

Over the course of the life span mental processing develops. With development, and as a result of experience or learning, new representations or patterns of thought and new processing skills or mechanisms are acquired. Different types of change take place through different mechanisms (Demetriou & Raftopoulos, 1999). There is a huge spectrum of sources from where changes may be derived. Change origin may be traced in a very specific action, experience or thought, or it may be located in a very general system of thought. Mental representations can be transformed, differentiated, integrated with each other, abolished, abandoned, or fade away as a result of such changes that aim at making the system more efficient. Mental processes, as well as their potential or capacity, expand systematically from birth to early adulthood, they stay in a more or less steady state during the period from early adulthood to middle age, and after middle age they start to decline. Obviously, the development of mental processing is dynamic and changes happen across the life span, in all directions and in all dimensions of human mind, at various rates and for various reasons. Acquisition of new representations may cause changes in processes and changes in processes may cause the transformation or better handling of representations. Moreover, change in mental capacity enhances the amount of representations and processes that can be handled and changes in processing strategies may result in more efficient use of capacity.

A comprehensive model of the mental architecture and development

Deriving from all three epistemological traditions that study the human mind, namely the experimental, the differential, and the developmental traditions, we propose a comprehensive model of the mental architecture of the mind. The mind is a three-level hierarchical structure. It involves three functionally distinguished levels: two levels comprising general-purpose mechanisms and processes, namely the *Processing Potentials* and the *Hypercognitive System*, and one level comprising specialized capacity systems, namely the *Specialized Domains of Thought*. Each level is itself a complex network of processes and systems involving multiple dimensions and tiers of organization, and each level is dynamically related to the other levels.

It is proposed that the facilitator for the dynamic communication between the levels is the *Processing Potentials Level*. It is considered the most basic level because it involves general processes and functions, such as speed and control of processing and working memory capacity, that define the processing potentials available at a given time which consequently constrain the condition and functioning of the systems included in the other two levels. The other two levels, namely the *Level of the Specialized Domains of Thought* and the *Hypercognitive Level* are *knowing* levels, in that they involve systems and functions underlying understanding, awareness and problem solving addressing both the surrounding physical and mental environment and the cognitive self. The first of these two *knowing* levels is primarily directed to the environment. It involves various specialized systems of cognitive functions or processes, abilities or operations and knowledge specializing in the representation and processing of the different aspects of the physical, the social and the mental environment, such as information, relations and problems. The other *knowing* level, namely the hypercognitive system, is directed to the self. It involves processes underlying self-monitoring, self-representation, and self-regulation. In other words, this level comprises processes underlying awareness and consciousness, intentionality, and self-control.

Understanding, learning, or performing any task, is effected as an outcome of the harmonic synergy of the processes involved in all three levels. Figure 4.1 shows an illustration of this model.

The proposed architecture of the mind will be presented below with a reference on supporting empirical evidence. Then, the development of and the dynamic interrelations between the various levels will be discussed. Special attention will be given to the development of the Processing Potentials Level.

Specialized domains of thought

Our research has identified six domains of thought. These are as follows: (1) The *categorical system* deals with similarity-difference relations. Forming concepts about class relationships is an example of the domain of this system.

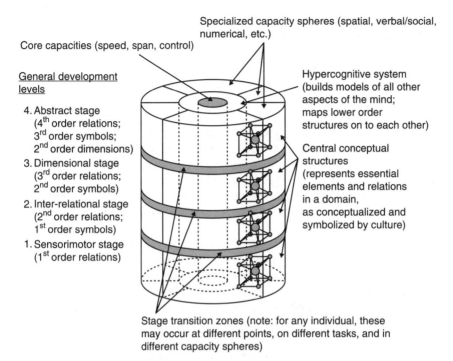

Specialized capacity spheres (spatial, verbal/social, numerical, etc.)

Core capacities (speed, span, control)

General development levels

4. Abstract stage
   (4th order relations;
   3rd order symbols;
   2nd order dimensions)
3. Dimensional stage
   (3rd order relations;
   2nd order symbols)
2. Inter-relational stage
   (2nd order relations;
   1st order symbols)
1. Sensorimotor stage
   (1st order relations)

Hypercognitive system (builds models of all other aspects of the mind; maps lower order structures on to each other)

Central conceptual structures (represents essential elements and relations in a domain, as conceptualized and symbolized by culture)

Stage transition zones (note: for any individual, these may occur at different points, on different tasks, and in different capacity spheres)

Figure 4.1 The general model of the architecture of the developing mind integrating concepts from the theories of Demetriou and Case (based on Figure 13 in Demetriou, Efklides, & Platsidou, 1993).

(2) The *quantitative system* deals with quantitative variations and relations in the environment. Mathematical concepts and operations are examples of the domain of this system. (3) The *causal system* deals with cause-effect relations. Operations such as trial-and-error or isolation of variables strategies that enable a person to decipher the causal relations between things or persons and ensuing causal concepts and attributions belong to this system. (4) The *spatial system* deals with orientation in space and the imaginal representation of the environment. Mental images and operations on them belong to this system. (5) The *propositional system* deals with the truth/falsity and the validity/invalidity of the flow of information in the environment and in systems of representation about the environment. Different types of logical relationships such as implication and conjunction belong to this system. (6) The *social system* deals with the understanding of social relationships and interactions. Mechanisms for monitoring non-verbal communication or skills for manipulating social interactions belong to this system (Demetriou, 1998a, 1998b, 2000; Demetriou & Efklides, 1985, 1988, 1989; Demetriou, Efklides, & Platsidou, 1993; Demetriou, Efklides, Papadaki, Papantoniou, & Economou, 1993; Demetriou & Kazi, 2001; Demetriou, Pachaury, Metallidou, &

Kazi, 1996; Demetriou, Platsidou, Efklides, Metallidou, & Shayer, 1991; Kargopoulos & Demetriou, 1998; Shayer, Demetriou, & Pervez, 1988).

We propose that the specialized domains of thought are systems or fields of thought that reflect and process the different fields of reality. They are domain specific in the sense that they specialize in the representation and the processing of a particular type of information and relations from the environment, they are procedurally specific in the sense that they involve mental operations and processes which reflect the peculiarities of the elements and the relations that characterize a specific part of reality, and they are symbolically biased in the sense that the symbolic systems used are the most conducive to the representation of the domain's own elements, properties and relations (Demetriou & Raftopoulos, 1999).

The specialized domains of thought are considered to be organized in three levels, each of which comprises different types of components or processes. Specifically, each domain involves (i) core processes, (ii) mental operations, processing skills, and rules and principles integrating their functioning and use, and (iii) acquired knowledge and formulated beliefs. Core processes can be innate or directly derived from maturational changes early in life. They are informationally encapsulated, i.e., they are not prone to any change due to learning. For instance, subitization, our ability to automatically perceive numerocity for sets of up to 3–4 elements, does not develop with age or experience. Rather the core processes act as inferential traps within each of the systems that respond to informational structures with core-specific interpretations that have adaptive value and "meaning" for the organism. A minimum set of conditions needs to be present in the input information, in order to activate the core processes to provide an interpretation of the input. Core processes are very fundamental processes since their presence and performance is important in the functioning of each domain and more specifically in the grounding of each domain into its respective environmental realm. During development, core processes are the first manifestations of the systems, and they are predominantly action and perception bound (e.g., color perception in the categorical system, subitization in the quantitative system, perception of causality in the causal system, depth perception in the spatial system, recognition of conspecifics in the social system). These processes are obviously the result of our evolution as a species, and they somehow characterize the cognitive functioning of other species as well (Rumbaugh & Washburn, 2003). Core elements form the background for the development of the other levels of the specialized domains of thought, namely the systems of the operating rules and processing skills and the development of the system of knowledge and beliefs that comes with age.

The operations, rules, and processing skills are systems of mental (or, frequently, physical) actions that are intentionally triggered when incoming information meets the criteria, or the minimum set of conditions, of the domain. At the initial phases of development, operations, skills, rules, and knowledge arise as a result of the dynamic interactions between domain-specific core processes, the informational structures of the environment, and the functioning of the hypercognitive system as this is manifested via the executive, the self-monitoring and the self-regulation processes. The systems of operations and processes within each domain emerge as a process of differentiation and expansion of the core processes when these do not suffice to meet the understanding and problem-solving needs of the moment. In other words, the initial inferential traps are gradually transformed into inferential ability that is increasingly self-guided and reflected upon to produce inferential patterns of thought (for example, categorization according to color in the categorical system, arithmetic operations in the quantitative system, isolation of variables in the causal system, mental rotation in the spatial system, perspective taking in the social system, rules of logic in the verbal system).

Finally, each system involves knowledge accumulating over the years as a result of the interactions between a particular system and its respective domain and beliefs formulated as a result of the exposure to and the experiences from the domain with which it is affiliated. The acquisition of new knowledge and the formation of new representations may, under certain circumstances (such as the condition of the processing efficiency parameters and the mental capacity of the system), drive changes in processes in such ways that the system can better and more efficiently deal with more aspects of the respective domain and, subsequently, changes in processes may cause the transformation or better handling of knowledge and representations that already exist in the system. Hypercognition plays a most important role in the functioning of this level. It monitors and orchestrates the learning process and knowledge acquisition as well as the formulation of the conceptual and belief structures. Along with hypercognition, executive control of processing contributes to a more efficient learning process as it allows the system to maintain dual representations, one of its own understanding and the other of new information to be registered (Kuhn & Pease, 2006). Table 4.1 presents the three levels of organization of each specialized domain of thought.

Clearly, the domains of quantitative, spatial, and verbal thought satisfy all three criteria discussed above. That is, each has a special function that involves characteristic operations and rules that can be easily discerned from those of the other domains, deals with a special type of information and relations in the environment, and is biased to a different symbol system (mathematical notation, mental images, and language, respectively). The other three domains (i.e., categorical, causal, and social reasoning) clearly satisfy the first two criteria (i.e., they are procedurally and domain specific) but not the third (that is, they are not symbolically specific; there is no symbol system distinctly associated with each of them) though one could argue that all three domains are increasingly based on inference and logical reasoning. Categorical reasoning needs deductive reasoning to specify the relations between classes or categories of things. Causal reasoning needs deductive reasoning to connect sequences of events and specify their cause-effect relations. Finally, social reasoning needs both inductive and deductive reasoning to connect the flow of verbal and social interactions between persons.

Table 4.1 The three levels of organization of each specialized domain of thought

Domain	Core processes	Mental operations	Knowledge and beliefs
Categorical	Perception according to perceptual similarity; inductive inferences based on similarity-difference relations	Specification of the semantic and logical relations between properties, classification; transformation of properties into mental objects; construction of conceptual systems	Conceptions and misconceptions about the world
Quantitative	Subitization; counting, pointing, bringing in, removing, sharing	Monitoring, reconstruction, execution and control of quantitative transformations	Factual knowledge about the quantitative aspects of the world; algebraic and statistical inference rules
Spatial	Perception of size, depth, and orientation; formation of mental images	Mental rotation, image integration, image reconstruction, location and direction tracking and reckoning	Stored mental images, mental maps and scripts about objects, locations, scenes or layouts maintained in the mind
Causal	Perception of overt and covert causal relations	Trial and error; combinatorial operations; hypothesis formation; systematic experimentation (isolation of variables); model construction	Knowledge, attributions and understanding of the reasons underlying physical and social events and the dynamic aspects of the world
Social	Recognition of conspecifics; recognition of emotionally laden facial expressions	Deciphering the mental and emotional states and intentions of others; organization of actions accordingly; imitation; decentering and taking the other's perspective	System of social attributions about other persons, their culture and their society
Verbal	Use of the grammatical and syntactical structures of language	Identifying truth in information; abstraction of information in goal-relevant ways; differentiation of the contextual from the formal elements; elimination of biases from inferential process; securing validity of inference	Knowledge about grammar, syntax and logical reasoning; metalogical knowledge about nature and justifiability of logical inferences; metacognitive awareness, knowledge, and control of inferential processes

All six domains of thought come out as distinct factors in factor analysis (Case, Demetriou, Platsidou, & Kazi, 2001; Demetriou & Kyriakides, 2006; Demetriou, Kyriakides, & Avraamidou, 2003). According to Case (1992), each of these domains involves its own semantic networks for the representation of domain-specific information and activates relevant actions and operations on the part of the reasoner. Furthermore, a cognitive analysis of these systems based on their logical structure revealed that they share some common logical processes to a considerable extent, while at the same time each maintains a unique set of logical principles and processes that remains an exclusive characteristic of the system (Kargopoulos & Demetriou, 1998). These logical and semantic differences between the Specialized Domains of Thought suggest that they are distinct cognitive entities in addition to being dimensions of systematic inter- and intra-individual differences. Therefore, it is clear that the psychometric methods of classical and modern confirmatory factor analysis that capture dimensions of individual differences converge with the cognitive methods of logical and semantic analysis that capture the formal and mental composition of cognitive domains.

Processing potentials

In this hierarchical model, the level of processing potentials is specified in terms of three cognitive parameters: *speed of processing, control of processing*, and *representational capacity*. *Speed of processing* refers to the maximum speed at which a given mental act may be efficiently executed. *Control of processing* is a cognitive ability strongly related to a broader mental ability, namely executive control, which refers to inhibiting attention to irrelevant stimuli, and prepotent or premature responses, to concentrating on goal-relevant information, to shifting focus to other information, if this is required, and to maintaining goal-relevant information and the appropriate mental rules in working memory (Zelazo, 2004), so that a strategic plan of action can be made that will lead to problem solving. *Representational capacity* is defined as the maximum amount of information and mental acts that the mind can efficiently activate at a given moment. Working memory is regarded as the functional manifestation of representational capacity. It is a hypothetical construct which comprises mental processes that keep a limited amount of information in an especially retrievable form, long enough for it to be used in ongoing mental tasks (Cowan, Morey, Chen, & Bunting, 2007). It is generally accepted that working memory involves central executive processes that are common across domains and modality-specific storage processes specializing in the representation of different types of information.

The hypercognitive system

Problem-solving creatures, other than humans, can draw inferences and they possess many domain-specific abilities, such as orientation in space, object recognition, quantification, etc. (Rumbaugh & Washburn, 2003). Even modern robots possess these abilities (Pfeifer & Scheier, 1999). However, possession of these abilities is not sufficient to credit these creatures with a mind. For this to be possible, a cognitive system must be able to reflect on its own reasoning, and to use the product of this reflection to organize complex reasoning processes. In other words, the system must be capable of *self-mapping*: record its own cognitive experiences and keep maps of them that can be used in the future, if needed (Demetriou, 2000; Demetriou & Efklides, 1989; Demetriou, Efklides, & Platsidou, 1993; Demetriou & Kazi, 2001, 2006; Demetriou, Kyriakides, & Avraamidou, 2003). This metacognitive ability to think about thinking, and to explicitly control the organization of one's reasoning processes is what accounts for a major part of the individual differences between reasoners of the same age, as well as for the age-related differences between children and adults (Moshman, 2004).

We postulate that creatures capable of self-mapping possess a second-order level of *knowing*. This is the *hypercognitive system*. It may be noted here that the adverb "hyper" in Greek means "higher than" or "on top of" or "going beyond," and when added to the word cognitive, it indicates the supervising and coordinating functions of the hypercognitive system. Thus, this term is preferable to the term metacognition, which is commonly used in the literature, because the adverb "meta" means after or later. The input to this system is information coming from the other levels of the mind (sensations, feelings, and conceptions caused by mental activity). This information is organized into the maps or models of mental functions to be described below. These are used to coordinate and control the functioning of the domain-specific systems and the processing potentials available. Thus, the hypercognitive system is defined by self-awareness and self-regulation knowledge and strategies and is conceived as the interface between (a) mind and reality, and (b) any of the various systems and processes of the mind. The hypercognitive system involves two central functions, namely the *working hypercognition* and the *long-term hypercognition*.

Working hypercognition revolves around a strong directive-executive function that is responsible for setting and pursuing mental and behavioral goals until they are attained. This function involves five basic components: (i) a directive function oriented to setting the mind's current goals; (ii) a planning function that proactively constructs a road map of the steps to be made toward the attainment of the goal; (iii) a comparator or monitoring function which regularly effects comparisons between the present state of the system and the goal; (iv) a negative feedback control function which registers discrepancies between the present state and the goal and suggests corrective actions; and (v) an evaluation function which enables the system to evaluate each step's processing demands vis-à-vis the available skills and strategies of the system so as to make decisions about the value of continuing or terminating the endeavor and evaluate the final outcome achieved. These processes operate recursively in such a way that goals and subgoals may be renewed according to the online evaluation of the system's distance from its ultimate objective. These regulatory functions operate under the current structural constraints of the system that define the system's current maximum potentials (Demetriou, 2000; Demetriou & Efklides, 1989; Demetriou & Kazi, 2001).

Consciousness is an integral part of the hypercognitive system. The very process of setting mental goals, planning their attainment, monitoring action vis-à-vis both the goals and the plans, and regulating real or mental action requires a system that can remember and review and therefore know itself. Therefore, conscious awareness and all ensuing functions, such as a self-concept (that is, awareness of one's own mental characteristics, functions, and mental states) and a theory of mind (that is, awareness of others' mental functions and states), are part of the very construction of the system. In fact, long-term hyper-cognition comprises the models and representations concerning past cognitive experiences that result from the functioning of working hypercognition. These models involve descriptions about the general structural and dynamic charac-teristics of the mind and prescriptions and rules about the efficient use of the functions – for instance, that excessive information requires organization if it is to be retained in memory or that rehearsal is needed if one is to learn quickly and permanently. Research on theory of mind (e.g., Fabricius & Schwanenflugel, 1994; Flavell, Green, & Flavell, 1986; Schneider, Lockl, & Fernadez, 2005; Wellman, 1990; Zelazo & Müller, 2002) and on implicit theories of intelligence (Grigorenko et al., 2001; Sternberg, Conway, Ketron, & Bernstein, 1981) sheds light on this aspect of long-term hypercognition. Moreover, research on self-evaluation and self-representation with regard to intellectual functioning is related to the evaluative and regulatory aspects of hypercognition (Demetriou & Bacrasevic, 2009; Demetriou & Kazi, 2001, 2006; Harter, 1999; Nicholls, 1990). Finally, we have shown that the hypercognitive system mediates the relations between cognitive processes and personality, enabling individuals to have an integrated cognitive-affective view of themselves that is accessible to conscious-ness (Demetriou, Kyriakides, & Avraamidou, 2003).

Therefore, long-term hypercognition involves the control and executive functions ascribed by Baddeley's model to the central executive and the epi-sodic buffer of working memory or by experimental researchers to functions underlying control of processing, inhibition, and selective attention. All these processes are usually referred to using the hypothetical constructs of selective attention, working memory, inhibition and sustained attention or alertness and are part of the generic construct of executive functions (Polderman et al., 2007). Ascription of these functions to the hypercognitive system rather than to working memory or control of processing conveys our assumption that self-awareness and control emanate from a higher-order system that special-izes in the surveillance and regulation of cognitive functions oriented to the environment. This system may have evolved from primary inhibition and control mechanisms associated with perception and automated action sequences (Demetriou, 2000; Demetriou & Bacracevic, 2009; Demetriou & Kazi, 2001, 2006; Gibson, 1966; Zelazo, 2004; Zelazo et al., 2003).

Davidson, Amso, Anderson, and Diamond (2006) place much value on the functions of working memory, inhibition, and cognitive flexibility and they postulate that mature cognition is characterized by the specific abilities which refer to these functions. As children enter adolescence and early adulthood they become increasingly more able to control their thoughts and actions (Huizinga, Dolan, & van der Molen, 2006). Specifically, their ability to select input from the environment that is relevant to their goals and suppress distracting or conflicting information, to hold that information in mind and to process it according to the demands of the task at hand, to inhibit inappropriate or premature reactions, and to maintain alertness during the problem-solving procedure is increasingly developed (Diamond, 1990; Zelazo, 2004; Zelazo et al., 2003).

Relations between the levels of mind

Several studies on the *three-level architecture of the mind*, which includes processing potentials as such, the specialized domains, and the hypercognitive system, have been conducted (see Demetriou, 2003, 2006; Demetriou & Kazi, 2001, 2006). One of them will be summarized here (Demetriou & Kazi, 2006). This study addressed all three dimensions of processing potentials, i.e., speed and control of processing and representational capacity (phonological, visual, and executive working memory), three domains of reasoning (verbal, quantitative and spatial reasoning) and self-awareness about the domains of reasoning mentioned above in a group of 11–15-year-old adolescents. The model that captures the relations between the levels of the mind is shown in Figure 4.2.

It can be seen that this model includes a first-order factor standing for processing efficiency and another first-order factor standing for working memory. These two factors are related to a second-order factor that stands for general mental capacity. Also, there are three first-order factors standing for performance on quantitative, verbal, and visuo-spatial reasoning. These three factors relate to another second-order factor that stands for general reasoning. Finally, there are three first-order factors standing for self-representation in each of the three reasoning domains. The three factors relate to another second-order factor that stands for general perceived competence. Obviously, these three second-order factors stand for the three main levels of the mental architecture proposed in our theory. These three second-order factors were regressed on a third-order factor, the G_{grand}. Attention is drawn to the relations between the three second-order factors and the G_{grand} factor. They are all very strong (all coefficients greater than 0.82), clearly suggesting that processing efficiency and representational capacity, inferential and problem-solving processes, and self-awareness about them, are all complementary and very strong components of the general psychometric factor of intelligence, *g*. All in all, this study shows clearly that all three types of processes are equally strong constituents of the human mind.

The *dynamic relations between the general and the specialized processes* are complex and bi-directional. On the one hand, general processes set the limits for the construction, operation, and development of the domain-specific systems. On the other hand, specialized processes provide the frame and raw material for the functioning of general processes. Thus, individual differences

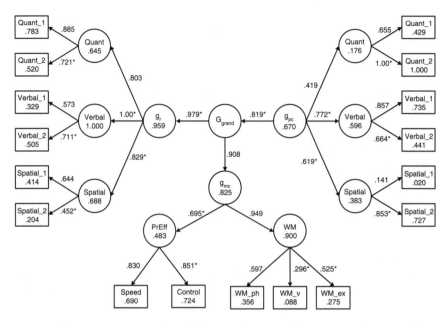

Figure 4.2 The confirmatory factor analysis for processing efficiency and capacity, and self-representation of the cognitive processes.

Notes
1 Free parameters are denoted by bold characters.
2 Significant coefficients are denoted by an asterisk.
3 Numbers in squares and circles indicate variance accounted for.

in the functioning of general processes reflect, to a large extent, differences in the specialized processes.

The models of the effects of general processes on specialized processes adopt a reductionist or bottom-up approach. That is, they assume that general-purpose processes constrain the condition of complex, and thus more specialized, processes, though there is no consensus yet on the exact nature of this relation and on the role of the various general-purpose processes in the functioning and development of specialized processes. For some scholars, speed of processing is the most important factor both for individual differences (Deary, 2000; Jensen, 1998) and intellectual development (Kail, 1991; Kail & Salthouse, 1994; Salthouse, 1996). For other scholars, attentional and executive control processes are more important factors in explaining individual differences and intellectual development (Bjorklund & Harnishfeger, 1995; Dempster, 1991, 1992; Engle, 2002; Harnishfeger, 1995; Schweizer, Moosbrugger, & Goldhammer, 2005; Stankov & Roberts, 1997; Zelazo, Qu, & Müller, 2005). Finally, for yet other scholars, working memory is the crucial causal factor underlying individual differences in intelligence (Cowan et al., 2007; Hale & Fry, 2000; Kyllonen & Christal, 1990; Oberauer, Süß, Schulze, Wilhelm, & Wittmann, 2000) and in intellectual development (Case, 1985, 1992; Halford, 1993; Halford & Andrews, 2004; Pascual-Leone, 1970, 1988; Rocadin, Pascual-Leone, Rich, & Dennis, 2007).

Obviously, the integrative theory to come will have to specify accurately the role of each of these processes. A series of studies in our laboratory tried to meet this challenge. The main methodological consideration guiding the design of these studies lies in the construction of the tasks. Specifically, tasks are constructed so as to differ systematically in their composition, from very simple to very complex, in such a way that tasks at each next level of complexity involve all of the processes of the previous level together with the processes that are specific to this particular level. Performance on such an array of tasks must conform to a simplex model, in terms of modern structural equation modeling. That is, a model where performance on the tasks of level L is regressed on performance on the tasks of the lower level $L - 1$ must fit the data very well because of the common components running through the sequence in the cascade fashion explicated above.

In one of these studies (Demetriou, Mouyi, & Spanoudis, 2008) we designed tasks dedicated to the following processes: speed of processing (SP), perceptual discrimination (PD), perceptual control (PC), conceptual control (CC), working memory (WM), information integration (InfI), and deductive and inductive reasoning (Reason). The first four processes address various aspects of processing efficiency by speeded performance tasks and the last three address representational and inferential processes. The tasks focused on these processes are assumed to include the components as specified in equations 1 to 6 shown below:

Perceptual Discrimination =   Speed + *perceptual discrimination processes*;   (1)

Perceptual Control =   Speed + PD + *control of perceptual attributes interference*;   (2)

Conceptual Control =   Speed + PD + PC + *control of interference from perceptual attributes to knowledge in long-term memory*;   (3)

Working Memory =   Speed + PD + PC + CC + *storage and retrieval processes*;   (4)

Information Integration =   Speed + PD + PC + CC + WM + *planning and integration processes*;   (5)

Reasoning =   Speed + PD + PC + CC + WM + InfI + *inferential processes*.   (6)

Speed of processing tasks addressed the ability to locate the position of a stimulus as fast as possible. *Perceptual discrimination tasks* studied the ability to specify which of two objects drawn to clearly differ in size (e.g., a leaf and a tree) is the bigger one. Therefore, it is assumed that perceptual discrimination reflects sheer speed of processing together with the processes required to discriminate between two simple stimuli and identify the target one. In the *perceptual control tasks* participants were presented with stimuli where one strong perceptual attribute interfered with a weaker but relevant attribute which was to be responded to. For instance, participants were presented with a big number digit, e.g., 7, composed of small 4s. Their task was to recognize the small component digit as fast as possible. Thus, it is assumed that perceptual control reflects the processes involved in perceptual discrimination and also the processes required for the control of the interference of the strong but irrelevant dimension of the stimulus condition in the identification of the weaker but relevant dimension. In *conceptual control tasks* participants were presented with pairs of objects or animals where their actual size relations were reversed, such as an ant bigger than a bear, and they were asked to choose which is bigger in reality. Therefore, conceptual knowledge (bears are bigger than ants) would have to dominate over the perceptual set up of the stimuli. Conceptual control is assumed to reflect all of the processes included in perceptual control and also the processes required to control interference from perceptual attributes to knowledge in long-term memory. *Working memory tasks* addressed both simple storage and executive processes using spatial, numerical and verbal information. Working memory is assumed to involve all of the processes above and also the processes required to store and recall information. In the *information integration tasks* participants were presented with a stimulus in the top right corner of the screen (e.g., a word) and they were asked to specify if its components (i.e., syllables), which were scrambled on the rest of the screen together with other stimuli, were all present. Information integration is assumed to involve all of the processes above and also the processes required to execute an action plan for the identification and integration of information as specified by the task requirements. Finally, *reasoning tasks* addressed various types of deductive and inductive reasoning in spatial, mathematical, and verbal relations. It is assumed that reasoning involves all of the processes above and also the inferential processes required to go beyond the information given in order to draw the relevant logically sound conclusions. These tasks were administered to 140 children about equally drawn from the six primary school grades, that is, children from 6.5 to 11.5 years old.

To test the model capturing the structural relations between the various processes specified above, a series of structural equation models were evaluated. Two of these models are presented in Figure 4.3. These models are built on the assumption, specified by equations 1 to 6, that processes are hierarchically organized so that the processes at each subsequent higher level in the hierarchy are largely based on the processes of the previous levels together with processes specific to this level. In the present case, the various processes

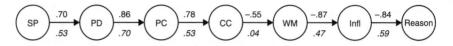

Figure 4.3 The simplex model of the structural relations between the factors.

Notes
1 The symbols in the figure are explicated in equations 1 to 6.
2 Coefficients in italics come from fitting the model after partialing out the effect of age. All coefficients are significant except the correlation between conceptual control (CC) and working memory (WM) when the age is partialed out.
3 Fit indices of the model before (X^2 (143) = 166.741, p = .085, CFI = .974, RMSEA = .045) and after partialing out the effect of age (X^2 (143) = 156.621, p = .206, CFI = .987, RMSEA = .034), respectively.

were represented by the seven first-order factors. Specifically, speed of processing, perceptual discrimination, perceptual control, conceptual control, working memory, information integration, and reasoning were identified by relating each of the corresponding sets of measures to a separate factor. These factors were regressed on each other in the cascade fashion shown in Figure 4.3. The fit of this model was excellent (see fit indices in Figure 4.3). It can be seen that all structural relations were significant and high. Therefore, it is clear that cognitive processes are hierarchically organized so that effects are carried over from one level of organization to the other where new processes are constructed in level specific fashion.

One might object that the relations captured by this model are spurious relations emanating from the operation of a powerful common factor that pulls the strings of the interaction between the various processes. One such factor is age, which represents the general maturational and experiential state and developmental direction of the organism. To test how age as such affects the relations between the various constructs, the model above was rerun after partialing out the effect of age. Technically, this was effected by regressing each of the observed variables involved in the model on age, in addition to the factors they are related to as specified above. The fit of this model was also excellent (see indices in Figure 4.3).

Naturally, the relations between factors did become weaker, suggesting that the force of development does bind the factors together, to some extent. However, most of the relations remained significant and generally high, suggesting that the cascade hierarchical structure of cognitive processes is part of their construction. Special attention, however, is drawn to the fact that this manipulation resulted in the annihilation of the relation between conceptual control and working memory. This finding reflects a division between the level of processing potentials and the representational level of the mind which is bridged by development. In other words, through development, the possibilities afforded by processing potentials are transformed into actual representational and inferential capabilities.

A second study confirmed and extended the findings of the study summarized above (Demetriou, Christou, Spanoudis, & Platsidou, 2002). This study included 120 children and adolescents from 8 to 14 years of age who were tested longitudinally for three consecutive years so that, by the end of the study, their ages ranged from 10 to 16 years old. The tasks used in this study overlapped with those used in the study summarized above only to some extent. Specifically, we used the perceptual discrimination and perceptual control PC tasks to examine processing efficiency. For memory, we used both tasks dedicated to short-term storage (STS) and executive control in working memory (ExWM). For reasoning, there were tasks addressed to three domains: deductive and inductive reasoning (Reason), as in the study above, and also quantitative (Math) reasoning (a series of numerical analogies and arithmetic operations tasks) and spatial (Spatial) reasoning (a series of mental rotation and coordination of perspectives tasks). A series of cascade models similar to the model presented above (Figure 4.3) was applied on this study as well. The general pattern of relations built into the model is shown in Figure 4.4A and B.

It can be seen in Figure 4.4A that each level was regressed on the previous level, except for the last three reasoning factors which were all regressed on the executive working memory factor. In the present case, however, we included in the model performance on perceptual discrimination and perceptual control of the first testing wave, performance on the short-term and executive working memory of the second testing wave, and performance on the three

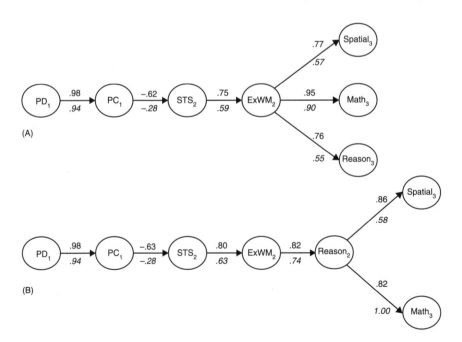

Figure 4.4 The simplex model of the structural relations of the longitudinal study.

reasoning domains of the third testing wave. This model is a very robust test of the structural relations between processes because each of the three main types of processes (processing efficiency, working memory, and reasoning) is measured at different points in time. That is, prediction here acquires its true meaning because we predict reasoning at time 3 from the condition of working memory at time 2, and we predict the condition of working memory at time 2 from the condition of processing efficiency at time 1. It can be seen that all relations are very strong and similar to the relations found by the first study. Moreover, partialing out the effects of age resulted in a mild reduction of the strength of the relations in all cases except the relation between perceptual control and short-term memory where the reduction was very large (from −.62 to −.28).

Figure 4.4B presents a slightly different version of the model explicated above. Specifically, the reasoning factor (of the second testing wave) was taken as a separate tier in this model. It can be seen that this factor was regressed on the executive memory factor (of the second testing wave), and the other two reasoning domains (of the third testing wave), that is, the domains of mathematical and spatial thought were regressed on this reasoning factor. Obviously, this manipulation conveys the assumption that the thought processes involved in spatial and mathematical thought build on and go beyond the deductive and inductive inferential processes. In other words, inferential processes are taken to be basic processes which are used for the construction of the domain-specific strategies, skills, and processes involved in the various domains. This model was found to hold well and, in fact, to be statistically more powerful than the model presented above.

The convergence between the two studies summarized above suggests the following conclusions. First, the separation between the level of processing potentials and the environment-oriented representational level is clear in both studies. Second, it is also clear that the first level functions as a developmental factor for the latter. This is suggested by the fact that partialing out the effect of age drastically diminishes the relation between processing efficiency and working memory, which suggests that these levels are connected by the developmental factors associated with age. Thus, changes in the dimensions of processing efficiency, that is, speed and control of processing, make changes in the various representational functions, such as information storage, integration, or inference possible. Attention is drawn to the fact that working memory seems to belong to the representational level of the mind's organization rather than the level of processing potentials. Attention is also drawn to the relations of the executive working memory factor with the three reasoning domains. It can be seen that these relations vary, reflecting differences between domains in the transformation of processing potentials and representational capacity into domain-specific skills, operations, and processes. Finally, it also seems to be the case that inferential processes as such form an extra tier in the architecture of the mind that intervenes between general executive processes and domain-specific computational and operational processes, strategies, and skills.

General developmental patterns

All of the processes mentioned above develop systematically with age. The structural models summarized suggest that there are strong developmental relations between the various processes, such that changes at any level of organization of the mind open the way for changes in other levels. Specifically, the simplex cascade models above suggest that changes in speed of processing open the way for changes in the various forms of control of processing. These, in turn, open the way for the enhancement of working memory capacity, which subsequently opens the way for development in inferential processes as such. Eventually, all of these changes result in the development of the various specialized domains through the reorganization of domain-specific skills, strategies, and knowledge and the acquisition of new ones. Other studies, to be summarized below, show that there is top-down escalation of change as well (Demetriou et al., 2002). Below we will summarize the basic developmental trends in each of the main levels of the mind.

Our research (Demetriou et al., 2008) shows that reaction times decrease with age in all of the *processing efficiency* functions described above (see Figure 4.5). Although absolute values vary depending upon the complexity of the process concerned, the pattern of change is exponential. Kail (1991) conducted a meta-analysis of 72 studies on speeded performance to provide additional evidence on the relation between the mean response times in groups of different ages. Kail showed that the mean reaction time of young children and adolescents is equal to the mean smallest reaction time (exhibited by young adults), multiplied with a slowing coefficient. The value of the slowing coefficient became smaller with age, in a nonlinear fashion: it changed substantially in early and middle childhood and more slowly thereafter. Overall,

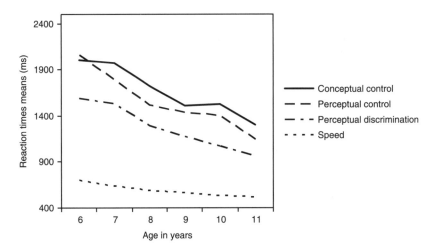

Figure 4.5 Processing efficiency as a function of age and process.

processing efficiency remains stable from early adulthood to the mid-50s, when it starts to decline systematically (Salthouse, 2004; Schaie, 1995).

Working memory is a hypothetical construct which comprises mental processes that keep a limited amount of information in an especially retrievable form, long enough for it to be used in ongoing mental tasks (Cowan et al., 2007). A consistent understanding of the function of working memory should successfully address both of its components, namely the storage component as well as the attention component (Conway, Cowan, Bunting, Therriault, & Minkoff, 2002) by studying its function in maintaining memory representations in the face of concurrent processing and under the plausible distractions and attention shifts (Ackerman, Beier, & Boyle, 2005; Engle, Tuholski, Laughlin, & Conway, 1999; Miyake & Shah, 1999). There are many ways to measure the capacity of working memory. This explains why scholars differ in their specification of the capacity of working memory at different periods of life.

According to our studies, all components of working memory (i.e., executive processes, numerical, phonological and visuo-spatial storage) increase with age (Demetriou, Efklides, & Platsidou, 1993; Demetriou et al., 2002, 2008). In fact, the development of the components of working memory seems to follow the same pattern of change and can be described by a logistic curve very similar to the exponential curve that describes the change of processing efficiency (Demetriou et al., 2005). This pattern of change of the components of working memory is illustrated in Figure 4.6.

It can be seen that there is an inverse trade-off in the development of the central executive and the storage buffers. That is, increasing involvement of executive processes leaves less storage capacity for domain-specific information, such as numbers, words, or mental images. This is so because executive operations themselves consume part of the available processing resources. However, with age, executive operations and information are chunked into integrated units. As a result, with development, one can store increasingly more complex units of information. For instance, primary school children can remember single numbers, whereas adolescents can store the products of operations applied on numbers. This pattern is in agreement with Case's (1985) claim that the development of operating space is inversely related to the development of short-term storage space. In line with the findings on processing efficiency, the various aspects of working memory remain stable from early adulthood to the 50s, and they start to decline thereafter (Salthouse, 2004; Schaie, 1995).

To account for this evidence, we proposed the functional shift model (Demetriou, Efklides, & Platsidou, 1993). This model presumes that when the mental units of a given level reach a maximum degree of complexity, the mind tends to reorganize these units at a higher level of representation or integration so as to make them more manageable. Having created a new mental unit, the mind prefers to work with this rather than the previous units due to its functional advantages. An example in the verbal domain would be the shift from words to sentences and in the quantitative domain from natural numbers to algebraic representations of numerical relations. The model suggests that

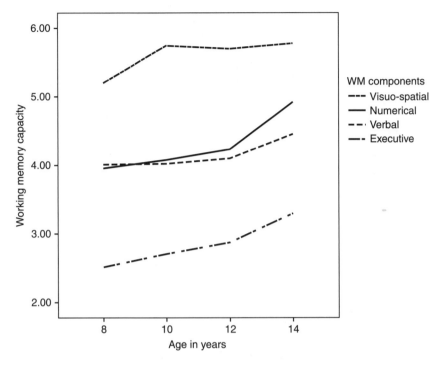

Figure 4.6 Short-term visuo-spatial, numerical, verbal and executive working memory as a function of age in a sample of Chinese children.

working memory cannot be disentangled completely from its content. By definition, then, working memory is representational in nature. This explains why in the models above working memory is tied to the representational rather than the efficiency level of the mind.

The *specialized domains* are developing through the life span both in terms of general trends and in terms of the modal characteristics of each domain. In the age span from birth to middle adolescence, changes are faster in all of the domains. This developmental profile of each specialized domain in the period between 3 and 15 years of age is outlined in Table 4.2. Inspection of Table 4.2 suggests that with development each of the domains moves from fewer and reality-referenced representations to more and reciprocally referenced ones.

As a result, concepts in each of the domains become increasingly defined in reference to rules and principles bridging more local concepts and creating new, broader concepts that are subject to change, should such a need occur. Moreover, understanding and problem solving in each of the domains evolve from global and less integrated to differentiated, but better integrated, mental operations. As a result, planning and operation from alternatives becomes increasingly part of the person's modus operandi, as well as the increasing

Table 4.2 Modal characteristics of the specialized domains with development

Age	Class	Number	Cause	Space	Verbal	Hyper
3 to 4	Proto-categories	Proto-quantitative schemes	Proto-causal schemes	Global images	Primary reasoning	Differentiation between modalities (perception vs. knowing)
5 to 6	Single criterion classes	Coordination of proto-quantitative schemes	Coordination of proto-causal schemes	Single spatial dimensions or operations	Permission rules	Understanding the stream of consciousness and inner speech
7 to 8	Logical multiplication	Number concepts and quantitative dimensions	Experience-based proto-theories	"Fluent" mental imagery	Explicit inference	Grasp of the constructive nature of thought
9 to 10	Logical multiplication on unfamiliar context	Construction of simple math relations	Testable theories in action	Representation of complex realities	Logical necessity	Differentiation between cognitive functions (memory vs. attention)
11 to 12	Flexible logical multiplication	Proportional reasoning Coordination of symbolic structures	Suppositions, isolation of variables	Imagination of the non real	Logical validity of propositions	Differentiation between clearly different domains (space vs. math)
13 to 14	Strategic classification including relevant-irrelevant information	Algebraic reasoning based on mutually specified symbol systems	Hypothesis driven experimentation	Originality in mental images	Grasp of formal relations	Awareness of specialized mental operations within a domain
15 to 16	Multilevel classes; networks of classification criteria	Generalized concept of variable	Integrated theory building	Personal imaginal worlds, aesthetic criteria	Reasoning on reasoning	Integrated cognitive theory

ability to efficiently monitor the problem-solving process. This offers flexibility in cognitive functioning and problem solving across the whole spectrum of specialized domains. Finally, as we will show in the next section, increasing reflection on cognitive and problem-solving processes, self-guidance, and self-awareness become part of the system.

Hypercognition develops along a number of different fronts (see Table 4.2), including the various functions of working hypercognition, such as the directive-executive function and self-evaluation, and the various dimensions of long-term hypercognition, such as the theory of mind, implicit theories of cognition and intelligence, and the self-concept. Space considerations do not allow a complete discussion of the development of these functions. Discussion here will focus on the development of awareness of cognitive processes because they are instrumental in the functioning and development of the other levels of the mind.

Demetriou and Kazi (2006) conducted a study to examine how, if at all, 3- to 7-year-old children are aware of the cognitive processes involved in tasks addressed to three domains of reasoning (i.e., spatial, quantitative and categorical reasoning). It was found that the judgements of similarity between processes activated by these tasks moved, with age, from the perceptual characteristics of the tasks to the mental operations involved. Specifically, pairs of cards, each of which showed a child trying to solve a task, were presented to participants who were asked to evaluate if the two tasks were similar and to justify their response. In some pairs, these model children were required to use the same processes, applied either on the same or on different objects. For example, two of the pairs addressed classification, two focused on counting, and two dealt with visuo-spatial reasoning. Finally, there were pairs where both children were required to use different mental processes, such as counting, classification or model figure reproduction. Judgements of similarity between processes in these self-awareness tasks moved, with age, from the perceptual characteristics of the tasks to the mental operations involved. Specifically, from 3 to 5 years, the majority of children based their judgements on perceptual similarity across all nine task pairs. More than half of 6-year-old children and more than two thirds of the 7-year-old children were able to recognize that pairs involving tasks belonging to different domains require different mental processes. However, it was only at the age of 7 years that the majority of children were able to recognize the mental process required by similar process tasks where the objects of application of the process differed. This pattern suggests that the development of self-awareness about mental processes develops with the development of reasoning processes as such (Demetriou & Kazi, 2006).

In another study, Demetriou and Kazi (2006) investigated the relations between self-concept and performance on reasoning in children from 11 to 17 years of age. Children were asked to solve tasks assessing four specialized domains (i.e., quantitative, causal, and social reasoning as well as drawing) and to evaluate their own performance by taking a self-representation inventory that probed general self-concept related to each domain. Table 4.3 shows

Table 4.3   Structural relations between reasoning, self-evaluation, and self-representation as a function of age

Age	Self-evaluation – Reasoning	Self-representation – Reasoning	Self-representation – Self-evaluation
11	.18	.00	.08
12	.33*	.06	.12
13	.78*	.01	−.10
14	.80*	.34*	−.30*
15	.97*	.54*	−.80*

* Significant at the 0.5 level.

the structural relations between the factors standing for reasoning, self-evaluation, and self-representation.

It can be seen that the relation of self-evaluation and reasoning is very low and non-significant at the age of 11 years and it then increases steadily and systematically until approaching unity at the age of 15–16 years ($r = 0.97$). Interestingly, the relation of self-representation and reasoning does follow the same trend but with a considerable age lag: it is very low until the age of 13, it rises to moderate and significant at the age of 14 ($r = 0.34$), and to high ($r = 0.54$) at the age of 15–16 years. In a similar fashion, the relation of self-representation and self-evaluation is very low until the age of 13 years, it rises to moderate and significant at the age of 14 ($r = -0.30$) and to very high at the age of 15–16 years ($r = -0.80$). The negative relation implies that with increasing accuracy in self-evaluations, adolescents become more conservative and strict in their self-representation.

The findings above suggest that self-awareness and self-evaluation of cognitive processes develop in a recycling fashion, which involves three major age-cycles: 3–7, 8–12, and 13–18. Within each phase of development, self-evaluation and self-awareness concerning the relevant mental operations are very low and inaccurate at the beginning, and they tend to increase and to become more accurate with development until the end of the phase. Entering the next phase resets both of them to an initial low level, from where they gradually take off again with the development of the new phase-specific problem-solving operations and skills. This pattern of change indicates that the thinker needs time and experience to acquire knowledge and sensitivity to the condition of the operations and processes of the new phase. It also indicates, as shown in the study summarized in Figure 4.2, that increasing self-awareness of cognitive processes becomes part of the very functioning of the processes concerned. As it will be shown below, this intertwining of cognitive functioning with awareness about it, which makes metarepresentation or, in other words, the explicit representation of cognitive processes possible, is in fact a very robust mechanism of cognitive development.

Metarepresentation as a mechanism of cognitive development

Metarepresentation is a significant mechanism of developmental change. It is a hypercognitive process which looks for, codifies, and typifies similarities between mental experiences to enhance understanding and problem-solving efficiency. So defined, metarepresentation is the constructive aspect of working hypercognition that integrates the contents of the episodic buffer, in Baddeley's (1990) terms, or the screen of conscience, in James' terms (1890), thereby generating new mental schemes and operations. In a sense, metarepresentation is inductive inference applied to mental experiences, representations, or operations, rather than to environmental stimuli and information as such. The distillation of this transformation process is the metarepresentations. Metarepresentations act as criteria that are activated any time the thinker needs to find a solution to a problem, monitor its implementation and evaluate its outcome in terms of its validity. We will explicate this process here in reference to the development of logical reasoning itself.

According to many theorists, reasoning reflects a universal language of thought that comprises a limited set of ready-made inference patterns. Both psychometric and developmental theorists would feel perfectly happy with the assumption of a universal language of thought. For psychometric theorists, it maps onto their construct of fluid intelligence as a system of general reasoning processes, such as Spearman's (1904) eduction of relations and correlates. For developmental theorists, it maps onto operative intelligence (Piaget, 1970), executive control structures (Case, 1985), skill structures (Fischer, 1980), or structure mappings (Halford, 1993).

We maintain that these general inference patterns do not exist at the beginning. Instead, they are constructed by mapping domain-specific inference patterns onto each other through the process of metarepresentation. Accommodating these general inference patterns, or the so-called metarepresentations, is effected by a general language of thought which, like the process of metarepresentation, is an emergent product of guided and reflected-upon domain-specific functioning. The general language of thought is gradually constructed when the patterns of thought are compared across domains and reduced to schemes that can be intentionally activated across domains. A good criterion of the power and the effectiveness of this general language of thought is logical necessity. That is, taking the conclusion of an inferential scheme as logically necessary implies that this scheme has been lifted from a context-bound processing frame to an advanced rule-bound organizer of relations, which does not allow any exceptions or knowledge and belief-based biases to intrude in the inferential process. Therefore, this general language of thought is a construction that gradually expands and stabilizes through the interaction between domain-specific processing and executive, self-awareness, and self-regulation processes of the hypercognitive system. It should be recognized that the development of this general logical language is confined by the potential of the processing system. We will elaborate on that later when we present recent experimental data on the relation of the logical reasoning developmental process with the processing efficiency and the representational parameters.

Natural language has a privileged relation with this emergent universal language of thought because it is the main symbol system that can be used to express and manipulate its constructions. Thus, natural language and the emergent language of thought are gradually intertwined and increasingly used to guide and facilitate inference and processing within each of the domains. Structural modeling shows that the relations between propositional reasoning as such and the other domains of thought become stronger with age. However, these relations always deviate considerably from unity, suggesting that there are other processes in these domains in addition to propositional reasoning (Demetriou, 2006). Thus, there is a dynamic interaction such that the functioning of domains feeds in the development of general inferential processes and these, once in place, guide and facilitate the functioning of the domains.

In conclusion, according to this theory, metarepresentation is the mechanism that drives the development of reasoning from stimulus-driven and content-bounded inference to explicit logical reasoning and ability to reflect on the process and its outcomes. Metarepresentation reminds one of Piaget's (1977/2001) reflective abstraction and Karmiloff-Smith's (1992) representational redescription. Like reflective abstraction, it abstracts general patterns from different mental functions or activities. Like representational redescription, it reorganizes them at a higher, more efficient representational level. However, its primary constituent is self-awareness. Although its accuracy and degree of involvement varies from age to age, since it is subject to development itself, self-awareness is always part of the abstraction and reconstruction processes which generate new concepts and schemes out of old ones. Our studies about self-evaluation and self-awareness summarized above suggest that moving across developmental phases is a product of increasing binding between actual cognitive processing and awareness about it. Moreover, there is accruing evidence that self-awareness and executive control are part of the learning process and that the efficiency of learning process changes during development because of changes in both of them (Kuhn & Pease, 2006). These processes ensure that future use of the new construct is under the intentional control of the thinker and not just under the control of external stimuli.

Reasoning development, processing efficiency, and representational capacity

In a recent study, Mouyi (2008) attempted to specify the relations between inductive and deductive reasoning development and the development of processing efficiency and representational capacity. Children from 7 to 12 years of age were examined by a large array of tasks addressed to inductive and deductive reasoning and also a large array of tasks addressed to speed and control of processing and various aspects of working memory, such as short-term storage and executive control. Rasch scaling of performance on the reasoning items revealed three levels for each type of reasoning. These are summarized below.

At the first level of inductive reasoning, inference based on concrete observations can be drawn. That is, children can identify patterns and formulate generalizations on the basis of a single dimension or relation. However, at this level, the child's experiences and specific knowledge may bias inference drawing against generalizations suggested by patterns. These biases suggest that control processes are not powerful enough to sustain the inferential processes against privileged knowledge and experiences. At the second level, inductive reasoning can handle *hidden* or *implied* relations that require the thinker to combine information present to the senses with knowledge stored in long-term memory. Mapping out the implied relation requires that non-relevant information in the premises or in long-term memory are inhibited. Moreover, inductive inferences based on the syntactical components of verbal premises can be drawn. Negative premises may be manipulated at this level. Thus, it is suggested that control processes at this level are powerful enough to direct the inferential process on target and protect representational capacity from overloading with irrelevant information. Finally, at the third level, inductive reasoning is based on theoretical supposition. That is, possibilities can be specified in advance and information in the premises is analyzed in reference to them. As a result, multiple parameters and relations can be simultaneously considered and manipulated. Generalizations can therefore be extracted from the relations and elevated to mental models.

In as far as deductive reasoning is concerned, the three levels are defined in terms of the four types of logical arguments: modus ponens, modus tollens, affirming the consequent, and denying the antecedent. Specifically, at the first level of deductive reasoning modus ponens inferences can be handled, simple at the beginning (involving only affirmative premises) and more complex later on (negations may be involved). Negation calls for the activation of the control processes ensuring that alternatives in meaning emanating from the negation are taken into consideration. Constructing, or retrieving from memory, the complement of a negation calls upon further cognitive resources allocation. At the second level, deductive reasoning can deal with modus tollens inferences. In comparison to modus ponens, modus tollens requires a model construction process which takes the modus ponens argument as a basis and then constructs alternative models which are compared to each other. Towards the end of this level, the denial of the antecedent and the affirmation of the consequent fallacies can be processed. Specifically, arguments with binary propositions can be solved. These higher reasoning functions are a big step forward because they enable the thinker to go beyond the obvious. Overall, reasoning at this level involves more steps and more operations. This poses higher needs to both representational capacity and control processes. Finally, at the third level of deductive reasoning, all fallacies can be solved. Fallacies place high demands on the system. Many alternatives must be retrieved from memory and processed. Moreover, the very nature of the outcome of processing is peculiar because the conclusion is that no conclusion can be reached. Therefore, the reasoner at this level must accept that not all arguments are determinate and thus uncertainty may be part of the reasoning process itself.

To specify the processing and representational profile of individuals at each of the three levels in the development of inductive and deductive reasoning, mean reaction time in speed and control of processing tasks and mean capacity for short-term storage and executive function of working memory were estimated. The relations between processing efficiency, working memory, and reasoning level are illustrated in Figure 4.7. It can be seen that there are very clear developmental trends in all dimensions. Reaction time to speed and control of processing tasks decreases and working memory capacity increases systematically across all three levels in both types of reasoning. Specifically, it can be seen that, at the first level, reaction times to speed and control of processing tasks are circa 650 ms and 1800 ms, respectively; at the third level these values drop to circa 530 ms and 1200 ms, respectively. The

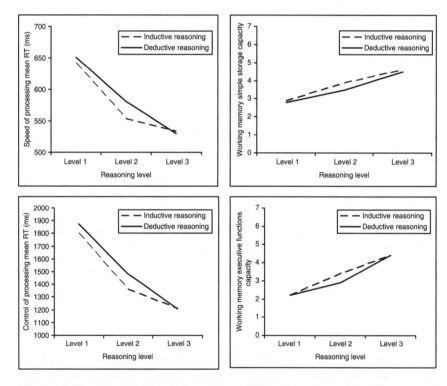

Figure 4.7 Developmental level of reasoning as a function of processing efficiency and working memory.

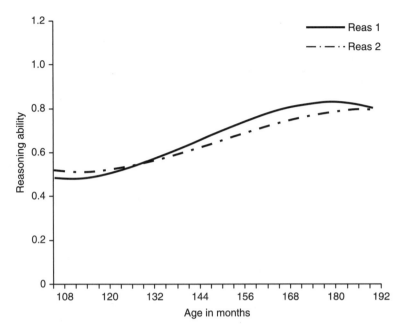

Figure 4.8 The cumulative effects of processing efficiency and working memory on reasoning ability.

Reas
1 Reasoning ability when influences from processing efficiency and working memory are assumed.
2 Reasoning ability when no influences from processing efficiency and working memory are assumed.

values for short-term and executive working memory at the first level are circa 3 and 2 units, respectively, and they rise to circa 4.5 units for both. Therefore, it is clear that ascension across these levels of reasoning development is associated with developments in processing efficiency and representational capacity.

In line with these findings, we have shown (Demetriou et al., 2002; see Figure 4.8) by means of dynamic systems modeling that the development of reasoning is slower when it is assumed to draw only upon itself than when it receives influences from any one of the processes involved in processing potentials (e.g., speed of processing or working memory). Moreover, development is considerably faster when it receives influences from both of these processes (i.e., speed of processing and working memory) than when it receives effects from one or none of them. It is also highly interesting that the contributions of each of these two potentiation factors to the growth of reasoning are different in their initiation and termination, due to their differences in growth rate. Development takes off and levels off considerably earlier when these effects are conjointly rather than separately active. In this kind of

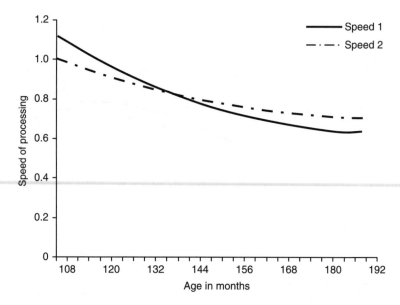

Figure 4.9 The effect of reasoning ability on the development of speed of processing.

Speed
1 Speed of proccessing when influence from reasoning ability is assumed.
2 Speed of processing when no influence from reasoning ability is assumed.

dynamic systems modeling, alternative models of change for a particular cognitive process are tested where different processes are assumed to contribute to the change of the target process. Thus, one can test mathematically and compare the form of alternative developmental curves where different combinations of processes interact. The mathematics of the models shown here is fully explicated in Demetriou et al. (2002). Of course, the models must, eventually, be tested against actual empirical evidence collected longitudinally.

In line with our assumption that development is synergic, we have shown that top-down effects are also present (Figure 4.9). That is, the development of reasoning does influence the development of processing efficiency. That is, we have shown that the development of processing efficiency and working memory is faster when they receive effects from reasoning than when they are supposed to capitalize only on their own capacity for development. Specifically, the curves of development for these two constructs are steeper, reflecting faster progression towards their end state, when effects from reasoning are assumed as compared to the curves reflecting the development of each of them alone. This means that changes in reasoning function as a mediator for the improvement of memory and processing efficiency.

Conclusions

This chapter aimed to integrate evidence and concepts from cognitive, differential, and developmental models of the human mind into an overarching theory. This theory aspires to be able at one and the same time to describe and explain mind's architecture, its development, and individual differences in regard to both architecture and development. With respect to mind's architecture, our findings support our assumption that both general and specialized capabilities and processes do exist. These are organized hierarchically so that more simple or general processes are embedded in more complex and specialized processes. This architecture, which is the culmination of more than a century of psychometric research (Carroll, 1993; Gustafsson & Undheim, 1996; Jensen, 1998), is largely consistent with findings in both the cognitive and the developmental tradition (Case et al., 2001; Demetriou et al., 2002). A large part of what is defined as psychometric *g* (i.e., the factors responsible for the positive correlations between all mental tests) includes mechanisms that have been of primary interest in research and theory in cognitive psychology, such as underlying processing efficiency, processing capacity, and directive-executive control. These very mechanisms seem able to explain, to a considerable extent, the person's state of understanding and problem solving at successive age periods, which is the object of developmental psychology and individual differences in regard to it.

In the proposed overarching model, intelligence is a function of a person's mental efficiency, flexibility, capability, insightfulness, both in regard to other individuals and in regard to a general developmental hierarchy. That is, excelling in understanding, learning, reasoning, and problem solving, in comparison to other individuals of the same age or in comparison to one's own performance in younger ages, is, to a considerable extent, a function of differences or increases in these processes. In psychometric terms, this is tantamount to saying that differences in the processes associated with *g* cause differences in general inferential and reasoning mechanisms. In developmental terms, this is tantamount to saying that changes in the processes underlying *g* result in the qualitative transformation of the general structures of thought underlying understanding and reasoning at successive ages so that more complex and less familiar problems can be solved and more abstract concepts can be constructed. It may be noted here that a general factor of intelligence was recently found able to explain differences in intellectual achievements between different primates (Deaner, van Schaik, & Johnson, 2006; Lee, 2006). These findings suggest that there has been a directional selection for general cognitive ability in the lineage leading to *Homo sapiens*. This is fully in line with recent research in the behavioral genetics of intelligence (Kovas & Plomin, 2006; Plomin & Spinath, 2002), suggesting that there are generalist genes that affect the organization and functioning of the brain as a whole.

Regarding change, the three traditions also seem to melt into this overarching model. On the one hand, transition mechanisms underlying development across developmental levels, as these are specified by developmental theory, are useful for differential theory because they highlight why and how change in mental age occurs. On the other hand, mechanisms of change underlying the automation of performance, as these are specified in cognitive theory or in models of learning, highlight how newly acquired developmental structures in a given phase may get established and consolidated, thereby preparing the way for the transition to the next developmental phase. Indeed, both these kinds of mechanisms may explain underlying cognitive differences between persons of different IQ.

The differentiation of development across domains is an integral part of the organization and functioning of the human mind. This is so because in each of the domains there are constraints directly coming from the particularities in the mental operations, the representations, and the skills that characterize each of the domains. Performance within and across persons may vary even if general processes are kept constant, because the dynamics of functioning and development differ across domains, and the mastering of these dynamics depends on both special domain-specific disposition and domain-specific experience. Domain-specific disposition is a multiplier of general potentials. If domain-specific disposition falls short of general potentials in a given domain, attainment in this domain will obviously prove to fall below the level of general potentials. For instance, visuo-spatial ability will fall below general potentials in the blind, even if general potentials are very high. If domain-specific disposition is high, such as a special proclivity in visualization, visuo-spatial ability will exceed the level expected from general potentials. Domain-specific experience is needed to give the chance to the developing person to customize, so to speak, the general possibilities and processes to particularities and constraints of each of the domains. Obviously, practice to the extreme in a domain will elevate this domain to the upper limit of general potentials. Overall, the particular combination of general potentials, domain-specific disposition, and domain-specific experience determines the momentum, stability, and direction of development in the individual.

It is hoped that this chapter suggests clearly that neither Gardner-like theories (e.g., Gardner, 1983), which postulate the existence of autonomous multiple intelligences, nor Jensen-like theories (e.g., Jensen, 1998), which stress the primacy of general processes, do justice to the complexity of the human mind. The human mind involves both general and specialized abilities, each of which functions as a dimension of intra- and inter-individual differences during both on-line functioning and developmental time. That is, general processes are everywhere, but they can never be seen alone, and specialized domains are the interfaces through which the mind interleaves with the different realms of the world. However, specialized processes involve general processes as part of their construction and they need them for their functioning and development. Developmental dynamics provide the melting pot where general and specialized processes get integrated and refined into world-relevant systems of understanding and action.

References

Ackerman, P. L., Beier, M. E., & Boyle, M. O. (2005). Working memory and intelligence: The same or different constructs? *Psychological Bulletin, 1*, 30–60.

Baddeley, A. D. (1990). *Human memory: Theory and practice.* Hillsdale, NJ: Erlbaum.

Bjorklund, D. F., & Harnishfeger, K. K. (1995). The evolution of inhibition mechanisms and their role in human cognition and behavior. In F. N. Dempster & C. J. Brainerd (Eds.), *Interference and inhibition in cognition* (pp. 141–173). New York: Academic Press.

Carroll, J. B. (1993). *Human cognitive abilities: A survey of factor-analytic studies.* New York: Cambridge University Press.

Case, R. (1985). *Intellectual development. Birth to adulthood.* New York: Academic Press.

Case, R. (1992). *The mind's staircase: Exploring the conceptual underpinnings of children's thought and knowledge.* Hillsdale, NJ: Erlbaum.

Case, R., Demetriou, A., Platsidou, M., & Kazi, S. (2001). Integrating concepts and tests of intelligence from the differential and the developmental traditions. *Intelligence, 29*, 307–336.

Conway, A. R. A., Cowan, N., Bunting, M. F., Therriault, D. J., & Minkoff, S. R. B. (2002). A latent variable analysis of working memory capacity, short-term memory capacity, processing speed, and general fluid intelligence. *Intelligence, 30*, 163–183.

Cowan, N., Morey, C. C., Chen, Z., & Bunting M. F. (2007). What do estimates of working memory capacity tell us? In N. Osaka, R. Logie, & M. D'Esposito (Eds.), *The cognitive neuroscience of working memory.* Oxford: Oxford University Press.

Davidson, M. C., Amso, D., Anderson, L. C., & Diamond, A. (2006). Development of cognitive control and executive functions from 4 to 13 years: Evidence from manipulations of memory, inhibition and task switching. *Neuropsychologia, 44*, 2037–2078.

Deaner, R. O., van Schaik, C. P., & Johnson, V. (2006). Do some taxa have better domain-general cognition than others? A metaanalysis of nonhuman primate studies. *Evolutionary Psychology, 4*, 149–196.

Deary, I. J. (2000). *Looking down on human intelligence.* Oxford: Oxford University Press.

Demetriou, A. (1998a). Nooplasis: 10 + 1 postulates about the formation of mind. *Learning and Instruction: The Journal of the European Association for Research on Learning and Instruction, 8*, 271–287.

Demetriou, A. (1998b). Cognitive development. In A. Demetriou, W. Doise, & K. F. M. van Lieshout (Eds.), *Life-span developmental psychology* (pp. 179–269). London: Wiley.

Demetriou, A. (2000). Organization and development of self-understanding and self-regulation: Toward a general theory. In M. Boekaerts, P. R. Pintrich, & M. Zeidner (Eds.), *Handbook of self-regulation* (pp. 209–251). New York: Academic Press.

Demetriou, A. (2003). Self-formations: Toward a life-span model of the developing mind and self. *Journal of Adult Development, 17*, 151–171.

Demetriou, A. (2006, July). *Mind, personality, and emotions: Deciphering their relations.* Keynote address presented at the 13th Conference of the European Association of Personality, Athens, Greece.

Demetriou, A., & Bacracevic, K. (2009). Cognitive development from adolescence to middle age: From environment-oriented reasoning to social understanding and self-awareness. *Learning and Individual Differences, 19*, 181–194.

Demetriou, A., Christou, C., Spanoudis, G., & Platsidou, M. (2002). The development of mental processing: Efficiency, working memory, and thinking. *Monographs of the Society of Research in Child Development, 67*, Serial Number 268.

Demetriou, A., & Efklides, A. (1985). Structure and sequence of formal and postformal thought: General patterns and individual differences. *Child Development, 56*, 1062–1091.

Demetriou, A., & Efklides, A. (1988). Experiential Structuralism and neo-Piagetian theories: Toward an integrated model. In A. Demetriou (Ed.), *The neo-Piagetian theories of cognitive development: Toward an integration* (pp. 173–222). Amsterdam: North-Holland.

Demetriou A., & Efklides, A. (1989). The person's conception of the structures of developing intellect: Early adolescence to middle age. *Genetic, Social, and General Psychology Monographs, 115*, 371–423.

Demetriou, A., Efklides, E., Papadaki, M., Papantoniou, A., & Economou, A. (1993). The structure and development of causal-experimental thought. *Developmental Psychology, 29*, 480–497.

Demetriou, A., Efklides, A., & Platsidou, M. (1993). The architecture and dynamics of developing mind: Experiential structuralism as a frame for unifying cognitive developmental theories. *Monographs of the Society for Research in Child Development, 58*, Serial Number 234.

Demetriou, A., & Kazi, S. (2001). *Unity and modularity in the mind and the self: Studies on the relationships between self-awareness, personality, and intellectual development from childhood to adolescence.* London: Routledge.

Demetriou, A., & Kazi, S. (2006). Self-awareness in g (with processing efficiency and reasoning). *Intelligence, 34*, 297–317.

Demetriou, A., & Kyriakides, L. (2006). A Rasch-measurement model analysis of cognitive developmental sequences: Validating a comprehensive theory of cognitive development. *British Journal of Educational Psychology, 76*, 209–242.

Demetriou, A., Kyriakides, L., & Avraamidou, C. (2003). The missing link in the relations between intelligence and personality. *Journal of Research in Personality, 37*, 547–581.

Demetriou, A., Mouyi, A., & Spanoudis, G. (2008). Modeling the structure and development of g. *Intelligence, 5*, 437–454.

Demetriou, A., Pachaury, A., Metallidou, Y., & Kazi, S. (1996). Universals and specificities in the structure and development of quantitative thought: A cross-cultural study in Greece and India. *International Journal of Behavioral Development, 19*, 255–290.

Demetriou, A., Platsidou, M., Efklides A., Metallidou, Y., & Shayer, M. (1991). Structure and sequence of the quantitative-relational abilities and processing potential from childhood and adolescence. *Learning and Instruction: The Journal of the European Association for Research on Learning and Instruction, 1*, 19–44.

Demetriou, A., & Raftopoulos, A. (1999). Modeling the developing mind: From structure to change. *Developmental Review, 19*, 319–368.

Demetriou, A., Zhang, X. K., Spanoudis, G., Christou, C., Kyriakides, L., & Platsidou, M. (2005). The architecture and development of mental processing: Greek, Chinese or Universal? *Intelligence, 33*, 109–141.

Dempster, F. N. (1991). Inhibitory processes: A neglected dimension of intelligence. *Intelligence, 15*, 157–173.

Dempster, F. N. (1992). The rise and fall of the inhibitory mechanism: Toward a unified theory of cognitive development and aging. *Developmental Review, 12*, 45–75.

Diamond, A. (1990). The development and neural bases of memory functions as indexed by the AB and delayed response tasks in human infants and infant monkeys. In A. Diamond (Ed.), *The development and neural bases of higher cognitive functions*. Annals of the New York Academy of Sciences: 608 (pp. 239–266). New York: New York Academy of Sciences.

Engle, R. W. (2002). Working memory capacity as executive attention. *Current Directions in Psychological Science, 11*, 19–23.

Engle, R. W., Tuholski, S. W., Laughlin, J. E., & Conway, A. R. A. (1999). Working memory, short-term memory, and general fluid intelligence: A latent-variable approach. *Journal of Experimental Psychology: General, 128*, 309–331.

Fabricius, W. V., & Schwanenflugel, P. J. (1994). The older child's theory of mind. In A. Demetriou & A. Efklides (Eds.), *Intelligence, mind, and reasoning: Structure and development* (pp. 111–132). Amsterdam: North-Holland.

Fischer, K. W. (1980). A theory of cognitive development: The control and construction of hierarchies of skills. *Psychological Review, 87*, 477–531.

Flavell, J. H., Green, F. L., & Flavell, E. R. (1986). Development of knowledge about the appearance-reality distinction. *Monographs of the Society for Research in Child Development, 51*, Serial Number 212.

Gardner, H. (1983). *Frames of mind. The theory of multiple intelligences.* New York: Basic Books.

Gibson, J. J. (1966). *The senses considered as perceptual systems.* London: Allen & Unwin.

Grigorenko, E. L., Geissler, P. W., Prince, R., Okatcha, F., Nokes, C., Kenny, D. A., et al. (2001). The organization of Luo conceptions of intelligence: A study of implicit theories in a Kenyan village. *International Journal of Behavioral Development, 25*, 367–378.

Gustafsson, J. E., & Undheim, J. O. (1996). Individual differences in cognitive functions. In D. C. Berliner & R. C. Calfee (Eds.), *Handbook of educational psychology* (pp. 186–242). New York: Macmillan.

Hale, S., & Fry, A. F. (2000). Relationships among processing speed, working memory, and fluid intelligence in children. *Biological Psychology, 54*, 1–34.

Halford, G. S. (1993). *Children's understanding: The development of mental models.* Hillsdale, NJ: Erlbaum.

Halford, G. S., & Andrews, G. (2004). The development of deductive reasoning: How important is complexity? *Thinking & Reasoning, 10*, 123–145.

Harnishfeger, K. K. (1995). The development of cognitive inhibition: Theories, definitions, and research evidence. In F. N. Dempster & C. J. Brainerd (Eds.), *Interference and inhibition in cognition* (pp. 175–204). New York: Academic Pres

Harter, S. (1999). *The construction of the self.* New York: The Guilford Press.

Huizinga, M., Dolan, C. V., & van der Molen, M. W. (2006). Age-related change in executive function: Developmental trends and a latent variable analysis. *Neuropsychologia, 44*, 2017–2036.

James, W. (1890). *The principles of psychology* (Vol. 1). New York: Hold.

Jensen, A. R. (1998). *The G factor: The science of mental ability.* New York: Praeger.

Kail, R. (1991). Developmental functions for speed of processing during childhood and adolescence. *Psychological Bulletin, 109*, 490–501.

Kail, R., & Salthouse, T. A. (1994). Processing speed as a mental capacity. *Acta Psychologica, 86*, 199–225.

Kargopoulos, P., & Demetriou, A. (1998). What, why, and whence logic? A response to the commentators. *New Ideas in Psychology, 16*, 125–139.

Karmiloff-Smith, A. (1992). *Beyond modularity: A developmental perspective on cognitive science.* Cambridge, MA: MIT Press.

Kovas, Y., & Plomin, R. (2006). Generalist genes: Implications for the cognitive sciences. *Trends in Cognitive Sciences, 10*, 198–203.

Kuhn, D., & Pease, M. (2006). Do children and adults learn differently? *Journal of Cognition and Development, 7*, 279–293.

Kyllonen, P., & Christal, R. E. (1990). Reasoning ability is (little more than) working-memory capacity? *Intelligence, 14*, 389–433.

Lee, J. J. (2006). A *g* beyond *Homo sapiens*: Some hints and suggestions. *Intelligence, 35*, 253–265.

Miyake, A., & Shah, P. (1999). *Models of working memory: Mechanisms of active maintenance and executive control.* Cambridge: Cambridge University Press.

Moshman, D. (2004). From inference to reasoning: The construction of rationality. *Thinking & Reasoning, 10*, 221–239.

Mouyi, A. (2008). *Developmental dynamics binding processing efficiency, working memory, and reasoning: A longitudinal study.* Unpublished doctoral dissertation, University of Cyprus, Nicosia, Cyprus.

Nicholls, J. G. (1990). What is ability and why are we mindful of it? A developmental perspective. In R. J. Sternberg & J. Kolligian, Jr. (Eds.), *Competence considered* (pp. 11–40). New Haven: Yale University Press.

Oberauer, K., Süß, H.-M., Schulze, R., Wilhelm, O., & Wittmann, W. W. (2000). Working memory capacity. Facets of a cognitive ability construct. *Personality and Individual Differences, 29*, 1017–1045.

Pascual-Leone, J. (1970). A mathematical model for the transition rule in Piaget's developmental stages. *Acta Psychologica, 32*, 301–345.

Pascual-Leone, J. (1988). Organismic processes for neo-Piagetian theories: A dialectical causal account of cognitive development. In A. Demetriou (Ed.), *The neo-Piagetian theories of cognitive development: Toward an integration* (pp. 25–64). Amsterdam: North-Holland.

Pfeifer, R., & Scheier, C. (1999). *Understanding intelligence.* Cambridge, MA: MIT Press.

Piaget, J. (1970). Piaget's theory. In P. H. Mussen, (Ed.), *Carmichael's handbook of child development* (pp. 703–732). New York: Wiley.

Piaget, J. (2001). *Studies in reflecting abstraction* (R. L. Campbell, Trans.). London: Psychology Press. (Original work published 1977.)

Plomin, R., & Spinath, F. M. (2002). Genetics and general cognitive ability (g). *Trends in Cognitive Sciences, 6*, 169–176.

Polderman, T. J. C., Posthuma, D., De Sonneville, L. M. J., Stins, J. F. Verhulst, F. C., & Boomsma, D. I. (2007). Genetic analyses of the stability of executive functioning during childhood. *Biological Psychology, 76*, 11–20.

Rocadin, C., Pascual-Leone, J., Rich, J. B., & Dennis, M. (2007). Developmental relations between working memory and inhibitory control. *Journal of the International Neuropsychological Society, 13*, 59–67.

Rumbaugh, D. M., & Washburn, D. A. (2003). *Intelligence of apes and other rational beings.* New Haven, CT: Yale University Press.

Salthouse, T. A. (1996). The processing-speed theory of adult age differences in cognition. *Psychological Review, 103*, 403–428.

Salthouse, T. A. (2004). What and when of cognitive aging. *Current Directions in Psychological Science, 13*, 140–144.

Schaie, K. W. (1995). *Intellectual development in adulthood: The Seattle Longitudinal Study*. New York: Cambridge University Press.

Schneider, W., Lockl, K., & Fernadez, O. (2005). Interrelationships among theory of mind, executive control, language development, and working memory in young children: A longitudinal analysis. In W. Schneider, R. Schumann-Hengsteler & B. Sodian (Eds.), *Young children's cognitive development* (pp. 259–284). Mahwah, NJ: Lawrence Erlbaum Associates.

Schweizer, K., Moosbrugger, H., & Goldhammer, F. (2005). The structure of the relationship between attention and intelligence. *Intelligence, 33*, 589–611.

Shayer, M., Demetriou, A., & Pervez, M. (1988). The structure and scaling of concrete operational thought: Three studies in four countries. *Genetic, Social, and General Psychology Monographs, 114*, 307–376.

Spearman, C. (1904). "General intelligence" objectively determined and measured. *American Journal of Psychology, 15*, 201–293.

Stankov, L., & Roberts, R. (1997). Mental speed is not the "basic" process of intelligence. *Personality and Individual Differences, 22*, 69–84.

Sternberg, R. J., Conway, B. E., Ketron, J. L., & Bernstein, M. (1981). People's conceptions of intelligence. *Journal of Personality and Social Psychology, 41*, 37–55.

Wellman, H. M. (1990). *The child's theory of mind*. Cambridge, MA: MIT Press.

Zelazo, P. D. (2004). The development of conscious control in childhood. *Trends in Cognitive Sciences, 8*, 12–17.

Zelazo, P. D., & Müller, U. (2002). Executive function in typical and atypical development. In U. Gowsami (Ed.), *Handbook of child cognitive development* (pp. 445–469). Oxford, UK: Blackwell.

Zelazo, P. D., Müller, U., Frye, D., Marcovitch, S., Argitis, G., Boseovski, J., et al. (2003). The development of executive function in early childhood. *Monographs of the Society for Research in Child Development, 68*, Serial No. 3.

Zelazo, P. D., Qu, L., & Müller, U. (2005). Hot and cool aspects of executive function: Relations with early development. In W. Schneider, R. Schumann-Hengsteler, & B. Sodian (Eds), *Young children's cognitive development: Interrelationships among executive functioning, working memory, verbal ability, and theory of mind*. Mahwah, NJ: Lawrence Erlbaum Associates.

5 Working memory capacity and its role in cognitive development

Are age differences driven by the same processes across the lifespan?

Anik de Ribaupierre, Delphine Fagot, and Thierry Lecerf

The main purpose of this chapter, in line with the other papers presented in this book, is to address the question of the development and the role of working memory capacity by relying on neo-Piagetian theories, and more particularly on Pascual-Leone's (1969, 1970, 1987) model, on the one hand, and on experimental cognitive psychology (e.g., Cowan's model, 1995), on the other hand. Neo-Piagetian and experimental approaches seem to be very different at first sight. The theoretical conception of working memory is *a priori* not the same, and the tasks developed were specific to each approach. Nevertheless, the findings obtained were highly convergent. Moreover, as we will develop below (see also de Ribaupierre, 2000; de Ribaupierre & Bailleux, 1994, 2000), in the last two decades strikingly similar hypotheses were advanced to explain age and individual differences in working memory capacity, not only in developmental psychology, but also across different fields, in particular in cognitive psychology and in neuropsychology.

Four studies will be presented as an empirical illustration of the convergence between a neo-Piagetian and an experimental approach as concerns the processes underlying cognitive development. In the first and second experiments, Working Memory span tasks, Processing Speed tasks, and Inhibition tasks were administered to children, young adults, and older adults. The main objectives were to assess the role of underlying processes of age differences in working memory capacity tasks, by using structural equation modeling, and to determine whether similar processes are at work across the lifespan by comparing results obtained with children, young adults, and older adults. In the third experiment, two neo-Piagetian tasks of attentional capacity, and three Piagetian tasks were administered to children. In the fourth experiment, the Raven's Progressive matrices (Raven, 1938) and Working Memory span tasks, together with other tasks, were administered. The goal of these two latter studies was to determine to what extent age-related variance in the Piagetian tasks or in the Raven's Progressive matrices can be accounted for by age differences in the neo-Piagetian or in working memory span tasks. It was also to verify that similar results could be obtained when administering tasks originally developed within a neo-Piagetian perspective or an experimental one. Of course, we believe that these tasks are very similar and should yield comparable results, as long as they are geared towards assessing attentional resources. However, it is often believed, in experimental cognitive psychology, that different tasks necessarily tap different processes or reciprocally that a same task invariably assesses the same processes, regardless of age or of familiarity, reflecting a confounding between task and processes (e.g., de Ribaupierre & Pascual-Leone, 1984).

Several definitions of working memory are available in the literature. There is, however, a consensus that working memory refers to a system or a set of processes responsible for the simultaneous storage and manipulation of information during cognitive tasks (Baddeley, 1986; Richardson, 1996), for temporary purposes. Most importantly, it is assumed that working memory capacity is limited. In other words, only a limited amount of information can be attentionally, or effortfully, simultaneously activated by attentional resources and this amount of information increases with age or varies across individuals (Cowan, 1995; Engle, Kane, & Tuholski, 1999; Engle, Tuholski, Laughlin, & Conway, 1999; Pascual-Leone, 1970, 1987). In the present framework, and following Pascual-Leone's or Cowan's propositions, we assume that the content of working memory consists of both activated long-term memory traces and representation of current information that requires attention, and serves to hold and attentionally process information relevant for the task being presently processed (e.g., de Ribaupierre, 2000; Engle et al., 1999). Moreover, we prefer to think in terms of working memory *tasks* rather than working memory per se, meaning thereby that there is no dedicated system to working memory; performance in such tasks depends on more general resources (such as attentional activation and inhibition) that are also at work in other cognitive tasks.

Neo-Piagetians have claimed for a long time (e.g., Case, 1985; Pascual-Leone, 1970, 1987) that the limits in attentional capacity and their gradual lifting with age under the effect of maturation and experience play an important role in cognitive development, by setting a ceiling on performance beyond which children of a certain level cannot perform, unless the task is facilitated (see also Chapman, 1990; Dasen & de Ribaupierre, 1987; de Ribaupierre, 2007; de Ribaupierre & Lecerf, 2006). By conducting task analyses, they were able to predict which cognitive tasks could be solved, given a certain level in attentional capacity. During the last years, adult developmentalists or cognitive aging theorists, and experimentalists have also stressed the central role played by working memory capacity in individual and developmental differences in higher cognitive abilities, such as language comprehension (Daneman & Carpenter, 1980), reasoning (Süß, Oberauer, Wittman, Wilhelm, & Schulze, 2002), or general ability (Engle et al., 1999). While developmental psychologists were more concerned with changes in working memory capacity with age, experimental psychologists were more interested in analyzing the processes that determine performance in the working memory span tasks themselves. Similar hypotheses were nevertheless formulated by both perspectives.

Within a lifespan developmental approach, two main hypotheses were formulated by developmental and by cognitive aging psychologists. Some authors suggested that the increase (decrease) of working memory capacity, and therefore age differences in working memory capacity, is due to an increase/decrease in the number of stimuli that can be maintained simultaneously (activation hypothesis). Others authors suggested that the increase of working memory capacity is due to an increase/decrease in the efficiency of inhibition (inhibition hypothesis). These two mechanisms, activation and inhibition, have often been suggested as exclusive alternatives. We would like to suggest, following Pascual-Leone's propositions, that both are conjointly at work (de Ribaupierre, 2001).

Attentional activation is a crucial factor for efficient working memory capacity, and individual and age differences have been shown to be related to the total amount of activation available, and thus to the total number of activated stimuli. In addition, we suggested previously that processing speed could be considered to be an indirect indicator of activation (de Ribaupierre, 2001). Within the field of cognitive aging, it has been shown repeatedly that age differences in working memory capacity can be accounted for by processing speed (de Ribaupierre & Lecerf, 2006; Salthouse, 1992a, 1992b, 1996; Salthouse & Meinz, 1995). The link between processing speed and activation is relatively straightforward to establish, although one does not know which is first: Faster processing allows for a larger number of stimuli to be maintained in working memory within a very short frame of time; reciprocally, if a larger number of items can be attentionally processed at the same time, processing will be faster. Within the field of experimental and cognitive psychology, hypotheses similar to those advanced by developmental psychologists were formulated as concerns the importance of processing speed for working memory capacity and fluid intelligence (Ackerman, Beier, & Boyle, 2002; Süß et al., 2002), and several studies reported evidence that the relationship between working memory capacity and fluid intelligence can be accounted for by processing speed (Fry & Hale, 1996; Jensen, 1998; Kail & Salthouse, 1994).

Although inhibition is considered by several authors to be a basic mechanism responsible for age differences in working memory capacity, there is relatively little direct empirical evidence supporting this hypothesis (Bjorklund & Harnishfeger, 1990). The role of inhibition is all the more difficult to demonstrate as a number of studies have now shown that it is not a unitary mechanism (Kramer, Humphrey, Larish, Logan, & Strayer, 1994; Shilling, Chetwynd, & Rabbitt, 2002), or that it appears to be domain specific (Palladino, Mammarella, & Vecchi, 2003). Hasher and Zacks (1988) proposed that if inhibitory mechanisms are inefficient, irrelevant information (distractors) overloads or clutters working memory; since then, they have shown in many studies that older adults are less efficient in inhibiting distractors. For instance, Zacks, Radvansky, and Hasher (1996) showed that older adults make more intrusion errors than younger adults, and intrusions were considered to reflect inefficient inhibitory mechanisms (de Beni, Palladino, Pazzaglia, & Cornoldi, 1998; de Beni & Palladino, 2000, 2004; Robert,

Borella, Fagot, Lecerf, & de Ribaupierre, 2009). In other words, age differences in the efficiency of inhibitory control are hypothesized to be related to age differences in working memory capacity, because goal irrelevant stimuli are more likely to have access to working memory, thereby reducing the probability for relevant information to be processed.

Taken together, the data indicate that both activation (or processing speed) and inhibition might account for age differences in working memory capacity. As mentioned above, we suggest considering them as two independent mechanisms, which can act jointly to influence performance in working memory tasks, or in other cognitive tasks, rather than as alternative explanations. It might also be the case that their relative role in accounting for performance in working memory tasks varies somewhat across life. Therefore, the main objective of a number of studies in our laboratory, some of which are summarized below, was to determine whether general processes, and more particularly processing speed and inhibition, are at work throughout the lifespan and might account for age differences in working memory capacity (e.g., Baltes, Staudinger, & Lindenberger, 1999; Schaie & Hertzog, 1986). In other words, their objective was to answer the question: "Are age differences driven by the same processes across the lifespan?" and to determine whether their relative weight varies in different age periods, by using the same tasks and comparing their relationships in children, young adults, and older adults. We assumed that both processing speed and inhibition would account for age differences in working memory capacity, but that their relative weight might vary. Although there is, as yet, no evidence in the extant literature, we hypothesized that the influence of inhibition would be more important for adults than for children. In order to test this hypothesis, structural equation models were used (Studies 1 and 2). Our hypothesis was, in both studies, that age would influence processing speed and inhibition, both of which would in turn influence working memory; we therefore tested a relatively simple model, using several tasks to measure each construct.

Secondly, and as suggested by neo-Piagetians and by some experimentalists, the increase of working memory capacity, that is a gradual increase in the quantity of information that can be processed simultaneously, is considered to be one of the main causal factors of cognitive development. Therefore, the second objective of this chapter is to present studies addressing this question, asking to what extent age-related variance in complex cognitive tasks such as Piagetian tasks (Balance, Islands, and Lines Folding) or Raven's Progressive matrices (a fluid intelligence measure) is accounted for by working memory span tasks or by neo-Piagetian attentional capacity tasks (CSVI and Peanut tasks). Even though tasks originated in different theoretical perspectives, similar findings should be obtained. The extent to which working memory capacity or attentional capacity explains age-related variance in Piagetian tasks or in Raven's task was assessed by means of regression and commonality analyses (Cohen & Cohen, 1983; Pedhazur, 1997). The influence of processing speed and inhibition was also considered in the last study.

Relationship between Working Memory, Inhibition, and Processing Speed: Studies 1 and 2

These two studies aimed at examining the relationship between the three constructs Working Memory, Inhibition, and Processing Speed, and to assess whether it would change with age across the lifespan. Our hypothesis was that Processing Speed and Inhibition[1] should be considered as accounting jointly for age differences in working memory and not as alternative, single predictors. Nevertheless, their respective role might change with age and/ or with individuals. Processing speed might play a relatively large role in some life periods (e.g., account more than Inhibition for age differences in working memory capacity during childhood) whereas Inhibition might be more important at some other ages (e.g., in older adulthood). The two studies were very similar, both using a large multivariate design, with several tasks (more than 20 in Study 2) supposed to reflect each of the three constructs, administered in an identical manner to school-age children, young adults, and older adults. They differed in the precise tasks used, in their amount, and in the age of the sample: Study 2 was meant to examine more closely the construct of Inhibition, and a larger sample of children (five age groups rather than three) was examined. It also included the Raven's Matrices task in order to link these three constructs with fluid intelligence.

Study 1[2]

1. Method

Participants. The sample consisted of 143 children (8, 10, and 12 years old), 102 young adults (18–35 years old), and 139 older adults (60–80 years old).

Tasks and procedure. This study included a dozen tasks, distributed into 3 groups (4 tasks of Working Memory, 4 tasks of Processing Speed, and 4 tasks of Inhibition), as well as a few other control tasks. All tasks were administered to all participants, in the same order and each participant was examined in two or three sessions.[3]

Processing Speed tasks. This construct was assessed by four tasks. *The Pattern Comparison task* and the *Letter Comparison task* were adapted from Salthouse (1992b). In these tasks, participants had to judge whether two stimuli (patterns or strings of letters) were identical. These tasks comprised two pages, and the time to complete each page was recorded. The score used in the present study was the total time to complete the two pages.

The Cross-out task was extracted from the Woodcock-Johnson Educational Battery – Revised (Woodcock & Johnson, 1989). In this task, geometric figures were presented. Participants were asked to indicate (by striking them) in a row of 21 figures those that matched a target presented to the left. The score was the number of rows completed correctly in 3 minutes.

In the computerized *Digit Symbol task* (Salthouse, 1992b; Wechsler, 1981), a coding key pairing numbers with symbols and a digit-symbol pair were presented, and participants had to decide whether the digit-symbol pair was identical or not to the coding key. The reaction time in milliseconds and the nature of responses (yes/no) were recorded for each stimulus. The score used in the present study was the mean reaction time across all correctly responded trials and the total of correct responses.

Working Memory span tasks. This construct was assessed by four tasks, three relying on visuo-spatial processing and one on verbal processing. *The Location-Spatial task* and *the Double-Color Span task* were adapted from Loisy and Roulin (1992; Lecerf & de Ribaupierre, 2005). Each of these tasks (together labeled the Matrices task below) involved showing a matrix (6*6 cells) on a computer screen, a number of target cells appearing in color on each trial. For the location-span task, all colored cells were red, and participants had to remember their location. For the double-color span task, target cells appeared in seven distinct colors and participants had to remember both the color and position of these cells. List-length, defined by the number of cells to remember, varied in an adaptive manner: It increased by one unit when all cells were correctly remembered and decreased by one unit when one or several cells were not reported. It was rarely higher than 4 cells to remember. The score used in the present study was the average number of correctly recalled positions and of correctly recalled positions and colors, respectively.

For *the Ghost-Peanut task* (de Ribaupierre & Bailleux, 1994; de Ribaupierre, Lecerf, & Bailleux, 2000) an array of 16 circles was shown on a computer screen, some of which appeared in color. On each trial, participants had to remember both their color and position. List-length, defined by the number of position/colors presented, ranged from two to six. The score used in the present study was the number of correctly recalled positions, the number of correctly recalled colors, and the number of correctly recalled associations (position and color, correctly recalled and matched).

The Reading Span task was adapted from Daneman and Carpenter (1980). In this task, a set of sentences was presented, and participants were required to decide whether or not the sentence was semantically correct, and to remember its last word. List-length, defined by the number of sentences in the series, ranged from two to five. The score used in the present study was the total number of words correctly recalled.

Inhibition. This construct was assessed by two tasks.[4] In the *Stroop-Color* (Stroop, 1935) *task* participants had to name color patches or read color words printed in black ink (control conditions), or to name the color of words printed in an incongruent ink color (i.e., the word "green" printed in yellow – incongruent condition). Stimuli were grouped by condition, on an A4 sheet of paper, and response time was manually recorded by page (3 pages by condition, 24 items per page). The score used in the present study is an index of interference, under the form of a relative difference: [(experimental condition – control condition)/control condition].

For *the Proactive Interference task*, participants were required to learn three sets of four lists of 10 words, two sets consisting of semantically related words, and one of phonologically related words. In the "semantic" condition, the first three lists belonged to the same category (e.g., Animals) and the fourth list belonged to a different category (e.g., Vehicles). In the "phonological" condition, the first three lists were based on a same phoneme (/ɛ̃/, as in "moulin") and the fourth list belonged to a different phoneme (/e/, as in "chalet"). The number of correctly recalled words was recorded, and the difference in performance across similar lists as well as the number of intrusions from the preceding lists was used as an index of interference.

2. Results and discussion

Descriptive statistics. To facilitate the comparison of the performance across tasks and across age groups, scores of each task were standardized, relatively to young adults. Thus, for each task, the young adults sample presents a mean of 0 and a standard deviation of 1; the scores of the other age groups reflect their position with respect to the young adults. Scores were then averaged across the tasks belonging to the same group, that is, Working Memory (Matrices, Ghost-Peanut and Reading span), Inhibition (Stroop-Color and Proactive interference), and Processing Speed (Pattern comparison, Letter comparison, Digit symbol, and Cross-out).

As can be seen in Figure 5.1 (panel A) age differences were large for all three constructs. However, the age trend was more pronounced for working memory and processing speed and smallest for inhibition. Thus, as concerns working memory tasks, 8-year-old children were, on average, located at –3.26 standard deviations from the young adults; 10-year-olds, 12-year-olds, older adults aged less than 70 years (young-olds), and older adults aged 70 years or more (old-olds) were respectively located at –2.04, –1.24, –1.30, and –1.68 standard deviations from young adults. Age differences were even larger for Processing Speed: from –7.18 standard deviations from young adults for the 8-year-old children, to –2.14 or –2.89 for the 12-year-olds or the young-old adults. In contrast, for the Inhibition tasks, 8-year-old children were, on average, located at –.81 standard deviations from the young adults, 10-year-old and 12-year-old children, young-old, and old-old adults were respectively located at –.64, –.60, –1.4, and –2.02 standard deviations from young adults. Nevertheless, despite these large age differences, interindividual differences were also very large; it is only for the two most extreme groups, i.e., 8-year-olds and young adults in Processing Speed tasks, that there was no overlap.

Structural-equation modeling. In order to address the construct generality issue and the relationship between these different variables, a structural equation modeling approach was used. First, it was verified, using confirmatory factor analyses, that the tasks supposed to measure a same construct did indeed correlate, both within each age group, or in terms of age differences. Two sets of analyses were run each time: children with young adults

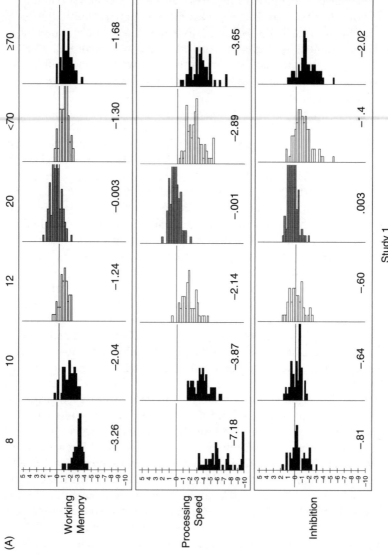

Study 1

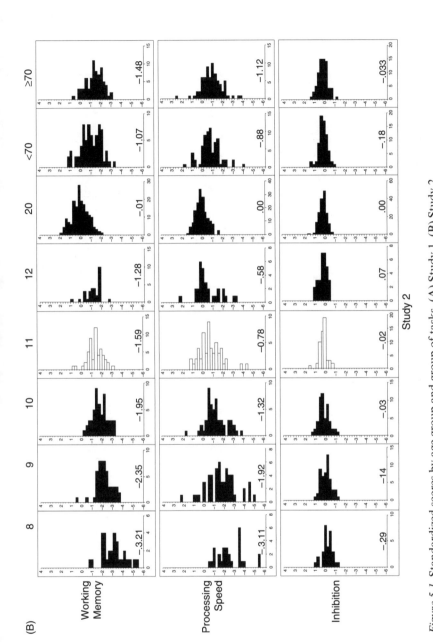

Figure 5.1 Standardized scores by age group and group of tasks. (A) Study 1. (B) Study 2.

(a subsample composed of half of the young adults), and older adults with young adults (the second half of young adults sample[5]). Then, several models were tested, to examine the relationships between the constructs. Figure 5.2 presents the theoretical model that was used to build the design and that

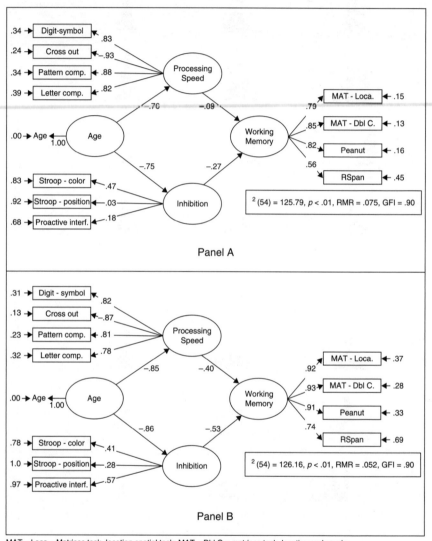

MAT – Loca = Matrices task, location spatial task; MAT – Dbl C = matrices task, location and words

Figure 5.2 Study 1: Age, Inhibition, Processing Speed, and Working Memory: A structural-equations model for children and young adults (Panel A) and for young and older adults (Panel B).

Note: MAT-Loca = Matrices task, location spatial mask; MAT-DblC = matrices task, location and words; RMR = Root Mean Square Residual; GFI = Goodness of Fit Index.

proved to be the most adequate for the two samples (Panel A: children and young adults; Panel B: young and older adults). It is worth stressing that a model with only one factor (confirmatory factor analyses) presented a much worse fit, as well as a model using a path Processing Speed → Inhibition → Working Memory. A multigroup model was also used, showing that even though the same model applies to both periods of the lifespan, the parameters cannot remain invariant. This result points to a configurational invariance across age groups but also to a lack of metric invariance (e.g., Schaie, Maitland, Willis, & Intrieri, 1998). Finally, it should also be stressed that the tasks supposed to tap Inhibition did not correlate strongly, as was already mentioned. First, only the interference index of the Stroop-Color task and the number of intrusions from the Proactive interference task could be used in the modeling; no such score could be used as concerns the Stroop-Position and the Negative priming tasks. Second, even for the two tasks that were retained, the amount of variance accounted for by the latent variable was very small. Nevertheless, it is noteworthy that the effect of Inhibition on working memory was somewhat larger for adults (Panel B) than for children (Panel A). In other words, age differences in children relative to young adults seem to be driven essentially by Processing Speed whereas Processing Speed and Inhibition both account for age differences observed in adulthood.

Study 2[6]

This study pursued the same objectives as Study 1, while focusing in more detail on the construct of Inhibition (in particular on the necessity to suppress information, see Borella et al., 2009), about which the previous study had raised some concerns. It also aimed at examining the relationship between Working Memory and fluid intelligence. Finally, we wanted to have a closer look at age differences within childhood, so that more age groups were included. As a result, more than 20 tasks were administered to all participants, among which there were three Processing Speed tasks, three Working Memory tasks, and ten Inhibition tasks; among the latter, only five will be presented here.

1. Method

Participants. The sample consisted of 220 children (8, 9, 10, 11, and 12 years old), 170 young adults (18–35 years old), and 143 older adults (60–88 years old).

Tasks and procedure. All tasks were administered to all participants, and each participant was examined during at least two sessions. The participants were administered a very large battery of tasks to address the three constructs of interest here (Processing Speed, Working Memory, and Inhibition).[7]

Processing Speed. This construct was assessed by three tasks. *The Pattern Comparison task* and *the Letter Comparison task* were adapted from Salthouse (1992b). These two tasks were identical to those administered in the first study.

The D2 task was adapted from Brickenkamp's test (1998), and consists of 10 test lines with 47 characters in each line, presented on an A4 sheet of paper. Participants were required to scan each line for 20 seconds (after which time they were required to go to the next line) and cross out all occurrences of the letter "d" with two dashes while ignoring all other characters. The score used in the present analyses was the total number of characters correctly crossed out on each of the last nine lines (D2+), as well as the number of errors (D2–).

Working Memory. This construct was assessed by two tasks, the Matrices task, itself composed of three subtasks, and the *Reading Span task*, which was identical to the task used in the first study.

The computerized *Matrices task* was adapted from Loisy and Roulin (1992). It differed from the one used in Study 1, in that it consisted in three subtasks which were successively presented. In the *Location-spatial subtask*, participants had to remember the location of cells (in a 5*5 matrix); it was identical to that presented in Study 1, except for the display that was simpler (25 cells rather than 36). The *Word-only subtask* required participants to remember lists of words presented in a columnar display. In the *double-verbal condition*, words appeared simultaneously in a 5*5 matrix, each in a different cell of the matrix, and participants had to recall both the words and their position. List-length varied in an adaptive manner, based on previous performance (number of correct word-position associations for the double-verbal task). The scores used in the present study were the number of locations correctly recalled, the number of words correctly recalled, and the number of correct word-position associations, in the double-verbal task.

Inhibition. This construct was assessed by ten different tasks, only five of which being part of the present study. Two computerized *Stroop tasks* were used, adapted from Stroop (1935). In each version, participants had to name the color of stimuli (words, signs, patches) appearing on the screen. In the *Integrated-Stroop task*, participants had to name the color of the stimulus itself (e.g., the color word Blue colored in blue = congruent; or in green = incongruent condition); it is the most frequently used form of the Stroop task.[8] In the *Dissociated-Stroop task*, participants had to name the color of a patch (target), while distractors (words) were presented above or below the patch color (e.g., a red patch accompanied by the word "blue" written in white). Four conditions were used in each task: two control ones (neutral words and signs), congruent (target and distractor printed in the same color), incongruent (target and distractor printed in different colors) and negative priming (pairs of incongruent trials in which the distractor to be ignored on the first trial became the target to be named on the next trial). Because the tasks were computerized, items of different conditions could be mixed, rather than grouped by condition as in Study 1. The scores used were response times for correctly responded trials, Stroop intrusions (giving the color of the distractor rather than the target) and a relative difference score ([(RT experimental – RT control)/RT control], where experimental refers to the condition of interest), to index interference, negative priming, or facilitation.

The Hayling task was adapted from Burgess and Shallice (1996). In this task participants were provided with lists of high-cloze sentences to be completed either with an expected word or with a word providing no meaning to the sentence, but grammatically correct with respect to case and gender. Scores were response times and number of correct responses.

The *Directed Forgetting Cueing task* (DF-Cueing task) was adapted from Bjork (1989) and Harnishfeger and Pope (1996). Each participant realized two computerized versions of the *DF-Cueing task*, in several conditions. In each version, participants had to learn a series of 20 words, which they were instructed, later in the course of the task, to forget or to remember. At the end of the task, recall was required for all the words, including those which were to forget, or only for those to be remembered. In *the Item-by-Item Cueing Directed Forgetting task*, instruction to remember or to forget appeared after each word; in *the Blocked-Cueing Directed Forgetting task* instruction appeared once, at half-list (i.e., after 10 words).

2. Results and discussion

Descriptive statistic. As for Study 1, in order to allow for an easier comparison of the performance of the different age groups across the different tasks, scores of each task were standardized, relatively to young adults. Figure 5.1 (panel B) presents the distribution of these standardized scores, averaged across the tasks indicative of each of the constructs of interest and for each age group. As can be seen in Figure 5.1, and like Study 1, age differences were large for Working Memory and Processing Speed; they were small for Inhibition. Thus, regarding working memory tasks, 8-year-old children were, on average, located at –3.21 standard deviations from the young adults; 9-, 10-, 11-, and 12-year-old children, young-old and old-old adults were respectively located at –2.35, –1.95, –1.59, –1.28, –1.07, and –1.48 standard deviations from young adults. Concerning Processing Speed, 8-year-old children were, on average, located at –3.11 standard deviations from the young adults; 9-, 10-, 11-, and 12-year-old children, young-old and old-old adults were respectively located at –1.92, –1.32, –.78, –.58, –.88, and –1.12 standard deviations from young adults. In contrast, age differences were much smaller for Inhibition: 8-year-old children were, on average, located at –.29 standard deviations from the young adults; 9-, 10-, 11-, and 12-year-old children, young-old and old-old adults were respectively located at –.14, –.03, –.02, –.07, –.18, and –0.33 standard deviations from young adults. One should also stress the magnitude of interindividual differences in all tasks, leading to a large overlap between the various age groups.

Structural-equation modeling. The approach and the theoretical model that was tested were similar to that of Study 1, that is, Processing Speed and Inhibition accounting for age differences in Working Memory (see Figure 5.3). This model proved the most adequate; adding direct paths, for instance, between Age and Working Memory did not improve the fit. Once again, the same model could be used for modeling age differences in both

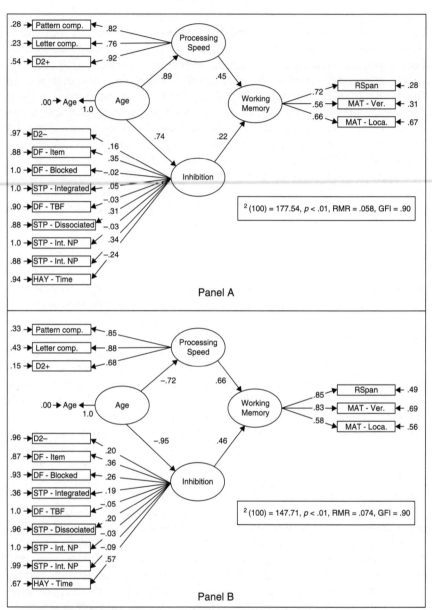

D2+ = D2 task, number of correct responses; D2– = D2 task, number of errors; DF-TBF = Directed forgetting task, number of words which were to be forgotten; STP-Integrated = Integrated-Stroop task; STP-Dissociated = Dissociated-Stroop task ;STP-Int_NP = Integrated-Stroop task, negative priming condition; HAY-Time = Hayling task, RTs; MAT-Ver = Matrices task, verbal condition; MAT-Loca = Matrices task, location spatial task.

Figure 5.3 Study 2: Age, Inhibition, Processing Speed, and Working Memory: A structural-equations model for children and young adults (Panel A) and for young and older adults (Panel B).

the young sample (Panel A: children and young adults) and the older sample (Panel B: young adults and older adults). However, the multigroup approach demonstrated that it was not possible to fix the parameters to identical values, either to define the latent variables and/or to model the relationships between the constructs. Therefore, results point to a configurational invariance, but not to a metric invariance, implying that the same variables are at work across the lifespan, but that their strict definition and their relative weight change across the lifespan.

To what extent does working memory account for age differences in cognitive tasks: Studies 3 and 4

Study 3

In order to address the possible influence of working memory capacities on cognitive capacities, the present study investigated whether working memory capacity accounts for age differences in Piagetian tasks. This study was part of a larger five-year longitudinal project on the development of working memory, during which a number of cognitive tasks were administered to children (de Ribaupierre & Bailleux, 1994, 1995). Here we will focus only on two working memory tasks: the CSVI (Compound Stimuli Visual Information; Pascual-Leone, 1970, 1987), and the Peanut tasks (Case, 1985; de Ribaupierre, Neirynck, & Spira, 1989). Further, we will investigate three Piagetian tasks: the Balance task (adapted from Inhelder & Piaget, 1955; Case, 1985; de Ribaupierre, 1975; Siegler, 1981), the Island task (Piaget, Inhelder, & Szeminska, 1948) and the Lines Folding task (Piaget & Inhelder, 1966). Only the results of the second, third and fifth year of the longitudinal study will be presented here, because these are the years at which Piagetian tasks were administered.

1. Method

Participants. For the second year of the longitudinal study, the sample consisted of 104 children (6, 7, 9, and 11 years old). For the third year of the longitudinal study, the sample consisted of 100 children (7, 8, 10, and 12 years old). For the fifth year of the longitudinal study, the sample consisted of 98 children (9, 10, 12, and 14 years old).

Tasks and procedure. Each year, all tasks were administered to all partici-pants. The participants were given, among other tasks, three Piagetian tasks and two working memory tasks.

Piagetian tasks. The Balance task was adapted from Inhelder and Piaget (1955; de Ribaupierre, 1975). In this task, a balance was presented, with weights on each arm, and participants had to decide whether the balance would lean towards the right, towards the left, or remain stable. Two condi-tions were used: Items A (standardized items) in which the experimenter placed the weights (five items of different difficulty) and children had to decide whether the balance would remain stable but could not check whether their response was correct; and Items B (semi-standardized items) in which children placed the weights to make the balance level. For both Items A and B, justifications were requested and taken into account for scoring. The order of administration was identical for all participants: Items A were administered first, followed by Items B. Responses were scored into six ordered levels of performance, for each item, according to a scale based on theoretical analyses in terms of dimensions of transformation (see Thomas, Pons, & de Ribaupierre, 1996, for a complete description). A median score was then calculated for each type of item.

The Island task was adapted from Piaget (Piaget et al., 1948) and Rieben, de Ribaupierre, and Lautrey (1983). In this task, a compact wooden block was first presented. Children had to imagine that this block was a building (a "house") constructed on an island and had to reconstruct it with small wooden blocks. The new building had to contain the same volume as the model while built on islands of a different surface. The model corresponded to 36 wooden blocks ($3 \times 3 \times 4$), but compact with no block indication, and was placed on a 3×4 island. The surfaces (islands) on which the children had to reproduce this volume were 1×3, and 2×2. For each reconstruction, children had first to give a verbal response by anticipation (i.e., announce how high their construction would be) and then to realize this construction (which had to be 12 and 9 floors high, respectively). As in the Balance task, children were systematically required to justify their response/action. Each item was scored using a scale of six ordered levels of performance. The levels of performance were defined in terms of the dimensions of transformation proposed by Rieben, de Ribaupierre, and Lautrey (1983, 1990). A median score was computed for the entire task.

The Lines Folding task was adapted from Piaget and Inhelder (1966) and Rieben et al. (1983). Children had to imagine the folding of a transparent sheet of paper on which colored, geometrical figures were drawn. The children's task was to draw the resulting figure (with the correct colors), that is the figure which would be visible when the paper was folded in half. As for the other Piagetian tasks, children's responses were scored using a scale of six ordered levels of performance, based on the dimensions of transformation proposed by Rieben et al. (1983, 1990). For each child a median score was computed across items.

Working Memory. This construct was assessed by two neo-Piagetian attentional capacity tasks which are considered to be similar, in that they draw on limited attentional resources, to the working memory tasks used in adult, cognitive psychology. *The Compound Stimuli Visual Information task* (CSVI) was adapted from Pascual-Leone (1970). In this computerized version, children learned to associate a simple visual stimulus (e.g., square shape, large size, red color, etc.) with one key of a specially designed keyboard. Nine simple stimulus-response key associations were to be learned. In the test phase, compound stimuli, composed of a number of the simple stimuli learned previously, were presented and children had to respond, by pressing on the corresponding keys, to all the simple stimuli they detected. Complexity was defined by the number of simple stimuli, and ranged from two to seven simple stimuli embedded in the compound one. The task varied somewhat across the longitudinal study, in particular in terms of complexity and of presentation time, but space is not sufficient here to report on these details. The score used in this paper was the number of correct responses (i.e., the simple stimuli presented which were correctly detected) by class of complexity, averaged across the task.

The Peanut task was adapted from Pascual-Leone (de Ribaupierre et al., 1989; de Ribaupierre, Lecerf, & Bailleux, 2000) and Case (1985). A clown figure (Mr. Peanut) was presented on a sheet of paper, with colored spots on it. The children's task was to recall the location of spots by placing colored chips on a blank clown figure. Two versions were administered: a *Purple-Peanut* in which all spots were of the same color and a *Color-Peanut* in which spots were of different colors (seven possible colors). In the colored version, children had to recall both the color and the location. Complexity, defined by the number of positions to recall, ranged from two to six. The score used was the total number of correct trials.

2. Results and discussion

For reasons of space, we present here only the results relevant to the question raised, namely the extent to which working memory capacity accounts for age differences in each of these Piagetian tasks. Following a method widely used by Salthouse (1992b; see also Pedhazur, 1997), regression and commonality analyses were run.[9]

In a first step, Age and working memory tasks were entered as predictors (alone, and then together), to assess three parts of the variance in the Piagetian task: the variance accounted for by Age alone, the variance accounted for by the working memory tasks alone (entered together) and the common variance accounted for by both predictors. The sum of these three components of variance is equal to the total R^2 that is obtained when the predictors are entered all at once. For instance, as concerns the total variance of Items A of the Balance task (see Figure 5.4, panel A), the total R^2 obtained when using the three working memory tasks and Age as predictors was .59; R^2 was equal to .488 when only Age was entered as a single predictor (age-related variance), and to .573 when the only predictor was working memory. On the basis of these three parameters, it can be estimated that the unique variance due to Age was .015, the unique variance due to working memory was .10, and the variance that both tasks jointly accounted for was .47, leaving 41% of the variance not accounted for by these variables. Now, to respond to the question of how much of the age differences were accounted for by the working memory tasks, the same approach was used with respect to the age-related variance, showing that 97% of it was accounted for by the working memory tasks. Thus, almost all of the age-related variance in this task was accounted for by the three working memory tasks.

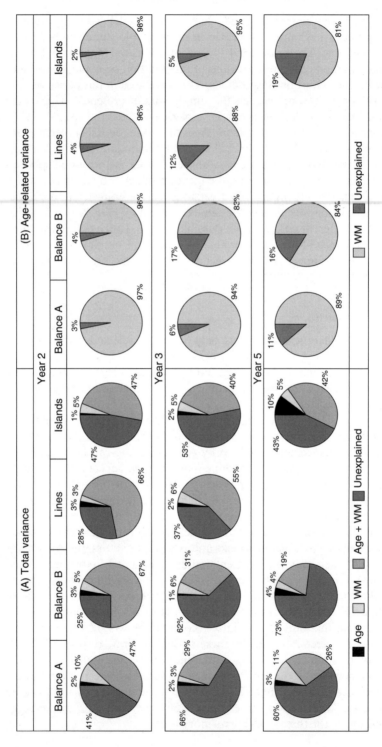

Figure 5.4 Study 3: Decomposition of the total variance (A) and the age-related variance (B) accounted for by working memory tasks, by task and by year of the longitudinal study.

Figure 5.4 presents the results for each of the three years and each of the three tasks,[10] with respect to the total variance in the Piagetian task (panel A) or the age-related variance (panel B). First, the part of the total variance not accounted for by Age and/or working memory varied from task to task, and from year to year. It was relatively small in Year 2 (varying from 25% in Balance B to 47% in Islands), but higher in Year 3 (37% in Lines to 66% in Balance A) and Year 5 (43% in Islands to 73% in Balance B). This means that age differences were more important the first time that these tasks were administered, and that individual differences tended to increase with familiarity with the tasks, and/or increased age.

As concerns the age-related variance, which is the question raised here, it can be seen that almost all of it was accounted for by the three working memory tasks combined (see Figure 5.4, panel B), and it decreased only slightly across the years. For instance, regarding Items A of the Balance task, the working memory capacity tasks accounted for 97% of the age-related variance in Year 2, 94% in Year 3, and 89% in Year 5. Considering all tasks, results show that more than 80% of age differences (regardless of how large age differences are) were explained by age differences in the working memory capacity tasks. It should be noted that regression analyses were also run the other way around, that is, using the Piagetian tasks as predictors of age-related variance in the working memory capacity tasks. Clearly, the amount of variance that Piagetian tasks explained in the working memory tasks was lower. This makes sense, as we will discuss in the conclusion.

Study 4

The objective of this last cross-sectional study was, as in Study 3, to assess if working memory capacity influences cognitive capacities; it was actually part of Study 2, described above. More precisely, the main purpose of Study 4 was to estimate to what extent the working memory capacity tasks account for age differences in intelligence (cognition). Relative to Study 3, the interesting question lies with the difference in the type of tasks used, and with the possibility of these two studies to demonstrate similarities across research traditions (see also de Ribaupierre & Lecerf, 2006). The working memory tasks are those used in cognitive psychology teams working with adults, rather than tasks developed within a neo-Piagetian perspective. Likewise, cognitive performance was assessed with the Raven's Matrices task, more commonly used than Piagetian tasks. Also, other variables were used, such as Processing Speed and Inhibition, which makes it possible to assess the relative role of working memory in accounting for age differences. Finally, older adults were also studied, which allows us to draw some conclusions with respect to age differences across the lifespan.

Four groups of tasks were used: Working Memory tasks (Reading Span and Matrices), Processing Speed tasks (Letters or Patterns Comparison, D2),

Inhibition tasks (Stroop, Directed Forgetting, Hayling), and fluid intelligence (Raven Standard Progressive Matrices).

1. Method

Participants. The sample consisted of 220 children (8, 9, 10, 11, and 12 years old), 170 young adults (18–35 years old), and 143 older adults (60–88 years old).

Tasks and procedure. All tasks were administered to all participants, and each participant was examined twice or more. This study being a substudy of Study 2, most tasks have already been described above. Hence, all tasks addressing the three aforementioned constructs (Processing Speed, Working Memory, and Inhibition) were the same as in the second study.

Fluid intelligence. The Raven Standard Progressive Matrices task was used as indicated in the manual (Raven, 1938). In this experiment, the task was applied without a time limit. The score used in the current paper was the total number of correct responses.

2. Results and discussion

As in Study 3, regression and commonality analyses were used. However, this time, there were four sets of independent variables which could be used as predictors: Age, Working Memory, Processing Speed, and Inhibition, while the score in the Raven's Matrices was used as a dependent variable. The predictors were entered alone (e.g., Age alone, or Working Memory), in combination two by two (e.g., Age with Working Memory tasks or Age with Inhibition tasks), in combination three by three (e.g., Age with Working Memory and Processing Speed tasks), and all together.[11]

Table 5.1 presents the results, for children and young adults (left column), and for young and older adults (right column). The decomposition of the total variance is reported in panel A, and the decomposition of the age-related variance in panel B. For instance, all variables together accounted for almost 70% of the observed variance in the Raven's Matrices in children and young adults (31% unexplained variance), which is rather sizeable. Most of this total variance was accounted for by combined variables rather than by unique variances. Thus, whereas almost 51% of the variance was linked to Age, in one way or another, the unique variance due to Age was almost 0; the unique variance due to Working Memory was 4%, while it was almost 5% for Processing Speed and 1% for Inhibition. In contrast, Age, Processing Speed, and Working Memory jointly accounted for about 35% of the variance. Results were similar for older adults, except for the fact that, this time, 41% of the total variance was not accounted for by the variables used as predictors.

Once again, the question we raised lies with the decomposition of the age-related variance (Table 5.1, panel B). It is of interest to note that the

Table 5.1 Study 4: Decomposition of the total variance (panel A) and the age-related variance (panel B) in the Raven's Matrices task, by age groups

	Children and young adults N = 262	Young and older adults N = 205
(A) Total variance		
Age	0.00%	3.40%
Speed	4.80%	1.30%
WM	3.60%	7.10%
Inhibition	1.30%	1.90%
A+S	6.10%	3.50%
A+WM	0.70%	4.40%
A+I	0.00%	0.20%
S+WM	5.20%	4.30%
S+I	0.30%	0.40%
WM+I	1.60%	2.90%
A + S + WM	34.10%	18.40%
A + S + I	0.00%	0.00%
A + WM + I	0.00%	1.50%
S + WM + I	1.40%	1.80%
All	9.40%	8.80%
Unexplained	31.50%	40.10%
(B) Age-related variance		
Speed	12.00%	9.00%
WM	1.00%	11.00%
Inhibition	0.00%	0.00%
S+WM	68.00%	46.00%
S+I	0.00%	0.00%
WM+I	0.00%	4.00%
S + WM + I	3.00%	4.00%
Unexplained	16.00%	26.00%

age-related variance represented approximately 51% of the total variance in the young sample (children and young adults) and 40% in the adult sample. The largest part of this age-related variance was accounted for by a combination of Processing Speed and Working Memory in the young sample (68%); Processing Speed alone accounted for 12%; Inhibition, whether alone or in combination with another variable, played a negligible part. In the older sample, the picture was slightly different. Processing Speed and Working Memory together still accounted for the largest part of the age-related variance (46%). Processing Speed alone and Working Memory alone played an almost equal role (9% vs. 11%); Inhibition, while still not very important, seemed to play a larger role than in the young sample.

General discussion

Four studies relying on multivariate designs were presented. These experiments aimed at understanding further the developmental and individual differences in working memory capacity, and, more generally, in fluid cognition, assuming that they might relate to age differences in Processing Speed and in Inhibition. The objective of presenting these studies was also to illustrate the potentialities of combining various theoretical perspectives, in particular the neo-Piagetian approach, lifespan developmental psychology, and cognitive experimental psychology.

Studies 1 and 2 showed first that it was possible to construct latent variables of Working Memory, Processing Speed, and Inhibition, although it proved more difficult for the latter. Such latent variables, subject to age differences, attest to the presence of somewhat global mechanisms, as developmentalists have suggested. Even though these latent variables correlated, in both studies a model with three factors fit the data better than a model with only one general variable. Thus, a single general developmental factor is not sufficient to explain cognitive development, in conformity with the proposal that development is multidimensional (e.g., Baltes et al., 1999; de Ribaupierre, 1993). It should be stressed that the latent variables did not account for all of the variance in the tasks, in particular as concerns Inhibition. The present results are thus consistent with the (relative) specificity of processes underlying the tasks used, which cognitive psychologists frequently choose to underline.

Structural equation modeling supported the hypothesis that age differences in working memory capacity are driven by age differences in Processing Speed and Inhibition, in line with the hypothesis of both neo-Piagetians (e.g., Pascual-Leone, 1987) and lifespan developmental researchers. Because the same model could be applied to account for differences between children and young adults on the one hand, and for differences between young and older adults on the other hand, it can be inferred that the same processes are at work throughout the lifespan. However, only a general configurational invariance was observed. This implies that either the latent variables do not have an identical meaning in the different age groups and/or that they differ in their relative weight. This is congruent with Reuchlin's proposal that individual or developmental differences can be accounted for by vicarious processes (Lautrey, 1990; Reuchlin, 1978), that is, by processes that exist in all individuals but with a varying degree of evocability. While Processing Speed explained a larger part of age differences in working memory capacity than Inhibition, at all ages, the results showed nevertheless that Inhibition accounted for a somewhat larger part of age difference in older adulthood than in childhood.

Studies 3 and 4 aimed at showing the role of working memory capacity in cognition, whether in Piagetian tasks (Study 3) or in fluid cognition as assessed by the Raven's Matrices (Study 4). Neo-Piagetian models as well as several theories of cognitive psychology contend that working memory plays an important role in accounting for age and/or individual differences. In particular, Pascual-Leone (1987) suggested that an increase in attentional capacity is one of the main causal factors of cognitive development, while it is itself driven by a change in activation power, in inhibition, and in executive efficiency. Engle showed that individual differences in working memory capacity, in young adults, are closely and positively linked to individual differences in cognitive tasks, including fluid intelligence, while working memory capacity itself is related to individual differences in attentional resources, and notably in inhibition (e.g., Engle, Kane, & Tuholski, 1999). The present results demonstrated that, despite the fact that the tasks originated in different theoretical perspectives – whether the predicting working memory tasks or the tasks assessing general cognition – most of the age-related variance (over 90% in most cases) was accounted for by working memory capacity. It should be noted, once again, that there remained a non-negligible part of the total variance in the tasks which was not captured by age and working memory capacity. Thus, on average, 35% of the total variance in the Piagetian tasks on Year 2 (55% and 59% for Years 3 and 5, respectively) was left unexplained by age and working memory. This attests again, if necessary, that performance in these tasks does not depend only on age differences, but that individual differences play an important role (Rieben et al., 1990), as well as other, more specific processes. Nevertheless, age differences remained important and were accounted for by working memory capacity, while the reverse did not hold. Likewise, a large part of the age-related variance (more than 50%) in the Raven's Matrices was accounted for by working memory capacity, and by working memory capacity combined with Processing Speed. Interestingly, Study 4 further showed, like Studies 1 and 2, that age differences in adulthood are driven by processes similar to those underlying age differences in childhood; however, Inhibition appeared to play a slightly larger role in adulthood. Also, it pointed to the importance of Processing Speed in both age groups, in conformity with Salthouse's findings (Kail & Salthouse, 1994; Salthouse, 1996).

In conclusion, we would like to argue that our findings (and methodology) contribute to bridging several traditions in psychology. First, they are convergent with both neo-Piagetian and cognitive psychology models which suggest that limited attentional resources, such as those indexed by working memory capacity tasks, play an important role in cognition, although certainly not the only one. In addition, whether elaborated by developmental psychologists (e.g., the CSVI or the Peanut tasks), or by cognitive psychologists (e.g., the spatial and verbal Matrices task, or the Reading span task[12]), working memory capacity tasks appear to tap the same construct. This is of course rather trivial in as much as one analyzes the processes at work in a task, but it is unfortunately often the case that certain types of tasks are considered to be related, or even to be reserved to a given tradition in psychology. Moreover, Studies 1 and 2 showed that working memory capacity tasks appear to be partly driven, at least as concerns age differences, by general constructs such as Processing Speed and Inhibition. That is, they do not index a specific cognitive system, but share processes with other cognitive tasks. Let us remind the reader that Baddeley himself (Baddeley, 1993) suggested that "working memory" could be considered analogous with "working attention" or that Moscovitch (1992) proposed to relabel "working memory" as "working with memory." Finally, Study 3 showed that age and individual differences in Piagetian tasks can be accounted for by working memory capacity, just as other cognitive tasks. We suggested elsewhere (de Ribaupierre & Lecerf, 2006) that Piagetian tasks are similar to fluid intelligence tasks. If Processing Speed tasks and/or Inhibition tasks had been used in that longitudinal study, there is little doubt for us that they would have behaved like they did in Studies 1 and 2; that is, they would have accounted for a large part of the age differences in the CSVI and in the Peanut tasks, the latter accounting in turn for age differences in the Piagetian tasks. This remains to be established empirically.

Notes

This paper is based on research made possible by several grants from the Fonds National Suisse de la Recherche Scientifique from 1997 to 2004.

1 It is very difficult, if not impossible, to empirically distinguish between inhibition and sensitivity to interference (see de Ribaupierre, Borella, & Delaloye, 2003); nevertheless, the term "inhibition" will systematically be used in the present chapter.
2 Geneva lifespan study (1995–1997) financed by the Fonds National Suisse de la Recherche Scientifique (Grant No 114-040465.94).
3 The tasks will be only very briefly presented: For more information, see the website: http://www.unige.ch/fapse/psychodiff/index.html.
4 Two other tasks, a Stroop-Position task and a Negative priming task (Tipper, 1985), were also administered. However, they were not used in the present analyses because they could not be used in the structural models presented below as they did not correlate with the other tasks supposed to measure inhibition.
5 The equivalence of the two subgroups of young adults on all tasks, including control tasks, was verified.
6 Geneva dimensionality of inhibition study (1997–2004) financed by the Fonds National Suisse de la Recherche Scientifique (Grants No 1114-52565.97 and 1213-065020.01).
7 The tasks will be briefly presented; for more information see the website: http://www.unige.ch/fapse/psychodiff/index.html.
8 It is actually the same, canonical, Stroop-Color task as in Study 1. However, in order to clearly differentiate this version of the task from the Dissociated-Stroop task which is also used in this study, we will refer to the Stroop-Color task as the "Integrated-Stroop task" here.
9 This method has been criticized by Lindenberger and Pötter (1998) because it presents risks of over interpretation when the mediator and the dependent variable are correlated. Results should therefore be considered with caution as regards exact values, but nevertheless point to the very important part of variance in cognitive performance accounted for by the working memory capacity tasks.

10 The Lines Foldings was used on Year 1, 2, and 3 of the longitudinal study, but not on Year 5, because of ceiling effects.
11 As in Study 3, it was judged preferable to enter tasks belonging to a same set as a "package" rather than computing an average score; this allows for each task to retain its relative weight.
12 Note, however, that the Reading span task proposed by Daneman and Carpenter (1980) was initially developed to be very similar to Case's Counting span task (Case, Kurland, & Goldberg, 1982).

References

Ackerman, P. L., Beier, M. E., & Boyle, M. O. (2002). Individual differences in working memory within a nomological network of cognitive and perceptual speed abilities. *Journal of Experimental Psychology: General, 131(4)*, 567–589.
Baddeley, A. D. (1986). *Working memory*. Oxford: Oxford University Press.
Baddeley, A. (1993). Working memory or working attention? In A. Baddeley & L. Weiskrantz (Eds.), *Attention: Selection, awareness, and control. A tribute to Donald Broadbent* (pp. 152–170). Oxford: Clarendon Press.
Baltes, P. B., Staudinger, U. M., & Lindenberger, U. (1999). Lifespan psychology: Theory and application to intellectual functioning. *Annual Review of Psychology, 50*, 471–507.
Bjork, R. A. (1989). Retrieval inhibition as an adaptative mechanism in human memory. In F. I. M. Craik (Ed.), *Varieties of memory and consciousness* (pp. 309–330). Hillsdale, NJ: Erlbaum.
Bjorklund, D. F., & Harnishfeger, K. K. (1990). The resources construct in cognitive development: Diverse sources of evidence and a theory of inefficient inhibition. *Developmental Review, 10*, 48–71.
Borella, E., Delaloye, C., Lecerf, T., Renaud, O., & de Ribaupierre, A. (2009). Do age differences between young and older adults in inhibitory tasks depend on the degree of activation of information? *European Journal of Cognitive Psychology, 21(2–3)*, 445–472.
Brickenkamp, R. (1998). *D2: test d'attention concentrée: manuel*. Paris: ECPA.
Burgess, P. W., & Shallice, T. (1996). Response suppression, initiation and strategy use following frontal lobe lesions. *Neuropsychologia, 34(4)*, 263–273.
Case, R. (1985). *Intellectual development. Birth to adulthood*. New York: Academic Press.
Case, R., Kurland, D. M., & Goldberg, J. (1982). Operational efficiency and the growth of short-term memory span. *Journal of Experimental Child Psychology, 33*, 386–404.
Chapman, M. (1990). Cognitive development and the growth of capacity: Issues in neo-Piagetian theory. In J. T. Enns (Ed.), *The development of attention: Research and theory* (pp. 263–287). Amsterdam: Elsevier Science Publishers.
Cohen, J., & Cohen, P. (1983). *Applied multiple regression/correlation for the behavioral sciences* (2nd ed.). Hillsdale, NJ: Lawrence Erlbaum Associates.
Cowan, N. (1995). *Attention and memory: An integrated framework*. New York: Oxford University Press.
Daneman, M., & Carpenter, P. A. (1980). Individual differences in working memory and reading. *Journal of Verbal Learning and Verbal Behavior, 19*, 450–466.
Dasen, P. R., & de Ribaupierre, A. (1987). Neo-Piagetian theories: Cross-cultural and differential perspectives. *International Journal of Psychology, 22*, 793–832.

de Beni, R., & Palladino, P. (2000). Intrusion errors in working memory tasks: Are they related to reading comprehension ability? *Learning and Individual Differences*, *12*, 131–143.

de Beni, R., & Palladino, P. (2004). Decline in working memory updating through ageing: Intrusion error analyses. *Memory*, *12*, 75–89.

de Beni, R., Palladino, P., Pazzaglia, F., & Cornoldi, C. (1998). Increases in intrusion errors and working memory deficit of poor comprehenders. *Quarterly Journal of Experimental Psychology*, *51A*, 305–320.

de Ribaupierre, A. (1975). *Mental space and formal operations*. Unpublished doctoral dissertation, University of Toronto, Canada.

de Ribaupierre, A. (1993). Structural and individual differences: On the difficulty of dissociating developmental and differential processes. In R. Case & W. Edelstein (Eds.), *The new structuralism in cognitive development: Theory and research on individual pathways* (pp. 11–32). Basel: Karger.

de Ribaupierre, A. (2000). Working memory and attentional control. In W. J. P. A. Grob (Ed.), *Control of human behavior, mental processes, and consciousness: Essays in honor of the 60th birthday of August Flammer* (pp. 147–164). Mahwah, NJ: Lawrence Erlbaum Associates.

de Ribaupierre, A. (2001). Working memory and attentional processes across the lifespan. In P. G. N. Otha (Ed.), *Lifespan development of human memory* (pp. 59–80). Cambridge, MA: MIT Press.

de Ribaupierre, A. (2007). Modèles néo-piagétiens du développement cognitif et perspective psychométrique de l'intelligence: y a-t-il convergence? *L'Année Psychologique*, *107*, 257–302.

de Ribaupierre, A., & Bailleux, C. (1994). Developmental change in a spatial task of attentional capacity: An essay toward an integration of two working memory models. *International Journal of Behavioral Development*, *17(1)*, 5–35.

de Ribaupierre, A., & Bailleux, C. (1995). Development of attentional capacity in childhood: A longitudinal study. In F. E. Weinert & W. Schneider (Eds.), *Memory performance and competencies: Issues in growth and development* (pp. 45–70). Mahwah, NJ: Lawrence Erlbaum.

de Ribaupierre, A., & Bailleux, C. (2000). The development of working memory: Further note on the comparability of two models of working memory. *Journal of Experimental Child Psychology*, *77(2)*, 110–127.

de Ribaupierre, A., Borella, E., & Delaloye, C. (2003). Inhibition et variabilité individuelle: généralité ou spécificité des processus inhibiteurs. In S. Moutier (Ed.), *Inhibition neurale et cognitive (Traité des sciences cognitives)* (pp. 103–124). Paris: Lavoisier.

de Ribaupierre, A., & Lecerf, T. (2006). Relationships between working memory and intelligence from a developmental perspective: Convergent evidence from a neo-Piagetian and a psychometric approach. *European Journal of Cognitive Psychology*, *18(1)*, 109–137.

de Ribaupierre, A., Lecerf, T., & Bailleux, C. (2000). Is encoding a non verbal task necessarily non verbal? *Cahiers de Psychologie Cognitive/Current Psychology of Cognition*, *19(2)*, 135–170.

de Ribaupierre, A., Neirynck, I., & Spira, A. (1989). Interactions between basic capacity and strategies in children's memory: Construction of a developmental paradigm. *Cahiers de Psychologie Cognitive/Current Psychology of Cognition*, *9*, 471–504.

de Ribaupierre, A., & Pascual-Leone, J. (1984). Pour une intégration des méthodes en psychologie: approches expérimentale, psycho-génétique et différentielle. [Towards an integration of approaches in psychology: Experimental, developmental and differential.] *L'Année Psychologique, 84(2)*, 227–250.

Engle, R. W., Kane, M. J., & Tuholski, S. W. (1999). Individual differences in working memory capacity and what they tell us about controlled attention, general fluid intelligence, and functions of the prefrontal cortex. In A. Miyake & P. Shah (Eds.), *Models of working memory: Mechanisms of active maintenance and executive control* (pp. 102–134). New York: Cambridge University Press.

Engle, R. W., Tuholski, S. W., Laughlin, J. E., & Conway, A. R. A. (1999). Working memory, short-term memory, and general fluid intelligence: A latent-variable approach. *Journal of Experimental Psychology: General, 128(3)*, 309–331.

Fry, A. F., & Hale, S. (1996). Processing speed, Working memory, and fluid intelligence: evidence for a developmental cascade. *Psychological Science, 7*, 237–241.

Harnishfeger, K. K., & Pope, R. S. (1996). Intending to forget: the development of cognitive inhibition in directed forgetting. *Journal of Experimental Child Psychology, 62(2)*, 292–315.

Hasher, L., & Zacks, R. T. (1988). Working memory, comprehension, and aging: a review and a new view. In G. M. Bower (Ed.), *The psychology of learning and motivation. Advances in research and theory* (Vol. 22). New York: Academic Press, Inc.

Inhelder, B., & Piaget, J. (1955). *De la logique de l'enfant à la logique de l'adolescent: essai sur la construction des structures opératoires formelles.* Paris: Presses Universitaires de France.

Jensen, A. R. (1998). *The g factor: The science of mental ability.* New York: Praeger.

Kail, R., & Salthouse, T. A. (1994). Processing speed as a mental capacity. *Acta Psychologica, 86*, 199–225.

Kramer, A. F., Humphrey, D. G., Larish, J. F., Logan, G. D., & Strayer, D. L. (1994). Aging and inhibition: Beyond a unitary view of inhibitory processing in attention. *Psychology and Aging, 9(4)*, 491–512.

Lautrey, J. (1990). Esquisse d'un modèle pluraliste du développement cognitif. In M. Reuchlin, J. Lautrey, C. Marendaz, & T. Ohlmann (Eds.), *Cognition: l'universel et l'individuel* (pp. 185–216). Paris: Presses Universitaires de France.

Lecerf, T., & de Ribaupierre, A. (2005). Recognition in a visuospatial memory task: The effect of presentation. *European Journal of Cognitive Psychology, 17(1)*, 47–75.

Lindenberger, U., & Pötter, U. (1998). The complex nature of unique and shared effects in hierarchical linear regression: Consequences for cross-sectional developmental research. *Psychological Methods, 3(2)*, 218–230.

Loisy, C., & Roulin, J.-L. (1992). *Multiple short-term storage in working memory: A new experimental approach.* Paper presented at the Fifth Conference of the European Society for Cognitive Psychology.

Moscovitch, M. (1992). Memory and working-with-memory: A component process model based on modules and central systems. *Journal of Cognitive Neuroscience, 4*, 257–267.

Palladino, P., Mammarella, N., & Vecchi, T. (2003). Modality-specific effects in inhibitory mechanisms: The interaction of peripheral and central components in working memory. *Brain and Cognition, 53(2)*, 263–267.

Pascual-Leone, J. (1969). *Cognitive development and cognitive style: A general Psychological integration.* University of Geneva, Switzerland.

Pascual-Leone, J. (1970). A mathematical model for the transition rule in Piaget's developmental stages. *Acta Psychologica, 32,* 301–345.

Pascual-Leone, J. (1987). Organismic processes for neo-piagetian theories: A dialectical causal account of cognitive development. *International Journal of Psychology, 22,* 531–570.

Pedhazur, E. J. (1997). *Multiple regression in behavioural research. Explanation and prediction* (3rd ed.). Harbor Drive: Harcourt Brace College Publishers.

Piaget, J., & Inhelder, B. (1966). *L'image mentale chez l'enfant.* Paris: Presses Universitaires de France.

Piaget, J., Inhelder, B., & Szeminska, A. (1948). *La géométrie spontanée chez l'enfant.* Paris: Presses Universitaires de France.

Raven, J. C (1938). *Standard progressive matrices* (revision 1956). Editions Scientifiques et Psychotechniques. Issy-les-Moulineaux, France.

Reuchlin, M. (1978). Processus vicariants et différences individuelles. *Journal de Psychologie, 2,* 133–145.

Richardson, J. T. E. (1996). Evolving issues in working memory. In J. T. E. Richardson, R. W. Engle, L. Hasher, R. H. Logie, E. R. Stoltzfus, & R. T. Zacks (Eds.), *Working memory and human cognition* (pp. 120–154). Oxford: Oxford University Press.

Rieben, L., de Ribaupierre, A., & Lautrey, J. (1983). *Le développement opératoire de l'enfant entre 6 et 12 ans. Elaboration d'un instrument d'évaluation.* Paris: Editions du CNRS.

Rieben, L., de Ribaupierre, A., & Lautrey, J. (1990). Structural invariants and individual modes of processing: On the necessity of a minimally structuralist approach of development for education. *Archives de Psychologie, 58,* 29–53.

Robert, C., Borella, E., Fagot, D., Lecerf, T., & de Ribaupierre, A. (2009). Working memory and inhibitory control across the life span: Analyses of intrusion errors in the reading span task. *Memory and Cognition, 37,* 336–345.

Salthouse, T. A. (1992a). Working-memory mediation of adult age differences in integrative reasoning. Special Issue: Memory and cognition applied. *Memory and Cognition, 20(4),* 413–423.

Salthouse, T. A. (1992b). *Mechanisms of age-cognition relations in adulthood.* Hillsdale, NJ: Lawrence Erlbaum Associates.

Salthouse, T. A. (1996). The processing-speed theory of adult age differences in cognition. *Psychological Review, 103(3),* 403–428.

Salthouse, T. A., & Meinz, E. J. (1995). Aging, inhibition, working memory, and speed. *Journals of Gerontology Series B Psychological Sciences and Social Sciences, 50b(6),* 297–306.

Schaie, K. W., & Hertzog, C. (1986). Toward a comprehensive model of adult intellectual development: Contributions of the Seattle longitudinal study. In R.J. Sternberg (Ed.), *Advances in the psychology of human intelligence* (Vol. 3, pp. 79–118). Hillsdale, NJ: Erlbaum.

Schaie, K. W., Maitland, S. B., Willis, S. L., & Intrieri, R. C. (1998). Longitudinal invariance of adults psychometric ability factor structures across 7 years. *Psychology and Aging, 13(1),* 8–20.

Shilling, V. M., Chetwynd, A., & Rabbitt, P. M. A. (2002). Individual inconsistency across measures of inhibition: An investigation of the construct validity of inhibition in older adults. *Neuropsychologia, 40(6),* 605–619.

Siegler, R. S. (1981). Developmental concepts within and between sequences. *Monographs of the Society for Research in Child Development, 46*, 6.

Stroop, J. R. (1935). Studies of interference in serial verbal reactions. *Journal of Experimental Psychology: General, 18*, 643–662.

Süß, H. M., Oberauer, K., Wittman, W. W., Wilhelm, O., & Schulze, R. (2002). Working-memory capacity explains reasoning ability – and a little bit more. *Intelligence, 30*, 261–288.

Thomas, L., Pons, F., & de Ribaupierre, A. (1996). Attentional capacity and cognitive level in the balance task. *Cahiers de Psychologie Cognitive/Current Psychology of Cognition, 15*, 137–172.

Tipper, S. P. (1985). The negative priming effect: Inhibitory priming by ignored objects. *Quarterly Journal of Experimental Psychology, 37A*, 571–590.

Wechsler, D. (1981). *Manual for the Wechsler Adult Intelligence Scale-Revised.* New York: The Psychological Corporation.

Woodcock, R. W., & Johnson, M. B. (1989). *Woodcock-Johnson psycho-educational battery-Revised*: Allen, TX: DLM Teaching Resources.

Zacks, R. T., Radvansky, G., & Hasher, L. (1996). Studies of directed forgetting in older adults. *Journal of Experimental Psychology. Learning, Memory, and Cognition, 22(1)*, 143–156.

Part II

Underlying processes of working memory development

6 New insights into an old problem
Distinguishing storage from processing in the development of working memory

Nelson Cowan, Candice C. Morey,
Angela M. AuBuchon, Christopher
E. Zwilling, Amanda L. Gilchrist,
and J. Scott Saults

Working memory (Baddeley & Hitch, 1974; Miller, Galanter, & Pribram, 1960) is the small amount of information held in mind at any time. It is often critical for the successful completion of cognitive tasks including language comprehension, reasoning, and problem-solving. In this chapter, we will briefly review the neo-Piagetian approach to cognition and describe some research advancing our understanding of a basic principle within that approach, the coordination of working memory storage and processing. Many researchers have remained skeptical of the neo-Piagetian conclusion that the basic storage capacity of working memory increases during childhood (e.g., Pascual-Leone, 1970). New research confirms that working memory matures not only because processing capabilities improve, but also because storage capacity increases.

Neo-Piagetian approaches to the development of cognition and working memory

One of the most basic questions about cognitive development is the nature of the tremendous increase in the intellectual capabilities of a human being during maturation from infancy to early adulthood. This question fascinated Jean Piaget, as one can observe and even emotionally feel in the wonderful, self-narrated film, *Piaget on Piaget* (Van Effenterre & Graham, 1977). Piaget was astonished by the growth of the child and deeply probed the basis of that growth, influencing developmental psychology profoundly. Nevertheless, no scientific enterprise starts within an individual or ends with that individual. At various points in his life, Piaget freely acknowledged various influences on his thinking, such as Alfred Binet, for whom he helped developed psychometric tests, and James Mark Baldwin, who wrote on evolutionary and developmental stages.

After Piaget, the question of the nature of intellectual development was approached at a more fine-grained level of analysis. Piaget had noticed increasing access to logic as the child matured. Age-related progressions in logical structures were shown to underlie maturation in the fundamental qualities of thought and behavior. Pre-operational children display a somewhat magical quality of thought, which tends to become rigidly logical in the concrete operational stage at age 7 or so, and later become more flexible and hypothetical around adolescence with the onset of a formal operational stage of thought. Discovering that progression, though, need not be the end of the investigation. Like a young child relentlessly asking "why," one can ask what it is that causes an improvement in the structure of logical thinking, and what drives that change. In doing so, the level of analysis becomes more fine-grained.

What is called neo-Piagetian thought can be viewed as a merger of Piaget's approach with other aspects of the cognitive science revolution. The latter is sometimes said to have begun in 1956 at a conference that allowed the exchange of ideas about mental structure between various disciplines including psychology, linguistics, and computer science (Gardner, 1985). Researchers at that time could begin to see that a computer has a limited speed of computation directly related to how much memory is available to carry out operations and how efficiently the central processor operates. Theoretical work suggested that neural activity operates in an all-or-none manner, like computer memory locations (McCulloch & Pitts, 1943), and helped inspire computer programs simulating complex human problem-solving (Newell & Simon, 1956). Miller (1956) focused on the limitations of humans viewed as information transmission devices, but with a unique human strength in grouping information in a meaningful way to improve memory and communication. Broadbent (1958) sketched out a model of human information processing in which a flood of sensory information gave rise to temporary, conscious memories at a limited rate and then a permanent memorial record of these events in the brain. This intellectual climate must have influenced the neo-Piagetian researchers, including Juan Pascual-Leone (1970; Pascual-Leone & Smith, 1969), who tried to analyze the maturation of complex thought into the underlying growth of basic processes including immediate memory, attention, and strategizing.

In Pascual-Leone's (1970) theoretical approach, a child's central computing ability is equal to $M=a+k$, where a is the ability to hold the task instructions and understand the task demands. If the task is developmentally appropriate, a is constant across age groups. The value k grows with age and the total M is the number of meaningful items or chunks (in the terminology of Miller, 1956) that the child can hold in mind. This total includes both processing and storage. Pascual-Leone explained developmental improvement in cognitive tasks by a developmental increase in M. In the terms of cognitive psychology, that suggestion amounts to a developmental increase in working memory storage capacity.

An increase in M is, however, theoretically not the only way to explain developmental increases in performance on working memory tasks. Another way is to assume only that the processing becomes more efficient and takes up less capacity, which leaves more capacity free to store data. This theoretically could occur with no developmental change in storage capacity. That alternative hypothesis was most famously adopted by Robbie Case, though only during the central part of his career. In his published report based on his dissertation, Case (1972) supported Pascual-Leone's theory. He came from that tradition and his acknowledgements included his "chairman, Carl Bereiter, and committee members, Glen Evans and Juan Pascual-Leone." Later on, though, Case, Kurland, and Goldberg (1982) provided formidable evidence favoring the processing efficiency or "operational efficiency" interpretation. Still later, he had second (or third) thoughts about whether efficiency was enough of an explanation without developmental increases in capacity (Case, 1995).

In their first experiment, Case et al. (1982) measured memory span for lists of words in children 3 to 6 years old, and they also measured operational efficiency. The latter was measured by the average speed with which spoken, tape-recorded words could be repeated into a microphone connected to a voice key and timer. The correlation between reaction time and span was an impressive –.74, and within an age group it was still significant at –.35. In a second experiment, adults were tested with nonsense syllables, which caused their operational efficiency to be diminished to a level equivalent to that of the children with real words. The result was adults' memory span was reduced accordingly. Experiments 3 and 4 followed the same logic using what was called a counting span task, in which each test trial involved series of arrays to be counted and then recall of the series of final counts (in Experiment 4, adults had to use newly-learned nonsense words to count and recall). The results were very similar to the first two experiments. The conclusion was that the operational efficiency increases with age and explains the ordinary increase in working memory span performance with age.

Although these data are strong, they are primarily correlational, not causal. Moreover, even the strongest correlation only accounts for about half the variance. The other half could be random error, or it could be due to a developmental increase in storage capacity. Distinguishing between theoretical accounts may make a big difference in practical terms. To the extent that storage capacity increases with age, educational materials must be developmentally appropriate and the introduction of certain concepts must await the necessary development of storage capacity. To the extent that operational efficiency increases with age, though, it may be that educational efforts could go toward practice that may improve the efficiency.

This debate among neo-Piagetians is still echoed among current researchers of adult individual differences in working memory. Several theorists have advanced the notion that differences in working memory task performance occur because individuals with low spans operate inefficiently and, in particular, that they do not maintain the goal of the task in the face of interference or incorrect but attractive response possibilities; and that low spans' working memories are cluttered by irrelevant information (Engle, 2002; Hasher, Stolzfus, Zacks, & Rypma, 1991; Kane et al., 2007; May, Hasher, &

Kane, 1999; McNab & Klingberg, 2008; Rosen & Engle, 1998; Vogel, McCollough, & Machizawa, 2005).

A recent developmental theory of working memory span starting from a neo-Piagetian approach is that of Barrouillet et al. (2009). Memory representations were said to decay unless they are refreshed through a rehearsal process. The speed with which refreshing takes place increases with age and was said to account to a large degree for developmental improvements in working memory. Yet, in Barrouillet's article the possibility that storage capacity could increase was not negated. Both storage and refreshment of items were said to benefit from a developmental increase in attentional capacity, and the detailed relation between storage and refreshment was left for future work.

The emphasis on operational efficiency is certainly understandable given the limitations of the available research methodology. It is not hard to show that a change in working memory task demands affects the number of items recalled. It is much more difficult to use performance on a working memory task somehow to estimate how much of that performance depends on information storage, or to measure that information storage. One problem in measuring storage can be traced back to the seminal work of Miller (1956). He showed that adults could recall lists of about seven items no matter whether the items were words, numbers, letters, or other well-known units or chunks. He also showed, however, that items could be combined to form new chunks. One example is the combination of the letters *U, S,* and *A* to form the single acronym standing for the United States of America. What he seems to have overlooked is the possibility that the limit of seven items itself results from some amount of on-line chunking; the digits in a seven-digit phone number might be combined into two or three smaller groups that can be memorized. Based on situations in which on-line chunking and verbal rehearsal cannot take place, other researchers have placed the fundamental capacity limit at only 3 or 4 items (Broadbent, 1975; Cowan, 2001). In general, it is quite difficult to be certain of how many chunks are formed from the materials presented for recall. Therefore, it is difficult to measure working memory storage capacity.

Another aspect of the uncertainty in measuring capacity is that one has to make assumptions about the operating schemes that are necessary to carry out the task. Pascual-Leone (2001) assumes that one can analyze the task demands and come up with a non-negligible amount of working memory storage capacity that is involved in just about any cognitive task. Cowan (2001), on the other hand, assumed that tasks that are fairly simple and are repeated for many trials become automatic (Shiffrin, 1988) and thereafter do not use appreciable capacity. Another issue is that it is not clear whether the correct count of what is stored in working memory involves the number of items or the complexity of associations between features within the items (Halford, Cowan, & Andrews, 2007), or between items and the context in which they appear.

It is with these difficulties in mind that one should evaluate the recent advances in understanding working memory development that we will describe. We include two recent studies of the development of capacity and one study of the development of operating efficiency.

Recent studies of the development of storage capacity

As we mentioned above, a lot of recent work on adults suggests that individuals with low working memory span are unable to keep irrelevant items out of working memory (e.g., Vogel et al., 2005). There is one study, though, indicating that this factor may not be as pervasive as one might think. Gold et al. (2006) examined the visual working memory performance of normal individuals and those with schizophrenia in a task in which the stimuli to be remembered were mixed with stimuli to be ignored. In one experiment, for example, participants were instructed to attend to the orientations of red bars and ignore green bars. Usually they were tested on the stimuli that they were supposed to attend to but, occasionally, they were tested on the stimuli that they were supposed to ignore. The data for each trial type were scored according to a formula that yields an estimate of the number of items in working memory (Cowan, 2001; Cowan et al., 2005, Appendix A). The Gold et al. study yielded two types of evidence: (1) The total number of items in working memory could be estimated from the *sum* of estimates for the attended and ignored items and (2) The tendency to attend to the assigned stimuli and ignore the other stimuli could be estimated from the *difference* between estimates for the attended and ignored items; far more items should be recalled from the attended set. Contrary to what most researchers would have expected, the main difference between individuals with versus without schizophrenia was not in the ability to ignore irrelevant stimuli, but in the total number of items in working memory. The groups differed mostly in the sum of estimates, with comparable slopes across the attended versus ignored stimuli.

We (Cowan, Morey, AuBuchon, Zwilling, & Gilchrist, 2010) adapted this procedure of Gold et al. to the study of developmental differences, using children 7–8 and 12–13 years old (who were in first and sixth grades, respectively) and college students. Our basic procedure is illustrated in Figure 6.1. To make the task fun for children, the colored shapes within a briefly flashed array were to be interpreted as "children" sitting in "seats" (the small squares) within a "classroom" (the array). The array was followed by a probe and the participant was to click on the spot where the probed shape belonged within the array; in the example shown, the shape belonged in a different location. On some trials, the probe shape was identical in shape and color to the item that had been at that spot in the array, and the correct answer was to click on the spot where the probe was shown. On other trials, the probe was not the same as any item in the array and the correct answer was to click the door to the right. In the cover story for that event, the "child" in the probe display did

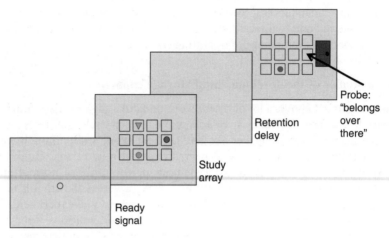

Probe:
"belongs
over
there"

Retention
delay

Study
array

Ready
signal

Instructions: When the probe object appears, mouse
click the location where it belongs.

Figure 6.1 Illustration of a trial in the procedure used by Cowan et al. (redrawn from
2010, *Developmental Science*). See text for further explanation.

not belong in the classroom and was to be sent to the principal. This procedure yielded a rich set of error types but, to allow our main analysis in which
capacity estimates were needed, we simplified the responses to indicate the
proportions of correct detection of a change when one had occurred (hits)
and incorrect detection of a change when none had occurred (false alarms).

The capacity estimate (Cowan, 2001) is based on the assumption that if the
item at the probed array location is in working memory, the participant will
know whether it has changed or not. If the item at the probed array location
is not in working memory, the participant will guess that it has changed with
some probability. This yields the equation for the number of items in working
memory, $k=S[p(hits)-p(fa)]$, where S is the array size, $p(hits)$ is the proportion of hits out of all change trials, and $p(fa)$ is the proportion of false
alarms out of all no-change trials.

After Gold et al. (2006), Cowan et al. (2010) varied the need for attention
to one shape or another between blocks of trials. In *1-set* trial blocks there
was only one shape. In *100%* trial blocks, there were two shapes but the participant was always tested with a probe location corresponding to an item in
the array in the shape that the participant had been instructed to attend to
during the trial block. In *80%–20%* trial blocks the instructions were the
same, but on 20% of the trials the tested location corresponded to an item of
the shape that the participant had been instructed to ignore during that trial
block. Finally, in *50%–50%* trial blocks, attention was to be divided between
the shapes and each one was tested on half the trials. These trial blocks

allowed capacity estimates for five trial types. Arranged from highest to lowest attention, they are *1-set, 100%, 80%, 50%*, and *20%* conditions.

There were several different set sizes but the results were clearest when there were only 2 items in the tested shape; except for the 1-set condition, these trials also included 2 items in the other shape as well. Figure 6.2 shows the results for that number of items. It is clear that all of the age groups showed a decline in capacity as the amount of attention dedicated to the tested shape declined; moreover, there was no difference between the slopes of these functions. This suggests that age did not improve the ability to focus on the relevant items and filter out the less-relevant items. What did change with age is that the total number of items recalled increased dramatically between the younger and older children. This suggests that there was a basic capacity increase during that age transition between first and sixth grades.

When there were 3 items in the tested shape and 3 in the untested shape, the results were a bit different. Then there appeared to be better filtering in the older children and adults than in the younger children, in addition to the marked increase in capacity between the younger and older children. Cowan et al. (2010) speculated that the age-related increase in basic

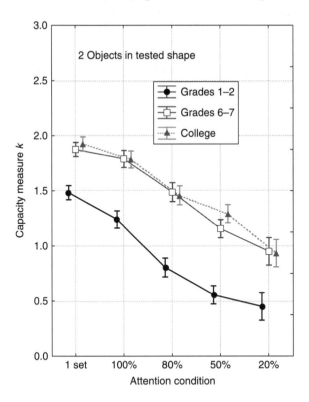

Figure 6.2 Some of the results of a visual array experiment with distracting items, Cowan et al. (redrawn from 2010, *Developmental Science*).

capacity tends to affect filtering ability. When capacity is sufficient, filtering is adequate, just as one might expect on the basis of the analysis by Pascual-Leone (1970).

A very different investigation of the development of working memory capacity was undertaken by Gilchrist, Cowan, and Naveh-Benjamin (2009), using sentence stimuli (cf. Allen & Baddeley, 2009; Tulving & Patkau, 1962). Instead of just providing items with a theoretically-based analysis of how they are combined into chunks (cf. Burtis, 1982; Pascual-Leone, 1970), Gilchrist et al. were able to measure the cohesion of the chunk. On every trial, a list of spoken and digitally-recorded sentences was presented. The list could include (1) 4 short, unrelated sentences, such as "*Thieves took the painting; Our neighbor sells vegetables . . .*" and so on; (2) 8 short, unrelated sentences; (3) 4 long sentences, each composed of two clauses, such as "*Our neighbor sells vegetables but he also makes fruit juice,*" again with no relation between the 4 sentences; or (4) 4 random pseudo-sentences, such as "*a close football your cheese,*" with each pseudo-sentence presented in its own sentence-like intonation and no relation between them. The materials presented as long sentences for some participants were broken into short sentences and random pseudo-sentences for other participants, and vice versa; nobody received the same materials in more than one condition and the assignment of materials to conditions was balanced across participants. Notice that there was a match between the phonological length of Conditions 2 and 3, and between Conditions 1 and 4, whereas the number of independent chunks in the stimuli differed between the conditions within these pairs.

Gilchrist et al. expected that each short sentence should tend to provide a cohesive unit, given that the vocabulary and sentence structure were within the abilities of even the youngest participants. Each long sentence might also provide a cohesive unit, but perhaps not inasmuch as the relation between the two clauses within the sentence provided only a weak constraint.

A measure of how many clause units were held in working memory was taken as the number of clauses *accessed*, which was defined as the number of clauses for which at least one content word was recalled. In turn, a measure of the cohesiveness of the clause was the proportion of clause *completion*, which was defined as the proportion of words recalled within accessed clauses. For these analyses, each random pseudo-sentence spoken under a single intonation was considered a clause.

The results are shown in Figure 6.3. The top panel shows that, systematically across conditions, there was a developmental increase between first and sixth grade in the number of clauses accessed. The bottom panel shows, however, that there was no sign of an overall developmental increase in the completion of accessed clauses. The coherence of clauses was therefore just as good for young children as for older children or adults. We take this finding to indicate that, in this instance at least, the sizes of chunks in working memory were similar across age groups and the developmental effect was entirely in the developmental growth in the number of units held in working memory.

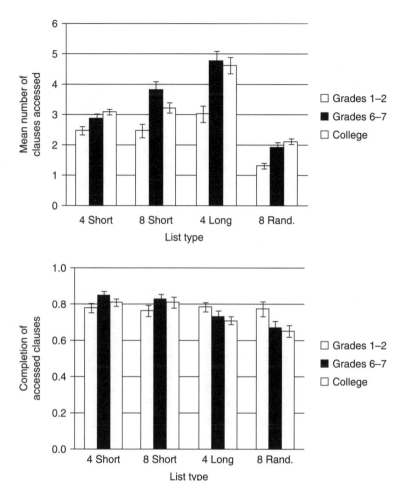

Figure 6.3 Results redrawn from Gilchrist, Cowan, and Naveh-Benjamin (2009). Top, clauses accessed; bottom, clause completion. See text for further explanation.

A recent study of the development of working memory strategies

It has been difficult to examine the growth of working memory storage capacity in a convincing manner, which is why we have highlighted our recent research on that topic. It would be unfortunate, though, if our research kept the pendulum swinging between storage capacity and operational efficiency as explanations for developmental growth when, in fact, there may now be sufficient evidence to conclude that both factors play important roles. Therefore, we conclude with a recent study in which we were able to pinpoint a developmental improvement in the use of strategies that result in more operational efficiency in older participants. It occurred within a test of the association between verbal and spatial materials (Cowan, Saults, & Morey, 2006), one example of the types of information that led Baddeley (2000) to propose the existence of an episodic buffer.

The procedure of Cowan et al. (2006) is illustrated in Figure 6.4. The participants were third- or sixth-grade children or college students; we deemed this procedure too difficult for first-graders, unlike the procedures to examine capacity explained above. On every trial, an array of 3 to 7 pentagons (representing houses) was presented, followed by names that appeared in the houses one at a time. Then a name was presented centrally and the task was to drag it to the house in which it had appeared. This was followed by task feedback.

We considered that participants actually could carry out the task in at least two different ways. First, as shown at the top of Figure 6.5, an associative strategy could be used. Each name could simply be associated with the location in which it appeared. This, of course, was the type of storage that we wanted to observe in the first place.

We had to consider, though, that it also would be possible for the task to be carried out with the parallel-codes strategy shown at the bottom of Figure 6.5. The participant could hold a verbal list of the names in the order they were presented, along with a spatial map of the house locations in the order they were used. Then, at the time of test, the participant would have to determine that it was the nth word that was presented so that the correct answer was the nth location on the spatial map. This strategy might be advantageous because it might require fewer attentional resources than the associative strategy inasmuch as verbal rehearsal of a list and spatial map retention both seem to be relatively effortless activities.

In order to distinguish between strategies, we therefore included two kinds of trials, always with exactly as many names as there were houses (3 to 7, depending on the trial). There were some trials (called *1-to-1* trials) in which

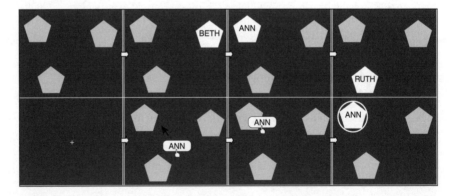

Figure 6.4 Illustration of the method of Cowan et al. (redrawn from 2006, *Journal of Memory and Language*). See text for further explanation.

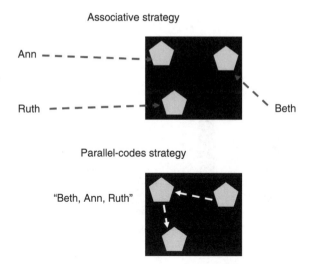

Associative strategy

Ann

Ruth

Beth

Parallel-codes strategy

"Beth, Ann, Ruth"

Figure 6.5 An illustration of two possible mnemonic strategies that could have been used by participants in Cowan et al. (redrawn from 2006, *Journal of Memory and Language*). See text for further explanation.

each house was used for exactly one name. There were other trials (called *uneven* trials) in which some houses were used for two names, not in immediate succession, and other houses were not used. In the latter kind of trial, the spatial map becomes convoluted, doubling back upon itself, which should make the parallel-codes strategy less useful. The uneven trials could be further divided into those in which the name being tested was the only one that appeared in a particular house and those in which the name being tested appeared in a house that was shared by one other name.

The proportions correct for each age group are shown in Figure 6.6. The right-hand cluster of bars represents a second group of college students who were required to recite the word *the, the, the* during the task to suppress rehearsal. The basic finding was that the pattern changed qualitatively during development. The third-grade children did better overall in the uneven condition than in the 1-to-1 condition, as would be expected on the basis of a predominant use of the associative strategy. In contrast, the college students did better overall in the 1-to-1 condition than in the uneven condition, as would be expected on the basis of a predominant use of the parallel-codes strategy. Moreover, rehearsal suppression made the college students' pattern change to look very similar to the third-grade children, except at a slightly higher level.

The theoretical interpretation was that young children tended to use the associative strategy, whereas college students tended to use the parallel-codes strategy that frees up some extra attention that can be used for mnemonic purposes. When the parallel-codes strategy was used, it was not as advantageous for the uneven condition as for the 1-to-1 condition. College students

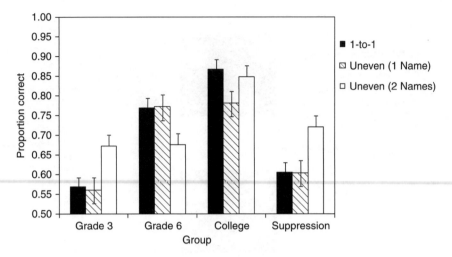

Figure 6.6 The results of a verbal-spatial association memory experiment, Cowan et al. (redrawn from 2006, *Journal of Memory and Language*).

under suppression, moreover, could not carry out the parallel-codes strategy. These data of Cowan et al. (2006), then, provide some striking support for the notion that adults sometimes can find strategies that improve their operational efficiency relative to children.

Concluding observations

Different theories of development have fallen in and out of favor over time. The Piagetian tradition is an especially rich one because of the highly logical, epistemological theoretical framework tying together various developmental findings. More recent scientific work has documented that children show signs of various intellectual skills earlier than Piaget might have expected them to and, as an unfortunate consequence, mainstream cognitive-developmental researchers do not seem to discuss the ideas of Piaget as much as they used to. They are still searching for an overarching theoretical framework to tie together various new findings.

Theoretical analyses that may be considered neo-Piagetian in spirit can play an important role in cognitive developmental psychology today (e.g., Andrews, Halford, Bunch, Bowden, & Jones, 2003; Johnson, Im-Bolter, & Pascual-Leone, 2003; Zelazo, 2004). The information processing framework has proven fruitful in the long run and will be important as a basis to understand new results. Behavioral research on working memory in adults already has guided investigations of genetics (Friedman et al., 2008) and brain imaging (Majerus et al., 2006; Todd & Marois, 2004) and the developmental research on working memory capacity may soon follow suit.

References

Allen, R. J., & Baddeley, A. D. (2009). Working memory and sentence recall. In A. Thorn & M. Page (Eds.), *Interactions between short-term and long-term memory in the verbal domain* (pp. 63–85). Hove, East Sussex, UK: Psychology Press.

Andrews, G., Halford, G. S., Bunch, K. M., Bowden, D., & Jones, T. (2003). Theory of mind and relational complexity. *Child Development, 74*, 1476–1499.

Baddeley, A. (2000). The episodic buffer: a new component of working memory? *Trends in Cognitive Sciences, 4*, 417–423.

Baddeley, A. D., & Hitch, G. (1974). Working memory. In G. H. Bower (Ed.), *The psychology of learning and motivation* (Vol. 8, pp. 47–89). New York: Academic Press.

Barrouillet, P., Gavens, N., Vergauwe, E., Gaillard, V., & Camos, V. (2009). Working memory span development: A time-based resource-sharing model account. *Developmental Psychology, 45*, 477–490.

Broadbent, D. E. (1958). *Perception and communication.* New York: Pergamon Press.

Broadbent, D. E. (1975). The magic number seven after fifteen years. In A. Kennedy & A. Wilkes (Eds.), *Studies in long-term memory* (pp. 3–18). Oxford: John Wiley & Sons.

Burtis, P. J. (1982). Capacity increase and chunking in the development of short-term memory. *Journal of Experimental Child Psychology, 34*, 387–413.

Case, R. (1972). Validation of a neo-Piagetian mental capacity construct. *Journal of Experimental Child Psychology, 14*, 287–302.

Case, R. (1995). Capacity-based explanations of working memory growth: A brief history and reevaluation. In F. E. Weinert & W. Schneider (Eds.), *Memory performance and competencies: Issues in growth and development* (pp. 23–44). Mahwah, NJ: Erlbaum.

Case, R., Kurland, D. M., & Goldberg, J. (1982). Operational efficiency and the growth of short-term memory span. *Journal of Experimental Child Psychology, 33*, 386–404.

Cowan, N. (2001). The magical number 4 in short-term memory: A reconsideration of mental storage capacity. *Behavioral and Brain Sciences, 24*, 87–185.

Cowan, N., Elliott, E. M., Saults, J. S., Morey, C. C., Mattox, S., Hismjatullina, A., et al. (2005). On the capacity of attention: Its estimation and its role in working memory and cognitive aptitudes. *Cognitive Psychology, 51*, 42–100.

Cowan, N., Morey, C. C., AuBuchon, A. M., Zwilling, C. E., & Gilchrist, A. L. (2010). Seven-year-olds allocate attention like adults unless working memory is overloaded. *Developmental Science, 13*, 120–133.

Cowan, N., Saults, J. S., & Morey, C. C. (2006). Development of working memory for verbal-spatial associations. *Journal of Memory and Language, 55*, 274–289.

Engle, R. W. (2002). Working memory capacity as executive attention. *Current Directions in Psychological Science, 11*, 19–23.

Friedman, N. P., Miyake, A., Young, S. E., DeFries, J. C., Corley, R.P., & Hewitt, J. K. (2008). Individual differences in executive functions are almost entirely genetic in origin. *Journal of Experimental Psychology: General, 137*, 201–225.

Gardner, H. (1985). *The mind's new science: A history of the cognitive revolution.* New York: Basic Books.

Gilchrist, A. L., Cowan, N., & Naveh-Benjamin, M. (2009). Investigating the childhood development of working memory using sentences: New evidence for the growth of chunk capacity. *Journal of Experimental Child Psychology, 104*, 252–265.

Gold, J. M., Fuller, R. L., Robinson, B. M., McMahon, R. P., Braun, E. L., & Luck, S. J. (2006). Intact attentional control of working memory encoding in schizophrenia. *Journal of Abnormal Psychology, 115*, 658–673.

Halford, G. S., Cowan, N., & Andrews, G. (2007). Separating cognitive capacity from knowledge: A new hypothesis. *Trends in Cognitive Sciences, 11,* 236–242.

Hasher, L., Stolzfus, E. R., Zacks, R. T., & Rypma, B. (1991). Age and inhibition. *Journal of Experimental Psychology: Learning, Memory, & Cognition, 17,* 163–169.

Johnson, J., Im-Bolter, N., & Pascual-Leone, J. (2003). Development of mental attention in gifted and mainstream children: The role of mental capacity, inhibition, and speed of processing. *Child Development, 74,* 1594–1614.

Kane, M. J., Brown, L. H., McVay, J. C., Silvia, P. J., Myin-Germeys, I., & Kwapil, T. R. (2007). For whom the mind wanders, and when: An experience-sampling study of working memory and executive control in daily life. *Psychological Science, 18,* 614–621.

Majerus, S., Poncelet, M., Van der Linden, M., Albouy, G., Salmon, E., Sterpenich, V., et al. (2006). The left intraparietal sulcus and verbal short-term memory: Focus of attention or serial order? *NeuroImage, 32,* 880–891.

May, C. P., Hasher, L., & Kane, M. J. (1999). The role of interference in memory span. *Memory & Cognition, 27,* 759–767.

McCulloch, W. S., & Pitts, W. (1943). A logical calculus of the ideas immanent in nervous activity. *Bulletin of Mathematical Biophysics, 5,* 115–133.

McNab, F., & Klingberg, T. (2008). Prefrontal cortex and basal ganglia control access to working memory. *Nature Neuroscience, 11,* 103–107.

Miller, G. A. (1956). The magical number seven, plus or minus two: Some limits on our capacity for processing information. *Psychological Review, 63,* 81–97.

Miller, G. A., Galanter, E, & Pribram, K. H. (1960). *Plans and the structure of behavior.* New York: Holt, Rinehart and Winston, Inc.

Newell, A., & Simon, H. A. (1956). The logic theory machine: A complex information processing system. *IRE Transactions on Information Theory, 2,* 61–79.

Pascual-Leone, J. A. (1970). Mathematical model for the transition rule in Piaget's developmental stages. *Acta Psychologica, 32,* 301–345.

Pascual-Leone, J. (2001). If the magical number is 4, how does one account for operations within working memory? *Behavioral and Brain Sciences, 24,* 136–138.

Pascual-Leone, J., & Smith, J. (1969). The encoding and decoding of symbols by children: A new experimental paradigm and a neo-Piagetian model. *Journal of Experimental Child Psychology, 8,* 328–355.

Rosen, V. M, & Engle, R. W. (1998). Working memory capacity and suppression. *Journal of Memory and Language, 39,* 418–436.

Shiffrin, R. M. (1988). Attention. In R. C. Atkinson, R. J. Herrnstein, G. Lindzey, & R. D. Luce (Eds.), *Stevens' handbook of experimental psychology* (Vol. 2, pp. 739–811). New York: Wiley.

Todd, J. J., & Marois, R. (2004). Capacity limit of visual short-term memory in human posterior parietal cortex. *Nature, 428,* 751–754.

Tulving, E., & Patkau, J. E. (1962). Concurrent effects of contextual constraint and word frequency on immediate recall and learning of verbal material. *Canadian Journal of Psychology, 16,* 83–95.

Van Effenterre, J. (director), & Graham, P. (writer) (1977). *Piaget on Piaget* (film). New Haven: Yale University Media Design Studio.

Vogel, E. K., McCollough, A. W., & Machizawa, M. G. (2005). Neural measures reveal individual differences in controlling access to working memory. *Nature, 438,* 500–503.

Zelazo, P. D. (2004). The development of conscious control in childhood. *Trends in Cognitive Sciences, 8,* 12–17.

7   Factors of working memory development

The Time-Based Resource-Sharing approach

Valérie Camos and Pierre Barrouillet

One of the main constraints of our cognitive functioning is the limited capacity of working memory. Because working memory is the system devoted to the active maintenance of information while processing is running, any limitation of its capacity has a direct impact on the amount of information that can be processed, and thus on the complexity of the situations we can deal with. As a consequence, it has often been argued that the poor performance frequently exhibited by young children in complex cognitive tasks resulted at least in part from a limited working memory capacity, whose age-related increase would constitute one of the main factors of cognitive development. This was one of the main assumptions of theories of cognitive development known as neo-Piagetian theories such as Pascual-Leone (1970), Case (1985, 1992), or Halford (1982, 1993). Even if, as it appeared in the first part of this book, these theories propose different accounts of the way cognitive resources increase with age, they all agree that there is an age-related increase in working memory capacity. Accordingly, it has repeatedly been shown that performance on complex span tasks designed to assess working memory capacity strongly increases with age (Case, Kurland, & Goldberg, 1982; Gathercole, Pickering, Ambridge, & Wearing, 2004) and is related to high-level cognitive performance and academic achievement in children and adolescents, lending strong support to the idea that working memory plays a major role in cognitive development. However, despite a great variety of empirical approaches and theoretical models of adults' working memory, and although an extensive body of research has been devoted to working memory in children, Towse, Hitch, and Horton (2007) noted in their recent survey of the literature that it is not easy to discern a developmental model of working memory. The aim of this chapter is not to provide such a model, but more modestly to suggest some factors that could account for working memory development, and as a consequence for cognitive development. In these last years, our developmental investigations were conducted within the theoretical framework provided by our Time-Based Resource-Sharing model (TBRS, Barrouillet, Bernardin, & Camos, 2004). Though this model was mainly developed and tested in adults, it was initially inspired by unanticipated developmental phenomena (Barrouillet & Camos, 2001). In the following, we shall present the TBRS model, the main factors that determine working memory capacity within this theoretical framework, and recent developmental studies that tested the impact of these factors on working memory development.

An overview of the Time-Based Resource-Sharing (TBRS) model

To account for complex span-related phenomena and more generally for working memory structure and functioning, we have recently proposed a new model of working memory named the Time-Based Resource-Sharing model (Barrouillet et al., 2004; Barrouillet & Camos, 2007). This model is based on four main proposals. First, the model assumes that in most working memory span tasks, both processing and maintenance of information within working memory rely on the same limited resource, which is attention. This is the case for complex activities such as reading sentences, counting dots, or solving arithmetic equations that are frequently used as processing components within traditional working memory span tasks. These activities involve the maintenance of goals, subgoals, and intermediary results, the frequent selection of relevant information and responses as well as retrievals from long-term memory, all of these processes requiring attention (Conway, Kane, & Engle, 2003; Engle, Kane, & Tuholski, 1999; Kane & Engle, 2003). This is also the case for simpler activities such as reading series of letters or digits, which requires attention to achieve activation of the relevant declarative knowledge from long-term memory (Anderson, 1993; Anderson & Lebiere, 1998; Logan, 1988). Moreover, we assume that not only processing but also maintenance of information requires attention because short-term memory is that part of long-term memory activated above threshold through attentional focusing (Anderson, 1993; Cantor & Engle, 1993; Cowan, 1995, 1999; Engle & Oransky, 1999; Lovett, Reder, & Lebière, 1999). Thus, both processing and maintenance require attention, which is assumed to be a limited resource that must consequently be shared. These limitations concern attention involved in voluntarily controlled processes, a kind of attention referred to as controlled attention by Engle et al. (1999), or as attention directed by the central executive in Cowan (1999).

The second assumption is that many of the elementary cognitive steps involved in both processing and maintenance can only take place one at a time. We assume that this constraint can be indifferently described as an attentional or a central processing limitation. In the former account, the focus of attention can only select one element of knowledge at a time as the object of the next cognitive operation (Garavan, 1998; Oberauer, 2002, 2005). In the latter, the central processes would be constrained by a central bottleneck applying to a variety of mental operations such as response selection or memory retrieval (Pashler, 1998). Thus, we consider the two theoretical proposals as functionally equivalent, referring either to the occupation of the central bottleneck or to the attentional capture as the same process. The main point is that when the focus of attention or the bottleneck that constrains central processes is occupied by some processing episode, it is not available for processes related to the maintenance of memory items.

The third assumption is that memory items on which attention focuses receive activation but, as soon as attention is switched away, this activation suffers from a time-related decay (Cowan, 1995, 1999; Towse & Hitch, 1995). As a consequence, in working memory span tasks, but also in current working memory functioning, the memory traces of items to be maintained fade away when attention is occupied by processing. The refreshment of these items before their complete disappearance leads to their reactivation or reconstruction. It is worth noting that this reactivation does not necessarily involve a rehearsal process as Baddeley described in his model of phonological loop (Baddeley, 1986; Baddeley & Logie, 1999). Rather, as demonstrated by Cowan in the field of recall activities (Cowan, 1992; Cowan et al., 1994), individuals can engage in a rapid and covert retrieval process through attentional focusing. It is assumed that this kind of refreshing can take place even during short pauses that might occur while concurrent processing is running. This mechanism is very akin to the one described in Johnson's (1992) model (Raye, Johnson, Mitchell, Greene & Johnson, 2007; Raye, Johnson, Mitchell, Reeder, & Greene, 2002).

The fourth assumption is that, due to the limitation of attention to only one element at a time and the time-related decay of memory traces outside the focus of attention, the sharing of attention is achieved through a rapid and incessant process of switching of this focus from processing to maintenance. This switching strongly differs from that hypothesized by Towse, Hitch, and Hutton (1998) who suggested a task switching reflecting the structure of the working memory span task, without any attempt to ensure the maintenance of memory items during processing. By contrast, the rapid switching we hypothesize would occur during processing. We assume that a given task, however demanding it is, rarely induces a continuous capture of attention. Rather, attention can be frequently diverted, even for short periods of time, towards other thoughts and brought back to the current activity. This continuous switching of attention must be considered as a basic mental process underlying our phenomenal experience of thinking and permitting the coherence and cohesion of our mental life beyond the succession of changing thoughts.

This conception of working memory delineates in turn a conception of cognitive load that departs from more traditional conceptions that conflate cognitive load with complexity. As we noted earlier, the processing components of traditional working memory span tasks involve complex activities such as reading sentences, counting dots among distractors, solving complex equations or reasoning. The rationale of these tasks is to be found within the theoretical framework of resource-sharing and the hypothesized trade-off between processing and storage (Case, 1985): Because complex activities are especially resource demanding, they conflict with the concurrent maintenance of the memory items. There is thus a clear difference between simple span measures assessing short-term memory capacity (e.g., the digit span or the word span), and complex span measures involving storage plus processing that assess working memory capacity (e.g., counting or reading spans). Within this framework, the more complex and demanding the processing component, the better and the more reliable the working memory task.

As far as we know, Towse and Hitch (1995) were among the first to cast doubt on this conception by suggesting that the detrimental effect of processing on maintenance was not due to the cognitive load it would involve but to its duration. However, these authors proposed a simple effect of time by assuming that there would be no active maintenance of stored items while the processing component of the task is performed (Towse, Hitch, & Hutton, 2002). In this case, memory traces would suffer from an uninterrupted decay during the phases devoted to processing, recall performance depending on their total duration. Short processing phases would thus reduce the delay between storage and recall, resulting in better recall performance and higher spans.

The Time-Based Resource-Sharing model departs from both previous conceptions. It assumes that the cognitive load involved in an activity depends neither on its complexity per se, nor on the total duration of the activity. Those tasks that frequently capture attention for prolonged periods of time would have a highly detrimental effect on concurrent maintenance of information because they prevent the possibility of refreshing decaying memory traces. We argue that they involve a high cognitive load, the cognitive load corresponding to the proportion of time during which these tasks capture attention, thus impeding concurrent activities that require central processes such as refreshing memory traces. Within this framework, the cognitive load (CL) would correspond to the following:

CL = Duration of attentional capture / Total time allowed

It is important to note that complex activities are not required to involve a high cognitive load, as we already surmised in our first study on working memory (Barrouillet & Camos, 2001). Simple activities such as reading digits can efficiently block attention for prolonged periods of time if they are performed under time constraints. This theory of cognitive load was tested by Barrouillet et al. (2004) using a working memory task named the reading digit span task in which participants have to maintain and recall series of letters of ascending length while reading digits. The stimuli are presented in successive screens displaying either a letter to be remembered or a digit to be read. After each letter to be remembered, some digits are presented in succession at a fixed pace. Both the number of digits presented after each letter and the total time allowed to read them (i.e., the inter-letter interval) can be varied (Figure 7.1).

According to the TBRS model, recall performance should be an inverse function of the cognitive load involved by the reading digit task. Indeed, cognitive load being the proportion of time during which the activity occupies attention, any increase in this proportion should decrease the possibility of switching attention from processing to maintenance and of refreshing decaying memory traces. Thus, increasing the number of digits to be read within a fixed period of time, or reducing the time allowed to read a fixed number of digits should

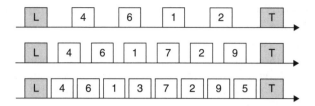

Figure 7.1 Series of screens displayed during a reading digit span task with increased paces from top to bottom.

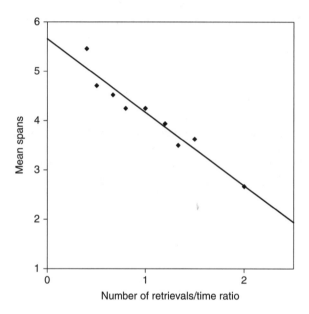

Figure 7.2 Mean span as a function of retrievals/time ratio in adults. Barrouillet, P., Bernardin, S., & Camos, V., Time constraints and resource sharing in adults' working memory spans. *Journal of Experimental Psychology: General, 133*(1), 83–100, 2004, APA, reprinted with permission.

result in an increased difficulty in switching attention to the decaying memory traces of the letters to be remembered and then in poorer recall. This is what Barrouillet et al. (2004) observed. To test the hypothesis that working memory span is a linear function of the cognitive load, we progressively increased this ratio. Nine groups of adult participants were presented with nine different values of the ratio (from 0.4 to 2) resulting from the combination of three different numbers of digits presented (4, 8, or 12) with three durations of the inter-letter intervals (6, 8, or 10 seconds). As it is shown in Figure 7.2, recall performance was highly correlated with this ratio, revealing a quasi-perfect trade-off between processing and storage (Barrouillet et al., 2004, Exp. 7).

In a subsequent series of experiment, Barrouillet, Bernardin, Portrat, Vergauwe, and Camos (2007) showed that the nature of the processing involved in the span tasks did not modify such a relationship between storage and processing. For example, when comparing two computer-paced span tasks in which the processing was either parity or location judgment, we found a monotonic and unique trend between the span and the cognitive load evaluated through the measure of processing times (Figure 7.3). Similarly, when we compared different working memory span tasks varying on the type of executive functions they involved (updating, response selection, inhibition or retrieval), we once again found a unique relationship between the cognitive load of the processing component and the storage capacity (Figure 7.4). However, as predicted by the TBRS, this relationship is only observed as far as the processing is attention demanding, like a Choice Reaction Time task (CRT). When a very low demanding task like a Simple Reaction Time task (SRT) is introduced as processing component, the concurrent storage capacity remains unchanged with the increased number of processing steps (Figure 7.5).

Finally, because our computer-paced working memory tasks hamper the use of sophisticated strategies to cope with the dual task requirements inherent to any working memory span task, we predicted that they would be better predictors of high-level cognitive performance like academic achievement than traditional self-paced working memory tasks such as the counting span (Case, Kurland, & Goldberg, 1982) or the reading span (Daneman & Carpenter, 1980)

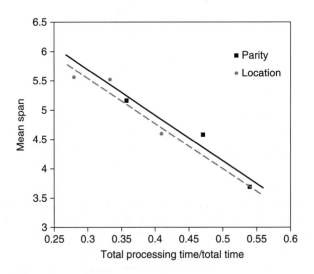

Figure 7.3 Mean span as a function of the cognitive load in adults when the processing component was either parity or location judgement task. Barrouillet, P., Bernardin, S., Portrat, S., Vergauwe, E., & Camos, V., Time and cognitive load in working memory. *Journal of Experimental Psychology: Learning, Memory, and Cognition, 33*(3), 570–585, 2007, APA, reprinted with permission.

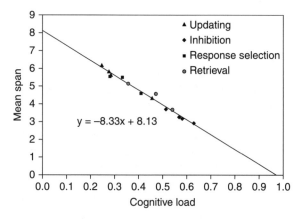

Figure 7.4 Relation between spans and cognitive load for different tasks involving executive function like memory updating, inhibition, retrieval and response selection (from Barrouillet, Portrat, & Camos, submitted).

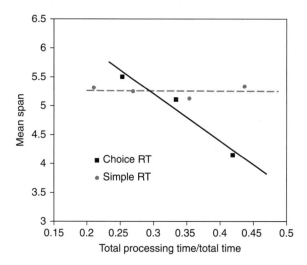

Figure 7.5 Mean span as a function of the processing time/total time ratio in adults for an attention demanding task (CRT) and a low demanding task. Barrouillet, P., Bernardin, S., Portrat, S., Vergauwe, E., & Camos, V., Time and cognitive load in working memory. *Journal of Experimental Psychology: Learning, Memory, and Cognition, 33*(3), 570–585, 2007, APA, reprinted with permission.

that allow participants to plan their activities and refresh memory traces. We observed this phenomenon in sixth graders whose academic achievement was better predicted by computer-paced working memory span tasks (Lépine, Barrouillet, & Camos, 2005; Barrouillet, Camos, Morlaix, & Suchaut, 2008).

Three factors to account for the development of working memory capacity

Though the seminal work of Baddeley and Hitch (1974) as well as further formulations of the model (Baddeley & Logie, 1999) did not involve any developmental consideration, the notions of resource and working memory have often been evoked to account for cognitive development. Many authors have argued that cognitive development mainly results from the age-related increase in some cognitive capacity. These capacity theories propose that children's performance depends on how much information they hold in mind at a given time, assuming that this capacity increases with age. For example, Pascual-Leone (1970) introduced the notion of mental power that can be understood as the maximum number of schemes that children can coordinate in thinking and solving problems, mental power increasing from 1 to 7 from early childhood to late adolescence. In the same way, Halford (1993) suggested that cognitive performance depends on the number of independent dimensions that can be simultaneously grasped, this number increasing with age due to some age-related increase in cognitive capacity. This increase in general capacity is assumed to be reflected in the strong age-related increase in children's working memory span (Cowan, Nugent, Elliott, & Saults, 2000; Swanson, 1996, 1999).

It could be argued that these accounts are rather vague in evoking some abstract and ill defined "capacity", but not all the theories remained so elusive, and attempts have been made to clarify the locus of this development in capacity. Case (1985) suggested considering working memory as a total processing space within which could be distinguished an operating space devoted to the processing of the secondary task, and a remaining short-term storage space available to maintain the items to be recalled. Case (1985) illustrated this resource-sharing hypothesis with a task called the counting span task, in which participants are asked to count dots on cards out loud, and then recall the number of dots on each card. The experimenter varies the number of cards to be counted, and consequently the number of values to be recalled after counting. The counting span is the maximum number of cards the participant is able to remember. Case, Kurland, and Goldberg (1982) observed that this counting span increases with age. Nevertheless, adults who were asked to perform a counting task using terms learned prior to the experiment instead of the traditional sequence of numbers exhibited a counting span equivalent to that of 6-year-old children. The authors then assumed that the developmental increase in working memory span is due to an improvement in the efficiency of the counting operation, which demands a smaller proportion of total processing space as the age of the participant increases. Many authors who developed working memory span tasks argued for this resource-sharing hypothesis related to variations in processing efficiency (Daneman & Carpenter, 1980, 1983; Turner & Engle, 1989).

Though increasing processing efficiency is in some way related to the capacity to process more information and to the age-related increase in working memory span, the precise nature of this relationship is still a subject of debate. To account for the developmental increase in working memory spans, Towse and Hitch (1995) put forward an alternative "memory decay" hypothesis. According to this hypothesis, the poor recall performance in the working memory span tasks is due to the fact that the memory traces of the items to be recalled suffer from a time-related decay. Because participants have to switch their attention from processing to storage when performing working memory span tasks, their recall performance depends on the duration of the processing which in turn determines the retention period during which memory traces fade away (see also Halford, Maybery, O'Hare, & Grant, 1994). The age-related increase in counting span would thus mainly result from faster counting in older children. In line with this hypothesis, Towse and Hitch (1995) observed that counting spans in children do not depend on the difficulty of the counting activity, but only on its duration. Towse, Hitch, and Hutton (1998) extended these results by varying the duration of the processing component in reading and operation span tasks. They observed that longer processing durations resulted in lower spans. These results have been replicated by Hitch, Towse, and Hutton (2001) in a longitudinal follow-up of Towse et al. (1998), and by Towse, Hitch, and Hutton (2000) in adults. Thus, Towse and Houston-Price (2001) concluded that the idea of resource capacity is superfluous in accounting for working memory span. As stressed by Towse et al. (2007), the task switching account suggests that an important limiting factor in working memory capacity is the persistence of memory representations, and it has been demonstrated that this persistence evolves with age (Cowan et al., 2000; Saults & Cowan, 1996).

Contrary to the task switching approach, other models have assumed that working memory spans reflect a capacity for controlled attention needed to activate relevant information and to resist interference by inhibiting irrelevant information (Engle et al., 1999). As we suggested (Barrouillet & Camos, 2001; Gavens & Barrouillet, 2004), the hypothesis of an age-related increase in attentional capacity could account for most of the developmental phenomena observed in working memory span (this point is developed in the next section). Because attention can be considered as a source of activation (Anderson, 1993), an increased capacity of attention would result in more activated and thus long-lasting memory representations, but also in faster processing, thus facilitating the persistence of information to be maintained. In the same way, greater attentional capacities would reduce the degree of interference due to representational overlap between items to be recalled and representations issued from concurrent processing (Saito & Miyake, 2004). More recently, Bayliss, Jarrold, Baddeley, Gunn, and Leigh (2005) used a componential analysis of complex working memory performance in children. As might be expected, processing efficiency was a contributor to working memory span but so was storage ability, which might correspond to the efficiency of the slave systems in Baddeley's working memory architecture, plus residual variance that was assumed to reflect the contribution of the central executive. In other words, Bayliss et al.'s (2005) study identified the three main factors that are usually assumed as underpinning working memory development: processing efficiency, memory-related capacity and a central resource that can be described as controlled attention. In summary, recent research has identified several factors that might underpin developmental increase in working memory capacity. However, as stressed by Towse et al. (2007), although an extensive body of research is devoted to complex span in children, producing a viable developmental model of working memory is, surprisingly, not straightforward.

Within the TBRS model, Barrouillet et al. (2004) identified three main factors that could limit working memory functioning and performance in complex span tasks. These factors could also underpin developmental changes. The first is the amount of available attention that produces activation. This limited supply restrains the processes involved in performing both the processing component of the task and the maintenance of memory traces. The second is the efficiency of the switching mechanism itself, whereas the third relates to the phenomenon of decay. Thus, our model assumes that age-related changes in these three factors could contribute to working memory development.

First, as already suggested by some authors like Pascual-Leone (1970), the amount of attention available for cognitive functioning might increase during development. Thus, for the same activities, older children would be able to process information faster than younger children. Within working memory span tasks, because the level of activation of the memory traces decreases during the processing steps, any reduction of the duration of these steps directly diminishes the time during which the traces decay, and consequently increases the time available for reactivation or refreshing before the next processing step. These two effects jointly induce a stronger activation of the traces and a better recall of the to-be-maintained items. Second, because the main hypothesis of the TBRS model is that there is a switching mechanism between processing and maintenance at a micro level (i.e., during the processing episodes), the efficiency of this mechanism should have a direct and strong impact on working memory functioning. An increase in the efficiency of the switching during childhood means that older children should take a greater advantage from the short pauses left free between each processing step and available for refreshing activities. The level of activation of the memory traces would be then higher for older than for younger children, resulting in the classically observed increase in span. As a consequence, age-related changes in the efficiency of this switching could play a central role in working memory development. In the same way, the speed at which memory traces decline and fade away should affect their retrieval during recall. A slower decay of the memory traces in older children should result in better recall performance in complex span tasks. Up to now, the developmental impact of two of these factors has been explored: the amount of available attention and the efficiency of the switching mechanism.

The amount of available attention

For our first study in children, we created the time-controlled paradigm we then used to develop our model in adults (Barrouillet & Camos, 2001). Following Towse and Hitch's (1995; Towse, Hitch, & Hutton, 2002) suggestion that the delay of retention between the presentation of the items and their recall is the determinant factor of complex spans, we compared two span tasks for which the duration of the processing episodes were equated, but that differed on attentional demand. In an operation span task, 9- and 11-year-old children were asked to maintain letters while they verified two- or three-operand additions. These operations were interleaved between the presentation of letters. In a "baba" span task, the arithmetic problems were replaced by the continuous aloud repetition of the syllable "ba" for a duration equal to the average time needed by children to verify the corresponding operation. Thus, the delay of retention was perfectly equated across the two tasks but the operation span task involved a higher attentional demand than the mere repetition of a syllable. Beside the expected increase in recall performance from 9 to 11, children were better able to maintain letters when they just had to repeat "ba" instead of verifying operations. This effect, which did not interact with age, was one of our first arguments in favour of the role of attention in working memory, and could lead to interpreting the developmental increase in spans as resulting from an increase in attentional resource. However, whereas verifying arithmetic problems like "4 + 7 + 8 = 19" induces an important attentional demand compared to the mere repetition of the same syllable, the resulting decrease in span was far from being dramatic (i.e., .7 at 9 and .42 at 11). This suggested that children were able to maintain active the memory traces while solving arithmetic problems. Thus, we reasoned that instead of switching their attention from processing to storage and from storage to processing as Towse et al. (1998) suggested, i.e., when presented with a memoranda and then when engaging in a new processing episode, children were able to switch their attention to reactivate the memory traces during processing, even when this processing is a demanding task. This intuition became one of the main assumptions of the TBRS model. Moreover, it would be over-simplistic to interpret such finding solely in terms of an increase in available attention. The effect of the attention demand suggested by the TBRS model can only partly account for children's working memory spans. The same task, here verifying operations, should be more demanding for younger than for older children. Thus, children would take longer to verify the same operations at 9 than at 11, older children benefiting from shorter processing times, i.e., shorter delays of retention. To clarify this issue, Gavens and Barrouillet (2004; Exp. 1) compared third and fifth graders' performance on complex span tasks when the duration of the processing component of the tasks was controlled and its difficulty equated across age.

In the first experiment of Gavens and Barrouillet (2004), the attention demand and the total duration of the processing task were manipulated in a factorial design by presenting 9- and 11-year-old children with either a continuous operation span task or a baba span task in which the duration of the processing component was either short or long. In the continuous operation span task, children had to maintain letters while solving running operations. After the presentation of each letter, children were presented with a digit (the root of the operation) followed by a series of sign-operand pairs (either +1 or –1) successively displayed on screen at a fixed pace. Children were asked to read the digit as well as the sign-operand pairs and to give the successive answers aloud. For example, for the series 6+1+1, children had to say "six plus one seven plus one eight". Each continuous operation contained either 2 sign-operand pairs in a short-duration condition or 4 pairs in a long-duration condition. In the baba span task, the digits and the sign-operand pairs were replaced by the syllable "ba" repeatedly displayed on screen at a fixed pace in such a way that children uttered the same number of syllables in both span tasks, equating the amount of articulatory suppression involved by the processing component of the tasks. As in Barrouillet and Camos (2001, Exp. 3), besides a strong age effect, recall performance was lower in the continuous operation span task than in the baba span task, with no interaction with age. Moreover, the short duration led to higher spans than the longer duration condition, this effect being only significant in the continuous operation span task but not in the baba span task. However, this effect of duration was quite small (7% of the experimental variance) compared to the effect of the attentional demand (73%). Thus, even when delays of retention were perfectly equated between the two types of tasks, continuous operation spans were far lower than baba spans, suggesting that the attentional demand of the processing component has a major impact on working memory spans. Moreover, though the duration of processing was kept constant across ages, older children still outperformed younger children. This suggested that the higher spans in older children do not entirely result, as Towse and Hitch (1995) surmised, from their faster processing and hence shorter delays of retention. However, this factor could not be totally discarded because keeping the duration constant seemed to have an effect on the developmental increase. The increase in baba spans observed between 9 and 11 years of age in this experiment (from 2.32 to 2.93) was less important than in Barrouillet and Camos (2001, Exp. 3; from 2.26 to 3.25) where younger children were subjected to longer periods of concurrent articulation than older children. This reduction of the age effect provided evidence that the developmental increase in working memory span could be partly accounted for by shorter delays of retention in older children as Towse and Hitch (1995) assumed.

In a further experiment, Gavens and Barrouillet (2004, Exp. 3) focused on this developmental issue. Is the developmental increase in working memory spans mainly due to faster processing in older children, as suggested by Towse and Hitch (1995), to an increase in processing efficiency as Case (1985) argued, or to an increase in the amount of cognitive capacity as Swanson (1996) and Halford, Wilson, and Phillips (1998) proposed? To answer this question, 9- and 11-year-old children were presented with a continuous operation span task in which the continuous operation had the same level of difficulty and the same duration in both age groups. The continuous operation span used in the previous Gavens and Barrouillet (2004; Exp. 1) experiment was modified in such a way that either 3 or 4 sign-operand pairs were presented between two letters to the younger and older children respectively during the same total duration of 9 s. In a pre-test, the authors verified that these conditions led to the same percentage of correct responses in both age groups. Once again, the continuous operation span task was compared to a baba span task leading to the same number of syllables being uttered (i.e., 10 and 13 repetitions for the younger and the older children respectively). While keeping duration and difficulty constant, the hypothesis of an age-related increase in attentional capacity predicts that older children still have higher working memory spans than younger children. Indeed, the mean span in the continuous operation task was significantly higher for the 11-year-old than for the 9-year-old children, though this developmental effect was less pronounced than in the baba span task, as testified by a significant age × task interaction. These results provided strong evidence for the role of processing efficiency in working memory development. As Case (1985) suggested, processing becomes less and less demanding with age, leaving an increasing part of cognitive resources available for storage. Accordingly, developmental differences were significantly reduced when processing efficiency was equated across age as suggested by the age × task interaction. However, the result also suggested that another factor underpins working memory development because age differences still remained significant in the continuous operation span. Gavens and Barrouillet (2004) proposed that this latter factor could be an overall increase in some cognitive resource.

The switching mechanism

We have seen that the specificity of our TBRS model is the role of the switching of attention between processing and storage in accounting for working memory functioning. As we suggested above, the efficiency of such a mechanism may also participate to the developmental change observed in working memory spans. Barrouillet, Gavens, Vergauwe, Gaillard, and Camos (2009) addressed this question in a series of experiments.

The increasing efficiency of switching from 8 to 14

The aim of the first experiment that we performed in children aged between 8 and 14 was twofold. First, we aimed at demonstrating that the rapid switching mechanism between processing and storage observed in adults is also functional in children who should be able to take advantage from the free pauses during processing to achieve maintenance of the items to be remembered. Second, we were interested in studying the age-related changes in the efficiency of this process of reactivation, and we assumed that older children should exhibit a higher capacity to take advantage from the pauses to refresh and reactivate memory traces. This assumption led to the counterintuitive

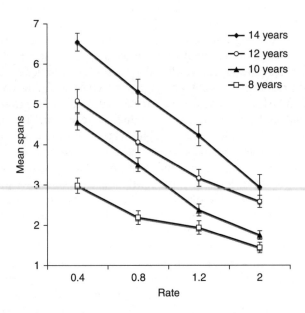

Figure 7.6 Mean spans as a function of the pace at which the processing component is performed (density of digits over time) in 8-, 10-, 12-, and 14-year-old children (Barrouillet et al., 2009, Experiment 1). Copyright © 2009 American Psychological Association. Reproduced with permission.

prediction that older children should be more affected than younger children by the variations in pace of the processing component of our computer-paced task. To test these hypotheses, Barrouillet et al. (2009, Exp. 1) presented children from 8 to 14 years of age with the reading digit span task described above, in which the digits were displayed at four different paces selected from the 9 used by Barrouillet et al. (2004, Exp. 7) in adults: in the inter-letter intervals, digits appeared at a rate of either 0.4, 0.8, 1.2, or 2 digits per second.

As can be seen in Figure 7.6, the results revealed two main phenomena. First, in each age group, recall performance decreased as the pace of the processing component (i.e., the rate at which the digits were presented) increased, even in the youngest group of 8-year-old children. Such an impact on maintenance of the density of the concurrent activity suggested that children in all age groups took advantage from the low presentation rates to refresh memory traces and achieve better recall. Second, we observed that the pace effect on spans was greater for older children, suggesting that they were more able to switch their attention from processing to storage whereas younger children were probably more passive, failing to efficiently reactivate memory traces. These results strongly suggested an age-related increase in the capacity to switch attention from one part of the task to the other. However, these first results could not discard the potential role of other factors in the observed developmental increase in working memory spans. For example, part of the developmental differences observed in the present experiment could result from the fact that older children were probably faster in reading the digits, thus benefiting from longer free pauses to refresh memory traces. As a consequence, the cognitive load involved in the secondary task, that is, the proportion of the inter-letter interval during which reading digits occupies attention, was probably weaker in older children.

In order to assess the potential role of this factor, Barrouillet et al. (2009) designed a second experiment in which the effects of age-related differences in processing speed were controlled. For this purpose, we used the same reading digit span task as in the previous experiment, but the time available to read each digit was tailored to the mean time needed to read digits at each age. For the sake of simplicity and in order to obtain a clear pattern of data about a potential interaction between age and cognitive load, the present experiment concentrated on the two extreme age groups (i.e., 8- and 14-year-old children). The mean digit reading times were assessed in a pre-test on two independent groups of children: As it could be expected, older children were far faster than younger children (mean reading times of 489 ms and 622 ms respectively). Three levels of cognitive load were created by presenting each digit in the reading digit span task for a duration equivalent to either 1, 2 or 4 mean reading times (e.g., for a reading time of 622 ms in the pre-test, each digit was presented during 622 ms, 1244 ms, or 2488 ms for the high, medium, and low level of cognitive load respectively). Moreover, in order to avoid exaggerated delays of retention, 12, 6 and 3 digits were presented in the high, medium and low conditions of cognitive load respectively, keeping constant the duration of the inter-letter interval across experimental conditions (i.e., 7464 ms and 5868 ms in younger and older children respectively). It is important to note that, in this experiment, and contrary to the previous one, the pace (i.e., the number of digits per second) varied between ages because the time available to read the same number of digits was longer in younger than in older children. By contrast, the reading digit task involved the same cognitive load between groups, because the reading activity occupied the same proportion of the inter-letter intervals in both ages (i.e., 100%, 50%, and 25% for the high, medium, and low levels of cognitive load respectively).

The TBRS model permits two main predictions. First, although the cognitive load of the secondary task was the same in both age groups, we still predicted higher spans in older children. Gavens and Barrouillet (2004) already observed that even when the difficulty of the processing component of a working memory span task was equated across ages, older children still outperformed younger children. The authors accounted for this phenomenon by assuming an age-related increase in cognitive resources leading to a higher level of activation of the to-be-remembered items at encoding, as well as a slower time-related decay of memory traces. As a consequence, we expected better recall performance in older children, even in the high cognitive load condition in which each digit was presented for a duration that did not exceed the time needed to read it, thus probably strongly impeding the reactivation of memory traces during processing. Second, an effect of cognitive load was expected with higher load resulting in lower recall performance in both age groups. However, our hypothesis of an age-related improvement in the reactivation process could lead to two different patterns of results. On the one hand, it could be assumed that the development of this process does not go beyond the general increase in processing speed and efficiency that affects most of the cognitive processes like memory search, mental rotation, name retrieval or visual search as observed by Kail (2001). In this case, the effect of cognitive load should be the same in both ages because the effects of differences in processing speed were controlled in this experiment. On the other hand, we can also suppose that the development of the refreshing process goes beyond a general increase in processing speed. For example, it could be assumed that the reactivation rate is higher in older children not only because they process information faster, but also because they have greater capacity to control their attention and are more able to switch their attention back and forth from processing to storage. In this case, even when controlling for age-related differences in processing speed, our paradigm should reveal a weaker effect of cognitive load in younger children who are less able to take advantage from the free pauses resulting from a low cognitive load.

As previously observed, the mean spans were higher in 14- than in 8-year-old children (2.88 and 1.80 respectively), and the cognitive load had a significant effect in spans (Figure 7.7). Though the effect of age steadily increased as

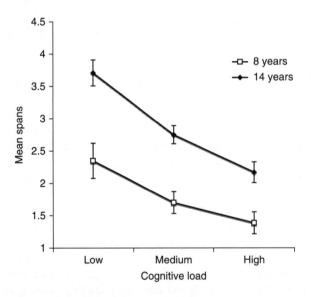

Figure 7.7 Mean spans as a function of age and cognitive load of the reading digit span task in Barrouillet et al. (2009), Experiment 2. Copyright © American Psychological Association. Reproduced with permission.

the cognitive load decreased, the age × cognitive load interaction was not significant. This suggests that a substantial part of the age × pace interaction observed in the previous experiment resulted from age-related differences in reading digit speed. This would mean in turn that, as we noted above, the development of the reactivation processes does not go beyond the general age-related increase in processing speed. However, variations in cognitive load had an effect proportionate to recall performance in both groups. Indeed, it was possible to estimate in each condition and age group the time available to refresh memory traces. Linear regressions of the spans on these available times revealed a quasi-perfect linear function in each age group, with a steeper slope in older than in younger children. Whereas 14-year-old children increased their recall performance by approximately 1 item for each additional second of time available after reading a digit, the same amount of time only yielded the half of this increase in 8-year-old children. This difference in slopes confirmed that older children were more efficient in refreshing memory traces (Figure 7.8).

A critical change from 5 to 7

The two previous experiments made clear that the refreshing mechanism is less efficient in young children as the slope of the function relating working memory spans to the pace at which the intervening task is performed becomes flatter as children involved in the study are younger. This developmental change suggests, as Hitch (2006) surmised, that there might be an age at which children do

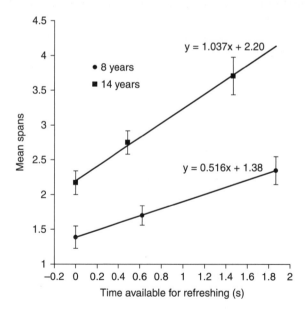

Figure 7.8 Mean spans as a function of age and free time available to refresh memory traces in Barrouillet et al. (2009), Experiment 2. Copyright © American Psychological Association. Reproduced with permission.

not switch their attention from processing to storage during the processing component of the task, adopting a serial control. What kind of recall performance pattern would result from such a working memory functioning? Suppose children who would not switch their attention during processing. Their attention would thus remain continuously occupied by, and stuck on, the processing part of the task except when items to be remembered are displayed on screen. Such a functioning would correspond to the task-switching described by Towse and Hitch (1995; Towse et al., 1998) in which the cognition is driven by the structure of working memory span tasks, that is by external events. In this case, memory traces should suffer from a continuous decay during processing without any attempt to refresh them. As a consequence, working memory spans should remain unaffected by the variation in cognitive load of the intervening task and any effect of pace should disappear because recall performance would only depend on the duration of this task. This is not to say that this intervening activity would not have any effect on maintenance and recall performance. Because attention is focused and remains stuck on the intervening task, the memory items leave primary memory and suffer from a time-related decay resulting in more difficult retrieval at recall (Unsworth & Engle, 2007). By contrast, when there is no intervening activity, attention can remain focused on the to-be-remembered items that benefit from higher levels of activation and are thus easier to retrieve. Thus, even if younger children's working memory span should remain unaffected by the variation in cognitive load of the intervening task because they do not switch their attention from processing to storage, their recall performance should nonetheless be poorer when an intervening task is to be performed.

We tested this hypothesis in two groups of 5- and 7-year-old children who performed a working memory span task in which they were presented with animals (drawings appearing on screen) to be remembered while naming the colour of smilies successively displayed on screen (Barrouillet et al., 2009, Exp. 3). We called this task the naming colour span task. The duration of the intervals between two successive memory items was constant whereas we varied the number of colours to be identified in each interval (either 0, 2, or 4 colours). The ages were chosen according to many studies demonstrating that before 7 years of age, children do not spontaneously use strategies to maintain memory items in short-term memory span tasks (Gathercole, Adams, & Hitch, 1994; Gathercole & Hitch, 1993; Hitch, Halliday, Dodd, & Littler, 1989). Due to the necessity to perform an intervening task, the naming colour span task is more complex than a simple span task and it is highly probable that 5-year-old children will not attempt to actively maintain memory items while performing this task. They should thus present a pattern of recall performance reflecting the task-switching process described by Towse and Hitch (1995) with attention being continuously occupied during the processing phases. Thus, in the younger children, the presence of an intervening task (i.e., 2 or 4 colours to be named) should disrupt recall performance compared to the 0-colour condition, because the resulting occupation of attention should remove the memory items from primary memory (Unsworth & Engle, 2007). However, the 2- and 4-colour conditions should elicit the same spans because the youngest children would not benefit from the pauses to refresh memory traces. By contrast, the micro-task switching mechanism described by the TBRS model might be efficient in 7-year-old children, leading to a smooth decrease in span as the cognitive load involved by the naming colour task increases, as we already observed in Barrouillet et al.'s (2009) Experiment 1.

The results revealed that before 7 years of age, the maintenance of items in working memory is impaired by an intervening task, but that the cognitive load induced by this task has no impact in recall performance. Indeed, whereas the working memory spans decreased smoothly in 7-year-old children as the number of colours to be named increased, recall performance in 5-year-old children remained unaffected when the number of colours increased from 2 to 4 (Figure 7.9). This suggests that, contrary to older children, 5-year-olds did not attempt, or were unable, to divert their attention from the processing component of the task. As soon as the first smiley appeared, they probably switched their attention to this part of the task and waited for the successive stimuli without any attempt to refresh memory until the next animal was displayed on screen. Thus, results suggest that the way they perform the working memory task reflects the task-switching process

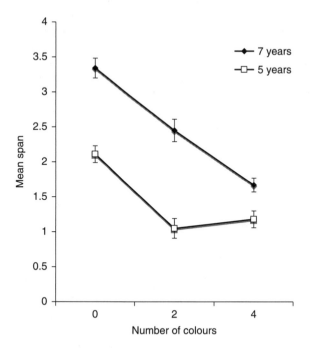

Figure 7.9 Mean spans as a function of age and number of colours to be named in Barrouillet et al. (2009), Experiment 3. Copyright © American. Psychological Association. Reproduced with permission.

described by Towse et al. (1998) who proposed that the main determinant of working memory span is the duration of the processing episodes rather than the cognitive load this processing involves. It can also be noted that the absence of any difference between the 2- and 4-colour conditions contradicts the idea that the effect of the amount of material to be processed in the intervening task is due to representation-based interferences.

By contrast, 7-year-old children's performance is in line with the TBRS model account of working memory, recall performance being a function of the proportion of time during which the processing component occupies attention. Thus, Barrouillet et al.'s (2009) third experiment indicates that the reactivation of memory traces through the rapid switching process hypothesized by our model is not a universal mechanism. It appears only somewhere between 5 and 7. As Barrouillet et al.'s (2009) Experiments 1 and 2 demonstrated, its efficiency and maybe its frequency of use increase with age until late adolescence, thus producing large developmental differences in the amount of information that can be maintained active, especially when the concurrent activities involve a moderate cognitive load that allows free pauses to reactivate memory items. As a consequence, this experiment lent also strong support to Hitch's (2006) hypothesis of a developmental switch from serial control and task switching to parallel processing, if we consider the rapid switching described by the TBRS model as a form of "parallel" processing, at least at a macro level of analysis.

A final experiment aimed at testing specifically Hitch's (2006) suggestion of the developmental change in the control or use of the switching process. At a young age, children's cognitive activity should mimic the structure of the working memory span task, and children would store and process information as it occurs in the task. On the contrary, after 7, children should be able to switch their attention to the stored memory traces during the processing episodes, as the TBRS proposes. Thus, on the one hand, recall performance in the younger children should entirely depend on the duration between the presentation of the items and their recall, i.e., the duration of the processing component. On the other hand, the cognitive load, i.e., the proportion of time the processing captures attention, should be the determinant of older children's span. We modified the naming colour span task described above to manipulate orthogonally the duration and the pace of the processing component. We presented either 1 or 2 colours within 2 s intervals, or 2 colours within 4 s. On the one hand, if there is no switching process, the duration of the processing component should determine recall performance. Thus, the first two conditions (2 s intervals) should not differ but lead to better recall than the 4 s condition. On the other hand, if young children switch their attention from processing to storage during the processing component of the task, their span should depend on the pace of this processing component, and presenting 2 colours in 2 s (i.e., 1 item per second) should induce a lower recall performance than the two other conditions (1 colour in 2 s and 2 colours in 4 s, i.e., 1 item every 2 seconds) that should not differ. The results first replicated that at 7 the working memory span depends on the pace and not on the duration of the processing component. However, in 5-year-old children, the reverse pattern was observed: recall performance decreased as the duration of the processing activity increased, whatever its pace. This reversal lends strong support to the hypothesis that a qualitative change intervenes between the ages 5 and 7 in the working memory processes responsible for the maintenance of information while concurrent processing is running.

Conclusion

The aim of the studies reported in this chapter was to shed light on some of the processes responsible for the developmental increase in working memory span. There is no doubt that working memory development results from the conjoined effect of a body of intricate factors that can only be distinguished in the light of a working memory theory. According to the TBRS model, working memory spans mainly depend on three factors. Whereas the developmental change in the speed of memory decay was documented for example by Cowan et al. (2000), the impact of two factors has been disputed in the present chapter. The first is the time during which attention is captured by the processing component of the task, which determines the time during which memory traces suffer from a time-related decay. The second is the efficiency of the mechanisms devoted to the reactivation of these memory traces as soon as attention can be diverted from processing activities to focus on them. One of the main problems is that both of these factors depend on several mechanisms.

The time during which attention is captured by processing depends on the efficiency of this processing, which depends in turn on a series of factors related to intrinsic characteristics of the subject but also to his or her environment and past experience. First, processing efficiency would depend on the amount of attention available to activate relevant declarative and procedural knowledge, this amount being a function of the maturational level of frontal brain areas (Fernandez-Duque, Baird, & Posner, 2000). This amount of attention determines the speed at which relevant information is retrieved and procedures instantiated, as well as the probability of success of these retrievals and of selection of the most appropriate procedure (Anderson, 1993). However, processing efficiency should also depend on previous experience, knowledge, and practice, all factors that would facilitate retrieval of relevant information and the use of efficient and robust procedures leading to faster processing. This development of strategies could result either from an increase in efficiency of a given strategy (e.g., an algorithmic strategy to solve arithmetic problems as in Turner and Engle's operation span) or from using faster and more effective strategies (e.g., by shifting from algorithmic strategies to a strategy of direct retrieval of the answer from memory, as described by Logan, 1988, or Siegler, 1996). We have seen that, as Case (1985) suggested, processing efficiency has a major impact in working memory spans and that the age-related increase in this efficiency accounts for an important part of working memory development. When equating the difficulty of the processing component across ages (Gavens &

Barrouillet, 2004), or when reducing the impact of processing efficiency by equating the cognitive load this processing involves (Barrouillet et al., 2009), we observed in both cases a strong reduction of developmental differences in working memory spans. However, and contrary to Case et al.'s (1982) prediction, these manipulations did not completely abolish developmental differences. The TBRS model could account for this phenomenon.

Case et al.'s (1982) prediction issued from Case's conception of working memory. He assumed that a total processing space (TPS) was divided into an operation space devoted to processing and a storage space devoted to maintenance. The more efficient the processing, the lower its cognitive demand and the amount of resources needed, and the larger the remaining space available for storage. Thus, the higher processing efficiency in older children would result in reduced cognitive demand and on the correlative increase in storage space, hence the developmental increase in working memory spans. Equating the processing demand of the tasks across ages should have resulted in equivalent spans. Why did this levelling in memory not occur, and where does the remaining developmental difference come from? Though we agree with Case that working memory is characterized by a resource sharing between processing and storage, our conception of the storage function differs. Case seemed to consider storage as a passive system, the number of items that can be maintained depending only on the available space. However, Barrouillet et al. (2009) observed that older children take a greater advantage than young children from equivalent periods of time available for maintenance activities, suggesting that storage is a dynamic system whose efficiency increases with age. This is the second factor assumed by the TBRS model as underpinning working memory spans.

The efficiency of this mechanism of reactivation of decaying memory traces is itself dependent on other factors. It can be supposed that this reactivation consists in an attention-based refreshing mechanism increasing the level of activation of memory traces through attentional focusing. The efficiency of this mechanism would thus depend on the amount of available attention as well as on the capacity to control attention and switch from processing to storage. However, it would also depend on knowledge, long-term memory facilitating the reintegration of decayed memory traces (Hulme et al., 1997). When verbal material is involved, the amount of information maintained would also depend on the efficiency of the articulatory mechanism described by Baddeley (1986; see Jarrold and Tam in this book). We recently established that these two mechanisms are independent, but can cooperate to maintain verbal information (Camos, Lagner, & Barrouillet, 2009). The results presented here indicate that an important part of developmental differences in working memory spans are attributable to the efficiency of these mechanisms of reactivation.

Thus, the increase in processing efficiency is only one part of the determinants of working memory development. Older children are also more able to maintain information active and to avoid its complete loss during processing. Such a developmental change could result from an age-related increase in attentional capacity, as suggested by Halford (1993; Halford, Cowan, & Andrews, 2007; see Andrews & Halford in this volume) and Pascual-Leone (1970; Pascual-Leone & Baillargeon, 1994; see Pascual-Leone & Johnson in this volume), as well as in the higher capacity to control attention, which has been assumed to play a major role in working memory functioning (Engle & Kane, 2004) and in cognitive development (Diamond, 2006; Zelazo, Müller, Frye, & Marcovitch, 2003). Thus, our research points towards an integrative approach of the different conceptions of working memory development proposed by the neo-Piagetian theories. As these theories assume, the capacity to maintain information active and ready for treatment dramatically increases with age, permitting children to cope with concepts, situations and problems of an increasing complexity.

References

Anderson, J. R. (1993). *Rules of the mind.* Hillsdale, NJ: Erlbaum.
Anderson, J. R., & Lebiere, C. (1998). *Atomic components of thought.* Hillsdale, NJ: Erlbaum.
Baddeley, A. D. (1986). *Working memory.* Oxford: Clarendon Press.
Baddeley, A. D., & Hitch, G. (1974). Working memory. In G. A. Bower (Ed.), *Recent advances in learning and motivation* (Vol. 8, pp. 647–667). New York: Academic Press.
Baddeley, A. D., & Logie, R. H. (1999). Working memory: The multiple-component model. In A. Miyake & P. Shah (Eds.), *Models of working memory: Mechanisms of active maintenance and executive control* (pp. 28–61). Cambridge: Cambridge University Press.
Barrouillet, P., Bernardin, S., & Camos, V. (2004). Time constraints and resource sharing in adults' working memory spans. *Journal of Experimental Psychology: General, 133*(1), 83–100.
Barrouillet, P., Bernardin, S., Portrat, S., Vergauwe, E., & Camos, V. (2007). Time and cognitive load in working memory. *Journal of Experimental Psychology: Learning, Memory and Cognition, 33*(3), 570–585.
Barrouillet, P., & Camos, V. (2001). Developmental increase in Working Memory Span: Resource sharing or temporal decay?, *Journal of Memory and Language, 45*(1), 1–20.
Barrouillet, P., & Camos, V. (2007). The time-based resource sharing model of working memory. In N. Osaka, R. Logie, & M. D'Esposito (Eds.), *The cognitive neuroscience of working memory* (pp. 59–80). Oxford: Oxford University Press.
Barrouillet, P., Camos, V., Morlaix, S., Suchaut, B. (2008). Compétences scolaires, capacités cognitives et origine sociale: Quels liens à l'école élémentaire? *Revue Française de Pédagogie, 162,* 5–14.
Barrouillet, P., Gavens, N., Vergauwe, E., Gaillard, V., & Camos, V. (2009). Working memory span development: A Time-Based Resource-Sharing model account. *Developmental Psychology, 45*(2), 477–490. The use of this information does not imply endorsement by the publisher.
Barrouillet, P., Portrat, S., & Camos, V. (submitted). Central executive and time constraints in working memory: An extended time-based resource-sharing model.
Bayliss, D. M., Jarrold, C., Baddeley, A. D., Gunn, D. M., & Leigh, E. (2005). Mapping the developmental constraints on working memory span performance. *Developmental Psychology, 41*(4), 579–597.

Camos, V., Lagner, P., & Barrouillet, P. (2009). Two maintenance mechanisms of verbal information in working memory. *Journal of Memory and Language, 61*(3), 457–469.

Cantor, J., & Engle, R. W. (1993). Working-memory capacity as long-term memory activation: An individual-differences approach. *Journal of Experimental Psychology: Learning, Memory, and Cognition, 25*, 1101–1114.

Case, R. (1985). *Intellectual development: Birth to adulthood.* New York: Academic Press.

Case, R. (1992). *The mind's staircase: Exploring the conceptual underpinnings of children's thought and knowledge.* Hillsdale, NJ: Lawrence Erlbaum Associates.

Case, R., Kurland, M., & Goldberg, J. (1982). Operational efficiency and the growth of short-term memory. *Journal of Experimental Child Psychology, 33*, 386–404.

Conway, A. R. A., Kane, M. J., & Engle, R. W. (2003). Working memory capacity and its relation to general intelligence. *Trends in Cognitive Sciences, 7*(12), 547–552.

Cowan, N. (1992). Verbal memory span and the timing of spoken recall. *Journal of Memory and Language, 31*, 668–684.

Cowan, N. (1995). *Attention and memory: An integrated framework.* New York: Oxford University Press.

Cowan, N. (1999). An embedded-process model of working memory. In A. Miyake & P. Shah (Eds.), *Models of working memory: Mechanisms of active maintenance and executive control* (pp. 62–101). Cambridge: Cambridge University Press.

Cowan, N., Keller, T. A., Hulme, C., Roodenrys, S., McDougall, S., & Rack, J. (1994). Verbal memory span in children: Speech timing clues to the mechanisms underlying age and word length effects. *Journal of Memory and Language, 33*, 234–250.

Cowan, N., Nugent, L. D., Elliott, E. M., & Saults, J. S. (2000). Persistence of memory for ignored lists of digits: Areas of developmental consistency and change. *Journal of Experimental Child Psychology, 76*, 151–172.

Daneman, M., & Carpenter, P. A. (1980). Individual differences in working memory and reading. *Journal of Verbal Learning and Verbal Behavior, 19*, 450–466.

Daneman, M., & Carpenter, P. A. (1983). Individual differences in integrating information between and within sentences. *Journal of Experimental Psychology: Learning, Memory, and Cognition, 9*, 561–584.

Diamond, A. (2006). The early development of executive functions. In E. Bialystok & F. I. Craik (Eds.), *Lifespan cognition: Mechanisms of change* (pp. 70–95). New York: Oxford University Press.

Engle, R. W., & Kane, M. J. (2004). Executive attention, working memory capacity, and a two-factor theory of cognitive control. In B. Ross (Ed.), *The psychology of learning and motivation* (Vol. 44, pp. 145–199). New York: Elsevier.

Engle, R. W., Kane, M. J., & Tuholski, S. W. (1999). Individual differences in working memory capacity and what they tell us about controlled attention, general fluid intelligence, and functions of the prefrontal cortex. In A. Miyake & P. Shah (Eds.), *Models of working memory: Mechanisms of active maintenance and executive control* (pp. 102–134). Cambridge: Cambridge University Press.

Engle, R. W., & Oransky, N. (1999). The evolution from short-term memory to working memory: Multi-store to dynamic models of temporary storage. In R. J. Sternberg (Ed.), *The nature of cognition* (pp. 515–556). Cambridge, MA: MIT Press.

Fernandez-Duque, D., Baird, J. A., & Posner, M. I. (2000). Executive attention and metacognitive regulation. *Consciousness and Cognition, 9*, 288–307.

Garavan, H. (1998). Serial attention within working memory. *Memory and Cognition, 26*(2), 263–276.

Gathercole, S. E., Adams, A. M., & Hitch, G. J. (1994). Do young children rehearse? An individual-differences analysis. *Memory and Cognition, 22*, 201–207.

Gathercole, S. E., & Hitch, G. J. (1993). Developmental changes in short-term memory: A revised working memory perspective. In A. Collins, S. E. Gathercole, M. A. Conway, & P. E. Morris (Eds.), *Theories of memory* (pp. 189–210). Hove, UK: Erlbaum.

Gathercole, S. E., Pickering, S. J., Ambridge, B., & Wearing, H. (2004). The structure of working memory from 4 to 15 years of age. *Developmental Psychology, 40*(2), 177–190.

Gavens, N., & Barrouillet, P. (2004). Delays of retention, processing efficiency, and attentional resources in working memory span development. *Journal of Memory and Language, 51*, 644–657.

Halford, G. S. (1982). *The development of thought*. Hillsdale, NJ: Lawrence Erlbaum.

Halford, G. S. (1993). *Children's understanding*. Hillsdale, NJ: Lawrence Erlbaum.

Halford, G. S., Cowan, N., & Andrews, G. (2007). Separating cognitive capacity from knowledge: A new hypothesis. *Trends in Cognitive Sciences, 11*, 236–242.

Halford, G. S., Maybery, M. T., O'Hare, A. W., & Grant, P. (1994). The development of memory and processing capacity. *Child Development, 65*, 1338–1356.

Halford, G. S., Wilson, W. H., & Phillips, S. (1998). Processing capacity defined by relational complexity: Implications for comparative, developmental, and cognitive psychology. *Behavioral and Brain Sciences, 21*, 803–864.

Hitch, G. (2006). Working memory in children: A cognitive approach. In E. Bialystok & F. I. Craik (Eds.), *Lifespan cognition: Mechanisms of change* (pp. 112–127). New York: Oxford University Press.

Hitch, G., Halliday, M. S., Dodd, A., & Littler, J. E. (1989). Development of rehearsal in short-term memory: Differences between pictorial and spoken stimuli. *British Journal of Developmental Psychology, 7*(4), 347–362.

Hitch, G., Towse, J. N., & Hutton, U. (2001). What limits children's working memory span? Theoretical accounts and applications for scholastic development. *Journal of Experimental Psychology: General, 130*(2), 184–198.

Hulme, C., Roodenrys, S., Schweickert, R., Brown, G. D. A., Martin, S., & Stuart, G. (1997). Word-frequency effects on short-term memory tasks: Evidence for a redintegration process in immediate serial recall. *Journal of Experimental Psychology: Learning, Memory, and Cognition, 23*(5), 1217–1232.

Johnson, M. K. (1992). MEM: Mechanisms of recollection. *Journal of Cognitive Neuroscience, 4*, 268–280.

Kail, R. V. (2001). Development of processing speed in childhood and adolescence. In H. Reese (Ed.), *Advances in child development and behavior* (Vol. 23, pp. 151–185). San Diego: Academic Press.

Kane, M. J., & Engle, R. W. (2003). Working memory capacity and the control of attention: The contributions of goal neglect, response competition, and task set to Stroop interference. *Journal of Experimental Psychology: General, 132*, 47–70.

Lépine, R., Barrouillet, P. & Camos, V. (2005). What makes working memory span so predictive of high level cognition?, *Psychonomic Bulletin & Review, 12*(1), 165–170.

Logan, G. D. (1988). Toward an instance theory of automatization. *Psychological Review, 95*, 492–527.

Lovett, M. C., Reder, L. M., & Lebière, C. (1999). Modeling working memory in a unified architecture: An ACT-R perspective. In A. Miyake & P. Shah (Eds.), *Models of working memory: Mechanisms of active maintenance and executive control* (pp. 135–182). Cambridge: Cambridge University Press.

Oberauer, K. (2002). Access to information in working memory: Exploring the focus of attention. *Journal of Experimental Psychology: Learning, Memory, and Cognition, 28*, 411–421.

Oberauer, K. (2005). Control of the contents of working memory: A comparison of two paradigms and two age groups. *Journal of Experimental Psychology: Learning, Memory, and Cognition, 31,* 714–728.

Pascual-Leone, J. A. (1970). A mathematical model for the transition rule in Piaget's developmental stage. *Acta Psychologica, 32,* 301–345.

Pascual-Leone, J., & Baillargeon, R. (1994). Developmental measurement of mental attention. *International Journal of Behavioral Development, 17,* 161–200.

Pashler, H. (1998). *The psychology of attention.* Cambridge, MA: MIT Press.

Raye, C. L., Johnson, M. K., Mitchell, K. J., Greene, E. J., & Johnson, M. R. (2007). Refreshing: A minimal executive function. *Cortex, 43,* 135–145.

Raye, C. L., Johnson, M. K., Mitchell, K. J., Reeder, J. A., & Greene, E. J. (2002). Neuroimaging a single thought: Dorsolateral PFC activity associated with refreshing just-activated information. *NeuroImage, 15,* 447–453.

Saito, S., & Miyake, A. (2004). On the nature of forgetting and the processing-storage relationship in reading span performance. *Journal of Memory and Language, 50,* 425–443.

Saults, J. S., & Cowan, N. (1996). The development of memory for ignored speech. *Journal of Experimental Child Psychology, 63*(1), 239–261.

Siegler, R. S. (1996). *Emerging minds: The process of change in children's thinking.* Oxford: Oxford University Press.

Swanson, H. L. (1996). Individual and age-related differences in children's working memory. *Memory and Cognition, 24,* 70–82.

Swanson, H. L. (1999). What develops in working memory? A life span perspective. *Developmental Psychology, 35,* 986–1000.

Towse, J. N., & Hitch, G. J. (1995). Is there a relationship between task demand and storage space in tests of working memory capacity? *Quarterly Journal of Experimental Psychology, 48A,* 108–124.

Towse, J. N., Hitch, G. J., & Horton, N. (2007). Working memory as the interface between processing and retention: A developmental perspective. *Advances in Child Development and Behavior, 35,* 219–251.

Towse, J. N., Hitch, G. J., & Hutton, U. (1998). A reevaluation of working memory capacity in children. *Journal of Memory and Language, 39,* 195–217.

Towse, J. N., Hitch, G. J., & Hutton, U. (2000). On the interpretation of working memory spans in adults. *Memory and Cognition, 28,* 341–348.

Towse, J. N., Hitch, G. J., & Hutton, U. (2002). On the nature of the relationship between processing activity and item retention in children. *Journal of Experimental Child Psychology, 82,* 156–184.

Towse, J. N., & Houston-Price, C. M. T. (2001). Reflections on the concept of central executive. In J. Andrade (Ed.), *Working memory in perspective* (pp. 240–260). Philadelphia, PA: Psychology Press.

Turner, M. L., & Engle, R. W. (1989). Is working memory task dependent? *Journal of Memory and Language, 28,* 127–154.

Unsworth, N., & Engle, R. W. (2007). The nature of individual differences in working memory capacity: Active maintenance in primary memory and controlled search from secondary memory. *Psychological Review, 114*(1), 104–132.

Zelazo, P. D., Müller, U., Frye, D., & Marcovitch, S. (2003). The development of executive function in early childhood. *Monographs of the Society for Research in Child Development, 68* (3), 1–137.

8 Rehearsal and the development of working memory

Chris Jarrold and Helen Tam

It seems intuitively obvious that when faced with the task of holding information actively in mind during a delay, participants will verbally rehearse this information wherever possible, in order to maximize their chances of remembering it successfully at the point of recall. For example, Spiker (1956) tested young children's memory during a delay by hiding a coin in one of two differently patterned boxes that were both fixed to a rotating disk. The disk was then rotated for 25 seconds at a speed at which it was impossible to visually track the baited box. Participants could therefore only find the coin by remembering which box had been baited initially. While some participants were required to do this solely on the basis of their memory of the visual pattern shown on the correct box, half of the participants were pre-trained to associate different verbal labels with each location. Children in the latter group showed superior recall, leading Spiker to suggest that "the possession of verbal names for the stimulus permits [the participant] to produce a representation of the absent stimuli during the delay period" (p. 111) or in other words, to verbally rehearse the identity of the target box.

Although one certainly can maintain information in a visual form in memory tasks (Logie, 1995; Pavio, 1971), participants tend to elect to maintain information verbally wherever possible. In part this may follow from the benefits that can be gained from a reduction of information by coding stimuli with simpler verbal labels; for example Glanzer and Clark (1962, 1963) proposed the "verbal loop hypothesis" which stated that participants engage in covert naming of visual stimuli in order to improve recall. However, it also appears that verbal rehearsal of information within immediate memory tasks is a relatively efficient way of maintaining this information for subsequent recall (Peterson & Peterson, 1959). Models of immediate, or short-term memory have therefore often included verbal rehearsal as a means of item maintenance (Atkinson & Shiffrin, 1968; Baddeley & Hitch, 1974), perhaps most explicitly in Baddeley's (1986) model of working memory.

In this model the phonological loop supports the short-term maintenance of verbal information, and consists of a limited capacity phonological store and a subvocal, phonologically mediated rehearsal process. According to Baddeley, rehearsal offsets forgetting of information that would otherwise be caused by trace decay. Two characteristic phenomena of the phonological loop result from this conception. First, items that take longer to rehearse, such as words of a long spoken duration, are subject to greater forgetting than items that take less time to rehearse, leading to the "word length effect" (Baddeley, Thomson, & Buchanan, 1975). Indeed, if adults are required to engage in concurrent articulation of other material, which is presumed to block rehearsal, the word length effect is eliminated (Baddeley, Lewis, & Vallar, 1984; though see Romani, McAlpine, Olson, Tsouknida, & Martin, 2005). Second, the faster an individual can rehearse material the less forgetting they experience. Subvocal rehearsal rates are assumed to relate to the rate at which individuals can overtly repeat verbal material (Landauer, 1962; Lovelace, Powell, & Brooks, 1973), and a correlation between speech rate and immediate memory span is therefore predicted by this model (Baddeley et al., 1975).

A third potential marker of rehearsal is the presence of a "phonological similarity effect" for visually presented material. The standard phonological similarity effect is the finding of poorer recall for phonologically confusable verbal items (e.g., hat, cat, mat, map, tap) than phonologically distinct items (Conrad & Hull, 1964). When such an effect is seen for visually presented stimuli it indicates that the participant has recoded the presented information into a phonological form. A number of authors have argued that the process of verbal recoding is analogous to rehearsal, as it involves the participant subvocally naming, or re-presenting, the information to themselves (Gathercole, 1998; Howard & Franklin, 1990; Vallar & Papagno, 1995; though see Crowder, 1976, p. 86).

The current chapter examines the development of rehearsal in two ways. First, it evaluates the evidence for each of the three potential markers of rehearsal in the short-term memory performance of children of different ages; and, in particular, focuses on evidence from studies from our research group that have been carried out among children showing atypical development. Second, it considers the impact of changes in the extent of children's rehearsal on their performance on working memory measures. While short-term memory refers to individuals' ability to maintain information actively in mind, working memory involves doing this in the face of additional potential distraction from processing requirements associated with the task (Jarrold & Towse, 2006). For example, while short-term memory is typically assessed using so-called "simple span" tasks that require the immediate recall of just presented storage items, working memory is often measured using "complex span" procedures that combine the presentation of to-be-remembered storage items with the requirement to complete additional processing operations (e.g., Daneman & Carpenter, 1980). As will be discussed below, working memory measures therefore tap a greater range of abilities than do short-term memory tasks, but both share the need to maintain storage materials (Bayliss, Jarrold, Gunn, & Baddeley, 2003; see also Unsworth & Engle, 2007a), and are therefore both open to the potential influence of rehearsal processes.

Before turning to these two main sections of the chapter, it is worth noting the relevance of Piagetian theory to this debate, given the context of the current volume. Work on the development of working memory has been influenced substantially by neo-Piagetian theories of the development of central resources, or *M*-space (Pascual-Leone, 1970). For example, Case, Kurland, and Goldberg (1982) were arguably the first to employ a complex span procedure with children, as part of Case's research into neo-Piagetian approaches to cognitive development. To our knowledge, Piaget himself did not deal directly with the question of rehearsal; however, he was characteristically prescient when he called for an analysis of the type of representation held in memory by children, writing: "It is customary to represent memory as a system of coding and decoding, which naturally assumes the intervention of a code. But curiously enough this code has been studied very little, as if it were taken for granted that the code stays the same throughout development" (Piaget, 1968, pp. 1–2). While Piaget's own work in this area focussed on the influence of the child's knowledge schemas on their ability to remember conceptual information (Piaget & Inhelder, 1968), one can certainly ask whether the "memory code" employed by children to maintain information in short-term or working memory changes with age. Indeed, psychologists have subsequently suggested that verbal rehearsal develops around the age of 7 years in children (Baddeley, Gathercole, & Papagno, 1998; Flavell, Beach, & Chinsky, 1966; Gathercole, 1998; Gathercole, Adams, & Hitch, 1994; Henry, 1991; Hitch, Woodin, & Baker, 1989). The suggestion of a qualitative developmental change in rehearsal status is clearly in line with the spirit, if not the detail, of Piagetian theory, and this claim will be evaluated in detail in the following and final sections of this chapter.

The development of rehearsal: Evidence from studies of short-term memory in typical and atypical development

The development of the word length effect

Although the presence of a word length effect in verbal short-term memory performance is potentially consistent with the notion that participants are rehearsing, the status of this phenomenon as a marker of rehearsal is a subject of considerable debate. Cowan et al. (1992) argued that word length effects, in part at least, might arise at output rather than because of rehearsal processes; as long words take longer to produce, greater forgetting of still to-be-output items might occur than when a string of short words have to be recalled (see also Dosher & Ma, 1998; though see Lovatt, Avons, & Masterson, 2002). Indeed, word length effects in adults may be attenuated when full output demands are removed from the task (Baddeley, Chincotta, Stafford, & Turk, 2002), though they are still observed (Baddeley et al., 2002; Campoy, 2008). Alternatively a number of authors have noted that the spoken duration of a given word is typically correlated with the number of phonemes it contains. Consequently, poorer recall for longer as opposed to shorter words could be driven by complexity effects or interference effects related to the greater information that needs to be maintained for longer words (Brown & Hulme, 1995; Campoy, 2008; Caplan, Rochon, & Waters, 1992; Hulme, Suprenant, Bireta, Stuart, & Neath, 2004; Lewandowsky & Oberauer, 2008; Lovatt, Avons, & Masterson, 2000; Neath & Nairne, 1995; Romani et al., 2005; Service, 1998). In addition, Campoy (2008) has recently shown that word length effects are observed in adults even under conditions of fast presentation rate, which, Campoy argues, should prevent the use of rehearsal.

There is therefore considerable evidence against the view that the word length effect necessarily reflects rehearsal processes. However, if a change in the size of the word length was seen in children of different ages, then not only would this be consistent with the view that rehearsal undergoes developmental change, but it would also be hard to reconcile with accounts that ascribe the word length effect to factors at the level of the stimulus rather than at the level of the participant (cf. Yuzawa, 2001). Studies by Henry and colleagues (Henry, 1991; Henry, Turner, Smith, & Leather, 2000; Turner, Henry, & Smith, 2000) appear to provide such evidence among typically developing individuals. These studies employed a probed recall design in which participants were presented with a list of items, either of long or of short spoken duration, and were then asked to recall one item from within the presented list, thereby minimizing any potentially confounding output demands. Memory for items was probed by the experimenter using nonverbal methods that either required the child to select the correct position in the presented list of a given item, or to identify the item at a given list position. All three of these studies found clear evidence of a word length effect among children aged 7 and above using this procedure, but not among younger individuals.

However, in recent work we have questioned the reliability of the probed recall procedure for looking at developmental changes in the size of short-term memory effects (Jarrold, Cocksey, & Dockerill, 2008). Marked recency effects are observed in probed recall procedures (Waugh & Norman, 1965) and so the effect of any manipulation is reduced or even eliminated when the final position in a list is probed. Consequently, if younger participants are given shorter lists than older participants, as was the case in Henry and colleagues' studies and all list positions are probed equally often, then relatively fewer trials will have the power to detect condition effects in younger individuals (Jarrold et al., 2008). It is also worth noting that in each of these probed recall experiments older individuals received more trials than did younger individuals, thereby further reducing the sensitivity of any task manipulation among younger participants.

However, these concerns do not apply to an earlier study by Allik and Siegel (1976), who tested probed recall of visually presented items among children of a variety of ages ranging from 4 to 10 years, and who presented

7-item lists to all participants, regardless of their age. Allik and Siegel found evidence of a reliable word length effect among children aged 8 and above, but not among children aged 6 and below, suggesting that while Henry and colleagues' design may well have been flawed, their conclusions might well be valid.

Comparable findings emerged from a study from our group that explored the size of the word length effect shown in probed recall of individuals with Down syndrome, plus a comparison sample of individuals with other learning difficulties and a group of typically developing children (Jarrold, Baddeley, & Hewes, 2000). Individuals in each group were matched for level of receptive vocabulary, and the average vocabulary mental age equivalent score for each group was around the four and a half year level; the mean chronological age of the individuals with Down syndrome and with other learning difficulties was around 13 and 10 years respectively. All individuals were presented with three item lists of words of either short or long spoken duration, and their memory for a single item was then probed, with probing occurring equally often at each serial position. The results showed no evidence of a reliable word length effect, and no suggestion of a significant word length by probed position interaction in the sample as a whole, or in any specific group. Indeed, an inspection of the data (see Figure 8.1) shows that while there was substantial recency in the data, leading to ceiling performance in both conditions for the final serial position, there was no evidence of a meaningful word length effect at the two earlier serial positions. Although further work is clearly needed to properly determine whether probed recall has the power to detect word length effects when children are given relatively short presentation lists, these data do suggest that young children do not show a word length effect when the confounding effects of output demands are eliminated (cf. Allik & Siegel, 1976). In addition, they show that among children with developmental delay, it is level of intellectual development and not age that predicts their performance. Consequently, to the extent that the word length effect under probed recall can be taken as an index of rehearsal, it appears that the development of rehearsal is linked to more general cognitive factors rather than occurring simply as a result of maturation (cf. Balthazar, 2003).

The development of the speech rate–span relationship

A relationship between the rate at which individuals can articulate words and their ability to remember those words in a short-term memory context has often been observed in adults (Baddeley et al., 1975; Cowan et al., 1998; Gathercole et al., 1994; Hulme, Maughan, & Brown, 1991; Schweickert & Boruff, 1986; Standing, Bond, Smith, & Isely, 1980; Standing & Curtis, 1989) and among children aged older than 7 years (Cohen & Heath, 1990; Cowan et al., 1994, 1998; Kail, 1992; Nicolson, 1981). As discussed above, such a relationship is clearly consistent with the notion that the speed of rehearsal constrains verbal short-term memory performance in these individuals,

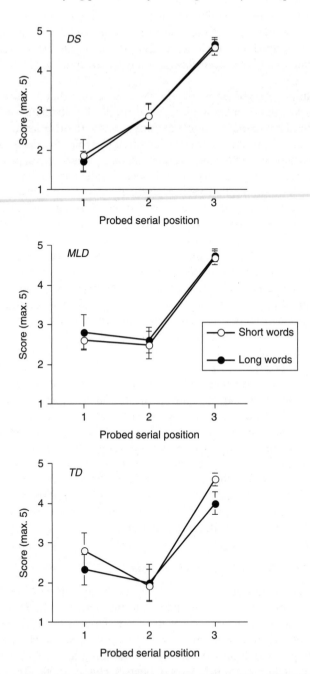

Figure 8.1 Probed recall for lists of short and long word length among individuals with Down syndrome (DS) and with moderate learning difficulties
(MLD), and among typically developing children (TD). Error bars
are +/–1 SE. Data redrawn with permission from Jarrold, Baddeley,
and Hewes (2000).

although it is worth noting that it might equally reflect the fact that speech rates correlate with word complexity (Brown & Hulme, 1995), rate of output from verbal short-term memory tasks, or general speed of processing (Ferguson & Bowey, 2005).

However, as discussed previously, evidence that younger children show no such relationship between speech rate and span would be difficult to account for using such domain-general explanations, and would appear to be more consistent with the notion that the relationship was mediated by rehearsal processes, assuming of course deficient rehearsal among younger individuals. For example, Gathercole and Adams (1993) found non-reliable correlations between these measures in 2- and 3-year-old children, a finding replicated by Gathercole et al. (1994) who also contrasted these null effects with a clear association between speech rate and span in adults. Ferguson, Bowey, and Tilley (2002) found a significant correlation between speech rate and span among 8- to 9-year-olds, but not among younger children, although it should be noted that the correlation between these measures for 10- to 11-year-olds was also non-significant. Having said this, Jarrold, Hewes, and Baddeley (2000) found that both 5- and 8-year-olds showed significant relationships between speech rates and span, while Cowan et al. (1994) also found a relia-ble relationship between these measures in 4-year-olds, albeit in the opposite direction to that predicted. Clearly, then, there is room for further work to explain these inconsistencies in the literature, and to properly determine the status of the speech rate–span relationship in young children. Nevertheless, the balance of current evidence appears to suggest that children younger than 7 show weaker, often non-significant, relationships between speech rate and span than do children older than 7.

The issue of a relationship between speech rate and span has been relevant to work from our group that has examined possible verbal short-term memory deficits among individuals with specific developmental disorders, particularly Down syndrome and Williams syndrome (see Jarrold, Baddeley, & Hewes, 1999). Individuals with Down syndrome have been shown to suffer from marked verbal short-term memory deficits relative to appropri-ately matched controls (see Jarrold, Purser, & Brock, 2006), and there is some evidence to suggest that individuals with Williams syndrome show subtle verbal short-term memory deficits (e.g., Laing, Hulme, Grant, & Karmiloff-Smith, 2001). In our study (Jarrold, Cowan, Hewes, & Riby, 2004) we com-pared the short-term memory performance of both individuals with Down syndrome and with Williams syndrome to that of two groups of typically developing children; each comparison group was matched to one of the clini-cal groups on the basis of receptive vocabulary mental age. The average verbal mental age of the individuals with Williams syndrome and their con-trols was around the 8-year level, while the individuals with Down syndrome and their controls were functioning around the 4- to 5-year level. In addition, each individual's speech rate for the items used in the short-term memory task was assessed.

The results showed that both clinical groups were impaired, relative to their controls, on the verbal short-term memory measure. In addition, each clinical group showed slower speech rates than their comparison individuals. However, among both individuals with Williams syndrome and their controls there was a significant relationship between speech rate and span. Furthermore, this relationship was similar in the two groups (see panel A of Figure 8.2), and, consequently, accounting for the reduced speech rates of individuals with Williams syndrome removed their deficit in verbal short-term memory (cf. Avons & Hanna, 1995; Raine, Hulme, Chadderton, & Bailey, 1991; Swanson & Ashbaker, 2000). In contrast, there was no reliable relationship between speech rate and short-term memory span for either the individuals with Down syndrome or their controls (see panel B of Figure 8.2). These findings therefore indicate that individuals functioning above the 7-year age equivalent level do show a reliable relationship between speech rate and span, while such a relationship is not readily observed among individuals functioning at around the 5-year level.

The development of the phonological similarity effect for visually presented material

Conrad (1971) is often credited as being the first researcher to specifically examine the process of verbal recoding of information in young children's short-term memory performance. Under the assumption that the presence of a phonological similarity effect would be evidence of phonological coding of items in memory, he presented children with sequences of pictures whose names had to be remembered. Memory for a set of images with phonologically dissimilar names was contrasted to that for a set of images with phonologically confusable labels (e.g., *cat, rat, tap*). Conrad showed that children aged 5 to 6 years and above showed significantly poorer recall of the set with similar names than of the set with non-confusable names, but no such difference was seen among 3- to 5-year-old children. However, what is less commonly reported is the fact that Conrad named the to-be-remembered pictures as they were presented, and so this study did not directly test children's ability to verbally recode (see also Alegria & Pignot, 1979).

When visually depicted items are presented without being named by the experimenter, children aged younger than 7 often fail to show a significant phonological similarity effect (Halliday, Hitch, Lennon, & Pettipher, 1990; Hayes & Schulze, 1977; Hitch, Halliday, Schaafstal, & Heffernan, 1991; though see also Al-Namlah, Fernyhough, & Meins, 2006; Ford & Silber, 1994; Palmer 2000a). For example, Hitch et al. (1989, Experiment 1) contrasted 5- and 11-year-olds' memory for the names of three types of visually depicted objects. In one condition the objects had phonologically similar names, in a second the names were phonologically distinct but the objects were drawn in a visually similar manner, and in a third control condition the items were neither phonologically nor visually confusable. Hitch et al. showed that 11-year-olds were detrimentally affected by phonological similarity but not by visual

Panel A

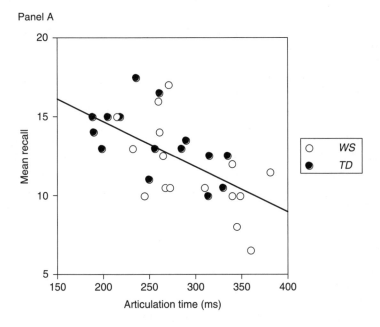

Panel B

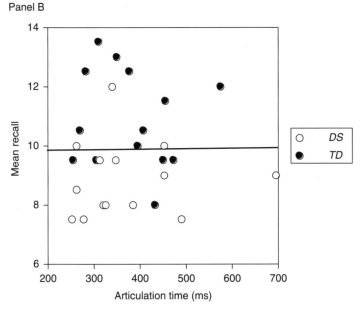

Figure 8.2 Relationship between articulation time and memory recall performance for individuals with Williams syndrome (WS) and matched typically developing controls (TD) (Panel A), and for individuals with Down syndrome (DS) and matched typically developing controls (TD) (Panel B). Lines of best fit are for all data points in each panel. Data redrawn with permission from Jarrold et al. (2004).

similarity, while, in contrast, 5-year-olds showed visual but not phonological confusions. This suggests that older children were inclined to recode the visually presented information in a phonological form, but that this option was not available to younger children, forcing them to adopt a visual approach to item maintenance. Indeed, when a further group of 11-year-olds were prevented from engaging in phonological recoding, by asking them to engage in articulatory suppression, their performance mirrored that of 5-year-olds.

Williams, Happé, and Jarrold (2008) recently applied Hitch and colleagues' methodology to a group of individuals with autism, in order to test the suggestion that autism is associated with deficits in the use of inner speech (Lidstone, Fernyhough, Meins, & Whitehouse, 2009; Whitehouse, Maybery, & Durkin, 2006); clearly if this were the case, then one would expect reduced phonological recoding of visually presented material. The recall of individuals with autism of names of visually presented objects in Hitch and colleagues' three categories – phonologically similar, visually similar, and control – was contrasted to that shown by a group of individuals with non-specific learning difficulties, of a comparable receptive vocabulary mental age. The two population groups did not differ reliably in their recall of object names across all three conditions. However, when the sample as a whole was divided in terms of receptive vocabulary level, into subgroups of individuals functioning above and below the 7-year level, a pattern of results emerged that entirely replicated Hitch et al.'s (1989) findings (see Figure 8.3). Specifically, individuals functioning above the 7-year level showed a clear phonological similarity effect but no visual similarity effect, while the opposite pattern was seen in

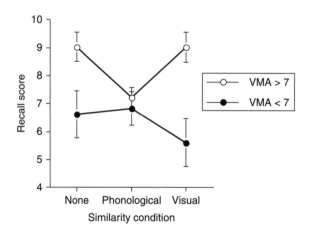

Figure 8.3 Short-term memory performance for individuals with and without autism combined for lists of visually presented items that are phonologically similar, visually similar, or neither phonologically nor visually similar (control). Separate lines for individuals with verbal mental ages (VMA) above and below 7 years. Error bars are +/–1 SE. Data redrawn from Williams et al. (2008).

participants whose mental age was less than 7. Once again, therefore, these data imply that it is developmental level, and not chronological age, that determines the degree to which potential evidence of rehearsal processes is seen in individuals showing atypical development.

The development of rehearsal in the context of working memory

The question of when children begin to engage in efficient phonological rehearsal is also relevant in the context of research into working memory, for two related reasons. First, and as discussed above, working memory tasks such as complex span tasks do require the participant to attempt to store information, and indeed evidence suggests that individuals' ability to maintain to-be-remembered items in short-term memory is one predictor of their performance on working memory measures (Alloway, Gathercole, & Pickering, 2006; Bayliss, Jarrold, Baddeley, Gunn, & Leigh, 2005; Bayliss et al., 2003; Engle, Tuholski, Laughlin, & Conway, 1999; Kane et al., 2004; Swanson, 2008; Unsworth & Engle, 2007a). Second, there is evidence to suggest that complex span tasks are better predictors of academic abilities, such as individuals' reading and mathematics skills, than are simple span tasks (Daneman & Merikle, 1996; Kane, Hambrick, & Conway, 2005; Oberauer, Schulze, Wilhelm, & Süß, 2005; though see Ackerman, Beier, & Boyle, 2005; Unsworth & Engle, 2007a). Complex span tasks combine processing and storage demands; for example, in Case et al.'s (1982) "counting span" task, participants were required to count the number of targets on successive presentation cards (the processing) while attempting to maintain the sequence of digit totals that resulted (the storage). Clearly then, the addition of processing is what differentiates complex and simple span tasks, and one possible reason why complex span tasks are often better predictors of academic attainment than simple span tasks is that this processing requirement affects the ease with which participants can rehearse. More specifically, it may be that the requirement to engage in processing temporarily "switches away" participants from rehearsal activities (Barrouillet, Bernardin, & Camos, 2004; Barrouillet, Bernardin, Portrat, Vergauwe, & Camos, 2007; Towse & Hitch, 1995, 2007), thereby placing a greater premium on rehearsal efficiency during the intervals within a task in which maintenance activity is possible. Alternatively, the addition of processing may block rehearsal completely, forcing the participant to retrieve storage items from long-term memory (Unsworth & Engle, 2006, 2007b).

Work with children who may or may not be rehearsing can therefore shed important light on this issue, and potentially illuminate the role of processing within working memory paradigms such as the complex span task. In our recent work (see Tam, Jarrold, Baddeley, & Sabatos-DeVito, 2010, Experiment 1 for full details) we have presented a variety of working memory measures to relatively large samples of 5- to 6-year-old children ($n = 117$), who one might expect not to be rehearsing, and to 7- to 8-year-olds ($n = 104$), who one might expect to be engaging in phonological rehearsal. Measures of reading and mathematics ability were also taken from 110 of the younger and 90 of the older children. In addition, each participant was given a test of the degree of phonological similarity effect shown for visually presented items in a short-term memory paradigm (cf. Hitch et al., 1989; Williams et al., 2008), to provide a measure of each individual's propensity to engage in phonological recoding, which in turn is assumed to relate to their ability to engage in phonological rehearsal (see above).

Four further working memory span measures were employed. In a simple span task participants were presented with increasingly long lists of to-be-remembered items, which were concrete words presented both auditorily and visually. They simply attempted to repeat the lists in correct serial order immediately following presentation. In a delayed span task the same presentation procedure was employed, but an unfilled interval was imposed between presentation and recall. The length of this interval was determined by the number of storage items in the presentation list, with 3 seconds unfilled delay being imposed per storage item. In a "Brown-Peterson" span task (Brown, 1958; Peterson & Peterson, 1959) storage items were presented in the same way, but a correspondingly long delay was filled with processing. Finally, in a complex span task the same storage and processing requirements were employed, but each successive presentation of a storage item was followed by a 3 second episode of processing. Following this, the next storage and processing pairing was presented, and so on.

The processing task employed in the Brown-Peterson and complex span tasks involved the participant making a forced-choice decision on the colour (silver or gold) of a series of visually presented circles. Clearly this processing was ostensibly nonverbal in nature, but work by Barrouillet and colleagues (Barrouillet et al., 2007; Portrat, Barrouillet, & Camos, 2008; Portrat, Camos, & Barrouillet, 2009; Vergauwe, Barrouillet, & Camos, 2010) has shown that such processing does disrupt the maintenance of verbal information. These authors argue that the need to make a forced-choice response captures attentional resources that might otherwise be devoted to the attentional "refreshment" of memory items. Whether such processing would also block phonological rehearsal was a question we wished to address using our design.

The results of the test of the phonological similarity effect with visual presentation produced an interaction between group and size of the similarity effect, consistent with previous literature. However, while the older group showed a clear phonological similarity effect, as would be expected, a reliable, albeit attenuated, similarity effect was also observed for the younger participants (cf. Ford & Silber, 1994). This suggests that phonological recoding, and by implication rehearsal, does develop over this age range, but that the onset of these abilities within a group of children may well be less discrete than has previously been suggested, a point that we return to below.

The older group unsurprisingly outperformed the younger children on all four of the other memory measures, but a reliable group by task interaction emerged from the analysis of these measures. First, a comparison of span scores for the simple span and delayed span tasks showed that the younger group were more affected by the imposition of an unfilled delay than the older group; a finding entirely consistent with the view that the younger participants employed rehearsal-related activities less efficiently during this delay. However, a similar comparison between performance across the delayed span and Brown-Peterson span tasks showed a similarly detrimental effect of the imposition of a processing load in both groups. This is a potential indication that nonverbal processing of the form employed here is sufficient to block non-phonological attentional refreshment of memory items, but does not affect the phonological rehearsal of memory items (cf. Hudjetz & Oberauer, 2007). Finally, both groups showed comparable performance on the Brown-Peterson span and complex span tasks. This implies that switching between processing and storage demands in the complex span task does not impose a cost on recall, although it should be noted that any switch cost present may have been obscured by a benefit to recall conferred by the greater "temporal discriminability" of the storage items in the complex span procedure (Brown, Neath, & Chater, 2007; Neath & Crowder, 1990).

Correlational analyses of the relationships between measures showed that the correlation between simple span and delayed span performance was particularly strong in both age groups. Among younger individuals simple span correlated significantly more strongly with delayed span than with either Brown-Peterson or complex span, and delayed span was significantly more strongly correlated with simple span than it was Brown-Peterson span. Among older individuals simple span was again significantly more closely related to delayed span than any other measure, and this correlation was significantly stronger than that between delayed span and either Brown-Peterson or complex span.

Among younger children, all four memory measures were comparable correlates of academic attainment. Among older individuals, Brown-Peterson and complex span scores were reliably related to academic ability, and to a similar extent to that seen in the younger group. More specifically, however, in these 7- to 8-year-olds, we found that academic ability was more strongly associated with simple and delayed span scores than with Brown-Peterson scores, or with complex span performance. In older children, delayed span may therefore be a significantly stronger predictor of reading and mathematics competence than either Brown-Peterson or complex span. Given that the delayed span task allows rehearsal to take place, it is perhaps unsurprising that delayed span performance also correlated significantly with the size of the phonological similarity effect in older, though not younger children.

In summary, this study suggests that children's rehearsal status does have an effect on their performance in working memory paradigms, and in turn therefore determines what "working memory" tasks really measure in children of different ages. Among the younger group assessed in this work there was some evidence of phonological recoding of visual information, and hence, rehearsal-related processes. However, this evidence was clearly less marked than in older individuals, and younger children were more likely to forget to-be-remembered items during an unfilled delay. If one accepts that rehearsal is relatively limited in children below the age of 7, then the imposition of a processing demand in the context of a working memory paradigm should have relatively little effect on such individuals, relative to their short-term memory performance (cf. Barrouillet, Gavens, Vergauwe, Gaillard, & Camos, 2009, Experiment 3). To some extent this was what was observed, and certainly, short-term memory measures such as simple span were equally strong predictors of academic ability as was complex span in this group. This contrasts with what is often seen in adult studies (though see Unsworth & Engle, 2007a), and would suggest that the relatively stronger predictive power of complex span among adults is related to the disruption of rehearsal by processing in such tasks (Cowan et al., 2005). Having said this, there was clear evidence that the older individuals assessed in this study were rehearsing, and yet complex span and Brown-Peterson span were not the strongest predictors of academic attainment in this group; rather simple and delayed span were stronger correlates of reading and maths. One explanation for this pattern is that though these individuals are rehearsing, rehearsal may be less efficient and less automated among 7- and 8-year-olds than in adults. Consequently there may be considerable individual variation in rehearsal efficiency or strategic use of rehearsal in this group, and this variation will be particularly well captured by tasks that maximize the opportunities for rehearsal, such as delayed span. Among such children, then, it may be that academic ability relates less to the use of rehearsal in the face of potentially disrupting processing, or the retrieval of material from long-term memory, but rather the ability to effectively maintain information in memory through efficient use of rehearsal strategies (Palmer, 2000b).

Conclusions: Evidence for a qualitative shift in rehearsal with age?

Piaget's theory of cognitive development is characterized by the notion that individuals, from infancy to early adulthood, pass through discrete stages each involving a qualitatively different form of mental representation. In a similar vein, research on rehearsal and its role in short-term and working memory development is often driven by the implicit notion that there is a qualitative change in the use of phonological rehearsal around 7 years of age. The two previous sections in this chapter present what might appear to be contradictory evidence concerning this issue. On the one hand, the evidence from typical and atypical development of the onset of the word length effect under probed recall, of the appearance of reliable speech rate–span correlations, and of the presence of a phonological similarity effect for visually presented materials, suggests that an approximate age of 7 years might well mark something of a watershed in the development of rehearsal. More precisely, children functioning below the 7-year age equivalent level often fail to show possible rehearsal-related phenomena, whereas children functioning above this level do show these effects. On the other hand, our study of working memory performance in large samples of 5- to 6- and 7- to 8-year-old children showed some evidence of rehearsal-related processes in the younger of these two groups.

The large sample size of young children employed in our study might go some way towards explaining this apparent contradiction, as the effect of phonological similarity for visually presented material seen in this group may well have been non-significant in a sample of the size more typically used in previous research. Indeed, Al-Namlah et al. (2006) have recently reported reliable phonological similarity effects for visually presented material among a relatively large sample ($n = 47$) of 4- to 6-year-old children. In addition, it is worth re-emphasizing that a reliable interaction between age and size of phonological similarity effect was observed in our working memory study, and hence these data are not completely inconsistent with previous work reviewed above.

However, our findings do question the assumption that children below the age of 7 years simply do not rehearse. In particular, they emphasize the obvious point that an apparently qualitative change in performance can arise from selective sampling of a quantitatively changing distribution. In other words, it may well be that the degree of rehearsal shown by an individual develops gradually, and continually with age between, say, 5 and 9 years, but that studies that have only assessed two non-adjacent age groups have imposed an artificial dichotomy on this developmental profile. In addition, if quantitative development were the case then one might well expect to see particularly small effect sizes for estimates of the word length under probed recall, the degree of association between speech rate and span, and the size of the phonological similarity effect under visual presentation among younger children. As noted, large sample sizes might be needed to see such effects, or these effects might "come and go" in the literature leading to an inconsistent pattern of findings for younger children. Certainly there is some evidence for this in the data on the development of rehearsal in short-term memory reviewed above, perhaps particularly in terms of the size of speech rate–span correlations.

Of course, no author would argue that all children develop rehearsal at exactly 7 years, and consequently even if one believed that an individual's rehearsal status undergoes something akin to qualitative change around 7, then one would not expect all 6-year-olds to not rehearse and all 8-year-olds to rehearse (cf. Conrad, 1971; Flavell et al., 1966). The key question for future research to address, therefore, is whether a given individual really does undergo qualitative change in their rehearsal status *as they develop*. To date, very few studies have looked at children's rehearsal status at the individual level (though see Al-Namlah et al., 2006; Palmer, 2000b), or have tracked the development of rehearsal-related phenomena longitudinally (though see Palmer, 2000a). Detailed studies of this kind, perhaps employing a microgenetic approach, are sorely needed in order to properly determine the shape and rate of age-related change in rehearsal in children.

A less direct way of distinguishing between qualitative and quantitative changes in rehearsal efficiency is to examine whether the development of memory span with age is non-linear in children. If rehearsal has any beneficial effect on recall at all, then one must predict that the onset of rehearsal confers an increase to memory span in older children. Even allowing for the fact that qualitative change at the individual level might occur across an age range within a sample, this leads to the prediction that there should be an observable discontinuity in the development of memory span with age. Individual variation in the onset of rehearsal would certainly "smooth" the developmental function, and so one would not necessarily expect a discrete step change in performance, but evidence of a completely linear development of memory span would be hard to reconcile with the notion of qualitative change.

In fact, existing data is much more suggestive of a linear rather than non-linear development of short-term memory performance from very young ages to adulthood (Alloway et al., 2006; Hulme, Thomson, Muir, & Lawrence, 1984; Gathercole, 1998, 1999; see also Alloway & Archibald, this volume). Given this, and the evidence of small but reliable effects of phonological similarity for visually presented material seen in 5- to 6-year-olds in our work, it may well be that previous notions of a qualitative change in verbal recoding and rehearsal, which would be consistent with a Piagetian model of development, need to be re-evaluated. This is not to deny, however, the evidence that rehearsal efficiency increases with age, and any study that selects discrete age groups will likely find evidence that the amount, efficiency, or quality of rehearsal seen differs across these age groups. This, in turn, will have implications for what any memory tasks given to these groups might measure. Among children where rehearsal is limited and inefficient, rehearsal will necessarily not be a major influence on task performance. Among adults where rehearsal is arguably maximally efficient, blocking rehearsal is likely to affect recall, but there may not be much variation in the size of these effects among individuals. In contrast, among children falling between these ages there may well be considerable individual variation in rehearsal efficiency, which in turn would lead to variation in what potential measures of working memory actually index in such individuals.

Finally, the fact that rehearsal status has such a clear effect on working memory performance is potentially problematic for any neo-Piagetian model of working memory that simply suggests that development of working memory capacity is driven by developmental changes in processing efficiency (cf. Case et al., 1982). It is increasingly clear that one factor that constrains performance in both children and adults on working memory measures such as complex span tasks is the opportunities that such tasks provide for rehearsal-like activity, coupled with individuals' ability to make use of these opportunities (Barrouillet et al., 2007, 2009). This implies that an individual's ability to maintain information in a working memory task is not solely driven by the efficiency with which they carry out the processing operations of the task, but also reflects their ability to reactivate memory representations when not engaged in processing (Barrouillet et al., 2009; Jarrold & Bayliss, 2007). Having said this, we are aware of one neo-Piagetian account that fits with these suggestions. Morra (2000) showed that both a neo-Piagetian capacity measure (*M*-capacity, Pascual-Leone, 1970) and articulation rate contributed separable variance to the prediction of children's short-term memory span (see also Morra & Camba, 2009). He therefore argued that "rehearsal skill may make an independent contribution to span" (Morra, 2000, p. 213) over and beyond an individual's operational capacity, but also predicted that the ability to employ a rehearsal strategy would be dependent on this operational capacity. This account therefore provides a capacity-based explanation for why rehearsal might be absent in younger children, although it still predicts essentially qualitative change in the use of rehearsal. This again emphasizes the need for further studies to map out in detail the shape of change of rehearsal processes with age and ability in children.

Author note

Correspondence concerning this article should be addressed to: Chris Jarrold, Department of Experimental Psychology, University of Bristol, 12a Priory Road, Bristol BS8 1TU, UK. Electronic mail: C.Jarrold@bristol.ac.uk. The preparation of this chapter was supported by a grant from the Economic and Social Research Council of the United Kingdom to Christopher Jarrold and Alan Baddeley on "The causes and consequences of forgetting in working memory" (RES-062-23-0148).

References

Ackerman, P. L., Beier, M. E., & Boyle, M. O. (2005). Working memory and intelligence: The same or different constructs? *Psychological Bulletin, 131*, 30–60.

Alegria, J., & Pignot, E. (1979). Genetic aspects of verbal mediation in memory. *Child Development, 50*, 235–238.

Allik, J. P., & Siegel, A. W. (1976). The use of the cumulative rehearsal strategy: A developmental study. *Journal of Experimental Child Psychology, 21*, 316–327.

Alloway, T. P., Gathercole, S. E., & Pickering, S. J. (2006). Verbal and visuospatial short-term and working memory in children: Are they separable? *Child Development, 77*, 1698–1716.

Al-Namlah, A. S., Fernyhough, C., & Meins, E. (2006). Sociocultural influences on the development of verbal mediation: Private speech and phonological recoding in Saudi Arabian and British samples. *Developmental Psychology, 42*, 117–131.

Atkinson, R. C., & Shiffrin, R. M. (1968). Human memory: A proposed system and its control processes. In K. W. Spence & J. T. Spence (Eds.), *The psychology of learning and motivation* (pp. 89–105). New York: Academic Press.

Avons, S. E., & Hanna, C. (1995). The memory-span deficit in children with specific reading disability: Is speech rate responsible? *British Journal of Developmental Psychology, 13*, 303–311.

Baddeley, A. D. (1986). *Working memory*. Oxford: Oxford University Press.

Baddeley, A. D., Chincotta, D., Stafford, L., & Turk, D. (2002). Is the word length effect in STM attributable to output delay? Evidence from serial recognition. *The Quarterly Journal of Experimental Psychology, 55A*, 353–369.

Baddeley, A., Gathercole, S., & Papagno, C. (1998). The phonological loop as a language learning device. *Psychological Review, 105*, 158–173.

Baddeley, A. D., & Hitch, G. J. (1974). Working memory. In G. Bower (Ed.), *The psychology of learning and motivation* (pp. 47–89). New York: Academic Press.

Baddeley, A. D., Lewis, V., & Vallar, G. (1984). Exploring the articulatory loop. *The Quarterly Journal of Experimental Psychology, 36A*, 233–252.

Baddeley, A. D., Thomson, N., & Buchanan, M. (1975). Word length and the structure of short-term memory. *Journal of Verbal Learning and Verbal Behavior, 14*, 575–589.

Balthazar, C. H. (2003). The word length effect in children with language impairment. *Journal of Communication Disorders, 36*, 487–505.

Barrouillet, P., Bernardin, S., & Camos, V. (2004). Time constraints and resource sharing in adults' working memory spans. *Journal of Experimental Psychology: General, 133*, 83–100.

Barrouillet, P., Bernardin, S., Portrat, S., Vergauwe, E., & Camos, V. (2007). Time and cognitive load in working memory. *Journal of Experimental Psychology: Learning, Memory, and Cognition, 33*, 570–585.

Barrouillet, P., Gavens, N., Vergauwe, E., Gaillard, V., & Camos, V. (2009). Working memory span development: A time-based resource-sharing model account. *Developmental Psychology, 45*, 477–490.

Bayliss, D. M., Jarrold, C., Baddeley, A. D., Gunn, D. M., & Leigh, E. (2005). Mapping the developmental constraints on working memory span performance. *Developmental Psychology, 41*, 579–597.

Bayliss, D. M., Jarrold, C., Gunn, D. M., & Baddeley, A. D. (2003). The complexities of complex span: Explaining individual differences in working memory in children and adults. *Journal of Experimental Psychology: General, 132*, 71–92.

Brown, G. D. A., & Hulme, C. (1995). Modeling item length effects in memory span: No rehearsal needed. *Journal of Memory and Language, 34*, 594–621.

Brown, G. D. A., Neath, I., & Chater, N. (2007). A temporal ratio model of memory. *Psychological Review, 114*, 539–576.

Brown, J. (1958). Some tests of the decay theory of immediate memory. *The Quarterly Journal of Experimental Psychology, 10*, 12–21.

Campoy, G. (2008). The effect of word length in short-term memory: Is rehearsal necessary? *The Quarterly Journal of Experimental Psychology, 61*, 724–734.

Caplan, D., Rochon, E., & Waters, G. S. (1992). Articulatory and phonological determinants of word length effects in span tasks. *The Quarterly Journal of Experimental Psychology, 45A*, 177–192.

Case, R., Kurland, D. M., & Goldberg, J. (1982). Operational efficiency and the growth of short-term memory span. *Journal of Experimental Child Psychology, 33*, 386–404.

Cohen, R. L., & Heath, M. (1990). The development of serial short-term memory and the articulatory loop hypothesis. *Intelligence, 14*, 151–171.

Conrad, R. (1971). The chronology of the development of covert speech in children. *Developmental Psychology, 5*, 398–405.

Conrad, R., & Hull, A. J. (1964). Information, acoustic confusion, and memory span. *British Journal of Psychology, 55*, 429–432.

Cowan, N., Day, L., Saults, J. S., Keller, T. A., Johnson, T., & Flores, L. (1992). The role of verbal output time in the effects of word length on immediate memory. *Journal of Memory and Language, 31*, 1–17.

Cowan, N., Elliott, E. M., Saults, J. S., Morey, C., Mattox, S., Hismjatullina, A., et al. (2005). On the capacity of attention: Its estimation and its role in working memory and cognitive abilities. *Cognitive Psychology, 51*, 42–100.

Cowan, N., Keller, T. A., Hulme, C., Roodenrys, S., McDougall, S., & Rack, J. (1994). Verbal memory span in children: Speech timing clues to the mechanisms underlying age and word length effects. *Journal of Memory and Language, 33*, 234–250.

Cowan, N., Wood, N. L., Wood, P. K., Keller, T. A., Nugent, L. D., & Keller, C. V. (1998). Two separate verbal processing rates contributing to short-term memory span. *Journal of Experimental Psychology: General, 127*, 141–160.

Crowder, R. G. (1976). *Principles of learning and memory.* Hillsdale, NJ: Lawrence Erlbaum Associates.

Daneman, M., & Carpenter, P. A. (1980). Individual differences in working memory and reading. *Journal of Verbal Learning and Verbal Behavior, 19*, 450–466.

Daneman, M., & Merikle, P. M. (1996). Working memory and language comprehension: A meta-analysis. *Psychonomic Bulletin and Review, 3*, 422–433.

Dosher, B. A., & Ma, J. J. (1998). Output loss or rehearsal loop? Output-time versus pronunciation-time limits in immediate recall for forgetting-matched materials. *Journal of Experimental Psychology: Learning, Memory and Cognition, 24*, 316–335.

Engle, R. W., Tuholski, S. W., Laughlin, J. E., & Conway, A. R. A. (1999). Working memory, short-term memory, and general fluid intelligence: A latent-variable approach. *Journal of Experimental Psychology: General, 128*, 309–311.

Ferguson, A. N., & Bowey, J. A. (2005). Global processing speed as a mediator of developmental changes in children's auditory memory span. *Journal of Experimental Child Psychology, 91*, 89–112.

Ferguson, A. N., Bowey, J. A., & Tilley, A. (2002). The association between auditory memory span and speech rate in children from kindergarten to sixth grade. *Journal of Experimental Child Psychology, 81*, 141–156.

Flavell, J. H., Beach, D. R., & Chinsky, J. M. (1966). Spontaneous verbal rehearsal in a memory task as a function of age. *Child Development, 37*, 283–299.

Ford, S., & Silber, K. P. (1994). Working memory in children: A developmental approach to the phonological coding of pictorial material. *British Journal of Developmental Psychology, 12*, 165–175.

Gathercole, S. E. (1998). The development of memory. *Journal of Child Psychology and Psychiatry, 39*, 3–27.

Gathercole, S. E. (1999). Cognitive approaches to the development of short-term memory. *Trends in Cognitive Sciences, 3*, 410–419.

Gathercole, S. E., & Adams, A. M. (1993). Phonological working memory in very young children. *Developmental Psychology, 29*, 770–778.

Gathercole, S. E., Adams, A. M., & Hitch, G. J. (1994). Do young children rehearse? An individual differences analysis. *Memory and Cognition, 22*, 201–207.

Glanzer, M., & Clark, W. H. (1962). Accuracy of perceptual recall: An analysis of organization. *Journal of Verbal Learning and Verbal Behavior, 1*, 289–299.

Glanzer, M., & Clark, W. H. (1963). The verbal loop hypothesis: Binary numbers. *Journal of Verbal Learning and Verbal Behavior, 2*, 301–309.

Halliday, M. S., Hitch, G. J., Lennon, B., & Pettipher, C. (1990). Verbal short-term memory in children: The role of the articulatory loop. *European Journal of Cognitive Psychology*, *2*, 23–38.

Hayes, D. S., & Schulze, S. A. (1977). Visual encoding in preschoolers' serial retention. *Child Development*, *48*, 1066–1070.

Henry, L. A. (1991). The effects of word length and phonemic similarity in young children's short-term memory. *The Quarterly Journal of Experimental Psychology*, *43A*, 35–52.

Henry, L. A., Turner, J. E., Smith, P. T., & Leather, C. (2000). Modality effects and the development of the word length effect in children. *Memory*, *8*, 1–17.

Hitch, G. J., Halliday, M. S., Schaafstal, A. M., & Heffernan, T. M. (1991). Speech, "inner speech", and the development of short-term memory: Effects of picture-labelling on recall. *Journal of Experimental Child Psychology*, *51*, 220–234.

Hitch, G. J., Woodin, M. E., & Baker, S. (1989). Visual and phonological components of working memory in children. *Memory and Cognition*, *17*, 175–185.

Howard, D., & Franklin, S. E. (1990). Memory without rehearsal. In G. Vallar & T. Shallice (Eds.), *Neuropsychological impairments of short-term memory* (pp. 287–318). Cambridge: Cambridge University Press.

Hudjetz, A., & Oberauer, K. (2007). The effects of processing time and processing rate on forgetting in working memory: Testing four models of the complex span paradigm. *Memory and Cognition*, *35*, 1675–1684.

Hulme, C., Maughan, S., & Brown, G. D. A. (1991). Memory for familiar and unfamiliar words: Evidence for a long-term memory contribution to short-term memory span. *Journal of Memory and Language*, *30*, 685–701.

Hulme, C., Suprenant, A. M., Bireta, T. J., Stuart, G., & Neath, I. (2004). Abolishing the word-length effect. *Journal of Experimental Psychology: Learning, Memory, and Cognition*, *30*, 98–106.

Hulme, C., Thomson, N., Muir, C., & Lawrence, A. (1984). Speech rate and the development of short-term memory span. *Journal of Experimental Child Psychology*, *38*, 241–253.

Jarrold, C., Baddeley, A. D., & Hewes, A. K. (1999). Genetically dissociated components of working memory: Evidence from Down's and Williams syndrome. *Neuropsychologia*, *37*, 637–651.

Jarrold, C., Baddeley, A. D., & Hewes, A. K. (2000). Verbal short-term memory deficits in Down syndrome: A consequence of problems in rehearsal? *Journal of Child Psychology and Psychiatry*, *41*, 233–244.

Jarrold, C. & Bayliss, D. M. (2007). Variation in working memory due to typical and atypical development. In A. R. A. Conway, C. Jarrold, M. J. Kane, A. Miyake, & J. N. Towse (Eds.), *Variation in working memory* (pp. 134–161). New York: Oxford University Press.

Jarrold, C., Cocksey, J., & Dockerill, E. (2008). Phonological similarity and lexicality effects in children's verbal short-term memory: Concerns about the interpretation of probed recall data. *The Quarterly Journal of Experimental Psychology*, *61*, 324–340.

Jarrold, C., Cowan, N., Hewes, A. K., & Riby, D. M. (2004). Speech timing and verbal short-term memory: Evidence for contrasting deficits in Down syndrome and Williams syndrome. *Journal of Memory and Language*, *51*, 365–380.

Jarrold, C., Hewes, A. K., & Baddeley, A. D. (2000). Two separate speech measures constrain verbal short-term memory in children. *Journal of Experimental Psychology: Learning, Memory, and Cognition*, *26*, 1626–1637.

Jarrold, C., Purser, H. R. M., & Brock, J. (2006). Short-term memory in Down syndrome. In T. P. Alloway & S. E. Gathercole (Eds.), *Working memory and neurodevelopmental disorders* (pp. 239–266). Hove, UK: Psychology Press.

Jarrold, C., & Towse, J. T. N. (2006). Individual differences in working memory. *Neuroscience, 139*, 39–50.

Kail, R. (1992). Processing speed, speech rate, and memory. *Developmental Psychology, 28*, 899–904.

Kane, M. J., Hambrick, D. Z., & Conway, A. R. A. (2005). Working memory capacity and fluid intelligence are strongly related constructs: Comment on Ackerman, Beier, and Boyle (2005). *Psychological Bulletin, 131*, 66–71.

Kane, M. J., Hambrick, D. Z., Tuholski, S. W., Wilhelm, O., Payne, T. W., & Engle, R. W. (2004). The generality of working memory capacity: A latent-variable approach to verbal and visuospatial memory span and reasoning. *Journal of Experimental Psychology: General, 133*, 189–217.

Laing, E., Hulme, C., Grant, J., & Karmiloff-Smith, A. (2001). Learning to read in Williams syndrome: Looking beneath the surface of atypical reading development. *Journal of Child Psychology and Psychiatry, 42*, 729–739.

Landauer, T. K. (1962). Rate of implicit speech. *Perceptual and Motor Skills, 15*, 646.

Lewandowsky, S., & Oberauer, K. (2008). The word length effect provides no evidence for decay in short-term memory. *Psychonomic Bulletin and Review, 15*, 875–888.

Lidstone, J., Fernyhough, C., Meins, E., & Whitehouse, A. (2009). Brief report: Inner speech impairment in children with autism is associated with greater nonverbal than verbal skills. *Journal of Autism and Developmental Disorders, 39*(8), 1222–1225.

Logie, R. H. (1995). *Visuo-spatial working memory*. Hove, UK: Lawrence Erlbaum Associates.

Lovatt, P., Avons, S. E., & Masterson, J. (2000). The word-length effect and disyllabic words. *The Quarterly Journal of Experimental Psychology, 53A*, 1–22.

Lovatt, P., Avons, S. E., & Masterson, J. (2002). Output decay in immediate serial recall: Speech time revisited. *Journal of Memory and Language, 46*, 227–243.

Lovelace, E. A., Powell, M., & Brooks, R. J. (1973). Alphabetic position effects in covert and overt alphabetic recitation times. *Journal of Experimental Psychology, 99*, 405–408.

Morra, S. (2000). A new model of verbal short-term memory. *Journal of Experimental Child Psycholgy, 75*, 191–227.

Morra, S., & Camba, R. (2009). Vocabulary learning in primary school children: working memory and long-term memory components. *Journal of Experimental Child Psychology, 104*, 156–178.

Neath, I., & Crowder, R. G. (1990). Schedules of presentation and temporal distinctiveness in human memory. *Journal of Experimental Psychology: Learning, Memory and Cognition, 16*, 316–327.

Neath, I., & Nairne, J. S. (1995). Word-length effects in immediate memory: Overwriting trace decay theory. *Psychonomic Bulletin and Review, 2*, 429–441.

Nicolson, R. (1981). The relationship between memory span and processing speed. In M. Friedman, J. P. Das, & N. O'Connor (Eds.), *Intelligence and learning* (pp. 179–183). New York: Plenum Press.

Oberauer, K., Schulze, R., Wilhelm, O., & Süß, H.-M. (2005). Working memory and intelligence – their correlation and their relation: Comment on Ackerman, Beier, and Boyle (2005). *Psychological Bulletin, 131*, 61–65.

Palmer, S. (2000a) Working memory: A developmental study of phonological recoding. *Memory, 8*, 179–193.

Palmer, S. (2000b). Development of phonological recoding and literacy acquisition: A four-year cross-sequential study. *British Journal of Developmental Psychology, 18*, 533–555.

Pascual-Leone, J. (1970). A mathematical model for the transition rule in Piaget's developmental stages. *Acta Psychologia, 32*, 301–345

Pavio, A. (1971). *Imagery and verbal processes.* New York: Holt, Rinehart & Winston.

Peterson, L. R., & Peterson, M. J. (1959). Short-term retention of individual verbal items. *Journal of Experimental Psychology, 58*, 193–198.

Piaget, J. (1968). *On the development of memory and identity.* Massachusetts: Clark University Press.

Piaget, J., & Inhelder, B. (1968). *Mémoire et intelligence.* Presses Universitaires de France.

Portrat, S., Barrouillet, P., & Camos, V. (2008). Time-related decay or interference-based forgetting in working memory? *Journal of Experimental Psychology: Learning, Memory, and Cognition, 34*, 1561–1564.

Portrat, S., Camos, V., & Barrouillet, P. (2009). Working memory in children: A time-constrained functioning similar to adults. *Journal of Experimental Child Psychology, 102*, 368–374.

Raine, A., Hulme, C., Chadderton, H., & Bailey, P. (1991). Verbal short-term memory span in speech-disordered children: Implications for articulatory coding in short-term memory. *Child Development, 62*, 415–423.

Romani, C., McAlpine, S., Olson, A., Tsouknida, E., & Martin, R. (2005). Length, lexicality, and articulatory suppression in immediate recall: Evidence against the articulatory loop. *Journal of Memory and Language, 52*, 398–415.

Schweickert, R., & Boruff, B. (1986). Short-term memory capacity: Magic number or magic spell? *Journal of Experimental Psychology: Learning, Memory and Cognition, 12*, 419–425.

Service, E. (1998). The effect of word length on immediate serial recall depends on phonological complexity, not articulatory duration. *The Quarterly Journal of Experimental Psychology, 51A*, 283–304.

Spiker, C. C. (1956). Stimulus pretraining and subsequent performance in the delayed reaction experiment. *Journal of Experimental Psychology, 52*, 107–111.

Standing, L., Bond, B., Smith, P., & Isely, C. (1980). Is the immediate memory span determined by subvocalization rate? *British Journal of Psychology, 71*, 525–539.

Standing, L., & Curtis, L. (1989). Subvocalization rate versus other predictors of the memory span. *Psychological Reports, 65*, 487–495.

Swanson, H. L. (2008). Working memory and intelligence in children: What develops? *Journal of Educational Psychology, 100*, 581–602.

Swanson, H. L., & Ashbaker, M. H. (2000). Working memory, short-term memory, speech rate, word recognition and reading comprehension in learning disabled readers: Does the executive system have a role? *Intelligence, 28*, 1–30.

Tam, H., Jarrold, C., Baddeley, A. D., & Sabatos-DeVito, M. (2010). The development of memory maintenance: Children's use of phonological rehearsal and attentional refreshment in working memory tasks. *Journal of Experimental Child Psychology, 107*, 306–324.

Towse, J. N., & Hitch, G. J. (1995). Is there a relationship between task demand and storage space in tests of working memory capacity. *The Quarterly Journal of Experimental Psychology, 48A*, 108–124.

Towse, J. N., & Hitch, G. J. (2007). Variation in working memory due to normal development. In A. R. A. Conway, C. Jarrold, M. J. Kane, A. Miyake, & J. N. Towse (Eds.), *Variation in working memory* (pp. 109–133). New York: Oxford University Press.

Turner, J. E., Henry, L. A., & Smith, P. T. (2000). The development of the use of long-term knowledge to assist short-term recall. *The Quarterly Journal of Experimental Psychology, 53A*, 457–478.

Unsworth, N., & Engle, R. W. (2006). Simple and complex memory spans and their relation to fluid abilities: Evidence from list-length effects. *Journal of Memory and Language, 54*, 68–80.

Unsworth, N., & Engle, R. W. (2007a). On the division of short-term and working memory: An examination of simple and complex span and their relation to higher order abilities. *Psychological Bulletin, 133*, 1038–1066.

Unsworth, N., & Engle, R. W. (2007b). The nature of individual differences in working memory capacity: Active maintenance in primary memory and controlled search in secondary memory. *Psychological Review, 114*, 104–132.

Vallar, G., & Papagno, C. (1995). Neuropsychological impairments of short-term memory. In A. D. Baddeley, B. A. Wilson, & F. Watts (Eds.), *Handbook of memory disorders* (pp. 135–165). Chichester: John Wiley & Sons.

Vergauwe, E., Barrouillet, P., & Camos, V. (2010). Do mental processes share a domain-general resource? *Psychological Science, 21*, 384–390.

Waugh, N. C., & Norman, D. A. (1965). Primary memory. *Psychological Review, 72*, 89–104.

Whitehouse, A. J. O., Maybery, M. T., & Durkin, K. (2006). Inner speech impairments in autism. *Journal of Child Psychology and Psychiatry, 47*, 857–865.

Williams, D., Happé, F., & Jarrold, C. (2008). Intact inner speech use in autism spectrum disorder: Evidence from a short-term memory task. *Journal of Child Psychology and Psychiatry, 49*, 51–58.

Yuzawa, M. (2001). Effects of word length on young children's memory performance. *Memory and Cognition, 29*, 557–564.

Part III

Working memory in typical and atypical development

9 The influence of working memory growth on reading and math performance in children with math and/or reading disabilities

H. Lee Swanson

Cognitive impairments are important correlates of functional outcome in children with reading disabilities (RD) and/or math disabilities (MD). Of these impairments, working memory (WM) has been the focus of extensive research efforts because it plays a central role in several domains of cognition including language comprehension, fluid intelligence, writing, arithmetic, and problem solving (Gathercole, Alloway, Willis, & Adams, 2006; also see Swanson & Siegel, 2001, for a review) as well as overall cognitive development (e.g., Case, 1995; de Ribaupierre & Lecerf, 2006). Further, WM impairments have been related to specific aspects of RD, such as problems in reading comprehension (Swanson, 1999b), as well as to specific aspects of MD, such as weaknesses in word problem solving (Swanson & Beebe-Frankenberger, 2004; Swanson, Jerman, & Zheng, 2008). We find, as do others, that children with normal intelligence but who suffer RD and/or MD experience considerable difficulty on WM tasks (e.g., Andersson, 2008; Bull, Johnston, & Roy, 1999; Chiappe, Hasher, & Siegel, 2000; De Beni, Palladino, Pazzaglia, & Cornoldi, 1998; de Jong, 1998; Gathercole et al., 2006; Passolunghi, Cornoldi, & De Liberto, 1999; Siegel & Ryan, 1989). There is also evidence that WM impairments may play a critical role in mediating some of the academic problems in children with RD and MD (e.g., see de Jong, 1998; Gathercole et al., 2006; Swanson & Berninger, 1995; Willcutt, Pennington, Olson, Chhabildas, & Hulslander, 2005). Although WM is integrally related to a number of academic behaviors, relatively few studies have been undertaken to systematically explore whether growth in WM underlies growth in reading and/or math performance.

The purpose of this chapter is to review some of our recent work that provides an empirical foundation for the view that reading disabilities (RD) and/or math disabilities (MD) reflect a fundamental deficit in the development of WM. We review evidence that suggests that these deficits, depending on task demands, manifest themselves as a domain-specific constraint (i.e., the inefficient accessing of phonological representations) or a domain-general constraint (i.e., capacity limitations in controlled attentional processing). That is, as an extension of research that localizes problems in RD to a phonological system (e.g., short-term memory or STM for words) or MD to constraints to number recall (e.g., short-term memory or STM for numbers), we think fundamental processing differences also emerge between children with specific learning disabilities in RD or MD that cut across tasks that involve the controlled-attentional processing of verbal and visual-spatial information. How constraints in the executive system operate independently and potentially interact with constraints in the phonological system will also be discussed.

Definition of terms

Before discussing the research linking RD and/or MD to WM, we provide our operational definition of RD/MD and WM. The concept of RD and/or MD rests on two assumptions: (a) reading and/or math difficulties are *not* due to inadequate opportunity to learn, general intelligence, physical or emotional disorders, but to basic disorders in specific psychological processes, and (b) these specific processing deficits are a reflection of neurological, constitutional, and/or biological factors. In our studies, we define RD samples by their primary academic difficulties in word recognition and then attempt to isolate problems in psychological processes. Because of the strong correlation between word recognition and comprehension, these children inevitably also suffer deficits in reading comprehension. Likewise, we operationally defined MD as those children who have general IQ scores on standardized tests above 85 and who have math scores below the 25th percentile on a standardized math achievement measure. Because of the strong correlation between calculation and word problems, these children inevitably also suffer deficits in word problem solving. An IQ-achievement test score discrepancy is not used in our studies because of serious problems with this type of definition of RD or MD (e.g., see Hoskyn & Swanson, 2000, for a review).

Working memory is defined as a processing resource of limited capacity, involved in the preservation of information while simultaneously processing the same or other information (e.g., Baddeley & Logie, 1999; Engle, Tuholski, Laughlin, & Conway, 1999; Just & Carpenter, 1992). Tasks that measure WM assess an individual's ability to maintain task-relevant information in an active state and to regulate controlled processing. For example, individuals performing WM tasks must remember some task elements and ignore, or inhibit, other elements as they complete task-relevant operations (see Barrouillet, Lépine, & Camos, 2008; Conway, Jarrold, Kane, Miyake, & Towse, 2007; Towse, Cowan, Hitch, & Horton, 2008, for a review of different models related to the competitive relationship between processing and memory activities). In addition, WM tasks are those that require some inference, transformation and/or monitoring of relevant and irrelevant information (Baddeley & Logie, 1999; Engle et al., 1999). In our studies, WM tasks typically engage participants in at least two activities after initial encoding: (1) a response to a question or questions about the material or related material to be retrieved, and (2) a response to recall item information that increases in set size. The first part of the task is a distractor of initial encoding items whereas the second part tests storage.

In contrast, tasks that measure STM typically involve situations that do not vary their initial encoding. That is, participants are not instructed to infer, transform or vary processing requirements. In those cases, participants are simply asked to recall a sequence of items in the order in which they were presented. Clearly both WM and STM tasks involve sharing some common activities on the participant's part (e.g., Colom, Abad, Quiroga, Shih, & Flores-Mendoza, 2008). For example, both STM and WM tasks invoke controlled processes such as rehearsal (e.g., see Gathercole, 1998, for a review). However, controlled processing on WM tasks emerges in the context of high demands on attention (e.g., maintaining a memory trace in the face of interference) and the drawing of resources from the executive system (see Engle et al., 1999, pp. 311–312, for discussion). Instructions in controlled processing emphasize maintaining information in the face of interference. Interference reflects competing memory traces that draw away from the targeted memory trace. In contrast, controlled processing on STM tasks attempts to maintain memory traces above some critical threshold (Cowan, 1995, 2005). This maintenance does not directly draw resources from the central executive system. Instructions in controlled processing may emphasize perceptual grouping or chunking skills, skills at phonological coding, and rehearsal speed (see Engle et al., 1999, for a review).

In elaborating the distinction between STM and WM, Cowan (1995) emphasized the role of attentional processes. WM is depicted as a subset of items of information stored in STM that are in turn submitted to limited attentional control processing (see also Engle et al., 1999). This assumes that when the contents of STM are separated from WM, what is left of WM is some form of controlled attention or processing related to the central executive system (also referred to as *the central executive component of WM*). Consequently, to understand the impact of WM to higher order processes, such as problem solving, in terms of controlled processing, the influence of STM must be partialed out (however, see Colom et al., 2008, for a competing interpretation).

Theoretical framework

The framework we used to capture WM performance as it applies to reading and math proficiency is Baddeley's multi-component model (1986, 1996, 2000, 2007). Baddeley (1986; Baddeley & Logie, 1999) describes WM as a limited central-executive system that interacts with a set of two passive storage systems used for temporary storage of different classes of information: the speech-based phonological loop and the visual sketchpad. The phonological loop is responsible for the temporary storage of verbal information; items are held within a phonological store of limited duration, and the items are maintained within the store via the process of articulation. The visual sketchpad is responsible for the storage of visual-spatial information over brief periods and plays a key role in the generation and manipulation of mental images. Both storage systems are in direct contact with the central executive system. The central executive system is considered to be primarily responsible for coordinating activity within the cognitive system, but also devotes some of its resources to increasing the amount of information that can be held in the two subsystems (Baddeley & Logie, 1999). A recent formulation of the model (Baddeley, 2000) also includes a temporary multimodal storage component called the *episodic buffer*.

Although the multicomponent model of Baddeley was primarily developed from research on adult samples, the model also has an excellent fit to the WM performance of children (Alloway, Gathercole, Willis, & Adams, 2004; Gathercole, Pickering, Ambridge, & Wearing, 2004). Further, there are correlates in the neuropsychological literature that complement the tripartite structure, suggesting that some functional independence exists among the systems (e.g., Jonides, 2000; Ruchkin et al., 1999). Functional magnetic resonance imaging (fMRI) studies suggest separate neural circuitry for the storage and rehearsal components of both the phonological and the visual-spatial system, with phonological system activity mainly located in the left hemisphere and visual-spatial system activity located primarily in the right hemisphere (Smith & Jonides, 1997). Executive control processes, on the other hand, are associated primarily with the prefrontal cortex (e.g., Reichle, Carpenter, & Just, 2000; Schretlen et al., 2000). Neuropsychological evidence also suggests that children with RD and/or MD experience difficulties related to these structures. Based on the type of task, of course, studies suggest that children with RD have processing difficulties related to regions of the frontal lobe (e.g., Lazar & Frank, 1998), left parietal lobe (e.g., Pugh et al., 2000; Shaywitz et al., 1998), as well as problems related to the interhemispheric transfer and coordination of information across the corpus callosum (e.g., Swanson & Mullen, 1983; Swanson & Obrzut, 1985). Likewise, a casual review of the literature shows that MD has been associated with the left basal ganglia, thalamus, and the left parieto-occipito-temporal areas (e.g., Dehaene & Cohen, 1995, 1997). Damage to these regions may be associated with difficulties in accessing number facts. Clearly, the biological correlates of the various subcomponents in WM in RD and/or MD samples are just beginning to be identified with advances in technology.

Linking growth in achievement to WM

Although WM is a fundamental component in many current theories of children's reading and math, no longitudinal studies (to the author's knowledge) have explicitly isolated those components of WM most directly related to growth in reading or math. Because WM is made up of three components (central executive, phonological loop, and visual-spatial sketchpad), the question arises as to whether WM as a whole constrains growth in reading or math, or whether a certain component is more important. Thus, although there is a strong interrelationship among these components, our more recent studies have sought to determine whether growth in certain components of WM is related to growth in reading and/or math.

Role of growth in WM and math disabilities

The first study reviewed (Swanson et al., 2008) examined the influence of cognitive growth in WM on mathematical problem solution accuracy in elementary school children (N = 353) with and without math disabilities. A battery of tests was administered over a three-year period that assessed problem solving, achievement, and cognitive processing (WM, inhibition, naming speed, phonological coding) in children in grades 1, 2 and 3. In this study we considered three models as an explanation of the role of WM in MD: one focused on the child's knowledge base for arithmetical calculations and components of word problems; another focused on the storage components of WM, primarily the phonological loop; and the third focused on the central executive system. The models were not necessarily exclusive of one another (each process can contribute important variance to problem solving to some degree), but suggested that some processes were more important than others. Based on these models, we considered three possibilities: (1) Growth in the relationship between WM and problem solving is primarily mediated by task specific knowledge and skills in mathematical calculation; (2) Growth in WM and problem solving is primarily mediated by the phonological loop; or (3) Growth in the executive component of WM, independent of the phonological system and resources activated in LTM, contributed unique variance to problem solving.

For this study, performance on measures of arithmetic calculation and recognition of problem solving components assessed long-term memory (LTM). Performance on measures of naming speed, phonological awareness and STM assessed the phonological system. Performance on WM tasks modeled after the format of Daneman and Carpenter's (1980) measure assessed executive processing. The WM tasks were assumed to capture at least two factors of executive processing: susceptibility to interference and manipulation of capacity in the coordination of both processing and storage (but see Towse, Cowan, Horton, & Whytock, 2008, for a competing interpretation). The approach used in this study (as well as in others, e.g., Engle, Cantor, & Carullo, 1992), to assess whether a particular system plays the major role in mediating differences in performance, was to remove statistically that system's influence from the analysis. In this study, the influence of the phonological system (e.g., naming speed, STM) or LTM was partialed via a hierarchical regression analysis between problem solving and WM. We reasoned that if WM and problem solving were primarily mediated by a phonological system and/or LTM, then the predictions of problem solving performance by performance on WM measures should be non-significant when measures related to the phonological system and LTM are entered (partialed) in the analysis. However, if growth in the central executive system (executive processing) mediated the relationship between WM and problem solving, then the correlations between these two variables were expected to remain significant when measures of phonological processing and LTM were partialed from the analysis.

The final model suggested that problem solving performance was related to executive processing, independent of the influence of the phonological system and LTM. This assumption followed logically from the problem solving literature suggesting that abstract thinking, such as comprehension and reasoning, requires the coordination of several basic processes (e.g., Engle et al., 1999; Kyllonen & Christal, 1990; Swanson, 2006). We assumed that measures of executive processing in this study were related to latent measures of WM and measures assumed to reflect some of the activities of the central executive system were inhibition (random generation of letters and numbers) and activation of LTM (composite measures of reading, arithmetic calculation, knowledge of problem solving components). We also assumed based on the work of Engle et al. (1999) and others (e.g., Cowan, 1995) that after storage processes (e.g., phonological loop and visual-spatial storage) were partialed from the analysis, the residual variance related to WM would capture a key process of the central executive system referred to as controlled attention.

Overall, the results showed that children identified as at risk for serious math problem solving difficulties in wave 1 showed less growth rate and lower levels of performance on cognitive measures than children not at risk at wave 3 (three years later). Additional important results are shown in Tables 9.1 and 9.2. The hierarchical regression analysis shown in Table 9.1 shows that several variables in wave 1 were used to predict word problem solving in wave 3. Also entered in the regression model were measures related to the knowledge of problem solving components and calculation ability at wave 3. As shown, both the WM executive system and visual-spatial sketchpad at wave 1 predicted wave 3 problem solving performance. The results in Tables 9.1 also show that WM contributed unique variance to problem solving beyond what phonological processes (e.g., phonological knowledge), reading skill, inhibition, and processing speed contributed. Additional analyses in the study showed that WM performance in wave 1 contributed approximately 36% of the variance to problem solving accuracy in wave 3 when entered by itself in the regression analysis. Thus, there was clear evidence that multiple systems of WM contributed important variance to problem solving performance three years later beyond processes related to speed, phonological knowledge, and reading skill.

Our results also showed that WM performance predicted problem solving accuracy when the hierarchical regression analysis included measures of LTM (reading, calculation, and knowledge of problem solving components). It has been argued that some of the functions of the central executive system include accessing information from LTM (e.g., Baddeley & Logie, 1999). Our results suggested, however, that although WM tasks may draw information from

Table 9.1 Predictions of year 3 problem solving accuracy based on wave 3 math calculation, problem solving knowledge and wave 1 fluid intelligence, reading and cognitive variables

Model	B	SE	β	t
Wave 3 predictors				
Problem solving				
Knowledge	0.25	0.11	0.12	2.13*
Calculation	0.3	0.08	0.27	3.42**
Wave 1 predictors				
Fluid intelligence (Raven)	0.13	0.04	0.16	2.85**
Reading	0.12	0.12	0.12	1.00
Phon. know.	–0.01	0.1	0.1	–0.09
Fluency	0.02	0.07	0.007	0.33
Speed	–0.004	0.06	–0.004	–0.06
Inhibition	0.09	0.06	0.07	1.6
Age	–0.15	0.06	–0.16	–2.39*
Sketchpad	0.15	0.04	0.14	3.23***
Phon. loop	0.12	0.06	0.09	1.85
Executive	0.19	0.08	0.15	2.34*
$F(12, 279) = 22.52; p < .001, R2 = .49.$				

Table adapted from Swanson et al., 2008.

Note: * $p < .05$, ** $p < .01$, *** $p < .001$.

LTM (e.g., knowledge of components related to problem solving), it may be the controlled attention (monitoring of attention) component of WM that plays a more important role in mathematical problem solving growth.

Table 9.2 shows the variables related to growth in WM that moderated growth in word problem solving. The table shows that the mean z score of the average age in the sample (9.7 years) at wave 3 was .47. The average unit of linear growth was .21. Hence, a 9.7 year old ended wave 3 with a z score of .47 and gained .21 units per testing session. More important, however, the results clearly showed that growth in the executive and phonological component of WM significantly moderated growth in problem solving accuracy.

Overall, our preliminary longitudinal work supports the notion that growth in WM is an important predictor of children's problem solving beyond the contribution of reading, calculation skills and individual differences in phonological processing, inhibition, and processing speed.

Growth in WM and reading disabilities

In the next longitudinal study we focus on children with RD (Swanson & Jerman, 2007). Prior to summarizing our findings, however, we briefly review previous studies. In one of the few developmental studies testing Baddeley's WM model in children with RD, Swanson (2003) compared RD and skilled readers (N = 226) across four (7, 10, 13, 20) age groups on WM tasks. As

Table 9.2 Contribution of working memory growth to problem solving

Conditional hierarchical model

	Estimate	SE	t-ratio
Fixed effects			
Intercept	.47	.02	17.49***
Linear growth	.21	.01	14.51***
Working memory			
Intercept			
STM	.14	.03	3.50**
Executive	.09	.02	3.23***
Sketchpad	.10	.02	4.50***
Growth (linear)			
STM	−.05	.02	−2.08*
Executive	−.10	.01	−5.51***
Sketchpad	.005	.01	.36
	Variance Estimate	*SE*	*Z*
Random effects (subject*teacher)			
Intercept	.07	.01	5.55**
Growth (linear)	.01	.004	3.95**
Residual	.09	.008	13.62**

Table adapted from Swanson et al., 2008.

Note: * $p < .05$, ** $p < .01$, *** $p < .001$.

expected, participants with RD were inferior to skilled readers at all age levels, but these differences increased with age. The age-related differences between ability groups were maintained under cuing conditions and when reading and mathematics skills were partialed from the analysis. Skilled readers showed age-related increases in WM, whereas the trajectory of growth for children with RD showed minimal age-related changes in span level across ages 7 to 20.

These findings raised questions as to whether constraints in WM growth constrained growth in reading. Although the literature is clear that impairments in WM in children with RD are related to reading performance, whether growth in WM underlies poor growth in reading skills has not been tested empirically. Gathercole, Tiffany, Briscoe, and Thorn (2005) have one of the closest studies on this issue. Although their research was not focused on RD per se, they initiated a longitudinal study that investigated the cognitive skills and scholastic attainments of children at 8 years of age who were selected on the basis of deficits in the phonological loop at age 4. The phonological loop was assessed by STM tasks that tapped the recall of verbal information. They investigated whether deficits in phonological STM performance during this developmental period had a direct consequence on children's attainment in the areas of language, mathematics, and literacy. The authors reasoned that if phonological memory was a significant deterrent to learning, then children with poor phonological memory should have low overall

achievement. The authors found that children who scored low on phonological STM measures assessed at 4 and 8 years of age performed at appropriate
levels in all areas of vocabulary, language, number skills, and literacy. The
authors concluded that children did not experience learning difficulties in key
domains over the early school years that could be attributed to poor phonological memory. However, a significant relationship was found between WM
abilities and learning during these early school years. Gathercole et al. found
that the relationship with WM and literacy was significant (r=.56).

As an extension of this earlier work, we (Swanson & Jerman, 2007) assessed
whether poor phonological memory and/or WM may underlie subsequent
growth in literacy in older children. We focused on older children because our
cross-sectional study (Swanson, 2003, 2006) suggested that growth on academic
tasks was more sensitive to WM constraints in older children as language abilities approach adult levels. There is also some literature suggesting that tasks
related to the phonological loop (i.e., STM) and executive system are not clearly
distinguishable in young children (i.e., high intercorrelation between WM and
STM measures, Alloway et al., 2004; Gathercole et al., 2004), and therefore the
phonological system may play a more important role in later academic performance when older children with RD are included in the sample. Furthermore,
Engle et al. (1999) suggested that STM and WM might not be distinguishable
in young children whose rehearsal processes are unstable (used inconsistently).

Thus, our longitudinal study (Swanson & Jerman, 2007) determined
whether (a) subgroups of children with reading disabilities (RD) (children
with RD-only, children with both reading and arithmetic deficits, and low
verbal IQ readers) and skilled readers varied in working memory (WM) and
short-term memory (STM) growth, and (b) whether growth in an executive
system and/or phonological storage system mediated growth in reading performance. A battery of memory and reading measures were administered to
84 children (ages 11 to 17) across three testing waves spaced one year apart.
The four subgroups were matched on fluid intelligence (Raven Progressive
Matrices Test), age, ethnicity, and gender at wave 1. We report on the first
three years of the study. We used three subgroups of children with RD
because some studies have suggested that children who have combined deficits in reading and math (referred to as the comorbid group in this study)
reflect more generalized deficits related to the executive system than do
RD-only children who have deficits only related to reading (e.g., van der
Sluis, van der Leij, & de Jong, 2005). Thus, this study examined whether children identified with only deficits in reading had isolated deficits in the development of phonological STM and children with comorbid deficits in both
reading and math had deficits in both STM and WM.

Figure 9.1 shows the level of performance and growth on measures of
WM. The analyses showed that memory growth for skilled readers differed
significantly from subgroups of children with RD. However, the analyses
showed no significant differences in growth curves among subgroups of
children with RD on a latent measure of WM (or STM in a separate

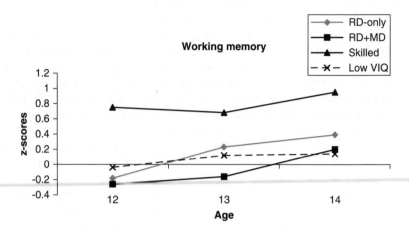

Figure 9.1 Growth among subgroups of children with reading disabilities (RD) on a
latent measure of working memory as a function of age (adapted from
Swanson & Jerman, 2007).

Note: RD-only = children with reading disabilities; RD+MD = children with reading and math
disabilities; Skilled = skilled readers; Low VIQ = low verbal IQ.

analysis). Thus, although the results showed that skilled readers yielded
higher WM growth estimates than the RD groups, no significant differentiation between subgroups of children with RD on growth measures emerged.

The growth model of reading for the total sample is shown in Table 9.3.
STM, WM, and verbal IQ were moderators. As shown, only WM growth
significantly moderated growth in reading comprehension and word fluency.
The negative estimate indicated that growth in WM was nonlinear. The
important finding, however, was that WM (controlled attention) growth,
rather than STM (phonological loop), significantly moderated growth in
reading comprehension and fluency.

Overall, these analyses supported the notion that deficient growth in
some executive component of WM was a common problem among children
with reading problems. Thus, in contrast to studies (e.g., van der Sluis
et al., 2005) that have suggested that RD children exhibit no problems in
executive function, whereas children who show reading plus arithmetic
difficulties have problems in executive processing, we did not find that to be
the case. The findings coincide with our earlier work on children with RD
suggesting that their WM deficits operate somewhat independent of their
STM deficits. That is, problems in WM have been found to persist in
children with RD even after partialing out the influence of verbal articulation
speed (Swanson & Ashbaker, 2000), reading comprehension (Swanson,
1999b), STM (Swanson, Ashbaker, & Lee, 1996), or IQ scores (Swanson &
Sachse-Lee, 2001b).

Table 9.3 Hierarchical linear modeling of growth in reading with STM and WM as moderators

Conditional growth model

	Reading comprehension		Fluency	
Fixed effects	*Estimate*	*SE*	*Estimate*	*Variance*
Intercept	.14**	0.06	.32**	0.08
Growth	.13**	0.03	.17**	0.04
Moderating variables				
RD classification	.10*	0.05	.27**	0.04
Starting age at wave 1	–0.02	0.03	–0.05	0.004
Verbal intelligence	.009**	0.002	0.003	0.002
Fluency	.19**	0.04	–	–
STM	0.06	0.04	0.03	0.06
WM	0.09	0.05	.22**	0.07
Linear growth				
STM growth	–0.008	0.01	–0.02	0.02
WM growth	–.04**	0.02	–.05*	0.02

Table adapted from Swanson and Jerman (2007).

Note: * $p < .05$, ** $p < .01$.

Synthesis of the RD / MD literature

In both of the aforementioned longitudinal studies, we found that WM predicted performance on the criterion measure (e.g., reading comprehension, word problem solving) even when measures of STM, vocabulary, naming speed, and inhibition were entered into the regression analysis. We thought these findings may be peculiar to our laboratory work, and thus we used a meta-analysis to synthesize other STM and WM studies on MD and RD. Of interest to us was whether MD and RD share the same WM problems. We (Swanson & Jerman, 2006) completed a quantitative synthesis of the literature comparing the cognitive functioning of children with MD with (1) average achieving children, (2) children with reading disabilities (RD), and (3) children with comorbid disabilities (RD+MD) on this question.

These effect sizes (ESs) ranged in terms of magnitude according to Cohen's (1988) classification of large (.80), moderate (.50), and small (.20). Approximately 194 effect sizes compared children with MD with average achievers ($M = -.52$, $SE = .01$), 58 effect sizes compared MD and children with RD ($M = -.10$, $SE = .03$), and 102 effect sizes compared children with MD to children with MD+RD ($M = .26$, $SE = .02$). We found that average achievers outperformed children with MD-only on measures of verbal problem solving ($M = -.58$), naming speed ($M = -.70$), verbal WM ($M = -.70$), visual-spatial WM ($M = -.63$) and long-term memory (LTM, $M = -.72$). The magnitude of these ESs was persistent across age and severity of math disability. The results further indicated that children with MD outperformed children with comorbid disabilities (MD+RD) on measures of literacy ($M = .75$), visual-spatial problem solving ($M = .51$), LTM ($M = .44$), STM for words ($M = .71$) and verbal WM ($M = .30$). Interestingly, we found that children with MD could only be differentiated (although weakly) from children with RD on measures of naming speed (–.23) and visual-spatial WM (–.30). More important, our analysis [hierarchical linear modeling (HLM, Bryk & Raudenbush, 1992)] showed that the magnitude of effect sizes in overall cognitive functioning between MD and average achievers was related to WM deficits when the effects of all other variables (e.g., age, IQ, reading level, other domain categories) were partialed out. The ESs as a function of ability group, STM and WM measures are shown in Table 9.4.

In general, our results suggested that MD and RD children share common memory deficits. We also found in our HLM analysis of ESs that WM was the strongest moderator related to the magnitude of the ESs in MD vs. average achievers. However, processes that underlie MD could not be clearly separated from children with RD. These findings are consistent with Shalev,

Table 9.4 Weighted effect sizes, standard error, confidence intervals and homogeneity of categories for comparisons between MD (math disabled) and non math disabled (MD/NMD), MD and reading disabled (MD/RD), and MD and RD+MD (CMOR) (corrected for outliers).

Comparison	K	Effect size[a]	Standard error	Lower	Upper	Homogeneity Q
		STM-Words				
MD/NMD	16	–.45	.06	–.58	–.32	44.78***
MD/RD	3	.16	.13	–.10	.42	7.33*
MD/CMOR	4	.71	.12	.46	.96	12.61**
		STM-Digits/numbers				
MD/NMD	11	–.26	.07	–.41	.10	48.94***
MD/RD	4	.03	.14	–.24	.32	6.35
MD/CMOR	9	–.08	.11	–.30	.13	110.57***
		WM-Verbal				
MD/NMD	43	–.70	.04	–.79	–.61	83.84***
MD/RD	19	–.07	.06	–.19	.04	139.95***
MD/CMOR	20	.30	.06	.17	.42	86.49**
		WM-Visual-spatial				
MD/NMD	13	–.63	.07	–.77	–.48	28.14**
MD/RD	13	–.30	.07	–.44	–.16	35.43**
MD/CMOR	13	.23	.07	.08	.38	14.10

Table adapted from Swanson and Jerman (2006).

Note: MD = Math Disabled only, NMD = non math disabled-average achiever, RD = reading disabled, CMOR = comorbid group with both low reading and low math; K = number of measures, Lower and Upper = 95% level of confidence range. [a] Positive effect sizes favor MD and negative effect sizes favor comparison group. * $p < .05$, ** $p < .01$, *** $p < .001$.

Manor, and Gross-Tsur (1997) who found no quantitative differences between children with RD and MD. Our results suggest that children with RD and MD were differentiated only on measures of naming speed and visual-spatial WM. However, the magnitudes of these ESs were small (−.23 and −.30, respectively). We found only moderate support for the notion that groups can be differentiated on measures of visual memory.

Of course the question emerges as to whether weak support for the notion that distinct processes separate children with MD from children with RD means that such children share a common set of mental resources. One could argue that the similarities between MD and RD children become much more reliable with greater manipulations of phonological information (a position consistent with Hecht, Torgesen, Wagner, & Rashotte, 2001). Phonological STM is believed to be composed of rehearsal components and phonological skills that are deficient in children with MD and RD. We found in our meta-analysis, however, that the two groups could not be differentiated on measures attributed to phonological memory (STM for digits and words). That is, the ESs between these two groups was .16 for STM-words and .03 for STM-digits. A further difficulty with the phonological explanation is that we found an advantage for RD in terms of naming speed, a measure assumed to tap phonological processing. Thus, although we do not discount the fact that RD and MD children share similar deficits in phonological processing, some disadvantages emerged for children with MD in the memory areas not attributed to phonological skills (i.e., visual-spatial WM). Thus, we would argue that if a common processing deficit exists between these two groups, it would be related to executive processes.

We have also completed a meta-analysis of findings on STM and WM focusing primarily on children with RD (Swanson, Zheng, & Jerman, 2009). The results are shown in Table 9.5. The purpose of the present study was to synthesize research that compared children with and without RD on measures of short-term memory (STM) and working memory (WM). We compared children with RD and average readers on STM tasks and WM tasks (one that followed the Daneman and Carpenter format). We computed effect sizes (ESs) across a broad age, reading and IQ range, yielding a mean ES across studies of −.89 (SD=1.03). The moderate range for STM measures consisted in 255 ESs (M= −.61, 95% confidence range of −.65 to −.58) and 320 ESs were in the moderate range for WM measures (M=−.67, 95% confidence range of −.68 to −.64). The results indicated that children with RD were distinctively disadvantaged compared to average readers on (a) STM measures requiring the recall of phonemes and digit sequences and (b) WM measures requiring the simultaneous processing and storage of digits within sentence sequences and final words from unrelated sentences. No significant moderating effects emerged in the HLM analysis for age, IQ, or reading level when predicting memory effect sizes. The findings indicated STM and WM differences between ability groups persisted across age, suggesting that both a phonological and executive system underlies RD.

Table 9.5 Effect size as a function of categorical variables for children with reading disabilities when compared to chronological age and IQ matched children

Category	Number of studies	M	SD	K	Unweighted effect size	Weighted effect size	SE	95% CI for effect size		Homogeneity Q
								Lower	Upper	
Short-term memory										
1. Phonological	7	−0.83	1.15	22	−0.75	−0.39	0.05	−0.50	−0.29	116.29***
2. Pictures	17	−0.90	1.13	53	−0.68	−0.57	0.04	−0.65	−0.49	311.34***
3. Words	25	−0.50	0.66	76	−0.50	−0.55	0.03	−0.61	−0.48	260.35***
4. Digits	11	−1.49	2.2	55	−0.98	−0.63	0.03	−0.69	−0.56	377.09***
5. Letters	4	−1.06	0.52	13	−0.91	−1.10	0.07	−1.24	−0.95	36.95***
Divided attention										
6. Backwards	16	−0.70	0.45	59	−0.64	−0.69	0.03	−0.74	−0.63	244.43***
7. Preload	3	−0.53	0.27	7	−0.57	−0.49	0.12	−0.73	−0.26	4.44
8. Sorting	1	−0.52	.	30	−0.52	−0.52	0.04	−0.60	−0.44	8.41
Working memory-D&C format										
9. Counting	10	−0.88	0.55	32	−0.85	−0.78	0.03	−0.84	−0.73	75.34***
10. Listen/Sentence	19	−1.51	1.21	57	−1.21	−0.84	0.03	−0.89	−0.79	318.92***
11. Visual-matrix	26	−0.69	0.63	72	−0.70	−0.80	0.03	−0.85	−0.74	490.85***
12. Complex visual.	6	−0.52	0.17	20	−0.54	−0.48	0.05	−0.57	−0.39	20.6
13. Semantic assoc.	10	−0.81	0.44	31	−0.56	−0.37	0.04	−0.44	−0.30	244.05***
14. Digit/sentence	10	−1.47	2.25	24	−0.89	−0.58	0.05	−0.68	−0.48	146.39***
15. Story retelling	4	−0.80	0.7	9	−0.65	−0.37	0.07	−0.50	−0.24	49.12***
16. Phonol/rhyming	7	−0.62	0.32	13	−0.60	−0.61	0.06	−0.74	−0.49	10.26

D&C=Daneman and Carpenter task format, K=number of dependent measures.

Note: *** $p < .001$.

Summary

Our previous results suggest that WM is a major cognitive deficiency in children with RD and MD. We now examine our previous laboratory studies that attempt to tease out more specifically the components and processes that may play an important role in RD and/or MD. We will divide out findings along the dimensions of Baddeley's multicomponent model. Because the majority of our previous research focused on children with RD, we focus on those studies directly.

Executive system

The central executive monitors the control processes in WM. There have been a number of cognitive activities assigned to the central executive, including coordination of subsidiary memory systems, control of encoding and retrieval strategies, switching of attention in manipulation of material held related to the verbal and visual-spatial systems, and the retrieval of information from LTM (e.g., Baddeley, 1996; Miyake, Friedman, Emerson, Witzki, & Howerter, 2000). Although the executive function has separable operations (e.g., inhibition, updating), these operations share some underlying commonality (e.g., see Miyake et al., 2000, for a review).

As stated when reviewing our longitudinal studies, we think that a crucial component of the central executive as it applies to RD is controlled attention. We briefly review some of our studies that have implicated deficits in executive processing for children with RD, particularly as it applies to controlled attention. The involvement of executive processing activities is inferred from three outcomes: (a) poor performance on complex divided attention tasks, (b) poor monitoring, such as an inability to suppress (inhibit) irrelevant information, and (c) depressed performance across verbal and visual-spatial tasks that require concurrent storage and processing.

Divided attention

Our results suggest that RD children can be distinguished from average achievers in how they handled attentional demands. For example, in one of our experiments (Swanson, 1993b, Exp. 1), a concurrent memory task, adapted from Baddeley (Baddeley, Eldridge, Lewis, & Thomson, 1984), was administered to RD and skilled readers. The task required subjects to remember digit strings (e.g., 9, 4, 1, 7, 5, 2) while they concurrently sorted blank cards, cards with pictures of nonverbal shapes, or sorting of cards with pictures of items that fit into semantic categories (e.g., vehicles – car, bus, truck; clothing – dress, socks, belt). Demands on the central executive capacity system were manipulated through the level of difficulty (3 vs. 6 digit strings) and type of sorting required (e.g., nonverbal shapes, semantic categories, blank cards). Sorting activities that placed demands on the verbal storage (phonological system) included the categorization of pictures into semantic categories, whereas sorting activities that made demands on the visual store (i.e., visual-spatial sketchpad) include discrimination among complex non-verbal shapes. Baddeley et al. (1984) found that in such activities the main task difficulty (sorting) interacts with concurrent memory load, but only with a memory load of 6 digits. Performance for the 6-digit memory load condition places processing demands on the central executive, thereby interfering with the main task. Swanson's (1993b) results indicated a clear effect for memory load. The results showed that RD readers can perform comparably to their chronological age (CA)-matched counterparts on verbal and visual-spatial sorting conditions that included 3-digit strings (low demands), and that only when the coordination of tasks becomes more difficult (6-digit strings) do ability group differences emerge. More important, the results for the high memory load condition (6-digit strings) showed that RD readers were inferior to the CA-matched readers (and reading matched controls for ordered recall) in their ability to recall digits during both verbal and nonverbal sorting. Because recall performance for RD readers was not restricted to a particular storage system (i.e., verbal storage), compared with the performance of CA-matched skilled readers, one can infer that processes other than a language-specific system accounted for the results.

Attention to relevant and irrelevant information

We have also explored RD children's selective attention toward word features. For example, Swanson and Cochran (1991) compared 10-year-old children with RD and children without RD (NRD) matched on chronological age on their retrieval of word features within and across the cerebral hemispheres that required dichotic listening. Participants were asked to recall words organized by semantic (e.g., red, black, green, orange), phonological (e.g., sit, pit, hit), and orthographic (e.g., sun, same, seal, soft) features presented to either the left or right ear. The study included two experiments. Experiment 1 compared recall with different orienting instructions to the word lists. One orienting instruction told children about the organizational structure of the words, while the other condition (nonorienting) did not. For the orienting condition, children were told to remember all words, "but to specifically remember words that go with _____" (e.g., colors) or "words that rhyme with ____" (e.g., it) or "words that start with the letter _____" (e.g., s) so that the words go with certain categories (such as animals and furniture) or sounds (rhymes). For the nonorienting condition, children were told to remember all words but no mention was made of the distinctive organization features of the words. Experiment 2 extended Exp. 1 by implementing a cued recall condition. In both experiments, children were told they would hear someone talking through the earphone in either the right or left ear. They would also hear words in the other ear. They were told that when they stopped hearing the information in the designated ear and the non-designated ear, they were to tell the experimenter all the words they could remember.

For both experiments, NRD children had higher levels of target recall and nontargeted recall than RD children. More important, ability group differences emerged in "how specific word features" were selectively attended to. The selective attention index focused on the targeted words in comparison to the background words (targeted word recall minus background word recall) from other lists within the targeted ear, as well as background items in the contralateral ear. Regardless of word features, whether competing word features were presented within ear or across ear conditions, or whether retrieval conditions were noncued or cued, RD children's selective attention scores were smaller (the difference score between targeted items and nontargeted items was closer to zero) than NRD readers. Thus, when compared with RD children, NRD children were more likely to ignore irrelevant information in the competing conditions. Taken together, the results of this study, as well as those of three earlier dichotic listening studies (Swanson & Mullen, 1983) suggest that RD children suffer processing deficits related to resource monitoring (attention to relevant information, suppression of irrelevant information) regardless of the type of word features, retrieval conditions, or ear presentation.

Combined processing and storage demands

Several of our studies (Swanson, 1992, 1994, 2003; Swanson et al., 1996; Swanson & Ashbaker, 2000) have also assessed executive processing via tasks that follow the format of Daneman and Carpenter's Sentence Span measure. This task is assumed to tap central executive processes related to "updating" (Miyake et al., 2000). Updating requires monitoring and coding information for relevance to the task at hand and then appropriately revising items held in WM. As shown in Table 9.5, a meta-analysis of the literature on RD children (Swanson et al., 2009) indicated that such children vary from the average reading counterpart on a host of measures that follow the Daneman and Carpenter (1980) format. As shown, effect sizes vary from .62 to 1.51 across verbal and visual-spatial material.

Summary

We have selectively reviewed studies suggesting that RD children's WM deficits may, depending on the task and materials, reflect problems related to the executive processing system. Although our research suggests that isolated difficulties related to updating and the suppression of irrelevant information underlie RD, we also want to emphasize that several activities that involve executive processing are very much intact for children with RD. Some of these intact executive processes relate to planning. For example, although planning (such as mapping out a sequence of moves) is considered a component of the executive system (however, see Miyake et al., 2000, p. 91), we have not found overall solution differences between RD and NRD students on such tasks (see Swanson, 1988, 1993a). Likewise, studies that have examined performance on complex executive-processing tasks, such as the Tower of Hanoi, have not produced reliable differences between RD and NRD children. In one study, Swanson (1993a) compared RD children, average readers, and children with high IQ on the Tower of Hanoi task, as well as two problem-solving tasks (Combinatorial, Pendulum). As expected, an advantage in solution times was found for the intellectually gifted children. In contrast, no significant differences in solution time or number of steps to solution were found between average achievers and RD children (children with reading scores below the 15th percentile) with comparable IQs on the three problem solving measures. However, "think aloud" protocols revealed that gifted and average achievers placed a heavy emphasis on domain-specific strategies whereas children with RD used a more general heuristic (see Swanson, 1993a, p. 883 for a discussion).

In summary, several studies suggest that some participants with RD, matched to NRD participants on psychometric IQ measures, are deficient on some tasks that measure specific components of executive processing. Those activities of the executive system that we think are particular candidates for difficulty in individuals with RD are related to updating (e.g., Siegel & Ryan, 1989; Swanson et al. 1996) and the inhibition of dominant or prepotent responses (e.g., Chiappe et al., 2000). Those components of the executive system that are relatively intact are related to "planning, self-regulation, or decision making" (e.g., Swanson, 1993a).

We will now turn our attention to the phonological system.

Phonological loop

In Baddeley's and Logie's model (1999), the phonological loop is specialized for the retention of verbal information over short periods of time. It is composed of both a phonological store, which holds information in phonological form, and a rehearsal process, which serves to maintain representations in the phonological store (see Baddeley, Gathercole, & Papagno, 1998, for an extensive review). Thus, the ability to retain and access phonological representations has been associated with verbal STM – but more specifically the phonological loop. The phonological loop has been referred to as STM because it involves two major components discussed in the STM literature: a speech-based phonological input store and a rehearsal process (see Baddeley, 1986, for review).

A substantial number of studies support the notion that children with RD experience deficits in phonological processing (e.g., see Stanovich & Siegel, 1994), such as forming or accessing phonological representations of information. This difficulty in forming and accessing phonological representations impairs their ability to retrieve verbal information from STM. Interestingly, this phonological impairment does not appear to have broad effects on general intellectual ability apart from the developmental consequences on language-related functions. Several recent studies suggest that deficits in the phonological loop may lie at the root of word learning problems in children with RD (e.g., see Siegel, 2003, for review). These findings build on earlier research that has shown that the manifestations of this phonological deficit are poor word recognition, poor performance on phonological awareness tasks, slow naming speed, and impaired verbal STM. The current research suggests that this deficit (1) predates the acquisition of literacy, (2) is independent of IQ, and (3) persists over time (e.g., Siegel, 1993).

In general, several studies suggest that difficulties in forming and accessing phonological representations impair the ability to learn new words in individuals with RD. As shown in Table 9.5, our recent quantitative synthesis (Swanson et al., 2009) shows that deficits in STM emerge across a host of measures. Our analysis shows that these deficits are primarily related to verbal information (also see O'Shaughnessy & Swanson, 1998, for an earlier synthesis) and persist across age.

Before we leave this section, a question emerges as to whether verbal STM and verbal WM are comparable constructs. Some authors have suggested that verbal STM and verbal WM are synonymous constructs in young children (e.g., Hutton & Towse, 2001). Hutton and Towse found, via a Principal Component Analysis, that both WM and STM tasks loaded on the same factor for children 8 to 11 years old. In addition, their results also showed that correlations related to WM and STM measures of reading and math were of the same magnitude (see Table 9.4), suggesting that WM and STM share the same construct (also see Cowan et al., 2003, for a similar finding).

Our research suggests, however, that a distinction between the two concepts may be necessary when applied to average achieving children (e.g., Swanson, 2008) and children with RD (Swanson, 1994). Although we assume that verbal WM tasks share some important variance with the phonological loop (STM), we also argue that the verbal WM tasks share important variance with the central system. For example, Swanson and Ashbaker (2000) tested whether the operations related to STM and WM operated independently of one another. In this study, they compared RD and NRD readers and younger reading level-matched children on a battery of WM and STM tests to assess executive and phonological processing, respectively. Measures of the executive system were modeled after Daneman and Carpenter's (1980) WM tasks, whereas measures of the phonological system included those that related to articulation speed, digit span, and word span. The study yielded two important results. First, although the RD group was inferior to the NRD group in WM, verbal STM, and articulation speed, the differences in verbal STM and WM revealed little relation with articulation speed. That is, reading-related differences on WM and STM measures remained when articulation speed was partialed from the analysis. These reading-group differences were pervasive across verbal and visual-spatial WM tasks, even when the influence of verbal STM was statistically removed, suggesting that reading-group differences are domain general. Second, WM tasks and verbal STM tasks contributed unique variance to word recognition and reading comprehension beyond articulation speed. These results are consistent with those of Daneman and Carpenter (1980) and others (e.g., Engle et al., 1999) who have argued that verbal STM tasks and WM tasks are tapping different processes.

Visual-spatial sketchpad

The visual-spatial sketchpad is specialized for the processing and storage of visual material, spatial material, or both, and for linguistic information that can be recoded into imaginable forms (see Baddeley, 1986, for a review). Measures of visual-spatial WM have primarily focused on memory for visual patterns (e.g., Logie, 1986). A major study by Gathercole and Pickering (2000a, 2000b) found that visual-spatial WM abilities, as well as measures of central executive processing, were associated with attainment levels on a national curriculum for children aged 6 to 7 years. Children who showed marked deficits in curriculum attainment also showed marked deficits in visual-spatial WM. Thus, there is a strong relationship between visual-spatial WM and academic performance in the younger grades. However, the literature linking RD to visual-spatial memory deficits is mixed. For example, several studies in the STM literature suggest RD children's visual STM is intact (see O'Shaughnessy & Swanson, 1998, for a comprehensive review). When visual-spatial WM (combined storage and processing demands) performance is considered, however, some studies find that visual-spatial WM in students with RD is intact when compared with their same age counterparts (e.g., Swanson et al., 1996, Exp. 1), whereas others suggest problems in various visual-spatial tasks (Swanson et al., 1996, Exp. 2). Most studies suggest, however, that depending on the type of academic disability, greater problems in performance are more likely to occur on verbal than visual-spatial WM tasks.

We found that the evidence on whether children with RD have any particular advantage on visual-spatial WM when compared to their normal achieving counterparts fluctuates with processing demands. Swanson (2000) proposed a model that may account for these mixed findings. There are two parts to this model. The first part of the model assumes that executive processes (domain-general system) are used to maintain associations across high demand processing conditions. The maintenance of associations across processing conditions is related to changes, via experimenter feedback (cues or probes), in WM performance. A child with a reading disability has difficulty efficiently maintaining these associations. The predictions of the first part of the model are consistent with current models of executive functions that are called into play only when the activities of multiple components of the cognitive architecture must be coordinated (e.g., Baddeley, 1996; Engle et al., 1992). The second part of the model assumes that when excessive demands are not made on the executive system, performance differences between children with RD and without RD are limited to the verbal system.

The second part of the model is consistent with earlier work suggesting that the visual-spatial system of RD children is generally intact, but when excessive demands are placed on the executive system, their visual-spatial performance is depressed compared with chronological age-matched readers (Swanson et al., 1996).

Explanations of the paradoxical findings

Taken together, there is evidence that children with RD and MD have problems in various components of the WM system. There is one finding, perhaps, that seems rather paradoxical: children with specific problems in reading and/ or math but with normal intelligence suffer deficits in domain-general processes related to the executive system. We consider three questions in this regard.

1. *Are problems in the executive system merely a manifestation of deficits in the phonological system?*

We have addressed this question in several studies (Swanson, 1994, 2003; Swanson & Ashbaker, 2000; Swanson & Berninger, 1995; Swanson & Sachse-Lee, 2001a, 2001b). Our conclusion is that executive processing deficits exist in children with RD independent of their deficits in phonological processing. A study by Swanson and Berninger (1995) examined potential differences between STM and WM by testing whether phonological STM and WM accounted for different cognitive profiles in RD readers. Swanson and Berninger used a double dissociation design to compare children deficient in reading comprehension (based on scores from the Passage Comprehension subtest of the Woodcock Reading Mastery Test), and/or word recognition (based on scores from the Word Identification subtest of the Woodcock Reading Mastery Test), on WM and phonological STM measures. Participants were divided into four ability groups: High Comprehension/High Word Recognition, Low Comprehension/High Word Recognition, High Comprehension/Low Word Recognition, and Low Comprehension/Low Word Recognition. The results were straightforward: WM measures were related primarily to reading comprehension, whereas phonological STM measures were related primarily to word recognition. Most critically, because no significant interaction emerged, the results further indicated that the comorbid group (i.e., children low in both comprehension and word recognition) had combined memory deficits. That is, WM deficits were reflective of the poor comprehension-only group and STM deficits were reflective of the poor recognition-only group.

2. *Are the executive processing problems attributed to RD merely a manifestation of attention disorders?*

Because executive deficits are manifestations of monitoring attention, it is easy to attribute any executive processing deficits that might arise related to children with RD as manifestations of Attention Deficit/Hyperactivity Disorder (ADHD). This is because RD and ADHD are comorbid in some epidemiological studies. Further, one can infer that problems in executive processes overlap with potential problems in attention (e.g., see Gathercole et al., 2008, for a review). A distinction can be made, however, in executive processing related to the self-monitoring of attention versus constraints in attentional capacity.

Studies that attribute executive deficits to ADHD primarily rely on measures related to various forms of planning, not measures of WM (Barkley, 1997). This distinction partly comes from the literature suggesting that children with ADHD do not suffer WM deficits (Siegel & Ryan, 1989; Willcutt, Pennington, Boada, & Ogline, 2001), whereas those with reading deficits do. For example, Siegel and Ryan (1989) found that ADHD children's WM span scores were not significantly different from normal achievers. In addition, the literature is clear that WM problems exist in individuals with RD who do not suffer from behavioral manifestations (e.g., inability to attend or focus for long periods, impulsivity) of attention deficits (Siegel & Ryan, 1989).

Thus, we assume that WM measures capture different aspects of executive functioning when compared to measures used in the clinical literature to assess executive functioning: competition for cognitive resources vs. planning and/or motor inhibition (e.g., Wisconsin Card Sorting task may reflect motor inhibition, Tower-of-Hanoi Task may reflect planning, see Miyake et al., 2000, p. 331). We would argue that the variance related to poor attention in ADHD are problems related to goal-directed or planning behaviors, whereas attention problems in children with RD are related to their capacity to maintain and hold relevant information in the face of interference or distraction. The symptoms attributed to ADHD children's poor attentional monitoring (impulsivity, distractibility, diminished persistence, diminished sensitivity to feedback, lack of planning and judgment) are intact (or normal) in RD children. In contrast to ADHD children, research with RD children has shown normal levels of planning and judgment on problem solving tasks (e.g., Tower of Hanoi, Swanson, 1993a), and signal detection measures (d') on vigilance tasks show comparable persistence (although less attentional capacity) as normal achievers in their use of attentional resources across time (Swanson, 1981, 1983).

3. *Are executive processing deficits secondary disorders to more fundamental problems in reading/math achievement or a limited knowledge base?*

In terms of achievement, a recent subgroup study found that independence (unique variance) exists between WM and reading achievement. Swanson and Sachse-Lee (2001a) subgrouped skilled and children with RD on a listening span measure modeled after Daneman and Carpenter (1980). The subgroups reflected (a) those children high in executive processing (high listening span), but with average reading skill, (b) those low in executive processing and reading, and (c) two additional subgroups of skilled and children with RD who were matched on listening span (moderate executive processing ability). The moderate executive processing skilled readers matched the high executive processing group on reading and the two subgroups of children with RD were also matched on poor reading performance. It is also important to note that for the two subgroups matched on moderate WM span, the poor readers had lower verbal IQ scores than the average readers. These four subgroups were compared on phonological, visual-spatial, and semantic WM tasks across noncued and cued WM conditions. As expected, the high executive processing group performed better than the low executive processing, and low executive processing and low reading subgroups underperformed the other subgroups on the phonological, visual-spatial, and semantic measures. However, the important results showed that the two reading groups matched on executive processing (moderate ability level) were statistically comparable in perform-ance on phonological, semantic, and visual-spatial measures. These findings suggest that executive processing problems operate independently of the influ-ence of reading achievement. These findings complement our other work showing that fundamental processing deficits exist in WM even when reading and/or math ability is partialed from the analysis (see Swanson, 1999a; Swanson & Sachse-Lee, 2001b).

In terms of children's knowledge base, we assume that knowledgeable chil-dren can outperform less knowledgeable children on WM tasks. Our work has evaluated the mediating role of accuracy and speed of retrieval of infor-mation from LTM on the relationship between WM span and reading com-prehension (Swanson, 1999b; see Table 9.4 for a test of the LTM mediation model). In one study (Swanson, 1999b), ability groups (RD, CA-matched, and reading level matched) were statistically matched (standard scores) on measures of fluid intelligence (Raven Colored Progressive Matrices Test). Ability groups were compared on measures of phonological accuracy and retrieval speed (phonemic deletion, digit naming, pseudoword repetition), measures of LTM accuracy and retrieval speed (semantic, orthographic and vocabulary) and executive processing (sentence span, counting span, visual-spatial span). There were two important findings in this study. First, entering LTM speed and accuracy, and phonological speed and accuracy, before executive processing (WM), in a hierarchical regression model did not elimi-nate the significant contribution of executive processing to reading compre-hension. Thus, there is important as well as unique variance related to WM measures above and beyond the contribution of LTM and phonological processing. Second, partialing out the influence of achievement (i.e., reading comprehension; see Table 9.5, Swanson, 1999a) does *not* eliminate perform-ance differences between RD and CA matched children on measures of speed for accessing phonological information *or* executive processing. Taken together, these findings are not consistent with the view that retrieval of domain-specific knowledge from LTM underlies ability group differences in executive processing.

Conclusion

We conclude that WM deficits are fundamental problems of children with RD and/or MD. We generally conclude that students with RD and/or MD suffer STM deficits related to the phonological loop, a component of WM that specializes in the retention of speech-based information. We argue, however, that this subsystem is not the only aspect of WM that underlies RD and/or MD. We find that in situations that place high demands on processing, which in turn place demands on controlled attentional processing (such as monitoring limited resources, suppressing conflicting information, updating information), children with RD and/or MD are at a clear disadvantage when compared with their chronological aged counterparts. Further these deficits are sustained when articulation speed, phonological processing, fluid intelligence and verbal STM are partialed from the analysis. We believe that RD and/MD students' executive system (and more specifically monitoring activities linked to their capacity for controlled sustained attention in the face of interference or distraction) is impaired. This impaired capability for controlled processing appears to manifest itself across visual-spatial and verbal WM tasks, and therefore reflects a domain-general deficit. These executive processing difficulties may include (a) maintaining task relevant information in the face of distraction or interference, (b) situations in suppressing and inhibiting information irrelevant to the task if necessary, and (c) accessing information from LTM. We also recognize that although these differences in controlled attention can be domain free, they can, based on the kind of task and processing demands, reflect domain-specific codes.

Author note

This chapter draws from previous discussions in Swanson (2003), Swanson et al. (2008), and Swanson and Siegel (2001), and the reader is also referred to those sources for additional information.

References

Alloway, T. P., Gathercole, S. E., Willis, C., & Adams, A. (2004). A structural analysis of working memory and related cognitive skills in young children. *Journal of Experimental Child Psychology*, *87*, 85–106.

Andersson, U. (2008). Working memory as a predictor of written arithmetical skills in children: The importance of central executive functions. *British Journal of Educational Psychology*, *78*, 181–203.

Baddeley, A. D. (1986). *Working memory*. London: Oxford University Press.

Baddeley, A. D. (1996). Exploring the central executive. *Quarterly Journal of Experimental Psychology*, *49A*, 5–28.

Baddeley, A. D. (2000). The episodic buffer: A new component of working memory? *Trends in Cognitive Sciences*, *4*, 417–422.

Baddeley, A. D. (2007). *Working memory, thought and action*. New York: Oxford University Press.

Baddeley, A. D., Eldridge, M., Lewis, V., & Thomson, N. (1984). Attention and retrieval from long-term memory. *Journal of Experimental Psychology: General*, *113*, 518–540.

Baddeley, A., Gathercole, S., & Papagno, C. (1998). The phonological loop as a language learning device. *Psychological Review*, *105*, 158–173.

Baddeley, A. D., & Logie, R. H. (1999). Working memory: The multiple component model. In A. Miyake & P. Shah (Eds.), *Models of working memory: Mechanisms of active maintenance and executive control* (pp. 28–61). New York: Cambridge University Press.

Barkley, R. A. (1997). Behavioral inhibition, sustained attention, and executive functions: Constructing a unified theory of ADHD. *Psychological Bulletin, 121*, 65–94.

Barrouillet, P., Lépine, R., & Camos, V. (2008). Is the influence of working memory capacity on high level cognition mediated by complexity or resource-dependent elementary processes? *Psychonomic Bulletin & Review, 15*, 528–534.

Bryk, A., & Raudenbush, S. W. (1992). *Hierarchical linear models.* Newbury Park, CA: Sage.

Bull, R., Johnston, R. S., & Roy, J. A. (1999). Exploring the roles of the visual-spatial sketch pad and central executive in children's arithmetical skills: Views from cognition and developmental neuropsychology. *Developmental Neuropsychology, 15*, 421–442.

Case, R. (1995). Capacity-based explanations of working memory growth: A brief history and re-evaluation. In. F. Weinert & W. Schneider (Eds.), *Memory performance and competencies: Issues in growth and development* (pp. 23–44). Mahwah, NJ: Erlbaum Associates.

Chiappe, P., Hasher, L., & Siegel, L. S. (2000). Working memory, inhibitory control, and reading disability. *Memory & Cognition, 28*, 8–17.

Cohen, J. (1988). *Statistical power analysis for the behavioral sciences* (2nd ed.). New York: Academic Press.

Colom, R., Abad, F. J., Quiroga, M. Ã, Shih, P. C., & Flores-Mendoza, C. (2008). Working memory and intelligence are highly related constructs, but why? *Intelligence, 36*, 584–606.

Conway, A. R. A., Jarrold, C., & Kane, M. J., Miyake, A., & Towse, J. (2007). *Variation in working memory.* New York: Oxford University Press.

Cowan, N. (1995). *Attention and memory: An integrated framework.* Oxford: Oxford University Press.

Cowan, N. (2005). *Working memory capacity.* New York: Psychology Press.

Cowan, N., Towse, J. N., Hamilton, Z., Saults, J. S., Elliott, E. M. Lacey, J. F., et al. (2003). Children's working memory processes: A response timing analysis. *Journal of Experimental Psychology: General, 132*, 113–132.

Daneman, M., & Carpenter, P. A. (1980). Individual differences in working memory and reading. *Journal of Verbal Learning and Verbal Behavior, 19*, 450–466.

De Beni, R., Palladino, P., Pazzaglia, F., & Cornoldi, C. (1998). Increases in intrusion errors and working memory deficit of poor comprehenders. *Quarterly Journal of Experimental Psychology: Human Experimental Psychology, 51*, 305–320.

Dehaene, S., & Cohen, L. (1995). Towards an anatomical and functional model of number processing. *Mathematical Cognition, 1*, 83–120.

Dehaene, S., & Cohen, L. (1997). Cerebral pathways for calculation: Double dissociation between rote verbal and quantitative knowledge of arithmetic. *Cortex, 33*, 219–250.

De Jong, P. (1998). Working memory deficits of reading disabled children. *Journal of Experimental Child Psychology, 70*, 75–95.

de Ribaupierre, A., & Lecerf, T. (2006). Relationships between working memory and intelligence from a developmental perspective: Convergent evidence from a neo-Piagetian and a psychometric approach. *European Journal of Cognitive Psychology, 18*, 109–137.

Engle, R. W., Cantor, J., & Carullo, J. J. (1992). Individual differences in working memory and comprehension: A test of four hypotheses. *Journal of Experimental Psychology: Learning, Memory and Cognition, 18,* 972–992.

Engle, R. W., Tuholski, S. W., Laughlin, J. E., & Conway, A. R. (1999). Working memory, short-term memory, and general fluid intelligence: A latent-variable approach. *Journal of Experimental Psychology: General, 128,* 309–331.

Gathercole, S. E. (1998). The development of memory. *Journal of Child Psychology and Psychiatry, 39,* 3–27.

Gathercole, S. E., Alloway, T. P., Kirkwood, H. J., Elliott, J. G., Holmes, J., & Hilton, K. A. (2008). Attentional and executive function behaviours in children with poor working memory. *Learning and Individual Differences, 18,* 214–223.

Gathercole, S. E., Alloway, T. P., Willis, C., & Adams, A. (2006). Working memory in children with reading disabilities. *Journal of Experimental Child Psychology, 93,* 265–281.

Gathercole, S. E., & Pickering, S. J. (2000a). Assessment of working memory in six- and seven-year-old children. *Journal of Educational Psychology, 92,* 377–390.

Gathercole, S. E., & Pickering, S. J. (2000b). Working memory deficits in children with low achievements in the national curriculum at 7 years of age. *British Journal of Education Psychology, 70,* 177–194.

Gathercole, S. E., Pickering, S. J., Ambridge, B., & Wearing, H. (2004). The structure of working memory from 4 to 15 years of age. *Developmental Psychology, 40,* 177–190.

Gathercole, S. E., Tiffany, C., Briscoe, J., & Thorn, A. (2005). Developmental consequences of poor phonological short-term memory function in childhood. *Journal of Child Psychology and Psychiatry, 46,* 598–611.

Hecht, S. A., Torgesen, J. K., Wagner, R., & Rashotte, C. (2001). The relationship between phonological processing abilities and emerging individual differences in mathematical computation skills: A longitudinal study of second to fifth grades. *Journal of Experimental Child Psychology, 79,* 192–227.

Hoskyn, M., & Swanson, H. L. (2000). Cognitive processing of low achievers and children with reading disabilities: A selective meta-analytic review of the published literature. *School Psychology Review, 29,* 102–109.

Hutton, U. M. Z., & Towse, J. N. (2001). Short-term memory and working memory as indices of children's cognitive skills. *Memory, 9,* 383–394.

Jonides, J. (2000). Mechanism of verbal working memory revealed by neuroimaging studies. In B. Landau et al. (Eds.), *Perception, cognition, and language* (pp. 87–104). Cambridge, MA: The MIT Press.

Just, M. A., & Carpenter, P. A. (1992). A capacity theory of comprehension: Individual differences in working memory. *Psychological Review, 99,* 122–149.

Kyllonen, P. C., & Christal, R. E. (1990). Reasoning ability is (little more than) working memory capacity? *Intelligence, 14,* 389–433.

Lazar, J. W., & Frank, Y. (1998). Frontal systems dysfunction in children with attention deficit/hyperactivity disorder and learning disabilities. *Journal of Neuropsychiatry & Clinical Neurosciences, 10,* 160–167.

Logie, R. H. (1986). Visuo-spatial processing in working memory. *Quarterly Journal of Experimental Psychology, 38A,* 229–247.

Miyake, A., Friedman, N. P., Emerson, M. J., Witzki, A. H., & Howerter, A. (2000). The unity and diversity of executive functions and their contributions to complex frontal lobe tasks: A latent variable analysis. *Cognitive Psychology, 41,* 49–100.

O'Shaughnessy, T., & Swanson, H. L. (1998). Do immediate memory deficits in students with learning disabilities in reading reflect a developmental lag or deficit? A selective meta-analysis of the literature. *Learning Disability Quarterly, 21,* 123–148.

Passolunghi, M. C., Cornoldi, C., & De Liberto, S. (1999). Working memory and intrusions of irrelevant information in a group of specific poor problem solvers. *Memory & Cognition, 27,* 779–790.

Pugh, K. R., Mencl, W. E., Shaywitz, B. A., Shaywitz, S. E., Fulbright, R. K., Constable, R. T., et al. (2000). The angular gyrus in developmental dyslexia: Task-specific differences in functional connectivity within posterior cortex. *Psychological Science, 11,* 51–56.

Reichle, E. D., Carpenter, P. A., & Just, M. A. (2000). The neural bases in strategy and skill in sentence-picture verification. *Cognitive Psychology, 40,* 261–295.

Ruchkin, D. S., Berndt, R. S., Johnson Jr., R., Grafman, J., Rotter, W., & Canoune, H. L. (1999). Lexical contributions to retention of verbal information in working memory: Event-related brain potential evidence. *Journal of Memory and Language, 41,* 345–364.

Schretlen, D., Pearlson, G. D., Anthony, J. C., Aylward, E. H., Augustine, A. M., Davis, A., et al. (2000). Elucidating the contributions of processing speed, executive ability, and frontal lobe volume to normal age-related differences in fluid intelligence. *Journal of the International Neuropsychological Society, 6,* 52–61.

Shalev, R. S., Manor, O., & Gross-Tsur, V. (1997). Neuropsychological aspects of developmental dyscalculia. *Mathematical Cognition, 3,* 105–120.

Shaywitz, S. E., Shaywitz, B. A., Pugh, K. R., Fulbright, R. K., Constable, R. T., Mencl, W. E., et al. (1998). Functional disruption in the organization of the brain for reading in dyslexia. *Proceedings of the National Academy of Sciences of the United States of America* (On-line), *95,* 2636–2641. Available: www.pnas.org/cgi/content/full/95/5/2636.

Siegel, L. S. (1993). Phonological processing deficits as a basis for reading disabilities. *Developmental Review, 13,* 246–257.

Siegel, L. S. (2003). Basic cognitive processes and reading disabilities. In H. L. Swanson, K. R. Harris, & S. Graham, (Eds.), *Handbook of learning disabilities* (pp. 158–181). New York: Guilford Press.

Siegel, L. S., & Ryan, E. B. (1989). The development of working memory in normally achieving and subtypes of learning disabled. *Child Development, 60,* 973–980.

Smith, E. E., & Jonides, J. (1997). Working memory: A view from neuroimaging. *Cognitive Psychology, 33,* 5–42.

Stanovich, K. E., & Siegel, L. (1994). Phenotypic performances profile of children with reading disabililities: A regression-based test of the phonological-core variable-difference model. *Journal of Education Psychology, 86,* 24–53.

Swanson, H. L. (1981). Vigilance deficits in learning disabled children: A signal detection analysis. *Journal of Child Psychology and Psychiatry, 22,* 393–399.

Swanson, H. L. (1983). A developmental study of vigilance in learning disabled and nondisabled children. *Journal of Abnormal Child Psychology, 11,* 415–439.

Swanson, H. L. (1988). Learning disabled children's problem solving: An information processing analysis of intellectual performance. *Intelligence, 12,* 261–278.

Swanson, H. L. (1992). Generality and modification of working memory among skilled and less skilled readers. *Journal of Educational Psychology, 84,* 473–488.

Swanson, H. L. (1993a). An information processing analysis of learning disabled children's problem solving. *American Education Research Journal, 30*, 861–893.

Swanson, H. L. (1993b). Executive processing in learning disabled readers. *Intelligence, 17*, 117–149.

Swanson, H. L. (1994). Short-term memory and working memory: Do both contribute to our understanding of academic achievement in children and adults with learning disabilities? *Journal of Learning Disabilities, 27*, 34–50.

Swanson, H. L. (1999a). What develops in working memory? A life span perspective. *Developmental Psychology, 35*, 986–1000.

Swanson, H. L. (1999b). Reading comprehension and working memory in skilled readers: Is the phonological loop more important than the executive system? *Journal of Experimental Child Psychology, 72*, 1–31.

Swanson, H. L. (2000). Are working memory deficits in readers with learning disabilities hard to change? *Journal of Learning Disabilities, 33*, 551–566.

Swanson, H. L. (2003). Age-related differences in learning disabled and skilled readers' working memory. *Journal of Experimental Child Psychology, 85*, 1–31.

Swanson, H. L. (2006). Cognitive processes that underlie mathematical precociousness in young children. *Journal of Experimental Child Psychology, 93*, 239–264.

Swanson, H. L. (2008). Working memory and intelligence in children: What develops? *Journal of Educational Psychology, 100*, 581–602.

Swanson, H. L., & Ashbaker, M. (2000). Working memory, STM, articulation speed, word recognition, and reading comprehension in learning disabled readers: Executive and/or articulatory system? *Intelligence, 28*, 1–30.

Swanson, H. L., Ashbaker, M., & Lee, C. (1996). Working-memory in learning disabled readers as a function of processing demands. *Journal of Child Experimental Psychology, 61*, 242–275.

Swanson, H. L., & Beebe-Frankenberger, M. (2004). The relationship between working memory and mathematical problem solving in children at risk and not at risk for serious math difficulties. *Journal of Educational Psychology, 96*, 471–491.

Swanson, H. L., & Berninger, V. W. (1995). The role of working memory and STM in skilled and less skilled readers' word recognition and comprehension. *Intelligence, 21*, 83–108.

Swanson, H. L., & Cochran, K. (1991). Learning disabilities, distinctive encoding, and hemispheric resources. *Brain and Language, 40*, 202–230.

Swanson, H. L., & Jerman, O. (2006). Math disabilities: A selective meta-analysis of the literature. *Review of Educational Research, 76*, 249–274.

Swanson, H. L., & Jerman, O. (2007). The influence of working memory on reading growth in subgroups of children with reading disabilities. *Journal of Experimental Child Psychology, 96*, 249–283.

Swanson, H. L., Jerman, O., & Zheng, X. (2008). Growth in working memory and mathematical problem solving in children at risk and not at risk for serious math difficulties. *Journal of Educational Psychology, 100*, 343–379.

Swanson, H. L., & Mullen, R. (1983). Hemisphere specialization in learning disabled readers' recall as a function of age and level of processing. *Journal of Experimental Child Psychology, 35*, 457–477.

Swanson, H. L., & Obrzut, J. E. (1985). Learning disabled readers' recall as a function of distinctive encoding, hemispheric processing, and selective attention. *Journal of Learning Disabilities, 18*, 409–418.

Swanson, H. L., & Sachse-Lee, C. (2001a). A subgroup analysis of working memory in children with reading disabilities: Domain general or domain specific deficiency? *Journal of Learning Disabilities, 34*, 249–263.

Swanson, H. L., & Sachse-Lee, C. (2001b). Mathematical problem solving and working memory in children with learning disabilities: Both executive and phonological processes are important. *Journal of Experimental Child Psychology, 79*, 294–321.

Swanson, H. L., & Siegel, L. (2001). Learning disabilities as a working memory deficit. *Issues in Education: Contributions from Educational Psychology, 7*, 1–48.

Swanson, H. L., Zheng, X., & Jerman, O. (2009). Working memory, short-term memory, and reading disabilities: A selective meta-analysis of the literature. *Journal of Learning Disabilities, 42*, 260–287.

Towse, J. N., Cowan, N., Hitch, G. J., & Horton, N. J. (2008). The recall of information from working memory: Insights from behavioural and chronometric perspectives. *Experimental Psychology, 55*, 371–383.

Towse, J. N., Cowan, N., Horton, N. J., & Whytock, S. (2008). Task experience and children's working memory performance: A perspective from recall timing. *Developmental Psychology, 44*, 695–706.

van der Sluis, S., van der Leij, A., & de Jong, P. F. (2005). Working memory in Dutch children with reading- and arithmetic-related LD. *Journal of Learning Disabilities, 38*, 207–221.

Willcutt, E. G., Pennington, B. F. Boada, R., & Ogline, J. S. (2001). A comparison of cognitive deficits in reading disability and attention-deficit/hyperactivity disorder. *Journal of Abnormal Psychology, 110*, 157–172.

Willcutt, E. G., Pennington, B. F., Olson, R. K., Chhabildas, N., & Hulslander, J. (2005). Neuropsychological analyses of comorbidity between reading disability and attention deficit hyperactivity disorder: In search of the common deficit. *Developmental Neuropsychology, 27*, 35–78.

10 Working memory in development

Links with learning between typical and atypical populations

Tracy Packiam Alloway and Lisa Archibald

Introduction

Working memory refers to the capacity to store and manipulate information for brief periods of time (Baddeley & Hitch, 1974; Just & Carpenter, 1992). It provides a mental workspace that is used in many important activities in learning, such as literacy (Gathercole, Alloway, Willis, & Adams, 2006; Siegel & Ryan, 1989) and numeracy (Geary, Hoard, Byrd-Craven, & DeSoto, 2004; Swanson, Ashbaker, & Lee, 1996; see also Cowan & Alloway, 2008, for a review). The functioning of the working memory system has also been implicated in groups of children with marked learning difficulties (e.g., Alloway et al., 2005a; Swanson & Saez, 2003). The extent to which deficits in specific cognitive mechanisms may underlie learning difficulties in developmental disorders is a matter of considerable interest in the fields of cognitive development and neuropathology. However, to date, few studies have provided a review of working memory profiles and the relationship to learning in students with different developmental pathologies, and it is the purpose of the present chapter to do so. The atypical groups included children with Specific Language Impairment, motor impairments (Developmental Coordination Disorder), behavioural problems (Attention Deficit and Hyperactive Disorder) and Autistic Spectrum Disorder. The extent to which deficits in subcomponents of working memory may differentiate these groups was explored by measuring memory skills systematically across the verbal and visuo-spatial domains.

There are several models of working memory (Baddeley, 1996; Barrouillet, Bernardin, & Camos, 2004; Case, Kurland, & Goldberg, 1982; Cowan, 2001; Engle, Kane, & Tuholski, 1999; Just & Carpenter, 1992). One common feature shared by the various models is that working memory is supported by a limited capacity resource which some theorists link with attention (Barrouillet et al., 2004; Cowan, 2001; Engle et al., 1999). For the purposes of the present review, we focus on the most widely used account of working memory based on the Baddeley and Hitch (1974) model. The central executive is the component responsible for controlling resources and monitoring information processing across informational domains (Baddeley, Emslie, Kolodny & Duncan, 1998; Baddeley & Hitch, 1974). This system is also responsible for a range of regulatory functions including the retrieval of information from long-term memory and attentional control. In this model, storage of information is mediated by two domain-specific slave systems: the phonological loop, which provides temporary storage of verbal information, and the visuo-spatial sketchpad, specialized for the maintenance and manipulation of visual and spatial representations (see Baddeley & Logie, 1999, for a review). A fourth component of this model has recently been added, the episodic buffer, responsible for binding information across informational domains and memory sub-systems into integrated chunks (Baddeley, 2000). This model of working memory has been supported by evidence from studies of children (e.g., Alloway, Gathercole, & Pickering, 2006; Alloway, Gathercole, Willis, & Adams, 2004; Bayliss, Jarrold, Gunn, & Baddeley, 2003), adult participants, neuropsychological patients (see Baddeley, 1996; Jonides, Lacey, & Nee, 2005, for reviews), as well as neuroimaging investigations (Vallar & Papagno, 2003).

Working memory capacity is measured by complex span tasks that require simultaneous short-term storage of information while processing additional, and sometimes unrelated, information. An example of such a task is reading span, in which the participant makes judgments about the semantic properties of sentences while remembering the last word of each sentence in sequence (Daneman & Carpenter, 1980). According to the Baddeley and Hitch account of working memory, the processing aspect of the task is controlled by a centralized component (i.e., the central executive), while the short-term storage aspect is supported by a domain-specific component – the phonological loop for verbal information and the visual/spatial sketchpad for visuo-spatial information. Working memory is related to, but distinguishable from, short-term memory. Whereas working memory involves both the storage and processing of information, short-term memory systems are specialized purely for the temporary storage of material within particular informational domains.

Working memory and learning

Individual differences in working memory capacity appear to have important consequences for children's ability to acquire knowledge and new skills. Verbal working memory skills are effective predictors of performance in many complex cognitive activities including reading (de Jong, 1998; Swanson, 1994), mathematics (Bull & Scerif, 2001; Mayringer & Wimmer, 2000; Siegel & Ryan, 1989), and language comprehension (Nation, Adams, Bowyer-Crane, & Snowling, 1999; Seigneuric, Ehrlich, Oakhill & Yuill, 2000), as well as attainments in National Curriculum assessments of English and mathematics (Alloway, Gathercole, Willis & Adams, 2005; Gathercole, Pickering, Knight, & Stegmann, 2004). In particular, marked deficits of verbal working memory correspond with the severity of learning difficulty experienced by a child (Alloway et al., 2005b; Pickering & Gathercole, 2004). Recent research has also established that poor verbal working memory skills, but not general intelligence or verbal short-term memory, are uniquely linked with both reading and mathematical abilities (Cain, Oakhill, & Bryant, 2004; Gathercole et al., 2006; Siegel, 1988). This asymmetry of associations provides a strong basis for identifying working memory as a specific and significant contributor to general learning difficulties.

The purpose of this chapter is to characterize the short-term and working memory impairments associated with a range of prevalent developmental disorders found in mainstream education. To this end, children with Specific Language Impairment (SLI), Developmental Coordination Disorder (DCD), Attention Deficit and Hyperactive Disorder (ADHD), and Asperger Syndrome (AS) were assessed on their memory skills using the Automated Working Memory Assessment (AWMA; Alloway, 2007a), a computerized test battery. The AWMA provides multiple assessments of verbal and visuo-spatial aspects of short-term memory and working memory. The tasks incorporated into the computerized battery were selected on the basis of providing reliable and valid assessments of verbal and visuo-spatial short-term and working memory in the relevant research literature. In line with this substantial body of prior evidence, verbal and visuo-spatial working memory were measured using tasks involving simultaneous storage and processing of information, whereas tasks involving only the storage of information were used to measure verbal and visuo-spatial short-term memory.

Of specific interest is to understand whether children with different developmental needs exhibit memory profiles unique to their disability. For example, do children with language impairments struggle more with verbal memory tasks, while children with motor difficulties exhibit deficits in visuo-spatial tasks? In children with attentional problems, current evidence regarding their memory profile is mixed. However, we might expect that memory tasks that require additional cognitive resources would be difficult for them. Finally, in children broadly identified as having social impairments, Asperger Syndrome, what would their working memory profile be like?

Specific Language Impairment (SLI)

Characteristics of this group

Specific Language Impairment (SLI) is an unexpected failure to develop language at the usual rate, despite normal general intellectual abilities, sensory functions, and environmental exposure to language. SLI is a relatively common developmental pathology, estimated to occur in approximately 7% of kindergarten children (Tomblin et al., 1997). For many children with SLI, deficits of language persist throughout childhood (Bishop & Edmundson, 1987; Tomblin, Zhang, Buckwalter, & O'Brien, 2003) and into adulthood (Snowling, Bishop, & Stothard, 2000; Stothard, Snowling, Bishop, Chipchase, & Kaplan, 1998). Even those whose language difficulties have apparently resolved and who perform in the average range on standard language measures may still be distinguishable from age peers on some measures (e.g., Conti-Ramsden, Botting, & Faragher, 2001). It should be noted that the language skills of individuals with SLI do not remain static over time; they change and improve, but age-appropriate language skills may not be achieved. This changing nature of the language difficulty over time can present a challenge when attempting to identify and compare individuals with SLI.

Children with SLI have been found to have difficulty with virtually every aspect of language that has been studied including lexical knowledge and semantics, word finding, grammatical and syntactical skill, and pragmatics (see Leonard, 1998, for a review). Impairments on nonlinguistic tasks have been reported also (e.g., Miller, Kail, Leonard, & Tomblin, 2001). One problem for researchers and clinicians attempting to identify and understand the disorder is that symptoms vary widely across affected individuals. This has led to widespread interest in establishing a clinical marker for SLI defined as a heritable deficit associated with the disorder present even when the condition no longer manifests itself and not present in unaffected individuals/family members (Gershon & Goldin, 1986). Two candidate measures have been proposed as clinical markers for SLI: nonword repetition (Bishop, North, & Donlan, 1996) and verb tense marking (Rice, 2003; Rice & Wexler, 1996). It is indeed the case that consistent SLI deficits have been reported over numerous studies for both nonword repetition (e.g., Conti-Ramsden, 2003; Dollaghan & Campbell, 1998; Ellis Weismer et al., 2000; Gathercole & Baddeley, 1990; Marton & Schwartz, 2003) and tense marking (Conti-Ramsden & Windfuhr, 2002; Leonard et al., 2003; Marchman, Wulfeck, & Ellis Weismer, 1999; Redmond, 2003). Interestingly, these two impairments have been found to be significantly heritable but have minimal genetic overlap suggesting that they represent distinct core deficits in SLI (Bishop, Adams, & Norbury, 2006).

Working memory profile

Nonword repetition has been proposed as a relatively pure index of verbal short-term memory (Gathercole & Baddeley, 1993; though see Bowey, 1996; Gathercole, 2006; Morra & Camba, 2009) leading to the suggestion that poor verbal short-term memory characterizes SLI (Gathercole & Baddeley, 1990). Converging evidence comes from studies demonstrating SLI deficits on a variety of verbal short-term memory tasks such as digit span and word list recall (e.g., Graham, 1980; Hick, Botting, & Conti-Ramsden, 2005). Verbal short-term memory has been specifically linked to the learning of the phonological forms of new words (Gathercole, Hitch, Service, & Martin, 1997), and as a result poor verbal short-term memory may be expected to disrupt language learning. Findings of a recent longitudinal study, however, suggest that a verbal short-term memory deficit alone is insufficient to account for pervasive and persistent language impairment of SLI: children with a history of very poor verbal short-term memory that extended between 4 and 8 years of age and low average working memory skills were found to have age-appropriate language abilities four years later (Gathercole et al., 2005; see also Im-Bolter, Johnson, & Pascual-Leone, 2006).

Another aspect of immediate memory implicated in more recent SLI research is working memory. Findings of SLI deficits on a number of processing-based tasks requiring either greater processing speed (e.g., Miller et al., 2001) or capacity (e.g., Ellis Weismer & Hesketh, 1993, 1996) have pointed the way to investigating working memory in SLI. Several studies have reported working memory impairments for SLI groups on tasks requiring the simultaneous storage and processing of verbal information (e.g., Ellis Weismer, Evans, & Hesketh, 1999; Hoffman & Gillam, 2004; Montgomery, 2000). The temporary storage and processing of nonverbal information has been the focus of only a few studies (Bavin, Wilson, Maruff, & Sleeman, 2005; Hoffman & Gillam, 2004); however, the use of unconventional tasks has made results of these studies difficult to interpret. The question of whether visuo-spatial memory skills are impaired in SLI is an important one as it addresses theoretical issues related to the general or specific nature of SLI deficits.

One of the first efforts to provide standardized assessments of short-term and working memory in SLI was reported by Archibald and Gathercole (2006a). Both short-term and verbal working memory were assessed in a group of school-age children with SLI. Group performance was markedly impaired on the verbal short-term and verbal working memory tasks with 70% and 95% of the group scoring in the deficit range, respectively. In contrast, the group achieved scores in the average range on the visuo-spatial short-term memory measures.

The advent of the standardized measures of visuo-spatial working memory (using the AWMA) provides an opportunity to investigate these skills in children with SLI (Archibald & Gathercole, 2006b). The children with SLI had marked and consistent deficits in verbal short-term and working memory deficits. In contrast, the group performed in the average range on visuo-spatial short-term and working memory tasks. These findings indicate that children with SLI have difficulty not only in retaining phonological information, but in processing verbal information as well. In fact, it may be that the verbal processing and storage tasks included in the AWMA present a particular challenge for children with SLI by combining two of the most difficult tasks – both storage and processing of verbal information. Nevertheless, children with SLI are impaired even on tasks requiring visuo-spatial storage when there is a simultaneous demand for the processing of verbal information (Archibald & Gathercole, 2007). It seems, then, that it is the processing of verbal information while attempting to hold in mind any information, regardless of modality, that is particularly problematic for children with SLI.

The finding of a modality-specific immediate memory impairment in SLI fits well with the working memory model. It is plausible from the present results to infer deficits in both verbal short-term memory and the central executive in SLI with visuo-spatial short-term memory relatively spared. The combined verbal short-term and working memory deficit also provides a possible mechanism for the persistent and pervasive language impairment that characterizes SLI. While poor verbal short-term memory alone may be insufficient to cause SLI (Gathercole et al., 2005), it is conceivable that a combined verbal storage and processing deficit could interfere with language learning significantly.

It is possible to argue that the linguistic deficit in SLI underlies the present findings of impairments on tasks requiring the storage and manipulation of verbal information. This is unlikely to be the case for two reasons: First, all of the children in the SLI group demonstrated task comprehension by completing at least the first level of all of the tasks. In addition, while the visuo spatial complex memory tasks included in the AWMA require the storage and processing of visuo-spatial information, the learning of the tasks requires some linguistic knowledge of concepts such as mirror image, rotation, and similar/dissimilar. The children with SLI in the present study were able to understand these tasks and complete them as expected for their age thus demonstrating their adequate linguistic ability for the AWMA tasks. It could also be suggested that the verbal working memory impairments observed in the present study arose as a result of the well-documented verbal short-term memory deficit in SLI. Findings from several studies, however, indicate the SLI impairment on complex memory tasks involving verbal short-term and working memory is significantly greater than what would be expected based on performance on the verbal short-term memory tasks alone (e.g., Archibald & Gathercole, 2007; Marton & Schwartz, 2003).

The profile of memory impairments characterizing SLI in this study differs from that of some of the other disorder groups described in this chapter. This is an especially exciting result as it suggests that working memory theory may provide a profitable avenue of inquiry for understanding the essential differences between common childhood pathologies. Such efforts have often been thwarted in the past due to the overlap in symptoms commonly observed in children from different disorder groups. The present findings suggest that attempting to process verbal information while holding any information in mind is difficult for children with SLI, and may be specifically linked to language learning.

Working memory and learning

The working memory profile for children with SLI described above suggests a possible mechanism for two important features of SLI: the general poverty of language knowledge and the inherent heterogeneity in the disorder. Verbal short-term memory reflected in tasks such as nonword repetition has been suggested to be an important mechanism in early vocabulary development (Gathercole, 2006). The accurate repetition of a novel phonological form is one way in which a new word begins its journey into the lexicon. Once vocabulary knowledge is established, however, this knowledge can support new learning of similar sounding words. Children with SLI are at a disadvantage on both counts. They fail to repeat novel phonological forms accurately resulting in slower early vocabulary development. At later stages of development, they then lack the lexical knowledge to support rapid new word learning. Previous research has suggested that this verbal short-term memory deficit in and of itself may not have a lasting impact (Gathercole et al., 2005). However, children with SLI also have difficulty simultaneously processing information and storing verbal material. Communication demands are constantly varying. For example, in the course of a single day, a child may be asked to produce the regular past tense form, "The dog rolled over", as a simple statement to describe a pet, embedded as a clause in response to the question "What do you think would happen if . . .", and as a written statement in a journal entry. Each instance comes with varying demands. Simple demands such as describing the action of a pet dog in front of the child may not exceed the working memory capacity of the child with SLI. Greater demands, however, such as producing the form in a clausal structure or as a written statement may lead to errors. The result of these varying demands may be considerable heterogeneity in the child's observable linguistic competency.

Developmental Coordination Disorder (DCD)

Characteristics of this group

The term Developmental Coordination Disorder (DCD) refers to children with "a marked impairment in the development of motor coordination . . . that significantly interferes with academic achievement or activities of daily living" (DSM-IV, APA, 1994, p. 53). DCD is a condition present from birth that affects the individual's ability to plan and control movements, which can lead to associated problems with language and perception. The nature of the condition is multifaceted, as the problem may be related to the integration of sensory and motor functions for some, while it could lie in the central motor or more peripheral neuromuscular apparatus for others. The causes of motor difficulties are equally varied and the origins of this motor planning disorder are still under debate (Sugden & Wright, 1998). It is believed to be due to a disruption in the development of the cortical control processes that inhibits efficiency of messages transmitted from the brain to the body, rather than the initial thought that it was caused by brain damage (e.g., Wilson, Maruff, & Lum, 2003). However, the underlying problem is unknown as this disturbance in message relaying may be caused by difficulty in collection, transmission or storage of motor information (see Alloway, 2006, for further discussion).

Labels such as developmental dyspraxia, minimal brain dysfunction, perceptual-motor dysfunction, physical awkwardness, and clumsiness have all frequently been used to describe individuals with motor difficulties, but it will be referred to as DCD in the present review (see Miyahara & Register, 2000; Peters, Barnett & Henderson, 2001). There is a 6% prevalence rate of DCD in children aged between 5 and 11, with a higher incidence of this disorder in boys (Mandich & Polatajko, 2003; Portwood, 1996).

DCD is a generalized problem that affects movement as well as perception (e.g., Visser, 2003). Observable behaviours in children with DCD include clumsiness, poor posture, confusion about which hand to use, difficulties throwing or catching a ball, reading and writing difficulties, and an inability to hold a pen or pencil properly (see Alloway, 2006, for a review). There are also reports of heterogeneity in motor profiles as some children have generalized motor problems, while other exhibit specific difficulties in fine motor tasks and balance (e.g., Wright & Sugden, 1996). DCD is also associated with difficulties in visual skills, speech, language, social skills, attention, and learning (Dewey, Kaplan, Crawford & Wilson, 2002; Piek & Dyck, 2004). Evidence indicates that DCD is not due to a neurological lag, and that the rate of progress in movement may not be made up over time (Barnett & Henderson, 1992). While some children are able to outgrow their motor difficulties without any intervention, others struggle with motor deficits even into adulthood resulting in socio-emotional struggles as well as perceptual and motor difficulties (Cousins & Smyth, 2003; Hellgren, Gillberg, Gillberg, & Enerskog, 1993).

Visual deficits are also characteristic of children with DCD. In visual tasks that do not include a motor component such as length discrimination, gestalt completion, and visual integration, common failures include inaccuracies in estimating object size (e.g., Lord & Hulme, 1988), and difficulties in locating an object's position in space (Schoemaker, Smits-Engelsman, & Jongmans, 2003). Visual tasks that do include some motor skills, such as Block Design and Object Assembly subtests from the WISC-III (Wechsler, 1992), are often good discriminators of children with DCD from controls.

Working memory profile

There is growing evidence that children with DCD struggle with working memory tasks. Alloway (2007b) indicated that almost half of the DCD sample achieved standard scores of less than 85 in the verbal short-term and working memory measures (42% and 49%, respectively). With respect to the visuo-spatial memory measures, a slightly larger proportion of the sample performed more poorly – 56% and 60% for visuo-spatial short-term and working memory, respectively.

There is also a degree of specificity to the working memory profiles of children with DCD. When compared with students with moderate learning difficulties, the working memory impairments varied as a function of special needs. The DCD group performed at significantly lower levels than children with learning difficulties in measures of verbal short-term memory, visuo-spatial short-term and working memory (Alloway & Temple, 2007). When comparing children with two different developmental pathologies, SLI and DCD, children with SLI showed marked impairments on verbal but not visuo-spatial measures of short-term and working memory whereas children with DCD had general deficits across verbal and visuo-spatial short-term and working memory. Performance on visuo-spatial working memory tasks alone was sufficient to successfully discriminate the two groups (Alloway & Archibald, 2008; Archibald & Alloway, 2008).

The profile of children with DCD indicates a specificity of memory impairments. In particular, their performance on visuo-spatial short-term and working memory tasks was significantly worse than on the verbal short-term memory ones. This profile fits well with several assumptions of the working memory model. First, verbal short-term memory and visual/spatial memory are managed by distinct cognitive resources. Data from neuropsychology as well as developmental studies support this dissociation (see Baddeley & Hitch, 2000, for a review). Second, visuo-spatial memory skills are linked with movement planning and control (e.g., Quinn, 1994; Smyth, Pearson, & Pendleton, 1988). The dynamic nature (i.e., sequential presentation of the stimuli) of the visual stimuli presentation could also have led to the deficit in visuo-spatial memory performance. Performance of typically-developing children is impaired on dynamic presentation formats of the visual and spatial tasks compared to static presentation formats (Pickering, Gathercole, Hall, & Lloyd, 2001). Similarly, children with DCD struggle more on tasks that involve active movement rather than passive movement (e.g., Wilson & McKenzie, 1998). The active condition of a motor test, rather than a passive one, is also able to significantly discriminate DCD children from a control group (Piek & Coleman-Carman, 1995).

Children with DCD seem to struggle with visuo-spatial memory tasks because of their difficulties with movement planning (such as mentally rotating objects in the Mr X and Spatial Span tasks and tracking movement in the Dot Matrix, Block Recall and Mazes Memory tasks). It is also likely that they perform poorly on these measures as a result of the combined processing and storage demands of these tasks. This view is substantiated by the finding that their performance on verbal working memory tasks, also requiring simultaneous processing and storage of information, is poor (see Alloway, 2007b, for further discussion). It is possible that the combination of motor activity and added processing demands of the tasks proved difficult for children with DCD.

Working memory and learning

There is evidence that poor working memory impairs learning in DCD children. Alloway (2007b) compared children with low visuo-spatial memory skills on standardized measures of reading and math. There was a significant difference in learning skills, even after IQ skills were statistically controlled.

Although children with DCD tend to struggle in nonverbal ability measures, these deficits have been explained in light of the motor components involved in tasks such as Block Design, rather than nonverbal intelligence per se (e.g., Coleman, Piek & Livesey, 2001). Correspondingly, Bonifacci (2004) found no relationship between motor abilities and nonverbal IQ when the IQ test did not involve motor skills (i.e., a matrices test). The unique link between visuo-spatial memory skills and learning is in line with recent findings that visuo-spatial memory can reliably discriminate Developmental Coordination Disorder children from children with learning difficulties but normal motor functioning (Alloway & Temple, 2007). Together, these findings suggest that visuo-spatial memory taps more than general ability and is not simply a reflection of motor involvement in a task. This provides a useful starting point in understanding how motor skills, memory and learning are linked in children with DCD.

More recently, Alloway and Warner (2008) investigated the transfer of gains made from an exercise-based intervention to academic attainment in those with DCD. The findings indicated that while motor skills improved, this effect did not transfer to reading and math scores. This is consistent with research indicating that task-specific training improved performance of DCD children on motor tasks but not academic tasks (Revie & Larkin, 1993; Reynolds, Nicolson, & Hambly, 2003, Wilson, 2005). Recent research on nutrition, learning, and motor difficulties supports the view that learning is not directly mediated by motor skills. Richardson and Montgomery (2005) found that fatty acid supplements improved reading but not motor skills, suggesting that the two skills are dissociable. On the basis of evidence of specific visuo-spatial memory deficits (Alloway, 2006; Alloway & Temple, 2007) and the link between visuo-spatial memory and learning in DCD children (Alloway, 2007b), a targeted intervention which focuses on training working memory in learning may be needed (see Discussion below).

Attention Deficit and Hyperactive Disorder (ADHD)

Characteristics of this group

The core features leading to a diagnosis of Attention Deficit and Hyperactive Disorder (ADHD) are significant levels of over-activity, inattention, and impulsiveness (DSM-IV, APA, 1994). Children with ADHD are usually seen as having great difficulty remaining seated when required to, and being much more active than their peers. They also find it hard to remember complex instructions, show poor attention to instructions, and find it hard not to interrupt with their comments. These symptoms can vary depending on the situation, which makes the diagnosis quite challenging at times, but the use of formal rating scales does give some objectivity to the assessment (Snyder et al., 2006). The ADHD assessment considers biological, psychological, and social factors, because children with ADHD usually show significant social, academic, and psychological difficulties at each stage of their development (Biederman, 2005).

The worldwide prevalence of ADHD is estimated to be 5% (Polanczyk, de Lima, Horta, Biederman, & Rohde, 2007), though in the UK research suggests a lower rate of 1–3% (Goodman, Ford, & Meltzer, 2002; McArdle, O'Brien, & Kolvin, 1995). In clinics, far more boys present with the disorder than girls, possibly because girls have lower ratings of externalizing problems than boys (Gershon, 2002). Within community samples, the gender ratio is approximately 3:1 (Szatmari, Offord, & Boyle, 1989). The presence of ADHD increases the risk of the child having oppositional defiance and conduct disorder considerably (Angold, Costello, & Erkanli, 1999), and it has a strong tendency to persist into adulthood (Rasmussen & Gillberg, 2001).

According to Barkley (1990), behavioural inhibition is a central impairment in those with ADHD (though see the motivational deficits theory, Sonuga-Barke, 2005). A key feature of Barkley's model is that inhibition serves as a trigger for secondary effects in various executive functions, including working memory (van Mourik, Oosterlaan, & Sergeant, 2005; Willcutt, Pennington, Chhabildas, Olson, & Hulslander, 2005). Although working memory shares a neuroanatomical association with the frontal lobes, current evidence suggests that in cognitive terms at least, it is distinct from other executive functions such as inhibition (Miyake, Friedman, Rettinger, Shah, & Hegarty, 2001).

Working memory profile

Children with ADHD typically perform within age-expected levels in short-term memory tasks, such as forward recall of letters (Benezra & Douglas, 1988), digits (Rucklidge & Tannock, 2002) or words (Roodenrys, Koloski, & Grainger, 2001). In cases where verbal short-term memory impairments have been reported, deficits are often nonsignificant after covarying for differences in IQ (Stevens, Quittner, Zuckerman, & Moore, 2002) and reading ability (Martinussen & Tannock, 2006; Roodenrys et al., 2001), suggesting that such impairments are not related to ADHD per se. Other studies reporting verbal short-term memory deficits in children with ADHD have typically used digit span tasks that incorporate both forward and backward digit recall (Mariani & Barkley, 1997; McInnes, Humphries, Hogg-Johnson, & Tannock, 2003). When performance on these tasks was investigated separately, ADHD children performed more poorly than controls on backward but not forward recall (Karatekin & Asarnow, 1998; McInnes et al., 2003). As backward digit recall involves both the manipulation and storage of digit sequences, these deficits are likely to reflect difficulty with managing the dual-nature of this task.

Previous research on visuo-spatial short-term memory and ADHD has also yielded mixed results. Some studies report average visuo-spatial memory skills on tasks involving immediate recall of spatial locations (Barkley, Edwards, Laneri, Fletcher, & Metevia, 2001; Cohen et al., 2000; Shue &

Douglas, 1992), while others report marked deficits (Karatekin & Asarnow, 1998; McInnes et al., 2003; Mehta, Goodyear, & Sahakian, 2004; Tripp, Ryan, & Peace, 2002) that persist after controlling for individual differences in age and IQ (Barnett et al., 2001).

With respect to measures of working memory, individuals with ADHD tend to perform below age-expected levels in tasks that measure their ability to control and sustain attention in the face of interference or distraction, independent of IQ or co-morbid language difficulties (e.g., Barnett et al., 2001; Martinussen & Tannock, 2006; McInnes et al., 2003; Willcutt et al., 2005). Specifically, visuo-spatial working memory deficits are more substantial than verbal ones (e.g., Martinussen, Hayden, Hogg-Johnson, & Tannock, 2005; Roodenrys, 2006). For example, performance falls within the typical range on verbal working memory tasks such as listening recall (Adams & Snowling, 2001; Kerns, McInerney, & Wilde, 2001; Rucklidge & Tannock, 2002; Shue & Douglas, 1992; Sonuga-Barke, Dalen, Daley, & Remington, 2002), but is markedly worse on visuo-spatial working memory tasks (Barkley, 1997; Barnett et al., 2001; Cornoldi et al., 2001). Of a range of executive function measures, visuo-spatial working memory tasks were found to be highly reliable in identifying students with ADHD from typically-developing controls (Holmes, Gathercole, Place, Alloway, & Elliott, 2010).

Most of the research on working memory in individuals with ADHD focuses on the combined subtype. However, there is a growing sentiment that the different subtypes of ADHD are characterized by dissociable cognitive and behavioural profiles (see Geurts et al., 2005). A recent study of students with inattentive symptoms, recruited via community sampling on the basis of teacher ratings of classroom behaviour, demonstrated that the combined and inattentive ADHD subtypes have similar working memory profiles and cannot be differentiated from one another on this criterion (Alloway, Elliott, Holmes, & Place, 2009). This finding extends previous neuropsychological evidence for the lack of distinctiveness between these two groups with respect to executive function skills (Barkley, Grodzinsky, & DuPaul, 1992; Chhabildas, Pennington, & Willcutt, 2001; Faraone, Biederman, Mennin, & Russell, 1998; Murphy, Barkley, & Bush, 2001).

Working memory and learning

How do attention difficulties and memory problems impact learning? Children with ADHD have been found to have significantly lower reading and mathematics scores than healthy controls (Holmes, Alloway, Gathercole, & Elliott, 2009). Two different patterns of performance might have been evidenced. First, according to the multiple deficit model, the additive effects of hyperactive/impulsive behaviour and working memory could have resulted in the children with ADHD-C performing worse than those with just poor working memory (Castellanos & Tannock, 2002). An alternative explanation is that regardless of the primary deficit, the presence of working memory impairment leads to learning difficulties. There is some support for this view in research on individuals with motor difficulties and language impairments (Alloway & Archibald, 2008). Although both groups had working memory impairments, students with motor difficulties achieved average levels on language measures. Despite this strength, they performed no better than their counterparts with language impairments in learning outcomes. This pattern can be interpreted as reflecting the link between working memory and academic attainment (Cowan & Alloway, 2008). Indeed, the working memory profiles of both the motor impaired and language impaired groups were significantly associated with reading and math.

Asperger Syndrome (AS)

Characteristics of this group

Autistic symptoms can be classified as follows: reciprocal social interactions, communication, imagination, and restricted interests and repetitive behaviours. *Social* symptoms include absent, diminished or atypical orientation toward their caregivers and peers. *Communication* symptoms include atypical reproduction of linguistic material without apparent communicative intent (echolalia), hyperlexia (in the written domain), and reduced ability to recode perceived language (stereotyped language). In rare instances, there is a complete absence of expressed oral language. In childhood, *imagination* difficulties include the absence of pretend play and in adulthood, there is an over-orientation toward the concrete aspects of the environment. *Restricted interests and repetitive behaviours* include hand flapping and focused and inflexible interest in objects or abstract domains of knowledge. In Asperger Syndrome, language is fluent, formal and overly detailed (see Belleville, Ménard, Mottron, & Ménard, 2006, for further discussion).

Working memory profile

Research on the memory profile of children with AS is relatively sparse, possibly due to the relative recency of this diagnosis (Belleville et al., 2006). AS is a common subgroup of the autistic spectrum and we can gain some insight into their memory profile from studies on Autistic Spectrum Disorder (ASD). To date, working memory research in ASD has taken the approach of investigating aspects of working memory (based on models of working memory) in isolation. For example, studies investigating verbal short-term memory have reported that individuals with autism show typical performance in the immediate serial recall in verbal tasks (Bennetto, Pennington, & Rogers, 1996; Russell, Jarrold, & Henry, 1996), typical recency effects (Boucher, 1978), and larger word length effects when using visual rather than auditory stimuli (Ménard, Mottron, Belleville, & Limoges, 2001). Closer inspection of the mechanisms involved in verbal short-term memory reveals that ASD persons tend to encode phonological and articulatory features of items more than semantic ones, compared to age-matched and IQ-matched participants (Mottron, Morasse, & Belleville, 2001). This focus on surface properties has been confirmed in samples of both low-functioning autistic persons (Russell et al., 1996) and high-functioning autistic persons (see Belleville et al., 2006).

With respect to visuo-spatial short-term memory, the majority of studies have reported typical performance in ASD persons. In tasks such as the Corsi block, where the participant had to recall locations on a matrix of squares, ASD participants performed at the same level as age-matched and IQ-matched individuals (Ozonoff & Strayer, 2001). However, in visuo-spatial memory tasks that involved saccade measurements, autistic participants exhibited greater errors relative to controls (Minshew, Luna, & Sweeney, 1999). This deficit also corresponded to decreased activation in brain regions thought to be associated in spatial working memory: the dorsolateral prefrontal cortex and posterior cingulate (Luna et al., 2002). However, caution is needed in interpreting whether these findings reflect a visuo-spatial memory deficit per se or limitations of executive resources that may mediate performance (see Belleville et al., 2006, for further discussion).

Working memory skills do not seem to be impaired in this population. However, the pattern of performance appears to depend on their general ability. For example, Russell et al. (1996) reported that low-functioning autistic adolescents performed more poorly than chronological age-matched participants, but did not differ from IQ-matched participants on measures of both verbal and visuo-spatial working memory. In contrast, Belleville, Rouleau, and Caza (1998) found that high-functioning autistic persons performed in a similar manner as age- and IQ-matched controls.

In a recent study, we examined memory skills in a cohort of high-functioning individuals with Asperger Syndrome, who did not have any disordered early language, cognitive, or self-help skills (DSM-IV, APA, 1994) and so represented those at the highest functioning end of the autistic spectrum (Rajendran & Alloway, 2009). As a group, the children with AS showed a pattern of performance of poor verbal short-term memory, alongside unaffected or spared performance in verbal working memory, visuo-spatial short-term and working memory. Inspection of individual profiles confirmed that 70% of the sample achieved standard scores less than 86 in verbal short-term memory, while only 30% scored less than 86 in verbal working memory and visuo-spatial short-term memory and 20% in visuo-spatial working memory.

One explanation for the poor performance on verbal short-term memory could be due to the computerized presentation of the material. In light of previous research indicating that autistic persons rely on phonarticulatory features (see Belleville et al., 2006 for a review), it is possible that they could not benefit from articulation to boost recall. Therefore, further research is needed to contrast the performance of individuals with AS in computerized assessments of working memory (e.g., the AWMA) against that of paper and pencil tests of working memory.

The AS children's poor verbal short-term memory skills may be linked to deficits in communication. Support for this view comes from Belleville et al. (2006) who suggest that lexical and semantic knowledge, which are also involved in the perception and production of language, contribute to successful verbal recall (see also Martin, Lesch, & Bartha, 1999). Evidence for this association in atypical populations is drawn from the close association between language impairments and poor verbal short-term memory skills in aphasic patients (Belleville, Caza, & Peretz, 2003).

In contrast, the relatively strong working memory performance in both verbal and visuo-spatial tasks could be due to the profile of the participants as they were high-functioning individuals with IQ in the normal range. Other studies have also found that verbal working memory skills are intact in high-functioning individuals with ASD (e.g., Williams, Goldstein, Carpenter, & Minshew, 2005). However, there are reports of a dissociation in performance between verbal and visuo-spatial working memory not evidenced in a recent study (Rajendran & Alloway, 2009). On the basis of eye movement studies, researchers have suggested that when there is no verbal scaffolding to support memory, autistic individuals struggle with greater processing demands, which affects accuracy of recall (Minshew et al., 1999; Williams et al., 2005). It is possible that in the present study, the high-functioning children used verbal recoding of spatial locations as a strategy to boost their visuo-spatial memory skills. An alternative explanation is that the task demands of the visuo-spatial memory tasks were not sufficiently taxing and so did not pose a problem for the ASD children. This is consistent with studies indicating that as task demands of working memory tasks increase, performance decreases (e.g., Minshew & Goldstein, 2001). Thus, tasks with modest demands result in performance comparable to typically developing populations (see Steele, Minshew, Luna, & Sweeney, 2007).

Discussion

The primary aim of this chapter was to understand the working memory profile of prevalent developmental disorders found in mainstream education. Although most of these groups have a diagnosis of a disorder not directly associated with learning difficulties, their difficulties nonetheless impact academic progress. Each of the developmental disorders considered in this review is associated with distinctive profiles of strengths and weaknesses across the range of aspects of working memory function. The areas of moderate and severe deficit in each case are summarized in Table 10.1.

Looking first at children with language impairments, consistent deficits in verbal short-term memory were found in this cohort. In most cases, this short-term memory deficit was accompanied by a sizeable impairment of verbal working memory. The deficits in visuo-spatial short-term and working

Table 10.1 Areas of memory deficit in different developmental disorders

Developmental disorder	Short-term memory		Working memory	
	Verbal	*Visuo-spatial*	*Verbal*	*Visuo-spatial*
Dyslexia		x	xx	x
Specific Language Impairment	x		x	
Developmental Coordination Disorder		x	x	x
ADHD		x	x	x
Autistic Spectrum Disorder	x			

Note: x = mean standard scores one standard deviation from the mean (<86); xx = mean standard scores two standard deviations from the mean (<71).

memory tasks could be attributed to poor verbal skills as children may have struggled with using phonological strategies to recode the information from the visuo-spatial domain to the verbal domain. In children with SLI, it is known that the working memory impairment is restricted only to verbal material, and does not extend to corresponding tasks employing visuo-spatial material. The dissociation of performance between verbal and visuo-spatial working memory tasks provides strong support for the suggestion that a combined storage and processing deficit in the verbal domain, rather than only poor verbal short-term memory skills, could result in language learning difficulties (see Archibald & Gathercole, 2007).

The memory profile of children with DCD reveals an interesting parallel with those with language impairments. The former is a disorder of movement and coordination, while the latter is a disorder of language. The specificity of the disorders on which the diagnosis is based in each case is reflected in the areas of disproportionate working memory weakness: SLI is associated with selective deficits in verbal short-term and working memory, and DCD with selective deficits in visuo-spatial short-term and working memory. In this respect, the two disorders mirror one another. It is commonly held that there is considerable heterogeneity amongst children with DCD (e.g., Hill, 2001; Visser, 2003). However, recent evidence suggests that despite substantial variability in language skills in DCD children, there was no drastic impact on performance on a variety of cognitive, memory, and attainment measures (Alloway & Archibald, 2008).

The profile of the ADHD group contrasts markedly with those with language disorders. Their impairments extend to visuo-spatial short-term memory, and both verbal and visuo-spatial working memory, with intact verbal short-term memory skills. It is possible that this profile of pervasive working memory deficits that extend across the verbal and visuo-spatial domains is a defining characteristic of children who have a core deficit in the central executive. This component of the working memory system is responsible for the control of attention and the coordination of activity across the system as a whole, and contributes to working memory tasks irrespective of the modality of the material to be remembered or mentally manipulated. In contrast, the specific impairments of working memory that are specific to a particular domain, such as in either SLI or DCD, are a secondary consequence of a core deficit that lies elsewhere, in the basic mental processing and manipulation of material of that particular kind.

Finally, in children with AS, poor performance was specific to verbal short-term memory tasks, with scores in the typical range for verbal working memory and visuo-spatial memory tasks. One possibility is that the verbal short-term memory deficits evidenced in the present study are the result of a computerized presentation of verbal stimuli as the ASD children were not able to benefit from phonarticulatory features available in spoken presentation. In contrast, the relatively strong performance in verbal working memory and visuo-spatial memory tasks suggests that these children do not struggle with the simultaneous task of processing and storing information. Other researchers who have found similarly good verbal working memory profiles in these populations propose that these skills do not drive impairments in associated executive function tasks such as planning and problem solving (e.g., Williams et al., 2005). This dissociation in performance supports the view that such deficits are intrinsic to skills underlying planning and problem solving tasks specifically, rather than a generalized executive function impairment. This proposal is distinct from that related to children with ADHD where working memory skills, particularly those related to attending to and updating information, are closely associated with performance on executive function tasks (e.g., Barnett et al., 2001; Martinussen & Tannock, 2006).

Testing working memory

In light of the extensive evidence that working memory is linked to learning outcomes through a student's academic career (see Cowan & Alloway, 2008), it is critical to support students who are struggling to learn by first identifying their working memory profile. The most effective and reliable way to do this is by using the Automated Working Memory Assessment (AWMA, Alloway, 2007a). The AWMA is a cognitive test that takes 10 minutes to administer and offers educators an informative first step in supporting a student's learning. To date, the AWMA has been translated into 15 languages to screen thousands of children throughout the world for working memory impairments. It provides the educator with a profile of a student's verbal and visuo-spatial working memory skills, as well as how this will impact their learning (see Alloway et al., 2009). For example, working memory difficulties lead to slower processing times and such students can benefit from both shorter activities in the classroom, as well as longer time for test taking. Given that 10% of children in a typical classroom have working memory difficulties, it is important that they are screened in order to determine who needs support and extra consideration during testing. Once we know the strength and weakness of a student's working memory, we can determine if they need cognitive training.

Supporting working memory

The use of the AWMA as a means of distinguishing between children with primary and secondary deficits of working memory on the basis of their working memory profiles may be valuable in assisting clinicians and educational psychologists in identifying what lies at the root of the problems faced by a particular child. For example, verbal short-term memory deficits could be compensated by areas of strength in visuo-spatial short-term memory through the use of memory aids such as note-taking. Conversely, weaknesses in visuo-spatial short-term memory can be boosted by relying on verbal strategies like rehearsal. Where working memory deficits are present, the child will struggle to hold in mind and manipulate relevant material in the course of ongoing mental activities. Support to prevent working memory overload and consequent task failure includes breaking down tasks into smaller components, simplifying the nature of the information to be remembered, and using long-term memory to assist recall (see Gathercole & Alloway, 2008, for further suggestions).

Training working memory

There is growing evidence that working memory can be trained (Jaeggi, Buschkuehl, Jonides, & Perrig, 2008). Findings from a recent study demonstrated that students who used a working memory training program (www. junglememory.com) improved, not only in their working memory skills, but in academic attainments as well (Alloway, 2009a). The control group did not perform much better without intervention, and in some instances they performed even worse (e.g., math, verbal and visual working memory). In contrast, the trial group who participated in the intervention demonstrated a clear gain not only in working memory tasks, but crucially in learning outcomes as well. For example, in spelling, their scores increased almost 10 standard scores points.

Are these increases in scores meaningful? Yes. One way to look at this gain is the difference between the grades of C and B, or between a B and an A. This is what students participating in the working memory training program experienced after just 12 weeks of training. Would they have made this improvement without training? No – there are two pieces of evidence to support this conclusion. The first is that the control group, who did not participate in the training program, showed no improvement and in fact performed worse in some cases (e.g., math and the working memory tests). The second piece of evidence demonstrating that students do not improve in either learning outcomes or memory scores without training comes from a study by the first author conducted on students with learning difficulties (Alloway, 2009b). A group of 8- to 10-year-olds who were all placed on the schools' SEN (special educational needs) registers for moderate learning difficulties were tested on a range of working memory, IQ, and learning (math, reading, and spelling) tests. These students were all receiving Individual Education Plans/Individual Education Programmes (IEPs) and continued to do so for a further two years. I retested them two years later on the same learning tests as at the first testing time. None of the students had improved. They started off at the bottom 10-percentile compared to their same-aged peers and remained there two years later despite receiving IEPs and special support in small groups. Both the data from the intervention study reported here and the longitudinal one I've described indicate that without cognitive training, a student with poor working memory will not "catch up" with their peers.

In summary, this chapter provides a summary of the strengths and weaknesses specific to memory function of different developmental disorders. We find distinct memory profiles associated with each disorder and reflect the nature of their deficit to some degree. The specificity of the diagnosis indicated by the AWMA identifies not only areas of deficit, but also areas of strength on which compensatory strategies can be effectively built. There is also exciting evidence emerging to demonstrate that the right type of training can improve not only working memory, but academic achievement as well.

Author note

This research was supported by a research grant awarded by the Economic and Social Research Council of Great Britain. We would like to thank Lee Swanson, Nelson Cowan, and Thusha Rajendran for helpful comments on an earlier draft of this chapter.

References

Adams, J. W., & Snowling, M. J. (2001). Executive function and reading impairments in children reported by their teachers as "hyperactive". *British Journal of Developmental Psychology*, *19*, 293–306.

Alloway, T. P. (2006). Working memory and children with developmental coordination disorders. In T. P. Alloway & S. E. Gathercole (Eds.), *Working memory and neurodevelopmental conditions* (pp. 161–186). London: Psychology Press.

Alloway, T. P. (2007a). *Automated Working Memory Assessment*. London: Psychological Corporation Europe.

Alloway, T. P. (2007b). Working memory, reading and mathematical skills in children with developmental coordination disorder. *Journal of Experimental Child Psychology*, *96*, 20–36.

Alloway, T. P. (2009a). Working memory: The new IQ. *Professional Association for Teachers of Students with Specific Learning Difficulties (PATOSS)*, *21*, 9–10.

Alloway, T. P. (2009b). Working memory, but not IQ, predicts subsequent learning in children with learning difficulties. *European Journal of Psychological Assessment, 25*, 92–98.

Alloway, T. P. & Archibald, L. M. (2008). A comparison of working memory and learning in children with developmental coordination disorder and specific language impairment. *Journal of Learning Disabilities, 41*, 251–262.

Alloway, T. P., Elliott, J., Holmes, J., & Place, M. (2010). Exploring the link between attention and working memory in clinical and community samples. *Child Neuropsychology*, *16*, 242–254.

Alloway, T. P., Gathercole, S. E., Adams, A. M., Willis, C., Eaglen, R., & Lamont, E. (2005a). Working memory and other cognitive skills as predictors of progress towards early learning goals at school entry. *British Journal of Developmental Psychology*, *23*, 417–426.

Alloway, T. P., Gathercole, S. E., & Pickering, S. J. (2006). Verbal and visuo-spatial short-term and working memory in children: Are they separable? *Child Development*, *77*, 1698–1716.

Alloway, T. P., Gathercole, S. E., Willis, C., & Adams, A. M. (2004). A structural analysis of working memory and related cognitive skills in early childhood. *Journal of Experimental Child Psychology*, *87*, 85–106.

Alloway, T. P., Gathercole, S. E., Willis, C., & Adams, A. M. (2005b). Working memory and special educational needs. *Educational and Child Psychology*, *22*, 56–67.

Alloway, T. P., & Temple, K. J. (2007). A comparison of working memory profiles and learning in children with developmental coordination disorder and moderate learning difficulties. *Applied Cognitive Psychology*, *21*, 473–487.

Alloway, T. P., & Warner, C. (2008). The effect of task-specific training on learning and memory in children with developmental coordination disorder. *Perceptual and Motor Skills*, *107*, 273–280.

American Psychiatric Association. (1994). *Diagnostic and statistical manual of mental disorders* (4th ed.). Washington, DC.

Angold, A., Costello, E. J., & Erkanli, A. (1999). Comorbidity. *Journal of Child Psychology and Psychiatry*, *40*, 57–88.

Archibald, L. M., & Alloway, T. P. (2008). Comparing language profiles: Children with specific language impairment and developmental coordination disorder. *International Journal of Communication and Language Disorders*, *43*, 165–180.

Archibald, L. M. D., & Gathercole, S. E. (2006a). Short-term and working memory in children with Specific Language Impairments. *International Journal of Language and Communication Disorders*, *41*, 675–693.

Archibald, L. M. D., & Gathercole, S. E. (2006b). Immediate visuospatial memory in Specific Language Impairment. *Journal of Speech, Language, and Hearing Research*, *49*, 265–277.

Archibald, L. M. D., & Gathercole, S. E. (2007). The complexities of complex span: Specifying working memory deficits in SLI. *Journal of Memory and Language*, *57*, 177–194.

Baddeley, A. D. (1996). Exploring the central executive. *Quarterly Journal of Experimental Psychology*, *49A*, 5–28.

Baddeley, A. D. (2000). The episodic buffer: A new component of working memory? *Trends in Cognitive Sciences*, *4*, 417–422.

Baddeley, A. D., Emslie, H., Kolodny, J., & Duncan, J. (1998). Random generation and the executive control of working memory. *Quarterly Journal of Experimental Psychology*, *51A*, 819–852.

Baddeley, A. D., & Hitch G. (1974). Working memory. In G. Bower (Ed.), *The psychology of learning and motivation* (pp. 47–90), *8*. New York: Academic Press.

Baddeley, A. D. & Hitch, G. J. (2000). Development of working memory: Should the Pascual-Leone and the Baddeley & Hitch models be merged? *Journal of Experimental Child Psychology*, *77*, 128–137.

Baddeley, A. D., & Logie, R. H. (1999). Working memory: The multiple-component model. In A. Miyake & P. Shah (Eds.), *Models of working memory: Mechanisms of active maintenance and executive control* (pp. 28–61). New York: Cambridge University Press.

Barkley, R. A. (1990). *Attention deficit hyperactivity disorder: A handbook for diagnosis and treatment*. New York: Guilford Press.

Barkley, R. A. (1997). *ADHD and the nature of self-control*. New York: Guilford.

Barkley, R. A., Edwards, G., Laneri, M., Fletcher, K., & Metevia, L. (2001). Executive functioning, temporal discounting, and sense of time in adolescents with Attention Deficit Hyperactivity Disorder and Oppositional Defiant Disorder (ODD). *Journal of Abnormal Child Psychology, 29*, 541–556.

Barkley, R. A., Grodzinsky, G., & DuPaul, G. J. (1992). Frontal lobe functions in attention deficit disorder with and without hyperactivity: A review and research report. *Journal of Abnormal Child Psychology, 20*, 163–188.

Barnett, A. L., & Henderson, S. E. (1992). Some observations on the figure drawings of clumsy children. *British Journal of Educational Psychology, 62*, 341–355.

Barnett, R., Maruff, P., Vance, A., Luk, E. S. L., Costin, J., Wood, C., & Pantelis, C. (2001). Abnormal executive function in attention deficit hyperactivity disorder: the effect of stimulant medication on age and spatial working memory. *Psychological Medicine, 31*, 1107–1115.

Barrouillet, P., Bernardin, S., & Camos, V. (2004). Time constraints and resource sharing in adults' working memory spans. *Journal of Experimental Psychology: General, 133*, 83–100.

Bavin, E. L., Wilson, P. H., Maruff, P., & Sleeman, F. (2005). Spatio-visual memory of children with specific language impairment: evidence for generalized processing problems. *International Journal of Language and Communication Disorders, 40*, 319–332.

Bayliss, D. M., Jarrold, C., Gunn, D. M., & Baddeley, A. D. (2003). The complexities of complex span: Explaining individual differences in working memory in children and adults. *Journal of Experimental Psychology: General, 132*, 71–92.

Belleville, S., Caza, N., & Peretz, I. (2003). A neuropsychological argument for a processing view of memory. *Journal of Memory and Language, 48*, 686–703.

Belleville, S., Ménard, E., Mottron, L., & Ménard, M-C. (2006). Working memory in autism. In T. P. Alloway & S. E. Gathercole (Eds.), *Working memory and neurodevelopmental conditions* (pp. 213–238). London: Psychology Press.

Belleville, S., Rouleau, N., & Caza, N. (1998). Effect of normal aging on the manipulation of information in working memory. *Memory and Cognition, 26*, 572–583.

Benezra, E., & Douglas, V. I. (1988). Short-term serial recall in ADDH, normal and reading-disabled boys. *Journal of Abnormal Child Psychology, 16*, 511–525.

Bennetto, L., Pennington, B. F., & Rogers, S. J. (1996). Intact and impaired memory functions in autism. *Child Development, 67*, 1816–1835.

Biederman, J. (2005). Attention-deficit/hyperactivity disorder: a selective overview. *Biological Psychiatry, 57*, 1215–1220.

Bishop, D. V. M., Adams, C. V., & Norbury, C. F. (2006). Distinct genetic influences on grammar and phonological short-term memory deficits: evidence from 6-year-old twins. *Genes, Brain and Behavior, 5*, 158–169.

Bishop, D. V. M., & Edmundson, A. (1987). Language-impaired 4-year-olds: Distinguishing transient from persistent impairment. *Journal of Speech and Hearing Disorders, 52*, 156–173.

Bishop, D. V. M., North, T., & Donlan, C. (1996). Nonword repetition as a behavioural marker for inherited language impairment: Evidence from a twin study. *Journal of Child Psychology and Psychiatry, 37,* 391–403.

Bonifacci, P. (2004). Children with low motor ability have lower visual-motor integration ability but unaffected perceptual skills. *Human Movement Science, 23,* 157–168.

Boucher, J. (1978). Echoic memory capacity in autistic children. *Journal of Child Psychology and Psychiatry, 19,* 161–166.

Bowey, J. A. (1996). On the association between phonological memory and receptive vocabulary in five-year-olds. *Journal of Experimental Child Psychology, 63,* 44–78.

Bull, R., & Scerif, G. (2001). Executive functioning as a predictor of children's mathematics ability. Shifting, inhibition and working memory. *Developmental NeuroPsychology, 19,* 273–293.

Cain, K., Oakhill, J., & Bryant, P. (2004). Children's reading comprehension ability: concurrent prediction by working memory, verbal ability and component skills. *Journal of Educational Psychology, 96,* 31–42.

Case, R., Kurland, D. M., & Goldberg, J. (1982). Operational efficiency and the growth of short-term memory span. *Journal of Experimental Child Psychology, 33,* 386–404.

Castellanos, F. X., & Tannock, R. (2002). Neuroscience of attention-deficit/hyperactivity disorder: the search for endophenotypes. *Nature Reviews/Neuroscience, 3,* 617–628.

Chhabildas, N., Pennington, B. F., & Willcutt, E.G. (2001). A comparison of the neuropsychological profiles of the DSM-IV subtypes of ADHD. *Journal of Abnormal Child Psychology, 29,* 529–540.

Cohen, N. J., Vallance, D. D., Barwick, M., Im, N., Menna, R., Horodezsky, N. B., & Isaacson, L. (2000). The interface between ADHD and language impairment: An examination of language, achievement, and cognitive processing. *Journal of Child Psychology and Psychiatry, 41,* 353–362.

Coleman, R., Piek, J. P., & Livesey, D. J. (2001). A longitudinal study of motor ability and kinaesthetic acuity in young children at risk of developmental coordination disorder. *Human Movement Science, 20,* 95–110.

Conti-Ramsden, G. (2003). Processing and linguistic markers in young children with specific language impairment. *Journal of Speech, Language, and Hearing Research, 46,* 1029–1037.

Conti-Ramsden, G., Botting, N., & Faragher, B. (2001) Psycholinguistic markers for Specific Language Impairment (SLI). *Journal of Child Psychology and Psychiatry, 42,* 741–748.

Conti-Ramsden, G., & Windfuhr, K. (2002). Productivity with word order and morphology: a comparative look at children with SLI and children with normal language abilities. *International Journal of Communication and Language Disorders, 37,* 17–30.

Cornoldi, C., Marzocchi, G. M., Belotti, M., Caroli, M. G., de Meo, T., & Braga, C. (2002). Working memory interference control deficit in children referred by teachers for ADHD symptoms. *Child NeuroPsychology, 7,* 230–240.

Cousins, M., & Smyth, M. M. (2003). Developmental coordination impairments in adulthood. *Human Movement Science, 22,* 433–459.

Cowan, N. (2001). The magical number 4 in short-term memory: A reconsideration of mental storage capacity. *Behavioral and Brain Sciences, 24,* 87–185.

Cowan, N., & Alloway, T. P. (2008). The development of working memory in childhood. In M. Courage & N. Cowan (Eds.), *Development of memory in infancy and childhood* (2nd ed., pp. 303–342). Hove, UK: Psychology Press.

Daneman, M., & Carpenter, P. A. (1980). Individual differences in working memory and reading. *Journal of Verbal Learning and Verbal Behaviour, 19*, 450–466.

de Jong, P. F. (1998). Working memory deficits of reading disabled children. *Journal of Experimental Child Psychology, 70*, 75–96.

Dewey, D., Kaplan, B. J., Crawford, S. G., & Wilson, B. N. (2002). Developmental coordination disorder: Associated problems in attention, learning, and psychosocial adjustment. *Human Movement Science, 21*, 905–918.

Dollaghan, C., & Campbell, T. F. (1998). Nonword repetition and child language impairment. *Journal of Speech, Language, and Hearing Research, 41*, 1136–1146.

Ellis Weismer, S., Evans, J., & Hesketh, L. (1999). An examination of working memory capacity in children with specific language impairment. *Journal of Speech, Language, and Hearing Research, 42*, 1249–1260.

Ellis Weismer, S., & Hesketh, L. (1993). The influence of prosodic and gestural cues on novel word acquisition by children with specific language impairment. *Journal of Speech and Hearing Research, 36*, 1013–1025.

Ellis Weismer, S., & Hesketh, L. (1996). Lexical learning by children with specific language impairment: Effects of linguistic input presented at varying speaking rates. *Journal of Speech and Hearing Resarch, 39*, 177–190.

Ellis Weismer, S., Tomblin, J. B., Zhang, X., Buckwalter, P., Gaura Chynoweth, J., & Jones, M. (2000). Nonword repetition performance in school-age children with and without language impairment. *Journal of Speech, Language, and Hearing Research, 43*, 865–878.

Engle, R. W., Kane, M. J., & Tuholski, S. W. (1999). Individual differences in working memory capacity and what they tell us about controlled attention, general fluid intelligence, and functions of the prefrontal cortex. In A. Miyake & P. Shah (Eds.), *Models of working memory: Mechanisms of active maintenance and executive control* (pp. 102–134). New York: Cambridge University Press.

Faraone, S. V., Biederman, J., Mennin, D., & Russell, R. L. (1998), Bipolar and antisocial disorders among relatives of ADHD children: parsing familial subtypes of illness. *Neuropsychiatry Genetics, 81*, 108–116.

Gathercole, S. E. (2006). Nonword repetition and word learning: The nature of the relationship. *Applied Psycholinguistics, 27*, 513–543.

Gathercole, S. E., & Alloway, T. P. (2008). *Working memory and learning: A practical guide*. London: Sage Publications.

Gathercole, S. E., Alloway, T. P., Willis, C., & Adams, A. M. (2006). Working memory in children with reading disabilities. *Journal of Experimental Child Psychology, 93*, 265–281.

Gathercole, S., & Baddeley, A., (1990). Phonological memory deficits in language disordered children: Is there a causal connection? *Journal of Memory and Language, 29*, 336–360.

Gathercole, S. E., & Baddeley, A. D. (1993). *Working memory and language processing*. Hove, UK: Erlbaum.

Gathercole, S. E., Hitch, G. J., Service, E., & Martin, A. J. (1997). Short-term memory and long-term learning in children. *Developmental Psychology, 33*, 966–979.

Gathercole, S. E., Pickering, S. J., Knight, C., & Stegmann, Z. (2004). Working memory skills and educational attainment: Evidence from National Curriculum assessments at 7 and 15 years of age. *Applied Cognitive Psychology, 18*, 1–16.

Gathercole, S. E., Tiffany, C., Briscoe, J., Thorn, A. S. C., & ALSPAC Team (2005). Developmental consequences of poor phonological short-term memory function in childhood: A longitudinal study. *Journal of Child Psychology and Psychiatry, 46*, 598–611.

Geary, D. C., Hoard, M. K., Byrd-Craven, J., & DeSoto, C. M. (2004). Strategy choices in simple and complex addition: Contributions of working memory and counting knowledge for children with mathematical disability. *Journal of Experimental Child Psychology, 88*, 121–151.

Gershon, J. (2002). A meta-analytic review of gender differences in ADHD. *Journal of Attentional Disorders, 5*, 143–154.

Gershon, E. S., & Goldin, L. R. (1986). Clinical methods in psychiatric genetics: robustness of genetic marker investigative strategies. *Acta Psychiatrica Scandinavica, 74*, 113–118.

Geurts, H. M., Verté, S., Oosterlaan, J., Roeyers, H., & Sergeant, J. A. (2005). ADHD subtypes: do they differ in their executive functioning profile? *Archives of Clinical NeuroPsychology, 20*, 457–477.

Goodman, R., Ford, T., & Meltzer, H. (2002). Mental health problems of children in the community: 18 month follow up. *BMJ.* 22, 1496–1497.

Graham, N. C. (1980). Memory constraints in language deficiency. In F. Margaret Jones (Ed.), *Language disability in children* (p. 69–94). Baltimore: University Park Press.

Hellgren, L., Gillberg, C., Gillberg, I. C., & Enerskog, I., (1993). Children with deficits in attention, motor control and perception (DAMP) almost grown up: General health at 16 years. *Developmental Medicine and Child Neurology, 35*, 881–893.

Hick, R., Botting, N., & Conti-Ramsden, G. (2005) Short-term memory and vocabulary development in children with Down syndrome and children with specific language impairment. *Developmental Medicine and Child Neurology, 47*, 532–538.

Hill, E. L. (2001). Non-specific nature of specific language impairment: a review of the literature with regard to concomitant motor impairments. *International Journal of Language and Communication Disorders, 36*, 149–171.

Hoffman, L. M., & Gillam, R. B. (2004). Verbal and spatial information processing constraints in children with specific language impairment. *Journal of Speech, Language, and Hearing Research, 47*, 114–125.

Holmes, J., Alloway, T. P., Gathercole, S. E., & Elliott, J. (2009). Working memory and executive function profiles of children with poor working memory and children with ADHD. Manuscript submitted for publication.

Holmes, J., Gathercole, S. E., Place, M., Alloway, T. P., Elliott, J., & Hilton, K.A. (2010). An assessment of the diagnostic utility of executive function assessments in the identification of ADHD in children. *Child & Adolescent Mental Health, 15*, 37–43.

Im-Bolter, N., Johnson, J., & Pascual-Leone, J. (2006) Processing limitations in children with specific language impairment: The role of executive function. *Child Development, 77*, 1822–1841.

Jaeggi, S., Buschkuehl, M., Jonides, J., & Perrig, W. (2008). Improving fluid intelligence with training on working memory. *Proceedings of the National Academy of Sciences, 105*, 6829–6833.

Jonides, J., Lacey, S. C., & Nee, D. E. (2005). Processes of working memory in mind and brain. *Current Directions in Psychological Science, 14*, 2–5.

Just, M. A., & Carpenter, P. A. (1992). A capacity theory of comprehension: Individual differences in working memory. *Psychological Review, 99*, 122–149.

Karatekin, C., & Asarnow, R. F. (1998). Working memory in childhood-onset schizophrenia and attention deficit/hyperactivity disorder (ADHD). *Psychiatry Research*, *80*, 165–176.

Kerns, K. A., McInerney, R. J., & Wilde, N. J. (2001). Time reproduction, working memory, and behavioural inhibition in children with ADHD. *Child NeuroPsychology*, *7*, 21–31.

Leonard, L. B. (1998). *Children with Specific Language Impairment*. Cambridge, MA: The MIT Press.

Leonard, L. B., Deevy, P., Miller, C., Charest, M., Kurtz, R., & Rauf, L. (2003). The use of grammatical morphemes reflecting aspect and modality by children with specific language impairment. *Journal of Child Language*, *30*, 769–795.

Lord, R., & Hulme, C. (1988). Visual perception and drawing ability in clumsy and normal children. *British Journal of Developmental Psychology*, *6*, 1–9.

Luna, B., Minshew, N. J., Garver, K. E., Lazar, N. A., Thulborn, K. R., Eddy, W. F., & Sweeney, J. A. (2002). Neocortical system abnormalities in autism: an fMRI study of spatial working memory. *Neurology*, *59*, 834–840.

Mandich, A., & Polatajko, H. J. (2003). Developmental coordination disorder: mechanisms, measurement and management. *Human Movement Science*, *22*, 407–411.

Marchman, V., Wulfeck, B., & Ellis Weismer, S. (1999). Productivity of past tense in children with normal language and specific language impairment. *Journal of Speech, Language, and Hearing Research*, *42*, 206–219.

Mariani, M. A., & Barkley, R. A. (1997). Neuropsychological and academic functioning in preschool boys with attention deficit hyperactivity disorder. *Developmental NeuroPsychology*, *13*, 111–129.

Martin, R. C., Lesch, M. F., & Bartha, M. C. (1999). Independence of input and output phonology in word processing and short-term memory. *Journal of Memory and Language*, *41*, 3–29.

Martinussen, R., Hayden, J., Hogg-Johnson, S., & Tannock, R. (2005). A meta-analysis of working memory impairments in children attention-deficit/hyperactivity disorder. *Journal of the American Academy of Child and Adolescent Psychiatry*, *44*, 377–384.

Martinussen, R., & Tannock, R. (2006). Working memory impairments in children with attention-deficit hyperactivity disorder with and without comorbid language learning disorders. *Journal of Clinical and Experimental NeuroPsychology*, *28*, 1073–1094.

Marton, K., & Schwartz, R. G. (2003). Working memory capacity limitations and language processes in children with specific language impairment. *Journal of Speech, Language, and Hearing Research*, *46*, 1138–1153.

Mayringer, H., & Wimmer, H. (2000). Pseudoname learning by German-speaking children with dyslexia: Evidence for a phonological learning deficit. *Journal of Experimental Child Psychology*, *75*, 116–133.

McArdle, P., O'Brien, G., & Kolvin, I. (1995). Hyperactivity: Prevalence and relationship with conduct disorder. *Journal of Child Psychology and Psychiatry*, *36*, 279–303.

McInnes, A., Humphries, T., Hogg-Johnson, S., & Tannock, R. (2003). Listening comprehension and working memory are impaired in attention-deficit/hyperactivity disorder irrespective of language impairment. *Journal of Abnormal Child Psychology*, *17*, 37–53.

Mehta, M. A., Goodyear, I. M., & Sahakian, B. J. (2004). Methylphenidate improves working memory function and set-shifting AD/HD: relationships to baseline memory capacity. *Journal of Child Psychology and Psychiatry*, *45*, 293–305.

Ménard, E., Mottron, L., Belleville, S., & Limoges, E. (2001). Executive and phono-articulatory processes of working memory in persons with autism. International Meeting for Autism Research, San Diego, CA.

Miller, C. A., Kail, R., Leonard, L. B., & Tomblin, J. B. (2001). Speed of processing in children with Specific Language Impairment. *Journal of Speech, Language, and Hearing Research, 44*, 416–433.

Minshew, N. J., & Goldstein, G. (2001). The pattern of intact and impaired memory functions in autism. *Journal of Child Psychology and Psychiatry and Allied Disciplines, 42*, 1095–1101.

Minshew, N. J., Luna, B., & Sweeney, J. A. (1999). Oculomotor evidence for neocortical systems but not cerebellar dysfunction in autism. *Neurology, 52*, 917–922.

Miyahara, M., & Register. G. (2000). Perceptions of three terms to describe physical awkwardness in children. *Research in Developmental Disabilities, 21*, 367–376.

Miyake, A. Friedman, N. P., Rettinger, D. A., Shah, P., & Hegarty, M. (2001). How are visual-spatial working memory, executive functioning, and spatial abilities related? A latent-variable analysis. *Journal of Experimental Psychology: General, 130*, 621–640.

Montgomery, J. (2000). Verbal working memory in sentence comprehension in children with specific language impairment. *Journal of Speech, Language, and Hearing Research, 43*, 293–308.

Morra, S., & Camba, R. (2009). Vocabulary learning in primary school children: working memory and long-term memory components. *Journal of Experimental Child Psychology, 104*, 156–178.

Mottron, L., Morasse, K., & Belleville, S. (2001). A study of memory functioning in individuals with autism. *Journal of Child Psychology and Psychiatry, 42*, 253–260.

Murphy, K. R., Barkley, R. A., & Bush, T. (2001).Young adults with attention deficit hyperactivity disorder: Subtype differences in comorbidity, educational, and clinical history. *The Journal of Nervous and Mental Disease, 190*, 147–157.

Nation, K., Adams, J. W., Bowyer-Crane, C. A., & Snowling, M. J. (1999). Working memory deficits in poor comprehenders reflect underlying language impairments. *Journal of Experimental Child Psychology, 73*, 139–158.

Ozonoff, S., & Strayer, D. L. (2001). Further evidence of intact working memory in autism. *Journal of Autism and Developmental Disorders, 31*, 257–263.

Peters, J. M., Barnett, A. L., & Henderson, S. E. (2001) Clumsiness, dyspraxia and developmental co-ordination disorder: how do health and educational professionals in the UK define the terms? *Child: Care, Health and Development, 27*, 399–412.

Pickering, S. J., & Gathercole, S. E. (2004). Distinctive working memory profiles in children with special educational needs. *Educational Psychology, 24*, 393–408.

Pickering, S. J., Gathercole, S. E., Hall, M., & Lloyd, S. A. (2001). Development of memory for pattern and path: Further evidence for the fractionation of visuo-spatial memory. *Quarterly Journal of Experimental Psychology, 54A*, 397–420.

Piek, J. P., & Coleman-Carman, R. (1995). Kinaesthetic sensitivity and motor performance of children with developmental coordination disorder. *Developmental Medicine and Child Neurology, 37*, 976–984.

Piek, J. P., & Dyck, M. J. (2004). Sensory-motor deficits in children with developmental coordination disorder, attention deficit hyperactivity disorder and autistic disorder. *Human Movement Science, 23*, 475–488.

Polanczyk, G., de Lima, M. S., Horta, B. L., Biederman, J., & Rohde, L. A. (2007). The worldwide prevalence of ADHD: a systematic review and meta-regression analysis. *American Journal of Psychiatry, 164*, 942–948.

Portwood, M. (1996). *Developmental dyspraxia: a practical manual for parents and professionals.* Durham, UK: Durham County Council.

Quinn, J. G. (1994). Towards a clarification of spatial processing. *Quarterly Journal of Experimental Psychology, 47A,* 465–480.

Rajendran, G., & Alloway, T. P. (2009). Working memory and cognitive skills in children with autism. Manuscript submitted for publication.

Rasmussen, P., & Gillberg, C. (2001). Natural outcome of ADHD with developmental coordination disorder at age 22 years: A controlled, longitudinal, community-based study. *Journal of the American Academy of Child and Adolescent Psychiatry, 39,* 1424–1431.

Redmond, S. M. (2003). Children's productions of the affixed in past tense and past participle contexts. *Journal of Speech, Language, and Hearing Research, 46,* 1095–1109.

Revie, G., & Larkin, D. (1993) Task specific intervention with children reduces movement problems. *Adapted Physical Activity Quarterly, 10,* 29–41.

Reynolds, D., Nicolson, R. I., & Hambly, H. (2003) Evaluation of an exercise-based treatment for children with reading difficulties. *Dyslexia, 9,* 48–71.

Rice, M. (2003). A unified model of specific and general language delay: Grammatical tense as a clinical marker of unexpected variation. In Y. Levy & J. Schaeffer (Eds.), *Language competence across populations: Towards a definition of specific language impairment* (pp. 63–94). Mahwah, NJ: Lawrence Erlbaum.

Rice, M., & Wexler, K. (1996). Toward tense as a clinical marker of specific language impairment in English-speaking children. *Journal of Speech and Hearing Research, 39,* 1239–1257.

Richardson, A. J., & Montgomery, P. (2005) The Oxford-Durham study: A randomized controlled trial of dietary supplementation with fatty acids in children with developmental coordination disorder. *Pediatrics, 115,* 1360–1366.

Roodenrys, S. (2006). Working memory function in attention deficit hyperactivity disorder. In T. P. Alloway & S. E. Gathercole (Eds.), *Working memory and neurodevelopmental disorders* (pp. 187–212). Hove and New York: Psychology Press.

Roodenrys, S., Koloski, N., & Grainger, J. (2001). Working memory function in attention deficit hyperactivity disordered and reading disabled children. *British Journal of Developmental Psychology, 19,* 325–337.

Rucklidge, J. R., & Tannock, R. (2002). Neuropsychological profiles of adolescents with ADHD: effects of reading and gender. *Journal of Child Psychology and Psychiatry, 43,* 988–1003.

Russell, J., Jarrold, C., & Henry, L. (1996). Working memory in children with autism and with moderate learning difficulties. *Journal of Child Psychology and Psychiatry, 37,* 673–686.

Schoemaker, M. M., Smits-Engelsman, B. C., & Jongmans, M. J. (2003). Psychometric properties of the movement assessment battery for children-checklist as a screening instrument for children with a developmental co-ordination disorder. *British Journal of Educational Psychology, 73,* 425–441.

Seigneuric, A., Ehrlich, M.-F., Oakhill, J. V., & Yuill, N. M. (2000). Working memory resources and children's reading comprehension. *Reading and Writing, 13,* 81–103.

Shue, K. L., & Douglas, V. I. (1992). ADHD and the frontal lobe syndrome. *Brain and Cognition, 20,* 104–124.

Siegel, L. S. (1988). Evidence that IQ scores are irrelevant to the definition and analysis of reading-disability. *Canadian Journal of Psychology, 42,* 201–215.

Siegel, L. S., & Ryan, E. B. (1989). The development of working memory in normally achieving and subtypes of learning disabled children. *Child Development*, 60, 973–980.

Smyth, M. M., Pearson, N. A., & Pendleton, L. R. (1988). Movement and working memory: Patterns and positions in space. *Quarterly Journal of Experimental Psychology*, *40A*, 497–514.

Snowling, M. J., Bishop, D. V. M., & Stothard, S. E. (2000). Is pre-school language impairment a risk factor for dyslexia in adolescence? *Journal of Child Psychology and Psychiatry*, *41*, 587–600.

Snyder, S. M., Hall, J. R., Cornwell, S. L., & Quintana, H. (2006). Review of clinical validation of ADHD behavior rating scales. *Psychological Reports*, *99*, 363–378.

Sonuga-Barke, E. J. S. (2005). Causal models of attention-deficit/hyperactivity disorder: From common simple deficits to multiple developmental pathways. *Biological Psychiatry*, *57*, 1231–1238.

Sonuga-Barke, E. J. S., Dalen, L., Daley, D., & Remington, B. (2002). Are planning, working memory, and inhibition associated with individual differences in preschool ADHD symptoms? *Developmental NeuroPsychology*, *21*, 255–272.

Steele, S., Minshew, N., Luna, B., & Sweeney, J. (2007). Spatial working memory deficits in autism. *Journal of Autism and Developmental Disorders*, 37, 605–612.

Stevens, J., Quittner, A. L., Zuckerman, J. B., & Moore, S. (2002). Behavioral inhibition, self-regulation of motivation, and working memory in children with attention deficit hyperactivity disorder. *Developmental NeuroPsychology*, *21*, 117–139.

Stothard, S. E., Snowling, M. J., Bishop, D. V. M., Chipchase, B. B., & Kaplan, C. A. (1998). Language-impaired preschoolers: A follow-up into adolescence. *Journal of Speech, Language, and Hearing Research*, *4*, 407–418.

Sugden, D. A. & Wright, H. C. (1998). *Motor coordination disorders in children*. London: Sage Press.

Swanson, H. L. (1994). Short-term memory and working memory: Do both contribute to our understanding of academic achievement in children and adults with learning disabilities? *Journal of Learning Disabilities*, *27*, 34–50.

Swanson, H. L., Ashbaker, M. H., & Lee, C. (1996). Learning-disabled readers' working memory as a function of processing demands. *Journal of Experimental Child Psychology*, *61*, 242–275.

Swanson, H. L., & Saez, L. (2003). Memory difficulties in children and adults with learning disabilities. In H. L. Swanson, S. Graham, & K. R. Harris (Eds.), *Handbook of learning disabilities*. New York: Guilford Press.

Szatmari, P., Offord, D. R., & Boyle, M. H. (1989). Ontario Child Health Study: prevalence of attention deficit disorder with hyperactivity. *Journal of Child Psychology and Psychiatry*, *30*, 219–230.

Tomblin, J. B., Records, N. L., Buckwalter, P., Zhang, X., Smith, E. & O'Brien, M. (1997) Prevalence of specific language impairment in kindergarten children. *Journal of Speech, Language, and Hearing Research*, 40, 1245–1260.

Tomblin, J. B., Zhang, X. Y., Buckwalter, P., & O'Brien, M. (2003). The stability of language disorder: Four years after kindergarten diagnosis. *Journal of Speech, Language, and Hearing Research*, *46*, 1283–1296.

Tripp, G., Ryan, J., & Peace, K. (2002). Neuropsychological functioning in children with DSM-IV combined type Attention Deficit Hyperactivity Disorder. *Australian and New Zealand Journal of Psychiatry*, *36*, 771–779.

Vallar, G., & Papagno, C. (2003). Neuropsychological impairments of short-term memory. In A. D. Baddeley, M. D. Kopelman, & B. A. Wilson (Eds.), *Handbook of memory disorders* (pp. 249–70). Chichester, UK: John Wiley & Sons.

Van Mourik, R., Oosterlaan, J., & Sergeant, J. A. (2005). The Stroop revisited: A meta-analysis of interference control in AD/HD. *Journal of Child Psychology and Psychiatry and Allied Disciplines*, *46*, 150–165.

Visser, J. (2003). Developmental coordination disorder: a review of research on subtypes and comorbidities. *Human Movement Science*, *22*, 479–493.

Wechsler, D. (1992). *Wechsler Intelligence Scale for Children – Third Edition UK*. London: The Psychological Corporation.

Willcutt, E. G., Pennington, B. F., Chhabildas, N. A., Olson, R. K., & Hulslander, J. L. (2005). Neuropsychological analyses of comorbidity between RD and ADHD: In search of the common deficit. *Developmental NeuroPsychology*, *27*, 35–78.

Williams, D., Goldstein, G., Carpenter, P., & Minshew, N. (2005). Verbal and spatial working memory in autism. *Journal of Autism and Developmental Disorders*, *35*, 747–756.

Wilson, P. H. (2005). Approaches to assessment and treatment of children with DCD: an evaluative review. *Journal of Child Psychology and Psychiatry*, *46*, 806–823.

Wilson, P. H., Maruff, P., & Lum, J. (2003). Procedural learning in children with developmental coordination disorder. *Human Movement Science*, *22*, 515–526.

Wilson, P. H., & McKenzie, B. E. (1998). Information processing deficits associated with developmental coordination disorder: A meta-analysis of research findings. *Journal of Child Psychology and Psychiatry*, *39*, 829–840.

Wright, H. C., & Sugden, D. A. (1996). The nature of developmental coordination disorder: Inter- and intragroup differences. *Adapted Physical Activity Quarterly*, *13*, 357–371.

Advances and issues
Some thoughts about controversial questions

Pierre Barrouillet and Vinciane Gaillard

The aim of this book was to offer an opportunity for both neo-Piagetian and working memory theorists to present and try to integrate their respective conceptions. We think that this book is indeed a promising step towards a fruitful dialog between both traditions. The different chapters provide us with an up-to-date account of neo-Piagetian theories of cognitive development, the role that working memory plays in this development, and how working memory itself develops. Though these contributions present original and unique conceptions issuing from various theoretical and methodological traditions, some points of agreement emerge about important questions concerning development. Interestingly, the variety of approaches endorsed by the different authors lead them to give a variety of answers to these main questions, making clear that these issues remain at the same time contentious. The present concluding chapter aims at discussing some of these issues by stressing both the points on which there is a large agreement and those that remain controversial. We will discuss in turn (a) the question of the units of cognition, their nature and the number of these units that children's thinking can grasp and manipulate at each developmental level, (b) the way cognitive capacities can be measured, (c) the factors underpinning both working memory and cognitive development, and (d) how atypical and typical development can be related and why neo-Piagetian theories could shed light on the questions raised by atypical development and remediation.

The units of cognition

Discovering the nature of the units of cognition has been a long-lasting quest for scientific psychology and a source of intense debate. As physicists have searched for centuries for the constitutive units of matter, psychologists have wondered for many times what are the units of thought and the elementary steps of cognition. Piaget has given one of the most influential answers to this question, suggesting that, from the very beginning of development, thinking involves schemes varying in nature (either perceptive, sensorimotor, symbolic, conceptual, or operational) and complexity, these schemes being differentiated and coordinated in structures of increasing complexity and efficiency. Pascual-Leone and

Johnson adopt this hypothesis, assuming that cognitive development results from the capacity to activate and coordinate schemes. Their maximum number would increase with age, culminating to 7 at the end of adolescence. Interestingly, other authors suggest their own conception of cognitive units. However, both the nature and the number of these units vary from one account to the other. Andrews and Halford assume that these units are dimensions that can be independently represented and coordinated within mental models, which are representations constructed to understand situations and solve problems. The maximum number of independent dimensions that can be represented would be 4. This same number of 4 is also proposed by Cowan et al. who consider the units of thought as chunks of information. Surprisingly, if the number of these chunks increases with age, their size does not seem to evolve with development.

How could the discrepancy between the magical numbers 7 and 4 be reduced? One of the possibilities would be to consider that the different authors do not consider the same aspects of mental functions. Pascual-Leone and Johnson seem to adopt a comprehensive view in evaluating the number of schemes involved in solving a given task, and consider both representational and procedural skills. This conception consists in taking into account both the figurative and the operative aspects of the cognitive functions as distinguished by Piaget. By contrast, both Andrews and Halford's and Cowan's accounts seem to concentrate on the figurative aspects. Their units are essentially units of representation that can be maintained active within a single focus of attention, but they do not consider the procedures that can be applied to these representations. This latter conception is closer to a widespread approach in cognitive psychology, which distinguishes between declarative and procedural knowledge. This theoretical framework assumes that the content of working memory consists only in declarative units, and that procedures act on these representations but cannot be represented. Thus, the units evoked by Andrews and Halford as well as by Cowan et al. seem to correspond to units of representation in working memory, whereas Pascual-Leone and Johnson adopt a more inclusive approach that goes beyond the limits of a working memory understood as the currently activated representations. It is interesting to note that a new conception of working memory has been recently put forward that encompasses both figurative and operative aspects by assuming the existence of a declarative and a procedural working memory (Oberauer, 2009). Thus, disagreements about the nature and number of mental units that can be activated at the same time could result from differences in the scope of processes that are taken into account, either restricted to the representational aspects of mental functioning, or extended to the procedural aspects.

It is worth noting that these questions concerning the units of thought and their maximum number do not have the same importance for all the authors. For example, Demetriou and Mouyi evoke the existence of units of information and executive operations that are integrated in more complex units with age, but they do not mention any fixed limitation of their number at each developmental level. This is probably due to the fact that Demetriou and

Mouyi consider that there are specialized domains of thought involving specific types of representations and processes that reflect the peculiarities of the elements and relations characterizing specific aspects of the environment. Within such a framework, it is quite difficult to imagine a quantification of the limitations of the cognitive system in terms of number of units, even if Demetriou and Mouyi assume that there is also a level of the cognitive architecture named Processing Potentials comprising general-purpose mechanisms such as processing speed, executive functions and representational capacity.

The nature of what has to be counted as units is an issue raised by Cowan et al. They note that one can concentrate on the number of items (whatever their nature, either chunks or schemes), or on the complexity of associations and relations between these items, as Andrews and Halford suggest doing. Despite a seeming commonality in these attempts to evaluate the number of "units" of thought that can be activated at once, it is fairly possible that these different accounts address different aspects of the cognitive functions, from the size of the focus of attention before any consolidation of information in working memory for Cowan, to the number of items and procedures that can be actively maintained and activated in working memory for Pascual-Leone and Johnson, whereas Andrews and Halford's proposal could be understood as an attempt to assess the complexity of the representation that results from the activation and coordination of the items represented in working memory. Thus, the different proposals gathered here could represent different approaches of different levels of the process of thought rather than real divergences in the way the limitations of our cognitive system and its development might be understood. Interestingly, it appears that the different estimations of the capacities available to activate these "units" of thought are given by different tasks that provide us with different measures of cognitive capacities.

Problems of measures

The discrepancies in conceptualizing the units of cognition are also reflected in the way their maximum number is measured. Pascual-Leone and Johnson present several tasks intended to measure M-capacity. In the Figural Intersection Task, children have to identify the common intersection of an increasing number of overlapping figures, whereas, in the Color Matching Tasks, children have to compare sets of colors successively presented in patterned figures. While the first task is akin to measures of attentional capacity, the second task involves a mnemonic component and is akin to the visual-array comparison studied by Cowan et al. (2005). The visual-array comparison is one of the tasks used by Cowan (2005) to establish that the size of the focus of attention is 4. The difference between this task and the Color Matching Tasks studied by Pascual-Leone and Johnson seems to reside in the time allowed for encoding. The arrays of colors used in the visual-array comparison task are usually presented briefly to avoid verbal encoding (Luck & Vogel, 1997), which is not the case for the Color Matching Tasks used by Pascual-Leone and Johnson, something that can explain the difference observed in the size of the arrays that can be successfully compared in the two tasks. For example, Cowan et al. in the present volume use a task comparable to the visual-array comparison task in which children are presented with an array of colored shapes and then with a single probe. They have to evaluate if this probe was previously presented in the same location, in another location or if it was not part of the array studied. Once more, the array under study was "briefly flashed," avoiding any strategy of memorization.

Pascual-Leone and Johnson also use verbal tasks such as the Mental Attention memory task, in which children are presented with arrays of consonants that they have to recall aloud and to dial using an old-fashioned rotary telephone. The authors assume that the need to search for the location of each consonant on the dial produces interference with recall. This searching task plays the same role as the processing component in working memory span tasks, in which processing is assumed to hinder strategies of active maintenance of information and to disrupt recall. The same phenomenon probably occurs in the Direction Following Task. In this task, children are given a list of directions of increasing complexity (e.g., "place a small blue square on a yellow space"). We can suppose that the attentional demands needed to follow a part of this direction (e.g., choosing the appropriate object) interfere with maintaining the location where this object has to be placed.

Finally, cognitive capacities in children are also assessed using simple memory tasks, such as Cowan et al. who present children with lists of sentences of various length, evaluating the number of clauses that can be "accessed" in a recall task. In this case, there is no concurrant task interfering with the memory task.

There is no doubt that each of these tasks assesses something that can be considered as a basic capacity, and the fact that Arsalidou (2008) has observed that the Color Matching Task and the Figural Intersection Task give the same M-scores at all the ages studied from 8 to 18 is very impressive. However, it is not really surprising that such a variety in the material used, in the processes involved, in the time allowed to study the material when memory is needed, and in the nature of the responses expected lead to divergent results and discrepant estimates of cognitive capacities. So, is this variety of tasks damageable for our understanding of cognitive and working memory development? Certainly not. Each of these tasks provides us with useful insights on the way cognitive capacities or resources, whatever their nature, increase with age, and on the factors underpinning these developmental changes. Not surprisingly, several hypotheses about the factors underpinning working memory development have been developed throughout the book. However, beyond this variety, some consensus emerges, leaving of course many issues unsolved.

Working memory development

The central theme of this book concerned the relationships between working memory and cognitive development as it is conceptualized by neo-Piagetian theorists. Within this tradition, Robbie Case had an influential role in suggesting that working memory capacity, and accordingly cognitive development, strongly relies on an increase in processing efficiency. This in turn allows the coordination of an increasing number of goals and sub-goals that permits more complex and efficient behavior with age. Case explained this relationship by assuming that, through maturation and exercise, the part of the total processing space devoted to operations decreases when processes become more efficient and less demanding, leaving more and more space available for storage purpose. A variant of this hypothesis is still defended by Camos and Barrouillet in their Time-Based Resource-Sharing (TBRS) model. According to this theory, the amount of information that can be held in working memory is a function of the cognitive load induced by the concurrent processing, this cognitive load being understood as the proportion of time during which processing occupies attention, thus impeding the refreshing of decaying working memory traces. The age-related increase in processing efficiency would reduce the time during which a given activity occupies attention and thus the cognitive load it induces. Accordingly, Camos and Barrouillet observe that when processing times are equated across ages, developmental differences in working memory capacity are strongly reduced.

Even though the TBRS hypothesis and Cases's account are akin, they differ in an important way. While Case assumes that processing consumes some space or cognitive resource that would continuously be shared with storage, the TBRS model does not retain this idea. Indeed, the effect of processing efficiency is mediated by a temporal factor (i.e., the duration of the occupation of attention), the TBRS model providing the link between processing speed and working memory capacity. Several other authors in this book suggest that processing speed is a causal determinant of processing efficiency. Based on correlational studies, Demetriou and Mouyi suggest that age-related changes in processing speed allow for more complex levels of cognition. De Ribaupierre, Fagot, and Lecerf also observe that processing speed accounts for unique variance in working memory and cognitive development, following a long-lasting tradition in psychology that has considered processing speed as a causal factor of development (Kail, 1991; Salthouse, 1996). However, Camos and Barrouillet suggest that the increase in processing speed results itself from an increase in attentional capacities.

Despite their importance and the number of studies documenting their effects, other factors than processing speed and efficiency are also put forward to account for working memory development. Because working memory has a dual role of processing and storage, the most natural idea is to suppose that both functions develop. Thus, though Case considered the increase in storage capacity as a mere by-product of the increase in processing efficiency, Cowan et al. question the role of an increase in basic storage capacity independent from processing efficiency. Both in the visuo-spatial and the verbal domain, they observe a development of storage capacity that is not the mere result of an increase in processing efficiency, something echoing the increase in

M-capacity hypothesized by Pascual-Leone and Johnson, though we have seen that there are divergences on the number of items that could be maintained. Concerning Cowan's conception, this development in storage capacity could result from an age-related increase in the size of the focus of attention (Cowan, 2005) associated with a decrease in the rate of passive loss of information from short-term storage (Cowan, Nugent, Elliot, & Saults, 2000).

Camos and Barrouillet also assume a development in storage capacity, but in a different way. They suggest that not only the time available for refreshing working memory traces, but also the efficiency of the mechanisms devoted to reactivate these traces plays an important role in working memory performance. Indeed, even when both the processing time and the time available for refreshing are equated across ages, there are still developmental differences, indicating that older children take a greater advantage of the time during which they can concentrate on storage and maintenance activities. This factor differs from the development of a basic storage capacity, and it is probable that both factors contribute to a greater storage capacity in older children, independent from processing efficiency. Of course, whether the efficiency of these refreshing processes develops independently from a general processing efficiency or not remains an open question. Though the results reported by Camos and Barrouillet in their chapter suggest that the two factors can be distinguished, further studies are needed to decipher this point: it remains possible that the processes specialized in reactivating memory traces do not develop independently from other processes, and that the efficiency of all these processes, whatever their nature, is under the dependence of a general processing speed factor.

The previous chapters raise also two important problems concerning working memory development. The first concerns the role of strategies. Studying young children, Camos and Barrouillet observe that, contrary to what is observed in older children and adults, working memory performance in children before 7 is not affected by variations in cognitive load, suggesting that these children do not use any strategy to refresh memory traces during processing. Working memory development would thus exhibit a qualitative change around the age of 7. This point is thoughtfully discussed by Jarrold and Tam who review several studies suggesting that the same qualitative change seems to occur in the use of the specific strategy of rehearsal for the maintenance of verbal information. However, a close scrutiny of this hypothesis and the use of large samples of participants suggest that while studies contrasting small groups often lead to this kind of conclusion, more fine-grained approaches suggest that the seemingly qualitative change could be quantitative in nature, and that children younger than 7 actually use rehearsal, albeit less efficiently than older children.

The second point concerns the role of inhibition. It has often been suggested that one of the main functions of working memory is to selectively focus on information relevant for the task in hand and to set aside irrelevant information by inhibiting those items activated through interference.

Accordingly, it has been proposed that a large part of working memory development would result from an increase in inhibitory capacities. This role of inhibition is here documented by de Ribaupierre et al. who observe that inhibitory capacities measured through Stroop tasks account for unique variance in working memory performance, especially in older adults. However, Cowan, using a particularly clever experimental procedure, does not observe any age-related change in the capacity to filter-out the less relevant items, whereas there is a clear development in the number of items that can be maintained. This suggests that development affects primarily the capacities to activate and maintain relevant information, rather than to inhibit irrelevant information.

Further studies are clearly needed to shed light on the developmental role of mnemonic strategies and inhibition. Nonetheless, the different contributions in this book delineate a complex picture of working memory development in which a plurality of factors intervene. Of course, as Case suggested, processing efficiency strongly determines the amount of information that can concurrently be held in working memory. This factor could mediate the role of processing speed that has been largely documented. However, there is no doubt that a basic capacity of storage must also be taken into account, as well as the efficiency of processes devoted to the active maintenance of information in face of decay and interference. The dual function of working memory, which coordinates processing and storage activities, is the reason why an increasing capacity to control and switch attention from one function to the other could also have a strong impact on working memory development, as Camos and Barrouillet suggest, even if the qualitative or quantitative nature of this change remains an open question (see Jarrold and Tam's contribution). Thus, what the different chapters of this book have made clear is that it is probably unfruitful to search for *the* unique factor accounting for working memory and cognitive development.

Typical and atypical development

It is well known that Piaget's interest in epistemic matters and universal developmental processes of a subject described as epistemic (as opposed to the psychological subject) led him to put little effort into the study of atypical development. Probably following the Piagetian tradition, neo-Piagetian theorists have yet paid little attention to the problems related to atypical development. This is all the more surprising given that the functionalist approach that they have adopted is particularly suited to propose a detailed description of the roots and mechanisms of several developmental disorders and learning difficulties. Indeed, the contributions gathered in the third part of this book demonstrate that working memory is an adequate theoretical framework to diagnose, analyze, and understand several manifestations of atypical development. Neo-Piagetian theories could thus have the potential to shed light on atypical development. Contrary to Piaget's theory, most of these theories conceive general factors and mechanisms of development, but also specialized systems and structures of knowledge. The structuralist theory of Robbie Case had a pioneering role in this domain by suggesting the existence of *Central Conceptual Structures* defined as networks of semantic and procedural knowledge that children have in a domain such as number, space, or social interactions (Case & Okamoto, 1996). A related idea is presented here by Demetriou and Mouyi with the notion of *Specialized Domains of Thought* dedicated to different domains of activity and specialized in the representation and processing of a particular type of information. Of course, these conceptions should be particularly suited to account for learning disabilities such as dyscalculia or dyslexia, even if Swanson demonstrates here that associating each learning disorder with the dysfunction of a specific and specialized system would be a simplistic approach.

Alloway and Swanson in their respective chapters show how Baddeley's theory of working memory provides us with a framework to understand and predict different developmental disorders that are associated with different profiles. Neo-Piagetian theories have the potential to account for most of the learning difficulties and developmental disorders by cumulating the strengths of the functionalist and the structuralist approaches. As Case (1993) noted, classical Piagetian theory had much to offer education, which could not be derived from the learning theories of its time. We could add that the current neo-Piagetian theories, by their capacity to address both the generality of the developmental mechanisms and the peculiarities of development within each domain of thought, have the potential to offer a renewed framework for understanding not only typical, but also atypical development.

The purpose of this book was to initiate a dialog between two streams of developmental psychology that, surprisingly, have until now remained relatively separated. The first is the neo-Piagetian approach, whose main originality has been to integrate the cognitive functionalist approach within the constructivist and structuralist conception of child development inherited from Piaget. The second is represented by psychologists who adopt a cognitive approach in studying the functioning and development of the central system of human cognitive architecture, working memory. As we have stressed in this concluding chapter, many points of consensus emerged through the different contributions, concerning the main role of working memory in human thinking, the constraints that its limited capacity places on development and learning, as well as the variety of factors that must be considered in order to account for cognitive development. We have also seen that several key questions remain unsolved, and we hope that the present book opens up as many avenues for future collaborative research.

Author note

The authors would like to thank Sergio Morra for having suggested addressing these issues as concluding remarks.

Advances and issues 271

References

Arsalidou, M. (2008). *Context, complexity, and the developmental assessment of attentional capacity*. Unpublished doctoral dissertation, York University, Toronto, ON, Canada.

Case, R. (1993). Theories of learning and theories of development. *Educational Psychologist, 28*, 219–233.

Case, R., & Okamoto, Y. (1996). The role of central conceptual structures in the development of children's thought. *Monographs of the Society for Research in Child Development, 61* (1–2, Serial No. 246).

Cowan, N. (2005). *Working memory capacity*. Hove, UK: Psychology Press.

Cowan, N., Elliott, E. M., Saults, J. S., Morey, C. C., Mattox, S., Hismjatullina, A., & Conway, A. R. A. (2005). On the capacity of attention: Its estimation and its role in working memory and cognitive aptitudes. *Cognitive Psychology, 51*, 42–100.

Cowan, N., Nugent, L. D., Elliot, E. M., & Saults, J. S. (2000). Persistence of memory for ignored lists of digits: Areas of developmental consistency and change. *Journal of Experimental Child Psychology, 76*, 151–172.

Kail, R. (1991). Developmental functions for speed of processing during childhood and adolescence. *Psychological Bulletin, 109*, 490–501.

Luck, S. J., & Vogel, E. K. (1997). The capacity of visual working memory for features and conjunctions. *Nature, 390*, 279–281.

Oberauer, K. (2009). Design for a working memory. *Psychology of Learning and Motivation: Advances in Research and Theory*, 51, 45–100.

Salthouse T. A. (1996). The processing-speed theory of adult age differences in cognition. *Psychological Review, 103*, 403–428.

Author index

Gross-Tsur, V., 215
Gunn, D. M., 159, 160, 178, 187, 234
Gusnard, D. A., 21
Gustafsson, J. E., 97

Hale, S., 80, 107
Halford, G. S., 2, 3–4, 41, 47, 47–68, 48,
 49, 50, 51, 52–54, 57, 59, 60–61, 62,
 80, 91, 140, 148, 151, 158, 159, 162,
 172, 264, 265
Hall, J. R., 242
Hall, M., 241
Halliday, M. S., 168, 184
Hambly, H., 242
Hambrick, D. Z., 62, 187
Hamidi, M., 62
Hanna, C., 184
Happé, F., 186, 188
Harnishfeger, K. K., 79, 107, 117
Harter, S., 77
Hasher, L., 107, 139–140, 203, 220
Hayashi, K. M., 63
Hayden, J., 244
Hayes, D. S., 184
Heath, M., 181
Hecht, S. A., 215
Heffernan, T. M., 184
Hegarty, M., 243
Heim, S., 63
Hellgren, L., 240
Henderson, S. E., 240
Henik, A., 15
Henry, L. A., 179, 180, 181, 245, 246
Hertzog, C., 108
Hesketh, L., 237
Hessels, M. G. P., 28
Hewes, A. K., 181, 183
Hewitt, J. K., 148
Hick, R., 236
Hill, E. L., 248
Hilton, K. A., 224
Hismjatullina, A., 141, 190, 265
Hitch, G. J., 2, 3, 5, 61, 137, 151, 153,
 154, 157, 158, 159–161, 162, 167, 168,
 170, 177, 179, 181, 183, 184–186, 187,
 188, 204, 233, 234, 236, 241
Hitzig, S., 39, 42
Hoard, M. K., 233
Hodkin, B., 55
Hoffman, L. M., 237
Hogg-Johnson, S., 243, 244
Hoijtink, H., 28
Holmes, J., 224, 244, 249
Holyoak, K. J., 62

Hongwanishkul, D., 77, 78
Honomichl, R. D., 64
Hopfinger, J. B., 15
Horodezsky, N. B., 243
Horta, B. L., 243
Horton, N. J., 3, 151, 159–160, 204, 207
Hoskyn, M., 204
Houston-Price, C. M. T., 159
Howard, D., 178
Howerter, A., 217, 219, 224
Hudjetz, A., 189
Huizinga, M., 78
Hull, A. J., 178
Hulme, C., 153, 172, 180, 181, 183, 184,
 192, 240
Hulslander, J. L., 203, 243, 244
Humphrey, D. G., 107
Humphries, T., 243, 244
Husserl, E., 13, 15–16, 20
Huttenlocher, P. R., 63
Hutton, U. M. Z., 153, 154, 159,
 160–161, 168, 170, 221

Ijaz, H., 24
Im, N., 243
Im-Bolter, N., 36, 37, 42, 148, 237
Inhelder, B., 119, 120, 179
Intrieri, R. C., 115
Isaacson, L., 243
Isely, C., 181

Jacques, S., 51
Jaeggi, S., 250
James, W., 15, 20, 21, 91
Jarrold, C., 2, 6, 159, 160, 172, 177–199,
 178, 180, 181, 183, 186, 187, 188, 193,
 204, 234, 245, 246, 268, 269
Jensen, A. R., 79, 97, 98, 107
Jensen, I. J., 59, 61
Jerman, O., 203, 207, 209, 210, 211,
 213–214, 215, 219, 221, 226
Jin, Z., 62
Johnson, J., 3, 13–46, 15, 16, 18, 20, 21,
 23, 24, 25, 26, 28, 29, 31, 33, 36, 37,
 38, 39, 41, 148, 172, 237, 264, 265,
 266, 268
Johnson, M. B., 109
Johnson, M. K., 153
Johnson, M. R., 153
Johnson, T., 179
Johnson, V., 97
Johnson-Laird, P. N., 47
Johnston, R. S., 203
Jones, M., 236

Subject index